Peril, Perseverance, and Perversion

Peril, Perseverance, and Perversion

Pastoral Reflections on Masculinity

Ryan LaMothe

CASCADE *Books* • Eugene, Oregon

PERIL, PERSEVERANCE, AND PERVERSION
Pastoral Reflections on Masculinity

Copyright © 2025 Ryan LaMothe. All rights reserved. Except for brief quotations in critical publications or reviews, no part of this book may be reproduced in any manner without prior written permission from the publisher. Write: Permissions, Wipf and Stock Publishers, 199 W. 8th Ave., Suite 3, Eugene, OR 97401.

Cascade Books
An Imprint of Wipf and Stock Publishers
199 W. 8th Ave., Suite 3
Eugene, OR 97401

www.wipfandstock.com

PAPERBACK ISBN: 978-1-6667-8592-0
HARDCOVER ISBN: 978-1-6667-8593-7
EBOOK ISBN: 978-1-6667-8594-4

Cataloguing-in-Publication data:

Names: LaMothe, Ryan, 1955–, author.

Title: Peril, perseverance, and perversion : pastoral reflections on masculinity / Ryan LaMothe.

Description: Eugene, OR: Cascade Books, 2025. | Includes bibliographical references and index.

Identifiers: ISBN 978-1-6667-8592-0 (paperback). | ISBN 978-1-6667-8593-7 (hardcover). | ISBN 978-1-6667-8594-4 (ebook).

Subjects: LCSH: Pastoral theology. | Men. | Masculinity. | Theology and literature.

Classification: BT83.63 L36 2025 (print). | BT83.63 (ebook)

VERSION NUMBER 01/14/25

For Cyn
and
for friendships that sustain life

Contents

Acknowledgments | ix

Introduction | xi

1. Mary Shelley's Frankenstein: The Horrors of Grief Gone Awry | 1
2. Ahab's Fatal Attraction: Defending against Loss and the Distortion of Care and Faith | 31
3. Scrooge and the Mammon Complex: The Agony of Loss, Masculine Invulnerability, and the Possibility of Redemption | 59
4. Toxic Masculinity and the Resistance of Ungovernable Selves in Daniel Black's Novel *The Coming* | 88
5. The Autobiography of Martin Luther King Jr.: Social Death, Sustaining Objects, and Radical Hope | 118
6. The Autobiography of Malcolm X: Being Aggrieved and the Emergence of an Anarchic Self | 150
7. Nelson Mandela, Transgression, and the Beauty of Becoming | 177
8. Western Men, the Ontological Rift, and Opportunities for Repair in Jack London's *Call of the Wild* | 207
9. Men and the Silence of Other Species: Traumatic Encounters and the Possibilities of Healing | 231

Bibliography | 257

Index | 271

Acknowledgments

There are moments in life when someone offers a thought or suggestion, seemingly in passing, that later begins to take root and grow. During a discussion of a paper I gave at a conference (the Philadelphia Group for Pastoral Theology with Boys and Men), Rubén Arjona, professor of pastoral care at Union Presbyterian Seminary in Richmond, Virginia, remembered my paper from the previous year and wondered if I was working toward a book. It had not occurred to me to do so, but the seed was planted. Thank you, Rubén. Some years later, I floated a book proposal to K. C. Hanson, editor-in-chief at Wipf and Stock Publishers, which was later accepted. I have worked with K. C. before on other projects. It has always been rewarding, and I am grateful to him and his staff.

I am indebted to Donald Capps and Robert Dykstra. Some years ago, they thought about gathering pastoral theologians from the U.S. and Canada to reflect on the experiences of boys and men. Because of Don's untimely death, Robert took the idea and labored to bring it to fruition. His consistent hospitality, kindness, and attention to detail made it possible for us to gather and engage in thoughtful and encouraging conversations. These were conferences where scholarship and friendship were present in equal measures. I am grateful for this, but, more importantly, I am thankful for Robert's friendship. I also deeply appreciate the participants in those conferences who provided helpful feedback on the articles that would later become chapters of this book. Let me mention a few: Robert Dykstra, Jaco Hamman, Phil Zylla, Rubén Arjona, Nathan Carlin, Danjuma Gibson, Adam Tietje, Joshua Morris, Jay-Paul Hinds, and Reggie Abraham. Lewis Rambo, who served as editor for the journal *Pastoral Psychology* for over three decades, enthusiastically supported publishing articles that came from these and other conferences. After Lewis's retirement, Kirk Bingaman took the reins of the journal and continued the support. I know I am not alone in offering deep appreciation for both Lewis and Kirk. They are consummate editors who have contributed much to the fields of pastoral theology, practical theology, and psychology of religion.

By the time this manuscript made it to Cascade Books, Kathy McKay had already provided her prodigious skills as a copyeditor. I have long appreciated and benefited from Kathy's work. Mary Jeanne Schumacher and Rev. Cynthia Geisen read, critiqued, and edited each of the chapters. They have also read and critiqued others of my works. A resounding thank you is hardly enough for all of this work. Let me add that Cindy not only edits my work, she is also my partner and friend. The last, but not least, thank you is for her.

Introduction

When I was five years old, I went downstairs with my brother and sisters to kiss and hug my mother and father. It was a nightly ritual. On that humid summer evening, after kissing and hugging my mother, I walked over to my father, who was reading on the couch. As I prepared to lean in, he stopped me, saying, "From now on, we will shake hands." I was confused and hurt. "Didn't my dad just hug and kiss my sisters?" I wondered. There was no explanation offered, then or later. My brother and I had our delightful revenge as adults. We would give my dad a big, playful, lingering embrace whenever we saw him, which he would reluctantly return.

Another memory. After graduating from West Point, I volunteered to attend Ranger Training at Fort Benning, Georgia. Once I completed the training, eleven of us signed in that very afternoon to Airborne training, also at Fort Benning. After what we had endured in Ranger School, we believed Airborne training would be a cakewalk. The Airborne instructors hazed the other recruits but knew to leave us alone. There was nothing that they could throw at us that we had not already experienced. After three weeks, while in the plane awaiting my last jump, and above the deafening roar of jet engines, I had an epiphany. A voice, clear and loud, said "Stop volunteering! You don't have to prove you are man enough." It had not occurred to me that volunteering for SERE (Survival, Escape, Resistance, and Evasion), Ranger School, and Airborne School had anything to do with proving I was a man. My more conscious motivation was a desire to be as well trained as possible, especially if I was going to lead, God forbid, soldiers in combat. But my epiphany revealed a more salient, powerful, unconscious motive—by making it through these ordeals, I felt I would somehow have proven that at age twenty-two I was a man. After that day, I never volunteered for any ordeal (except my dissertation defense) and have been at ease with never having to prove that I am a man.

What these two memories have in common are questions associated with masculinity. What does it mean to be a man in this culture, in this age? What are the markers for knowing when one is a man? What social or cultural rituals mark the transition from boyhood to manhood? How, as a boy or man, do I express love and affection to other men and women? Similarly, how do I handle my vulnerability as a man given life's sundry precarities? How, as a man, am I to dwell in the world? My father, for instance, probably thought that I needed to learn that men express affection by shaking hands, though it was okay (not shameful) to kiss and hug my mother—girls and women. This actually fit well with the macho environment of the Army, where vulnerability is equated with weakness and anxiety. These are transformed into aggression, though shame lingers silently in the background. This may be apt in preparing men (and women) for combat, but not for living day in and day out with loved ones.

"Masculinity" is deeply and wonderfully complex, varied, and contested. Simply stated, the Oxford Dictionary defines masculinity as the "qualities or attributes [and roles] regarded as characteristic of men or boys."[1] Just as I did at age five, we begin to learn in our homes what these nebulous qualities and roles are, as well as how we are to manage vulnerability and intimacy with persons of any gender. All of this begins long before we acquire language or self-consciousness. Studies of parents interacting with their infants reveal gender-related care.[2] Parents, in other words, communicate in thousands of ways what it means to be a boy or a girl—care is gendered and engendering. In addition, schools, sports, TV, media, etc., are other venues that comprise apparatuses[3] that inform us about what it means to be a boy or man. Long before my epiphany, I had learned what it was to be a man, which accompanied, in this culture, the unconscious shaming

---

1. Oxford Dictionary, "Masculinity," Oxford Languages, https://www.bing.com/search?q=definition+of+masculinity&toWww=1&redig=F1E97E3E4D474AB18B922BFA7874FB33.

2. See Dinkel and Snyder, "Exploring Gender Differences"; Neri et al., "Parenting Preterm Infants."

3. For Giorgi Agamben, the term *apparatus* refers to "a set of practices, bodies of knowledge, measures and institutions that aim to manage, govern, control, and orient—in a way that purports to be useful—the behaviors, gestures, and thoughts of human beings." Referencing Foucault, Agamben writes that "in a disciplinary society, apparatuses aim to create—through a series of practices, discourses, and bodies of knowledge—docile, yet free, bodies that assume their identity and their 'freedom' as subjects." The apparatuses associated with Christianity include its attending theologies, narratives, and rituals. Agamben, *What Is An apparatus?*, 13,19.

associated with those attributes and qualities linked to being a women or girl. Shame, especially when it lurks in the shadows of a culture or society, is a most powerful instructor. When shame is not acknowledged, confronted, and worked through, masculine attributes and roles take on the character of tyrants, fools, villains, rogues, sadists, rigid and self-righteous rebels and scholars, etc. These men, living lives of quiet desperation, transfer their fears and vulnerabilities rather than accept and transform them. If shame is confronted and worked through, vulnerability is transformed, enabling men to become collaborative, caring leaders; sages; reflective rebels or revolutionaries; healers/shamans; or even curious and humble scholars.

This book, drawing on novels and autobiographies, explores how men respond to the precarities of life. I endeavor to provide depictions of masculinities gone awry and their sources, as well as stories of men who find ways to adopt more life-enriching forms of relating to other men, women, and other species. One reason for using novels and autobiographies, instead of case studies, is that these are in the public realm and readily accessible. Another reason is that pastoral theologians and pastoral ministers listen to, analyze, assess, and respond to countless narratives. We are story-telling animals, and these stories often reveal and conceal our vulnerabilities, desires, fears, and anxieties.

I would also like to mention that five of the chapters, which have been thoroughly revised,[4] were presented initially as papers at conferences in Philadelphia (the Philadelphia Group for Pastoral Theology with Boys and Men) and later published in the journal *Pastoral Psychology*. The origin of this conference dates to the spring of 2015 and a conversation over lunch shared by Donald Capps and Robert Dykstra, colleagues in pastoral theology at Princeton Theological Seminary. They were impressed and aided in their seminary courses by rich, edited volumes on nuances of pastoral care around concerns specific to women. Donald and Robert began to wonder whether similar possible benefits might accrue from a focus by male pastoral theologians on contemporary struggles of boys and men. Sadly, Donald Capps died in a car accident in the late summer of 2015, leaving Robert to take the reins. He was assisted by Nathan Carlin, a pastoral theologian who teaches medical humanities at the University of Texas Medical School at Houston. This

---

4. Chapters 1 and 3 are based on my article "Male Pathological Grief in Mary Shelley's *Frankenstein* and Charles Dickens's *A Christmas Carol*: A Pastoral Psychological Perspective." Chapter 2 is based on the article "Literature and Social Pathologies: Ahab's Masculinity as a Distortion of Care and Faith." Chapter 5 relies on my article "Autobiography in the Face of Social Death: Martin Luther King Jr., Sustaining Object/Process, and Radical Hope/Redemption." Chapter 8 is based on "Men, the Ontological Rift, and the Possibility of Repair in Jack London's *Call of the Wild*: A Pastoral-Psychoanalytic Perspective."

conference, originally slated to be a one-off gathering, has met since 2015, except for two years during the most recent pandemic. Lewis Rambo, editor of *Pastoral Psychology*, and, later, Kirk Bingaman encouraged participants to publish their papers in the journal, which many of us did.

This book comprises three sections. The first three chapters depict how men can, for varied reasons, fail to mourn, leaving in their wake a wide path of misery and destruction. The first two chapters are tales of tragedy, ending with no hope of redemption. Frankenstein, devastated by his mother's death, seeks escape through study and the fanatical pursuit of reanimating life, resulting in numerous deaths and eventually his own death. After he loses a limb in a previous encounter with the white whale, Captain Ahab maniacally seeks revenge, relentlessly pursuing Moby Dick, ending in the deaths of all the crew save one—somebody had to survive to tell the story. The third chapter depicts the miserable life of Ebenezer Scrooge—a man who clearly avoided losses, stemming back to the death of his mother, his being shunted off to school, and the loss of a lover in early adulthood. Scrooge's story is not simply a tragic story of male grief gone awry; it is a tale of a process whereby losses are painfully faced, experienced, and worked through, creating the possibility of future relations of love and care. This is a story in which pain and vulnerability are initially transferred and later faced and transformed.

The second part of the book addresses a novel by Daniel Black, *The Coming*, and three autobiographies, by Martin Luther King Jr., Malcolm X, and Nelson Mandela. What they have in common are their experiences of the brutalities of racism. Black's novel portrays the untold horrors of the Middle Passage, perpetrated by white men. In this novel, we see how the intersection of capitalism, colonization, and racism perversely shape the subjectivities and actions of white men, which, in turn, impact enslaved persons and later men such as Malcolm X, King, and Mandela. In these chapters, I am also interested in portraying and understanding the resiliencies, resistances, and revolutionary responses of men who endure the persistent onslaughts of racism.

The third section of this book contains two chapters on novels by Jack London, namely, *Call of the Wild* and *White Fang*. Here, I shift to men's relationships to nature and, in particular, to other species—dogs and wolves. As I mentioned above, our relationships to other species reveals something about how we understand ourselves, as well as what it means to be a boy or man in relation to the Earth and its denizens. In the previous chapters, I briefly address the realities of climate change because the climate crisis exposes how we perceive and treat other species, which, by and large, in the West is deplorable and hugely destructive. For instance, Ahab's maniacal pursuit of Moby Dick takes place against the background of capitalism and imperialism, the apparatuses of which have distorted the subjectivities of boys and men and correspondingly their relations to other species and the Earth. London's novels, written long before there was any awareness of climate change, provide a more focused approach to men's relationships to other species and the Earth. More particularly, the novels describe the exploitative and brutal actions toward Buck, a dog abducted in California to be sold in Alaska, and White Fang, a wolf captured and treated horribly at the hands of Gray Beaver and Beauty Smith. Each novel also depicts men who see the sufferings of Buck and White Fang and respond by rescuing them from the hands of mendacious men. Once rescued, these men demonstrate a patient tenderness, care, and love that heal the physical and psychic traumas of Buck and White Fang. Mutual respect, trust, and care develop between the men and the dog and wolf they rescue, which render inoperative those apparatuses of capitalism and imperialism responsible for the destructive relations men have toward other species and the Earth. These novels, in one sense, invite us, men and boys, to examine critically our relations to other species and to consider more empathic, compassionate, and caring relations with them and ourselves.

Let me end by returning to my two memories. I certainly felt my dad loved me, but that screen memory reveals our, his and mine, struggles and anxieties about expressing tenderness and affection with each other and, later, as an adult with other men. Of course, there was a kind of tenderness and vulnerability in our handshake, but it was attenuated. This was also true in the Army. There were moments of masculine tenderness, more often than not coupled with machismo. What diminished this kind of masculine affection was unconscious anxiety and shame about being vulnerable. To be a man, I was told in countless ways, was to be strong in the face of precarity, but this strength rested on unacknowledged and anxious insecurity. It took the love of other men and women for me to re-learn that there is strength and courage in facing and dealing with the vulnerabilities of life together, which can open us to recognize empathically the singularities and vulnerabilities of all creatures. All life is precarious, and this reality, which is blatantly apparent in the climate crisis, is an invitation for us to care for other humans, other species, and the Earth.

1

Mary Shelley's Frankenstein
The Horrors of Grief Gone Awry

There are two forces in this world that propel our lives in opposite directions: the first is the power over life, and the second is the power of life.[1]

'Tis a fearful thing / to love what death can touch.[2]

Loss is an inevitable factor in human life, and Mary Wollstonecraft Shelley knew this well. When Mary was just a twelve-day-old infant, her brilliant feminist mother, Mary Wollstonecraft, who wrote *A Vindication of the Rights of Women* (and other publications), died.[3] Mary Wollstonecraft's partner was a well-known philosopher, William Godwin. We don't know how William responded to his wife's death, at least in the short term. Yet, as Walter Miller notes, Mary's father then "married a widow who clearly favored her own two children,"[4] which suggests further pain-

---

1. Kishik, *The Power of Life*, 100.
2. Halevi, "Tis a Fearful Thing."
3. Mary Wollstonecraft was and is well known for having authored the book *A Vindication of the Rights of Women*.
4. Miller, foreword, vii.

ful, though often subtle, childhood losses with regard to the attention and affection of her father and stepmother. When Mary was newly married to the poet Percy Shelley, her first child, Clara, died in 1815—less than two years after Mary had met Percy.[5] By June of 1816, when Percy suggested that Percy, Shelley, and Lord Byron each write a ghost story, young Mary was already well acquainted with loss and the precarity of life. Unfortunately, tragedy continued to dog her. By the time *Frankenstein* was published in 1819, Mary's second daughter and her son were dead. In 1822, Mary had a miscarriage and was saved by her husband, who "sat her down in an ice-bath until the doctor arrived."[6] Three weeks later, Percy himself died in a storm while sailing.

The death of her mother, the loss of affection and attention from her overly logical father and emotionally biased stepmother, and the deaths of her children and husband were not the only losses Mary experienced. As mentioned, her mother's publications "defended the French Revolution . . . [and] attacked the hierarchical system that required underpaid mechanics to support the rich and idle aristocracy and deprived women of any chance to realize their human potential."[7] Mary Wollstonecraft "demanded equal political rights for all English persons deprived of the vote—which meant at the time, most members of the middle-class, all workers, and all women regardless of class!"[8] I say this to highlight not only that Mary Shelley was heavily influenced by her mother's work and her father's belief in the education of women but also that she would have been keenly aware of the innumerable deeply felt and tangible losses associated with the marginalization and oppression of women in a patriarchal, capitalist society. At the same time, like women in any male-dominated society, Mary Shelley would have been educated in the ways of men, familiar with their machinations and privileges as well as their responses to grief and mourning. She certainly had firsthand experience of her father's ways of dealing with loss.

There are many possible themes (e.g., dangers of science, ideology of progress, fear of difference, patriarchy) in Mary Shelley's *Frankenstein*, though the one that is the focus of this chapter is on loss and how experiences of male grief and the process of mourning can go terribly awry. Since the main characters are Victor[9] Frankenstein and the being he created, the

---

5. Miller, foreword, ix.
6. Miller, foreword, xvii.
7. Miller, foreword, vii.
8. Miller, foreword, ix.
9. It is ironic that Shelley's main character is named Victor since he tries to defeat death only to end up utterly defeated.

focus here is on masculinity vis-à-vis grief. It is important to begin with a brief discussion about the notions of grief and mourning. This sets the stage for describing Victor's family and his experience of his mother's death, which is followed by a discussion of his subsequent responses that led him to an inordinate attachment to and faith in science[10] and to reanimating dead tissue[11] that resulted in the creation of the monster. Since Victor's pathological grief is inextricably yoked to the creature's responses to traumatic loss, I also turn my focus to the creature's grief responses. My point in including the creature is that grief gone awry, in the case of Victor, gives birth to another iteration of male pathological grief—envy and violence. Pathological grief, in other words, has devastating consequences in patriarchal societies, giving birth to all kinds of tragedies. Indeed, in my view, Mary Shelley's book is a witness, a testament to how patriarchy can give rise to destructive male grief.

Before beginning, I offer a few caveats and clarifications. First, on the manifest level, *Frankenstein* is a story about love and how grief can become distorted, having devastating ripple effects. On the latent level, distortions in grief and mourning cannot be adequately grasped without understanding the dominant narratives, rituals, and social-political and economic structures that provide the ground for love and responses to loss. While it is not possible to dive deeply into these factors, let me say that, in this case, the primary latent systemic contributor to pathological male grief in this story is patriarchy, which undergirds the political order, capitalism, and the sciences. Patriarchy refers to the rule—power and authority—of men over women, children, and other species. The term primarily refers to a type of political reality, but its tentacles reach into religion, culture, and science. A patriarchal society comprises apparatuses that produce and maintain male power, authority, and privileges, subordinating and, in some cases, subjugating women and children (and other species over which men are believed to have dominion). Mary Shelley, like her mother, would have experienced

---

10. Readers may not notice the relation between science and patriarchy. This relation does not mean identity, but it is important that science emerged in the context of Greek patriarchy. Aristotle, reputedly the first scientist, set up elaborate hierarchal taxonomies and dissected (probed, depersonalized) other species to learn about them. He had power over other species. Millennia later, Francis Bacon (1561–1626) reiterated this view, arguing that science had "the practical aim of improving humanity's lot [which depended on] the increased understanding and *control* of nature." Of course, not all scientists hold this view, but I would venture to say that most scientific practices reflect relations of power and control over othered human beings, other species, and the Earth. Grayling, *The History of Philosophy*, 197.

11. The fantasy of reanimating dead tissue came from Mary's own experiences. Miller writes that Mary "suffered from recurrent dreams that she had massaged her dead baby, Clara, until she was brought back to life." Miller, foreword, x.

patriarchy in routine daily events, as well as in the retreat of her father into rationality and his replacement of his deceased wife with another woman who was to take over the role of mother. More particularly, patriarchy is evident in the story itself. Women play a subordinate and supporting role in the narrative. Worse, Victor's treatment of his fiancée and later wife reveals a disturbing lack of concern for her safety and a prioritizing of his needs and desires over her desires and safety—unquestioned male privilege/entitlement. I add here that, during the time Shelley wrote, the trope "mother nature" would have been familiar to most people, which would have included scientists who pursued having increasing power and control over nature. We see this in the way Victor uses science to wield power over nature by attempting to reanimate dead tissue.

Second and relatedly, one may wonder about my focus on masculinity in this story when so much has changed since Mary Shelley's day. True, there have been numerous changes, but patriarchy and misogyny are alive and well today in the U.S. and elsewhere. Conservative Christian, Islamic, and Jewish communities are deeply patriarchal. Moreover, there is a rise in the U.S. of popular pseudo-academic opportunists like Jordan Peterson and conservative pundits who appeal to boys and men with their messages of male "leadership," which is simply a code for reinstituting patriarchy. Male privilege and entitlement are also evident in the bitterness and hatred toward girls and women expressed by boys and men who identify as incels—involuntary celibate. So, in my view, the pathological grief depicted in Mary Shelley's story is relevant today.

This moves me to a third point. I am not trying to universalize or essentialize male grief and mourning in relation to patriarchal apparatuses. In other words, I am not suggesting that patriarchy, in and of itself, "causes" pathological grief. Certainly, there are men in patriarchal systems who grieve well, just as there are instances of pathological grief manifested in other societies that are not patriarchal. I am, however, suggesting that patriarchy and its close connection to apparatuses[12] of power and privilege, whether they are political, economic, or scientific, provide the nutrients for the poisonous weeds of maladaptive grief to flourish. Fourth, by exploring the negative dynamics of male grief, I am not picking on men. Clearly, all

---

12. Just to remind readers, for Giorgi Agamben, the term *apparatus* refers to "a set of practices, bodies of knowledge, measures and institutions that aim to manage, govern, control, and orient—in a way that purports to be useful—the behaviors, gestures, and thoughts of human beings." Referencing Foucault, Agamben writes that "in a disciplinary society, apparatuses aim to create—through a series of practices, discourses, and bodies of knowledge—docile, yet free, bodies that assume their identity and their 'freedom' as subjects." The apparatuses associated with Christianity include its attendant theologies, narratives, and rituals. Agamben, *What Is an Apparatus?*, 13,19.

genders can manifest destructive grief. My interest is in trying to understand male grief gone awry in this novel with the aim of considering ways to empathically understand and to intervene when we encounter such grief, as well as how we might undermine the apparatuses that give rise to these maladaptive responses to loss, while creating or facilitating apparatuses that will help people of all genders deal with loss in more life-giving and life-affirming ways. Finally, I have another reason for delving into problems in loss. Today and in the near future, all of humanity faces catastrophic losses due to climate change. These losses include destruction of homes and habitats, failed states, extinction of species, and the very real possibility of human extinction.[13] I fear many individuals will deal with these losses by falling into male authoritarianism and barbarism—a barbarism of fear, hatred, and violence that represents profound failures in grief and mourning.[14] Perhaps if we recognize the signs of our griefs gone awry, we can change our attitudes and behaviors.

Grief and Mourning

Since grief and mourning are features of this and subsequent chapters, it is helpful to spend a bit of time not only defining terms but also situating grief and mourning within the existential realities of human life. Let me begin with William Worden's classic text on grief and mourning,[15] *Grief Counseling and Grief Therapy*, by pointing out that human animals (and other animals) develop and seek to maintain affectional bonds with attachment figures.[16] "Affectional bond" is another way of saying that human attachments are characterized by care and love,[17] whether between human animals

---

13. See LaMothe, *The Coming Jesus*; LaMothe, *Pastoral Care in the Anthropocene*.

14. See Stengers, *Making Sense in Common*.

15. William Worden, for over four decades, has explored and researched grief and loss. Worden, *Grief Counseling and Grief Therapy*. I suspect if he were going to add to his work he would address the realities of chronic sorrow, which is especially evident in current realities of climate change. Many people are aware of and grieve losses associated with climate change—losses that are individual, systemic, repeated, and longstanding. See Cunsolo and Landman, *Mourning Nature*; Pihkala, "Eco-Anxiety, Tragedy, and Hope."

16. Worden, *Grief Counseling and Grief Therapy*, 13.

17. Care is a seemingly mundane concept, but deeply complex and contested. While I will say more about care in chapter 2, for the purposes of this chapter, I use the following definition of care: care is everything we do to help individuals, families, communities, and societies to (1) meet the vital biological, psychosocial, existential, and spiritual needs of individuals, families, and communities; (2) develop or maintain basic capabilities with the aim of human flourishing; (3) facilitate participation in the polis; and (4)

or other-than-human animals (and inanimate objects). Care is existentially and developmentally vital and not some mere attribute of the attachment associated with childhood or confined to families.[18] Granted, to survive and thrive, children must be cared for by parents and other adults, which means that children are psychologically and physically vulnerable and dependent. Thus, children are motivated to maintain the affectional bonds with parents because of their need to survive. Of course, not all motivations for attachment, whether in childhood or adulthood, are based on the motivation to survive. There is also the pleasure of affection and friendship, which suggests that an affectional bond can be without utility and pursued for its own sake. Theodor Adorno, no doubt echoing Aristotle, makes a similar claim, saying that "tenderness between people is nothing other than the awareness of the possibility of relations without purpose."[19] We might say that this attachment adds to our thriving, but that is not necessarily the sole or primary motivation to maintain the attachment. Sometimes we love and tenderly care for the sake of the Other's survival and thriving, even when it is detrimental to ourselves.

Before defining and unpacking the terms of grief and mourning, it is necessary to highlight another related feature of affectional bonds and care, namely, faith. To return to the parent-child example, the parent's care for a child accompanies, necessarily, the reality of human faith.[20] Paren-

---

maintain a habitable environment for the common good of all. I add to this definition that care and pastoral care as political concepts necessarily involve shared critical and constructive reflection on how the structures (and their accompanying narratives and practices) of the state, governing authorities, and non-state organizations (e.g., businesses, labor unions, religious and secular communities, etc.), and other actors meet or fail to meet the four features of this definition of care. LaMothe, *Care of Souls*, 8.

18. Numerous feminist scholars and pastoral theologians have argued that care is a political concept. See Bubeck, *Care, Gender, and Justice*; Engster, *The Heart of Justice*; Hamington, *Embodied Care*; Held, *The Ethics of Care*; Helsel, *Pastoral Power*; Johnson, *Race, Religion, and Resilience*; LaMothe, *Care of Souls*; Oliner and Oliner, *Toward a Caring Society*; Ramsay, "Compassionate Resistance"; Robinson, *Globalizing Care*; Robinson, *The Ethics of Care*; Rogers-Vaughn, *Caring for Souls*; Rumscheidt, *No Room for Grace*; Sevenhuijsen, *Citizenship and the Ethics of Care*; Tronto, *Caring Democracy*; Tronto, *Moral Boundaries*.

19. Waggoner, *Unhoused*, 82.

20. Chapter 2 addresses the interrelation between care and faith, which will serve as a hermeneutical lens for addressing the pathological masculinity and grief of Herman Melville's Captain Ahab. For the time being, let me note that, for H. R. Niebuhr and other theologians, faith is constitutive to being human. Faith is, therefore, an anthropological category and not simply or solely a religious category. I find that Niebuhr's depiction of faith in terms of interrelated dialectical pairs, namely, belief-disbelief, trust-distrust, loyalty-disloyalty (I add hope-hopelessness), is helpful in understanding the pre-representational dynamics of faith in early childhood, as well as later, more

tal personal recognition and attunement enables the child's construction of pre-representational experiences of trust[21] and fidelity or loyalty.[22] Put differently, one could say the child develops—in light of the parent's consistent attunement—a pre-representational belief in the parent's trustworthiness and loyalty linked to parents' consistent attunement to children's needs. Of course, this is speculation, but as the child grows and attains the capacities for symbolization and narrative, it is clear that relational dynamics of care and faith are evident. Indeed, the struggles of faith (alienation, betrayal, distrust, hopelessness) and pleasures of faith (companionship, trust, loyalty, hope) are evident in the stories (e.g., fairy tales) children love. Care and faith, then, are intertwined in affectional bonds and are evident in grief and mourning. For instance, in the face of the death of a parent, children often feel betrayed and abandoned, which disturbs and disrupts their experiences of trust and hope.[23] In adulthood, divorce accompanies many losses, including the loss of relational trust and loyalty between partners.

The care and faith associated with affectional bonds take place against an inevitable anthropological reality, namely, finitude. The first line in Yehuda Halevi's poem ("'Tis a fearful thing to love what death can touch") reveals the inherent human vulnerability and dependency in our care for

---

complicated symbolic constructions. I add here that the notion of faith, like the notion of care, is a political concept, which is evidenced by the notion of the ecclesia and kingdom of God. Niebuhr, *Faith on Earth*.

21. Erik Erikson developed a psychosocial, stagewise developmental theory that highlighted relational struggles and achievements. The first stage in his schema is the parent-infant couple navigating trust-mistrust, with the successful outcome being the virtue of hope. The successful navigation of this and other stages does not mean that these are no longer issues in life. The struggle of trust-mistrust can be found throughout the life cycle. I mention this only because this first stage represents a feature of faith and this faith vis-à-vis the infant is organized semiotically but not yet symbolically. Erikson, *Childhood and Society*.

22. The term *pre-representational* means that the pre-symbolic infant is not able to form or use representations of objects. Donald Winnicott used the term *environmental mother* to refer to just this. Christopher Bollas's notion of transformational objects is similar to Winnicott's view, though he focuses more on process vis-à-vis pre-representational. Pre-representational organizations of experience are features of semiotic systems, which later include symbolic organizations of experience. As Charles Sanders Peirce makes clear, semiotic processes operate prior to more complicated symbolic processes. So, we can say that an infant organizes experience, at this period of development, semiotically, though without the capacity to form and use representations. Winnicott, *Playing and Reality*; Bollas, *The Shadow of the Object*; Peirce, *Peirce on Signs*; Peirce, *The Essential Peirce*.

23. Worden, *Grief Counseling and Grief Therapy*, 230–36.

others. Feminist philosopher Judith Butler rightly argues that precarity is an existential feature of human life, indeed of all finite beings.[24] To care, to love means dealing with the reality that while human agency and freedom are part and parcel of developing and maintaining affectional bonds, we have little control over the loss of these bonds through death or accident. Precarity pervades all life, and loss is a manifestation of this precarity. Consider that Mary Shelley would have had no conscious memory[25] of her mother's untimely death, though she would have eventually been conscious of this loss, as she was conscious of the loss of affection from her father and stepmother. Death and other losses, in other words, remind us that life is precarious, transient, and that helplessness, powerlessness, and vulnerability are aspects of human life, whether we are talking about childhood or adulthood. We may not like it, we may fear it, but precarity is part and parcel of what it means to be alive, and loss is just one feature of it.

There are two more key existential features of finitude, precarity, and loss vis-à-vis care and affectional bonds—key because they figure in the discussion below. The death of a loved one can evoke a sense of helplessness, as well as awareness of our own vulnerability, our own sell-by date. But there is something also frightening about death, our own or a loved one's. When Halevi says it is a fearful thing to love what death can touch, we might wonder about the source of that fear. To be sure, I want the person I love to continue to exist, to be part of my life, and might fear losing her. Yet, I think fear associated with death is rooted in the existential realities of impermanence and insignificance. All life is marked by impermanence, and the realities of climate exchange and mass extinctions bring this to the fore. Dinosaurs were impermanent and eventually so will we be, as will our sun and galaxy. This aspect of precarity is one of the most difficult to face—a reality that is often covered up by religious beliefs in eternal life, at least for some chosen human beings—all other species need not apply.

---

24. Butler, *Precarious Life*.

25. It would be a mistake to assume that because Mary (or anyone else) had no memory of the death of her mother that she would not have some unconscious pre-symbolic memory or pre-representational organizations of experience. Infant-parent researchers note that infants' experiences are organized semiotically, though symbolic and autobiographical cognitive operations have not come online. This suggests that Mary, as an infant, would have had semiotic organizations of the experience of her mother's absence. Interestingly, psychoanalyst Harry Hardin argues convincingly that Sigmund Freud, as a very young child, experienced significant losses associated with the care provided by his mother while she grieved the deaths of her father and second son. Hardin, "On the Vicissitudes of Freud's Early Mothering" [I and II.] See also Beebe and Lachmann, "The Contribution." Hardin and Hardin. "On the Vicissitudes of Early Primary Surrogate Mothering."

The reality of impermanence is closely associated with existential insignificance. Granted, human beings are signifying and valuing animals. Our loving other people, our affectional bonds, reveal their significance to us and their inestimable impermanent value. When they die, they remain significant for as long as we live and remember them. We assign significance, we hold on to the personal significance of the dead loved one, against the background of existential insignificance. By this I mean that, with regard to the cosmos, all life is insignificant because there is no external, independent being conferring significance—ontological or existential. Significance is contingent (on us), transient, impermanent, rather than timeless or ontological. It is, therefore, a mistake to believe that because we are signifying and valuing animals that what we value is ontological or eternal. Neither the universe nor creation assigns significance or permanence. When human beings become extinct, we, like the dinosaurs before us, will recede into existential insignificance. Religions and, in Victor's case, a preoccupation with science, can serve as soporifics—beliefs in our ontological significance—that deflect us from facing inevitable loss and precarity.

Affectional bonds, care, and faith are features of human existence, and human finitude/precarity reveals the existential impermanence and insignificance of these bonds, all of which are the existential foundations of grief and mourning. Put another way, there would be no grief and mourning if we did not care, had no faith, or were somehow invulnerable and eternal. Given that most human animals encounter loss, it is important to be clear about the terms. Worden makes a distinction between grief and mourning. He defines grief as the *experience of loss*, which comprises feelings, cognitions, physical sensations, and behaviors.[26] These components of grief vary widely across cultures, societies, religions, gender, individuals, etc. Moreover, feelings, thoughts, sensations, and behaviors vary in expression and intensity during the process of mourning. And sometimes, long after a loss has been experienced and worked through, feelings and thoughts may be reawakened. I wonder, for instance, if Mary Shelley's grief following the death of her husband reverberated with the death of her mother, the loss of her father's affection in childhood, and the deaths of her children.

The experience of grief is distinct but, of course, inseparable from mourning. Mourning, for Worden, is the process of working through loss. Instead of viewing this process in terms of stages or phases, Worden argues for understanding the process in terms of tasks: (1) accept the reality of loss, (2) process the pain of grief, (3) adjust to the world without the deceased, and (4) find an enduring connection with the deceased in the

---

26. Worden, *Grief Counseling and Grief Therapy*, 18–30.

midst of embarking on a new life.[27] These tasks reveal the arduous emotional-relational work of mourning. Indeed, mourning is work, and it is important to stress that this work is not simply or solely the work of an individual. If anything, the work of mourning is relational, familial, and communal, though, sadly and tragically, some people may experience loss and mourning in isolation. When this occurs, we can anticipate that the tasks of mourning may be impeded. It is also important to mention that other people and social-political apparatuses can be obstacles to experiencing loss and doing the work of mourning. Melissa Kelley discusses disenfranchised grief and mourning, which refers to losses that are not socially or culturally recognized (e.g., people with AIDs, pets, houseless people).[28] These losses are not grievable,[29] which can interfere with persons' obtaining the social-political recognition and support to work through the tasks of mourning.

Grief and mourning are inevitable in life, but human beings, for various conscious and unconscious reasons, find ways to defend against the pain of grief and the work of mourning. Understanding mourning that goes awry has long been of interest to psychologists and pastoral theologians.[30] Sigmund Freud, for instance, wanted to understand the differences between melancholia and common types of mourning.[31] The key mental features of melancholia are profound "dejection, cessation of interest in the outside world, loss of a capacity to love, inhibition of all activity, and a lowering of self-regarding feelings to a degree that finds utterances in self-reproaches and self-revilings, and culminates in a delusional expectation of punishment."[32] A melancholic patient, Freud proposed, "represents his ego to us as worthless, incapable of any achievement."[33] These patients are "perpetually taking offense and behaving *as if* they had been treated with great injustice. All this is possible only because the reactions expressed in their behavior still proceed from an attitude of revolt."[34] Freud argued that typical mourning, while painful, does not have these features, leaving one to conclude that melancholia is a maladaptive grief response.[35] While appreci-

27. Worden, *Grief Counseling and Grief Therapy*, 39–51.
28. Kelley, *Grief*.
29. Butler, *Precarious Life*.
30. Capps, *Men, Religion, and Melancholia*; Capps, *Men and Their Religion*; Kelley, *Grief*; Mitchell and Anderson, *All Our Losses*; Oates, *Grief, Transition, and Loss*; Park, *Pastoral Care for Survivors*.
31. Freud, *Mourning and Melancholia*.
32. Freud, *Mourning and Melancholia*, 242.
33. Freud, *Mourning and Melancholia*, 246.
34. Freud, *Mourning and Melancholia*, 248.
35. Donald Capps examined the lives and works of William James, Erik Erikson,

ating Freud's work, Worden argues that the research on grief and mourning demonstrates "a more continuous relationship between normal and abnormal grief reactions, between the complicated and uncomplicated, and that pathology is more related to the intensity of a reaction or the duration of a reaction than to the simple presence or absence of a specific symptom or behavior."[36] To return to the tasks of mourning, Worden argues that, in pathological types of mourning, one or more of the tasks of mourning are not completed, whether due to some psychosocial incapacity or a conscious or unconscious refusal to do the work of this or that task.

A great deal has been written about pathological mourning, and to view this literature would take me far afield. For my purposes, the male characters of Victor Frankenstein and the organism he created serve as illustrations of mourning gone awry. For now, though, I wish to briefly depict some general ideas about pathological mourning given Worden's tasks and notions of care and faith. Broadly speaking, pathological mourning emerges when a person (or group) refuses, consciously or unconsciously, to do the work of one or more of the tasks outlined by Worden. There may be many reasons and motivations for this, but I would suggest that we can understand this as a defense against anxieties and fears associated with vulnerability, the loss of relational care and faith, as well as a defense against experiencing and accepting the existential realities of our impermanence and insignificance. Put another way, persons unconsciously wish to be invulnerable, which protects them from the reality of their impermanence and insignificance and its accompanying suffering. By holding on to the dead loved person/object, one believes that care and faith (significance) are not subject to the constraints of precarity and finitude. Pathological grief, then, is the attempt to avoid impermanence and the maddening emotions and thoughts of loss.

Care and Faith: Victor's Family

To understand Victor's pathological mourning empathically, we need to delve into the story of his early life and relationships. Interestingly, the novel begins at the end of the line for Victor, when he knows he is dying. Captain Walton, whose crew rescued Victor from the ice, writes to his sister

---

Carl Jung, and Sigmund Freud, arguing they had a disposition toward melancholia, which, Capps believed, had roots in their early psychosocial development. The early felt loss of their mother's attention and affections shaped their stance and interest in religion. Melancholia, then, can be viewed as an inability or unwillingness to mourn. My interest, however, is not to confine problems in mourning under the rubric of melancholia. Capps, *Men, Religion, and Melancholia*.

36. Worden, *Grief Counseling and Grief Therapy*, 134.

Margaret about this strange encounter. Sailing in the frigid waters of the north, the crew encountered a half-dead man. Upon regaining some of his health, Victor[37] Frankenstein says to Captain Walton, "You have hope, and the world before you, and have no cause to despair. But I—I have lost everything and cannot begin life anew."[38] Victor reiterates that he has experienced "unparalleled misfortunes" and that "nothing can alter my destiny."[39] Victor previously decided to take his secrets to the grave, "having determined at one time that the memory of these evils should die with me."[40] But after being rescued and received the attentive and kindly ear of Captain Walton, Victor decides to begin his narrative.

Victor starts by telling Captain Walton about his origins (he is Genevese—from the environs of Geneva, Switzerland), parents, and childhood. Maladaptive male grief marks the very beginning of the story. His father had a very good friend, Beaufort, whom he dearly loved.[41] Beaufort fell into poverty and, after paying his debts, retreated to Lucerne with his daughter Caroline. Victor's father must have told him that Beaufort's "grief only became deeper and rankling when he had leisure for reflection, and at length it took so fast hold of his mind that at the end of three months he lay on a bed of sickness."[42] Despite his daughter's attentive care, Beaufort died. Victor's father went to the funeral and, seeing her poverty and grief, decided to take her to Geneva and place her under his protection. "Two years after this event," Victor says, "Caroline became his wife."[43]

Let me pause here to highlight this seemingly minor part of the story. As I will comment later, Caroline's care for her ill father, who was dying of grief, is another instance in the novel where women are portrayed as caretakers who sacrifice themselves for others. In my view, these subordinate characters represent women who are willing to face, experience, and deal with loss by caring for others. By contrast, Caroline's father, Beaufort, is so caught up in his grief—after the losses of his fortune and social

---

37. Phillip Wade argues that Mary Shelley's choice of the name "Victor" comes from her reading of *Paradise Lost*, wherein God is named "The Victor." In her story, Victor is playing God. Victor uses science to reanimate the dead, which is another way of considering resurrection as the overcoming of (victory over) impermanence and vulnerability. Wade, "Shelley and the Miltonic Element."
38. Shelley, *Frankenstein*, 13.
39. Shelley, *Frankenstein*, 14.
40. Shelley, *Frankenstein*, 14.
41. Shelley, *Frankenstein*, 17.
42. Shelley, *Frankenstein*, 18.
43. Shelley, *Frankenstein*, 18.

position—that he fails to accept and work through the reality of loss. This results in his abdicating his responsibility to love and care for his daughter.

To return to Shelley's narrative, one can imagine that there was a gap in age between Victor's father and his bride, which, Victor says, "seemed to unite them only closer in bonds of devoted affection."[44] Victor recalls, "There was a show of gratitude and worship in his attachment to my mother . . . for it was inspired by reverence for her virtues and a desire to be the means of . . . recompensing her for the sorrows she had endured."[45] Part of the father's devotion and care were due to "her weakened" or fragile condition.[46] Clearly, for Victor, his mother was equally devoted to and loving toward her husband.

Not long after they were married, they had a son. As the firstborn child, Victor said that as "much as they [his parents] were attached to each other, they seemed to draw inexhaustible stores of affection from a very mine of love to bestow upon me."[47] He recalls his mother's tender caresses and his father's benevolent smiles. "I was their plaything and their idol," he says, "and something better—their child."[48] In one of their travels, his mother rescues and adopts an orphan who becomes Victor's "beautiful and adored companion of all my occupations and my pleasures. Everyone loved Elizabeth."[49] As they grew up together, Victor remembers, "Harmony was the soul of our companionship, and the diversity and contrast that subsisted in our characters drew us nearer together."[50] Interestingly, Victor recalls his mother telling him that Elizabeth was a present for him. "I, with child seriousness, interpreted her words literally and looked upon Elizabeth as mine—mine to protect, love, and cherish,"[51] though in the end he fails miserably in fulfilling this obligation. Within a couple of years of Elizabeth's adoption, his parents had another child, a son. After this birth, the parents "gave up entirely their wandering life and fixed themselves to their native

---

44. Shelley, *Frankenstein*, 18.
45. Shelley, *Frankenstein*, 18.
46. This is an example of what Miller points out regarding the book, namely, that women are secondary characters and follow a typical patriarchal trope—women are caring and fragile.
47. Shelley, *Frankenstein*, 19.
48. Shelley, *Frankenstein*, 19.
49. Shelley, *Frankenstein*, 21.
50. Shelley, *Frankenstein*, 22.
51. Shelley, *Frankenstein*, 21. Despite the sentiment, this strikes me as yet another example of patriarchal trope wherein females are (fragile) *property* to be exchanged, protected, and cared for.

country."[52] This stability enabled Victor to form an intimate relationship with Henry Clerval, a fellow student and neighbor. Victor concludes, "No human being could have passed a happier childhood than myself."[53]

Victor's idealizations regarding his parents and childhood beg for psychoanalytic wariness, but for now I will simply say that his narrative to Captain Walton represents very close affectional bonds of deep interpersonal care and faith. Before moving to the crisis, it is important to mention Victor's interests in childhood, which will be key in his response to his mother's death. In the midst of all this love and affection, Victor curiously admits his "temper was sometimes violent, and my passion vehement."[54] Thankfully, these passions were directed toward learning and, in particular, a fascination for the "metaphysical, or in its highest sense, the physical secrets of the world."[55] Science and natural philosophy were areas that Victor was passionately interested in as a teenager. As he narrates: "Under the guidance of my new preceptors I entered with the greatest diligence into the search for the philosopher's stone and the elixir of life."[56] His fantasy, which presages his response to his mother's death, was to "banish disease from the human frame and render man *invulnerable* to any but a violent death!"[57]

By his account, Victor's childhood was filled with a deep sense of love and care between his parents and between the parents and the children. This care would have accompanied beliefs about his parents' care for him as well as considerable trust and fidelity from and toward them, between himself and Elizabeth, and toward his younger brother. Add to this his boyhood friendship with Henry. What is curious to me in all of this is Victor's omnipotent fantasy regarding creating an elixir that would render human beings invulnerable to death. Perhaps, this arose from facing the reality of his mother's fragile health or perhaps from the stories of his mother's experiences of loss associated with her father's death and their subsequent fall into poverty. Certainly, his mother would have experienced firsthand the precarity of life—existential insignificance (linked to the stigma of poverty) and impermanence (with regard to loss of wealth, social position, and death).

---

52. Shelley, *Frankenstein*, 22.
53. Shelley, *Frankenstein*, 23.
54. Shelley, *Frankenstein*, 23.
55. Shelley, *Frankenstein*, 23.
56. Shelley, *Frankenstein*, 25. The philosopher's stone refers to the practice of alchemy, which could refer to changing material substance into gold or to concocting an elixir that would rejuvenate life—immortality.
57. Shelley, *Frankenstein*, 26; italics mine.

Features of Grief Gone Awry: Victor's Response to His Mother's Death

The greater the love, the closer the ties, the deeper and more painful the loss, and Victor's loss occurs just before he is ready to depart for college. The first misfortune of his life, he recalls, occurred when Elizabeth became ill with scarlet fever. This is on the heels of his fantastic passion to discover an elixir to banish disease. This scare was followed quickly by another. Because of the infectious nature and severity of the illness, Victor and his father try to dissuade his mother from caring for Elizabeth. His mother, nevertheless, heroically decides to care for her, and the result is that Elizabeth "triumphed over the malignity of the distemper."[58] Unfortunately, his mother caught the disease, and it became clear that she was dying. She tells her children, "I regret I am taken from you; and, happy and beloved as I have been, is it not hard to quit you all? But these thoughts are not befitting me; I will endeavor to resign myself cheerfully to death and will indulge the hope of meeting you in another world."[59] Victor tells Walton that his mother "died calmly, and her countenance expressed affection even in death."[60]

The death of his mother was the second misfortune of Victor's young life and was profoundly painful and disturbing. "I need not," he says to Walton, "describe the feelings of those whose dearest ties are rent by that most *irreparable evil*, the void that presents itself to the soul, and the despair that is exhibited on the countenance."[61] Victor's comments about the initial experience of grief adhere to Worden's first task of mourning—accepting the reality of the loss. "It is so long," he continues, "before the mind can persuade itself that she whom we saw every day ... can have departed forever."[62] But there is an important twist in his narrative of grief. Victor goes on to say, "These are the reflections of the first days; but when the lapse of time proves

---

58. Shelley, *Frankenstein*, 28.

59. Shelley, *Frankenstein*, 28–29. I do not have time to explore the mother's response, but it is important to say that she held a belief in an afterlife wherein she would be reunited with her children and husband. This belief gave rise to her hope and both are over and against the background of existential insignificance and impermanence. The mother, in other words, unsurprisingly and understandably, wanted to extend finite significance (love for her husband and children) to the infinite and permanent. If we juxtapose Catherine's religious or spiritual belief and hope with Victor's belief and hope that science or alchemy offered the possibility of invulnerability, then we see two sides of the same coin. Religion and science, in this case, reflect a desire and a defense against existential insignificance and impermanence.

60. Shelley, *Frankenstein*, 29.

61. Shelley, *Frankenstein*, 29; italics mine.

62. Shelley, *Frankenstein*, 29.

the reality of the evil, then the actual bitterness of grief commences."[63] He then quickly moves to remark that "we still had our duties . . . we must continue our course,"[64] which means that not long after this terrible loss, life goes on, but, as we will see, derailed mourning undermines his life and the lives of others.

Before carrying on with the story, it is important to pause and take note of several key points here. Victor twice refers to his mother's death as evil—an irreparable evil. The link between death and evil was likely a common view of the time in Christian Europe. However, it is intriguing that this might suggest a link to his rage and despair that accompany her death, as well as his feelings of helplessness and powerlessness. One might imagine him sitting out of reach of his mother, who is dying, and his feelings of utter helplessness and powerlessness. These are common-enough feelings people have while sitting with a beloved person who is dying. Yet, Victor links the notion of evil to his mother's illness and death, which indicates to me that Victor has some nascent awareness of these feelings but does not allow himself to experience them. Instead, the term *evil* functions psychologically to transform or displace helplessness and powerlessness into anger/rage, despair, and bitterness and resentment toward death. In psychoanalytic parlance, helplessness and powerlessness are split off, remaining unconscious.

Linking evil to his mother's death further suggests Victor's attitude and stance toward life. If something is deemed to be evil, then it is wholly unacceptable and one is compelled to resist, fight against it, or acquiesce in despair. It is not something one accepts stoically and simply moves on, as his mother tried to do. For religious people confronting and coping with evil can mean trusting in God's love, care, and security for comfort and protection. It can also mean drawing on God's strength to resist the seemingly implacable realities of evil, which can mean accepting, in this case, death. Victor, however, does not turn to God, though as we will see he turns to science, where he can direct his hatred toward defeating death. Put differently, the appellation of evil signifies, in part, the refusal to accept the reality of existential precarity, and this refusal attends the wish for invulnerability. To defeat evil is to defeat death, which is not only a fantasy but one that obstructs the vulnerability necessary for the work of mourning. One cannot surrender to pain of loss if one is singularly bent on fighting an evil.

And this leads to another related point. Once the reality of the death sinks in (task #1), Victor speaks of the bitterness of grief. I think the bitterness of grief, which in some ways is understandable, is likewise linked to the

63. Shelley, *Frankenstein*, 29.
64. Shelley, *Frankenstein*, 29.

idea of death as evil. It may be that one becomes embittered when confronted with an implacable or irreparable reality and has difficulty holding on to and making use of past positive experiences of love, care, affection, etc. To put this another way, Victor has many positive memories of his mother's love and care and her trust and fidelity, but once she dies, he is only in touch with his anger, rage, bitterness, hatred, and despair, which are not mitigated by his positive memories. The appellation of evil removes the possibility of the balm and the comfort of memories of love and care. Evil must be faced and fought, necessarily leaving aside any vulnerability and openness to love and care—past and present. Indeed, Victor's self-imposed isolation[65] from his family for many months and his preoccupation with his studies and experimental attempts to reanimate dead tissue represents this move away from vulnerability, which is necessary for doing the work of mourning.

Let me add another thought about evil and grief/mourning. Recall Victor's youthful fantasy of creating an elixir. This desire to defeat death is a way of living that refuses to accept existential insignificance and impermanence. It is not, in my view, death and illness that Victor wishes to banish but rather the reality of his and his mother's insignificance and impermanence. This reality is what is evil. When he mentions these two misfortunes—Elizabeth's illness and his mother's death—the misfortune is not simply the threat or actual loss of the care and affection of both. Rather, it is facing the fact that the significance evident in loving relationships is impermanent. So, I would suggest here that one reason Victor never worked through the losses is that he never came to terms with the reality of existential insignificance and impermanence. He never gave up the fantasy that science could find an elixir to defeat illness and death. In other words, science became a tool to fight and defeat evil, and he associated evil not only with his mother's death and the realities of precarity and impermanence but also his terror at his own existential insignificance and impermanence.

In brief, I suggest that assigning the notion of evil to his mother's death is a symptom of failed grief in that Victor unconsciously refused to be in touch with his vulnerability, helplessness, and the impermanence of life. Indeed, impermanence and vulnerability are, in some ways, connected to his idea of evil—something to be overcome, as in the case of his grandiose desire to find the philosopher's stone. We also need to remember that he is telling Walton about a death that happened many years before, and yet, Victor's feelings, beliefs (e.g., about evil), and attitude are seemingly unchanged. In

---

65. I suggest that his retreat from family relations also represented his fear of vulnerability. His mother's death and his adopted sister's illness signified just how precarious love and life are. Isolating himself was a defense against experiencing vulnerability linked to precarity and loss.

Victor's story, there is no sense of his having worked through the other tasks of mourning, arriving at some other meaning(s) associated with death. His mother's death from beginning to end remains an evil. Let me stress that it is quite understandable for a young man to express his rage, powerlessness, and bitterness about the death of his beloved mother, but one would hope that this would be part of the first task of mourning that leads to doing the other tasks, which Victor does not do.

Several weeks after his mother's death, Victor travels to Ingolstadt to attend university. Here is where we see clear evidence of his maladaptive grief. Upon arriving at Ingolstadt, Victor is overcome by loneliness and aloneness, which he sets aside as he meets with his professors. Victor, for some years before his mother's death, had been reading passionately and tirelessly in the area of alchemy, which his father had earlier tried to dissuade him from and one professor, Krempe, later derided.[66] Bereft, Victor continues his studies, listening to another professor, Waldman, who capture his attention. During one lecture, Waldman remarks that teachers of science "penetrate into the recesses of nature and show how she works in her hiding-places. They ascend into the heavens; they have discovered how the blood circulates, and the nature of the air we breathe. They have acquired new and unlimited powers; they can command the thunders of heaven, mimic the earthquake, and even mock the invisible world with its own shadows."[67] We can imagine how this might excite a young man seeking the power to "penetrate" the mysteries of life with the aim of overcoming death. Victor visits Waldman, who does not dismiss Victor's previous studies but instead invites Victor to take up chemistry, which he readily accepts. In a moment of narcissistic grandiosity, Victor exclaims, "More, far more, will I achieve... I will pioneer a new way, explore unknown powers, and unfold to the world the deepest mysteries of creation."[68] Contrast this with the sense of melancholy and powerlessness he had experienced just days previously. Science and its prospects of glory (grandiosity) serve as a distraction from the distress of the work of mourning and experiences of loneliness from Victor's self-imposed isolation from his family.

For two years, Victor assiduously applies himself, astonishing his fellow students with his acumen and receiving the accolades of professors and the university for some discoveries he made. During these two years, he "paid no visit to Geneva, but was engaged heart and soul in the pursuit of

---

66. Shelley, *Frankenstein*, 24, 31.
67. Shelley, *Frankenstein*, 33.
68. Shelley, *Frankenstein*, 33.

some discoveries which I hoped to make."[69] This withdrawal from his stated affectional bonds represents a defense against experiencing the possibility of his loved ones' illness and death. Physical distance may have deflected Victor from the precarity of these affectional bonds, but he nevertheless was lonely. Yet, his loneliness could be managed by his preoccupation with science, which, in turn, functions to fuel the fantasy of discovering the process to reanimate dead tissue—a fantasy that represents a defense against existential vulnerability and attendant feelings of helplessness and powerlessness. Science is the god that will provide solace in the aim of defeating death. In brief, isolation and science serve as distractions from the emotional work of mourning, which signals distortions in care and faith. Care is distorted in that he does not demonstrate care and love for, nor fidelity to, his father, siblings, Elizabeth, William, Ernest, or Henry, his friend, though he affirms that he loves them. They are not forgotten, but their importance has been replaced by Victor's absolute trust in and fidelity to the power of science (and Victor's use of science for his own gains). Science, though, is much more than a mere distraction from mourning or displacement of his care and faith—it is an idol that can, in his imagination, defeat death. Science represents the possibility of salvation—permanence and existential significance.

Since science is so central in Victor's faith life, let's spend a little time explicating his work. In his studies and experiments, "The phenomenon which had peculiarly attracted my attention was the structure of the human frame . . . Whence, I often asked myself, did the principle of life proceed?"[70] Victor believes that to understand the principle of life, one must understand its decay, which leads him to the science of anatomy.[71] This directs him to burial vaults and charnel houses, where he could examine, with scientific detachment, all kinds of deaths and disease. In yet another peak of grandiosity, Victor remarks, "After days and nights of incredible labour and fatigue, I succeeded in discovering the cause of the generation of life."[72] Victor "thought that if I could bestow animation upon life-less matter, I might in the process of time (although I now found it impossible) renew life where death had apparently devoted the body to corruption."[73] Victor poured himself into this work, losing sleep and weight and distancing

---

69. Shelley, *Frankenstein*, 35.

70. Shelley, *Frankenstein*, 36.

71. One could say that Victor has confused "life" with living. His preoccupation with his idol interferes with his living—finding meaning, care, and fidelity in everyday relations.

72. Shelley, *Frankenstein*, 37.

73. Shelley, *Frankenstein*, 39.

himself even further from his family.[74] His physical and mental decline signify his lack of care for himself, as well as lack of care for his friends and family. Victor's absolute belief and trust in science represent his unconscious wish to overcome death and impermanence. Put differently, reanimating life represents a wish not simply to avoid the impermanence of life but a wish for invulnerability.

In the end, Victor is, in part, successful in reanimating life: "After days and nights of incredible labour and fatigue, I succeeded in discovering the cause of generation and life; nay, more, I became capable of bestowing animation upon lifeless matter."[75] He has a moment of moral hesitation "concerning the manner in which I should employ it."[76] Not surprisingly, Victor's hesitation recedes against the tidal wave of narcissistic grandiosity ("A new species would bless me as its creator and source").[77] After months of exhaustive work, Victor creates a being.

> I saw the dull yellow eye of the creature open; it breathed hard, and a convulsive motion agitated its limbs. How can I describe my emotions at this catastrophe, or how delineate the wretch whom with such infinite pains and care I had endeavored to form? . . . No mortal could support the horror of that countenance. A mummy again endued with animation could not be so hideous as that wretch . . . he was ugly then, but when those muscles and joints were rendered capable of motion, it became a thing such as even Dante could not have conceived.[78]

Victor, in disgust and despair, fled the apartment and upon returning found the creature had somehow left—much to his relief.

Before moving to the creature, I linger here to discuss aspects of Victor's failure to mourn. Victor's grandiose pursuit of the god of science to reanimate life is clearly linked to his mother's death and the evil he assigns to her death. If he can resurrect a dead person, he might never again have to experience the sufferings of loss with the added narcissistic benefit of being a savior, a rescuer. Put another way, instead of feeling powerless in the face of illness and death, Victor would now be powerful—a god. He would

---

74. Mary Shelley's depiction of the grandiosity, melancholia, and bursts of energy followed by depression all indicate a diagnosis of manic-depressive or bipolar illness. While this illness is a factor in Victor's failure to mourn, I am focused less on mental illness as the cause.

75. Shelley, *Frankenstein*, 37.

76. Shelley, *Frankenstein*, 38.

77. Shelley, *Frankenstein*, 38. The creature does indeed see Victor as his creator, his god, but he does not bless him, for reasons I will address below.

78. Shelley, *Frankenstein*, 42–43.

have defeated death—the evil—and made possible permanent significant relationships with those he loves. Precarity, vulnerability, impermanence, and insignificance would all fall before the power of reanimating life.

To further grasp Victor's preoccupation with science and its relation to maladaptive grief, I turn to Christopher Bollas's notion of "transformational object" and how it functions to obstruct the work of mourning, as well as impede and distort care and faith. For Bollas, the first transformational "object"[79] is the parent, who "alters the infant's environment to meet [the infant's] needs."[80] More precisely, the parent-object is "a process that alters the infant's experience" or subjectivity.[81] In other words, the "object is 'known' not so much by putting it into an object-representation, but as a recurrent *experience of being*."[82] This experience of being is contingent on the process of care and resulting relational trust, which provides the relationship and process or experiences necessary for infants to surrender to the parents' care. Naturally, these experiences are organized presymbolically, which means transformational objects lie outside consciousness—consciousness organized in relation to developmentally later symbolic processes.

For Bollas, transformational objects appear in adulthood. In terms of adult life, a transformational object or process "is pursued in order to surrender to it as a mechanism that alters the self, where the subject-as-supplicant now feels himself to be the recipient of *enviro-somatic caring*."[83] For instance, we might imagine surrendering to and being moved by a symphony, a sunset, moments of friendship. In these experiences, Bollas contends, there are traces of early presymbolic experiences of being. Of course, Bollas recognizes that transformational objects can go wrong, providing the example of Ahab's obsession or fanatical revolutionaries who seek to transform the world. Victor's turn to science strikes me as a transformational object or process used to avoid the pain of loss. To transform dead objects into life is to recover (permanently) the maternal love, devotion, and care that was ripped from his life. Death is evil, for Victor, because it obliterates experiences of being—of being significant in the eyes of his mother.[84] Vic-

---

79. Bollas acknowledges that the infant cannot yet differentiate between this or that object in the earliest phase of infancy. He views the "object" as pertaining to the process of parental caring and the infant's pre-representational organizations of this process.

80. Bollas, *The Shadow of the Object*, 15.

81. Bollas, *The Shadow of the Object*, 13.

82. Bollas, *The Shadow of the Object*, 13; italics mine.

83. Bollas, *The Shadow of the Object*, 14; italics mine.

84. If Victor was Christian, he might have turned to God, holding to the belief that his mother was still alive in heaven though gone from the Earth. In this instance, God would function as a transformational object whereby Victor could surrender to God to

tor does not surrender to science to obtain an enviro-somatic experience of being. Instead, he *uses* science to omnipotently (in his fantasy) transform the world into a world where illness and death are mostly defeated. Put differently, he uses science to avoid experiences associated with loss, namely, existential precarity and impermanence.

The negative transformational object, in the case of maladaptive grief, manifests a refusal to surrender to loss and associated feelings and thoughts. A refusal to surrender to loss, of course, is evident in the early stages of mourning when people may be in denial as they try to accept the reality of loss. However, if a person remains in denial and refuses to surrender to the experience of loss and the work of mourning, then we take note of the negative transformational object or process. This is the case in Victor's use of science as a tool to transform humanity so that he would not have to face the realities of illness and death. As with any negative transformational object, nothing is transformed. Instead, pain and suffering—insignificance and impermanence—are transferred, in this story to the dreaded creature. At the same time, the negative transformational object accompanies, in Victor's case, the unconscious desire to be invulnerable, which is closely associated with the fantasy of omnipotence. Put another way, the wished-for transformational object (science) would fundamentally alter his experiences of vulnerability, powerlessness, and helplessness in the face of death.

There is more to say about the consequences of an abortive transformational object or process vis-à-vis a failure to mourn. As noted above, Victor basically abandoned his friends and family in his pursuit of scientific knowledge. His father laments this distance, this lack of care, but Victor is undeterred from his goal of reanimating the dead. His faith in science is an idol—a science linked to Victor's fantasies of omnipotence, invulnerability, and permanence. He begins with an absolute trust in and fidelity to science. In the end, he gives up his scientific endeavors, but this does not mean he has lost his trust in science or belief in its powers. The idol remains. When in the thralls of his scientific pursuits, loyalty and trust in and care for family and friends, while not absent, recede into the background. What he cares about is science and himself—his goals, both conscious and unconscious. Indeed, his penchant to care more about his internal beliefs and desires is evident in his neglect of protecting the woman he loves, even as he has experienced and been warned about the creature's desire to cause him pain by killing those he loves (more on this later). Add to this his perfidy with

---

experience going on being vis-à-vis maternal care. Of course, God as a transformational object can function negatively as well. There are innumerable examples of religious people's maladaptive grief stemming from their rigid and certain belief that their loved one is in heaven, which can accompany the belief that death is evil.

regard to the being he has created. Victor expresses deep disgust and turns away (reflecting his faithlessness, lack of accountability, and the absence of care) from the creature.

Consequences of Grief Gone Awry

The failure to mourn almost always leads to a chain of tragic consequences for individuals and those around them. When we fail to face and work through our pain, our fears of loss, our anxieties about existential impermanence, then all of this is transferred to others, resulting in negative outcomes. In this novel, the creature, in my view, can be understood as a literary device representing the consequences of maladaptive male grief. While I have already mentioned Victor's distancing himself from family and friends as a result of his failure to mourn, in this section I want to focus on the creature to illustrate the destructive relational dynamics associated with grief and its transformational object gone awry.

Recall that Victor initially fled the scene when the creature began to come alive, only to return much later, relieved that it was no longer in his apartment. Victor's relief and meeting his friend Henry Clerval are momentarily restorative. Henry realizes that Victor is quite physically and emotionally ill and ends up caring for Victor for several months, nurturing him back to health.[85] Victor planned to return home in the fall but was delayed until the spring because of early snowstorms. Before leaving for home, Victor receives a letter from his father informing Victor that William, his brother, had been murdered while taking a walk in the mountains with his other brother, Ernest—who lost sight of William at some point. As Victor drew closer to his village, "Fear overcame me; I dared not advance, dreading a thousand nameless evils."[86] Victor stayed for two days in Lausanne before starting home again. After discovering the gates of the town were shut, Victor resolved to visit the place where William had been murdered. Despite the rain and lightning, Victor made his way and, in the midst of lamenting William's death, he "perceived in the gloom a figure . . . the filthy demon to whom I had given life."[87] In that moment, Victor knew with certainty that the creature had murdered William. He thought of pursuing the creature, but it climbed a vertical cliff with alacrity. Because of the improbability of

---

85. Shelley, *Frankenstein*, 46–47.
86. Shelley, *Frankenstein*, 58.
87. Shelley, *Frankenstein*, 59.

people being able to grasp or believe the monstrosity and power of this creature, Victor "resolved to remain silent."[88]

Victor returns home to find a household in mourning, as well as fearful and desperate because Justine, their cousin, has been arrested for William's murder. Justine, in hopes of avoiding execution, decides to confess, though clearly she is innocent. She is nevertheless condemned and, after her death, Victor experiences intense remorse for the deaths of William and Justine, as well as for the suffering of his father, Ernest, and Elizabeth.[89] Feeling responsible for these deaths and the suffering of his family members, Victor nevertheless keeps his role and the creature's deeds a secret—secrets that represent the maladaptive grief of emotional isolation, which only lead to further sufferings.

Before hearing the voice of the creature, let me stress that the relation between secrets and maladaptive grief is depicted in an encounter between Elizabeth and Victor. Elizabeth has been profoundly disillusioned by the execution of Justine. "Alas," she cries, "Victor, when falsehood can look so like the truth, who can assure themselves of certain happiness? I feel as if I were walking on a precipice . . . William and Justine were assassinated, and the murderer escapes; he walks about the world free, and perhaps respected. But even if I were condemned to suffer on the scaffold for the same crimes, I would not change places with such a wretch."[90] Her anger and disgust are not lost on Victor, for he realizes he is "the true murderer."[91] Elizabeth mistakes Victor's anguish over what she uttered for grief and responds lovingly. Instead of confessing his role, Victor again remains quiet, which further isolates him. Worse, by keeping Elizabeth in the dark, he eventually impedes her (and other family members) from protecting herself. Eventually, she too will be murdered, adding to the losses and remorse. Indeed, Victor plans to take the secret to his grave, but in the end he tells Captain Walton the sordid story of his betrayals. True to character, Victor, instead of sharing his grief and confessing his role in the deaths, leaves home alone to travel to a boyhood haunt, the village of Chamounix.

---

88. Shelley, *Frankenstein*, 61. I do not have time to delve into how Justine is accused of William's death and eventually is executed for this. The creature is implicated in her being found with evidence, but Victor feels powerless to save Justine because of his silence. This is yet another example of Victor not taking accountability for his actions or not having the integrity to face the consequences, even if that means incredulity or punishment.

89. Shelley, *Frankenstein*, 71.

90. Shelley, *Frankenstein*, 75. It is not an accident that "Justine" is closely associated with the notion of justice. Justice was executed on the scaffold, and Victor's silence is largely to blame. Maladaptive grief can result in the eclipse of justice.

91. Shelley, *Frankenstein*, 75.

It is in the mountains, while hiking, that Victor, with hatred and rage, espies the creature rapidly approaching. This is the place in the novel where the reader begins to hear the voice and appreciate the immense suffering of this creature. After raging at the "Devil," the creature responds:

> I expected this reception. All men hate the wretched; how, then, must I be hated, who am miserable beyond all living things! Yet you, my creator, detest and spurn me, thy creature, to whom thou art bound by ties only dissoluble by annihilation of one of us. You purpose to kill me. How dare you sport thus with life? Do your duty towards me, and I will do mine towards you and the rest of humanity. If you comply with my conditions, I will leave them and you at peace; but if you refuse, I will glut the maw of death, until satiated with the blood of your remaining friends.[92]

Victor responds by trying to attack him, but the creature easily eludes him. He again reminds Victor of his responsibility and reiterates his own suffering: "Everywhere I see bliss, from which I alone am irrevocably excluded. I was benevolent and good; misery made me a fiend."[93]

The creature is saying that he was created good, but the hatred, disgust, and fear of those he encountered, beginning with his abandonment by his creator, have led to extreme isolation, loneliness, and desperation. Only the bleak, craggy, windswept mountains have been "kinder to me than your fellow human beings." Indeed, the creature knows that "if the multitude of mankind knew of my existence, they would do as you do, and arm themselves for my destruction."[94] Before hearing about the specifics of the deal the creature and Victor make and its consequences, we need to hear more about the creature's journey.

The creature remembers becoming conscious in Victor's apartment. Being very cold, he donned on some of Victor's clothes, though they did not fit. He left for the darkened streets. "I was a poor, helpless, miserable wretch; I knew, and could distinguish nothing; but feeling pain invade me on all sides, I say down and wept."[95] His first perception of sunshine accompanied pleasure as he gradually began to experience and organize more sensations. Eventually the creature, hungry and in need of shelter, encountered an old man cooking a meal in his hut. When the old man saw the creature, he fled in terror.[96] After eating the shepherd's meager meal, the creature wandered down

---

92. Shelley, *Frankenstein*, 81.
93. Shelley, *Frankenstein*, 81–82.
94. Shelley, *Frankenstein*, 81.
95. Shelley, *Frankenstein*, 84.
96. Shelley, *Frankenstein*, 87.

to the village, where women fainted and children shrieked when they saw him. The "village was roused; some fled, some attacked me, until, grievously bruised by stones and many other kinds of missile weapons, I escaped."[97]

The creature found shelter in a low hovel connected to a cottage, which he feared entering given his last encounter with human beings. Here begins a lengthy narrative. The creature, unable to understand language or culture, begins to observe the family and their daily rhythms. In his initial observations, "What chiefly struck me was the gentle manner of these people, and I longed to join them, but dared not."[98] Unbeknownst to the family, they were educating the creature. He learned the language, how to read, and the family's daily rituals, and in this process he developed a sense of empathy for their lives. The creature also came to some painful revelations:

> O my creation and creator I was absolutely ignorant, but I knew that I possessed no money, no friends, no kind of property. I was, besides, endued with a figure hideously deformed and loathsome; I was not even of the same nature as man. I was more agile than they and could subsist upon a coarser diet. I bore the extremes of heat and cold with less injury to my frame: my stature far exceeded theirs. When I looked around I saw and heard none like me. Was I then a monster, a blot upon the earth, from which all men fled and whom all men disowned? I cannot describe to you the agony of these reflections inflicted upon me; I tried to dispel them, but sorrow only increased with knowledge.[99]

One can hear the profound loneliness, isolation, and shame that haunted this creature of Victor's grief. The evil Victor associates with death now confronts him as an embodied living thing—a monster he created.

The creature's story, his awakening and self-reflection, presage yet another painful encounter. After numerous months of hiding and observing, the creature decides, with much trepidation, to approach the old man, who is blind, while the rest of the family is away. The old man, De Lacey, greets him. The creature tells De Lacey that he is friendless and hopes "to claim protection of some friends, whom I sincerely love, and of whose favour I have some hopes."[100] He also mentions that this family has never seen him, exclaiming that "I am full of fears, for if I fail there, I am an outcast in the world forever."[101] The old man advises that he not despair: "to be friendless

97. Shelley, *Frankenstein*, 87.
98. Shelley, *Frankenstein*, 91.
99. Shelley, *Frankenstein*, 101.
100. Shelley, *Frankenstein*, 113.
101. Shelley, *Frankenstein*, 113.

is indeed to be unfortunate, but the hearts of men, when unprejudiced by any obvious self-interest, are full of brotherly love and charity."[102] Just as the two are nearing acceptance and a kind of intimacy, the family comes home and the young man attacks the creature. The creature knows he could tear the man apart but instead flees.

This is the final rejection. The creature rages in the woods, sinking into despair. In those moments, "I declared everlasting war against the species, and more than all, against him who had formed me."[103] He begins to formulate a plan, which becomes evident as the reason for the encounter with Victor in the mountains. Shunned and hated by humanity, the creature wants Victor to make a creature like himself—a being that would assuage his loneliness. Here is the deal; if Victor fails to fulfill it, the creature will "share my wretchedness" with Victor.[104] Victor initially agrees. He does so not out of empathy or compassion for the creature's losses and immense suffering but out of fear that the creature will kill more of his family and friends. In terms of the creature, Victor is the wished-for transformational object. The creature believes that his life will be transformed from loneliness to companionship. Later, Victor decides he cannot in good conscience do as the creature wishes.[105] The creature then proceeds to do what he promised and kills everyone Victor loves. They become bound by their mutual wretchedness as Victor pursues the creature to the ends of the earth. Between them there is only the aridity of carelessness, hatred, and perfidy.

It might be easy to see the creature as a monster, but, as he notes, he was not created this way. He was created to be loved and to give love, which he desperately longs for. Even his initial abandonment by Victor does not lead to destructive desires or behaviors. Moreover, the creature observes, listens, and learns from the family he observes. After taking the huge risk to become vulnerable, which is necessary in seeking and receiving love, the creature experiences yet another rejection—another instance of hatred, disgust, horror, and violence. This is a catastrophic loss and, for him, ungrievable. His murderous envy, in other words, represents an eclipse of care and faith, as well as an unwillingness to grieve. And why would he grieve? Human beings grieve to honor those they love, and in this grief there is a seed of hope that love will return in another form. Grief and mourning,

---

102. Shelley, *Frankenstein*, 113–14.
103. Shelley, *Frankenstein*, 116.
104. Shelley, *Frankenstein*, 82.
105. Remember, Victor keeps all of this a secret until meeting Captain Walton. Also, Victor decides to marry Elizabeth, even though this puts her squarely in the crosshairs of the creature's murderous envy. Victor's isolation from grief and failure to tell people he loves of what he has done strike me as manifestations of grief gone terribly awry.

which require vulnerability and surrender to the pains of loss, create a space for the possibility of a future love, which the creature has no hope of attaining—unless Victor produces another being.

It is not death that is evil, as we are led to believe in reading Victor's story. Evil arises and becomes embodied when Victor refuses to mourn, when he seeks invulnerability by trying to reanimate life with the omnipotent aim of defeating illness and death. Victor, in the face of the existential impermanence of life and love, refuses to accept this, and the creature represents the consequences of Victor's aborted grief and mourning. Aborted grief and mourning are incapable of giving birth to new life, new experiences of love. Only destruction remains. I add here that Victor and the creature are two sides of the same coin in that Victor's transformational object is science, which produces the creature. The creature's transformational object is Victor. Both objects are failures not because they are fantastic but because they function to obstruct the hard work of mourning lost love and accepting the existential impermanence of life and love. As the creature recognizes, only in their deaths will their interminable enmity end.

Conclusion

Victor flees the profound experience of helplessness and powerlessness that emerges in the face of the death of someone he loves by pursuing the power and glory of science and in the hubristic power of reanimating life. In his attempt to reanimate the dead, Victor wishes to avoid the pain of loneliness that follows the death of his beloved mother. By contrast, the creature, not unlike many human beings, experiences catastrophic loneliness. Perhaps, we could say this is a loneliness instilled by his creator, maybe even projected onto the creature by Victor, who refuses to face his own loneliness. The creature similarly is unwilling to face and work through this loneliness and accompanying existential helplessness and powerlessness. Instead, he demands his creator give him a mate and, when this fails, the creature trusts in his power to create in his creator the misery he feels—a misery he will not let go of and that fuels his bitterness and envy. They are locked in a tragic dance of refusing to grieve, to let go, to accept, if only reluctantly, the reality of existential precarity and impermanence. They have a faith relationship that reveals a marital vow, if you will—an arid and tragic vow that they will share in misery unto death.

While the focus in this chapter is on men, I do not think that grief gone awry is exclusive to men. But I wonder if patriarchal cultures, like the one Mary Shelley was writing in and experiencing, give rise to forms of masculinity that resist existential vulnerability and precarity by way of maintaining control, power, and privilege. Indeed, her story, in one sense, parallels the Oedipal story in which Tiresias, the prophet, tells King Laius that he will be killed by his son. Laius will have none of this and has his infant son taken out and killed. The son is found and ends up living—and later unwittingly kills his father and marries his mother. Here is yet another story of patriarchy in which a person refuses to grieve, to let go, and the result is tragedy. Patriarchy creates apparatuses that further the power and privileges of men over women (and over "mother" nature). Boys and men learn to depend on this power and their privileges for a sense of self-esteem, self-confidence, and self-respect. This power, in other words, undergirds male agency, which can at times mask or distract from the realities of existential precarity, insignificance, and impermanence. The seductions and distractions of power and privilege invariably impact and distort love and faith.

Victor's mother and later his wife are beloved yet are mere subordinate figures to Victor's desires and hopes. Victor's desire to reanimate the dead is but another iteration of power over and refusal to surrender to the reality of vulnerability and loss. The death of his mother is not simply a reminder of Victor's existential helplessness but a confrontation of the illusory power males have over "mother" nature. Victor cares only for what the creature can do for him, just as he loves and wants to hold on to his mother and wife for what they do for him. Put differently, Victor has no desire to create a being whom he will love and care for in itself, in its singularity; he desires to obtain power over the realities of nature, namely, insignificance and the impermanence of all living beings.

Lest we believe this is a story for a different time, we need only read the news today to take note of mainly white men who are misogynistic, incel, fascist, and rightwing Christian conservatives who seek to manage their existential precarity and vulnerability by seeking to subordinate women, marginalize people of color and LGBTQI persons, and follow authoritarian leaders who tell them what they want to hear. Are not these instances of persons failing to grieve, to let go of their preoccupation with power and privilege? Are not these instances of creating relationships whereby persons' misery, fear, insecurity, anxiety, and loneliness are projected onto marginalized individuals and communities? I suspect many readers can recall encountering people, in this case men, who refuse to let go of power and privilege and, in the process, leave a tragic trail of misery, carelessness, and perfidy.

Of course, it is difficult to do the work of empathic understanding when we encounter misogynists, authoritarians, etc.—men who refuse to let go of power over others and nature and, concomitantly, refuse to embrace existential insignificance and impermanence. I think this is the case because men who fail to grieve, more often than not, unwittingly share their unacknowledged misery, bitterness, loneliness, hatred, and fear with bystanders, making it understandably difficult for anyone to see the pain and loss behind the facades of power. In Shelley's story, the relationship between Victor and his creature manifests a dearth of empathy and compassion and an ocean of carelessness and perfidy. The creature attempts to elicit compassion from his creator, only to fail in the end. Yet, the reader is, in my view, invited to have empathy for both characters, recognizing the deeply tragic reality that is fostered not simply by Victor's acts and subsequently the creature's actions but also by the larger systems (e.g., patriarchal apparatuses in education, politics, and science) that are in the background. Our empathic understanding and care, however, do not mean we must accept or fail to hold people accountable. In our pastoral care to boys and men who fail to grieve, empathy is the first task. The second task is to find ways to intervene, to assist or invite boys and men to grieve, to let go, and to accept the existential vulnerability and the precarity of life.

2

Ahab's Fatal Attraction

Defending against Loss and the Distortion of Care and Faith

> The most terrible thing in life is that the possessions of which we have been deprived are not only missing, but they exist in us like upside down shadows, nocturnal and devastating powers . . . We are also what we are not.[1]
>
> Every kind of madness is a severance of my relation to others.[2]

I suspect many of us have, at one time or another, obsessed about work, relationships, religion, or some other feature of human life. Many times our obsessions are fleeting, while at other times they are more enduring and troubling. For those whose obsessions perdure, becoming part of their way of being in the world, it is likely that, in our day, they will need help in the form of therapy and/or medication. The term *obsess* comes from the Latin *ob* (opposite) and *sedere* (sit), which in late Middle English was associated with being haunted or possessed by an evil spirit. Today, in the West, we eschew the notion of evil spirits and instead rely on the *Diagnostic and Statistical Manual of Mental Disorders* (5th edition) for criteria to diagnose

---

1. Marcel, *The Existential Background of Human Dignity*, 61.
2. Mounier, *Personalism*, 20.

obsession. Yet, the idea of evil spirits conveys a phenomenological truth, namely, a sense that one is not in control or has lost one's capacity for agency and reason. Put another way, the evil spirit will not let go of the person and, therefore, the haunted individual needs a religious cure. In our present time, it is less about spirits and more about the obsessed person's experience of feeling incapable of letting go of the object or activity. While I am glad we have moved away from theological explanations of evil as a source of obsession, there is another truth to be gleaned here. Today, diagnoses tend to focus on the individual, offering psychological and medical explanations for obsession. But I think obsessed persons can be unwittingly caught in the grip of powerful systemic forces that shape their subjectivity and fuel their obsessions, leading to fatal attractions or, more broadly, tragic and painful attachments. Caught in the talons of these larger systems, we find the rationales for our obsessions, and these rationales screen our unconscious fears and anxieties, occlude our agency, and undermine our judgments. To be obsessed, in short, is a maniacal refusal to let go, to surrender to grief and mourning. This refusal and the resulting fatal attraction can be supported by larger systems and forces of meaning.

A classic tale of a fatal obsession is Herman Melville's *Moby-Dick*.[3] In the previous chapter, I explored Victor Frankenstein's refusal to grieve, arguing that this had roots in the larger patriarchal systems that, in Shelley's day, undergirded society, religion, and science. Melville's novel, written in the same century, offers another opportunity to examine masculinity and the failure to let go, though in this chapter I consider the relation between Ahab's[4] fatal attraction in terms of other systems of meaning and how they distort care and faith, giving rise to a pathological type of masculinity. More specifically, to understand this pathological masculinity, I situate Melville's novel in a society where liberalism, capitalism, and imperialism, which were dominant semiotic systems in the nineteenth century, served as key factors in shaping and supporting a type of masculinity[5] wherein one possesses a maniacal preoccupation with one's individual goals or self-interests that

---

3. Melville, *Moby-Dick*.

4. The name Ahab comes from the Hebrew *ahavah* and *aheb*, meaning to love. As I mention below, Ahab's mother dies when he is a young child, and the story itself reflects the distortion of love/care—a distortion that arises out of a failure to let go not only of the loss of his leg but also, I argue, of the earlier losses linked to the death of his mother. "Captain Ahab," Wikipedia, https://en.wikipedia.org/wiki/Captain_Ahab, accessed July 17, 2019.

5. Malte Ibsen explores the impact of the Frankfurt School of critical thinking. He notes that both Theodor Adorno and Max Horkheimer viewed capitalism as a dominant system that adversely shapes the subjectivity of residents of market societies. See Ibsen, *A Critical Theory of Global Justice*.

accompanies instrumentalized, conditional care, if present, and, correspondingly, an instrumental, contractual faith. There are two steps before moving to discuss the novel. First, I briefly define and depict the notions of care and faith since these concepts will serve as the hermeneutical lens. Second, I provide a concise overview of the sociopolitical and economic context of the nineteenth century to show that liberalism, capitalism, and Western imperialism were dominant representational systems shaping the lives of U.S. citizens. As I hope to make clear, these systems are in the background of the novel and serve as factors that inform Ahab's masculinity and his obsession.[6] These two steps are foundational for turning to the novel itself and the depiction and analysis of Ahab's masculinity and fatal attraction.

There are a few caveats and clarifications to attend to before setting sail. First, a literary work is a cultural artifact, often both disclosing and hiding aspects of the society, politics, and economics of the time. Edward Saïd, for instance, surveys Western literature in the nineteenth and twentieth centuries, revealing how "Orientals" were portrayed and consistently misrepresented.[7] These distortions were, Saïd argues, inextricably joined to Western imperialism and its violence and exploitation of people from the Mideast to China and Japan. Similarly, Saïd's contemporary, Stuart Hall, explores how people from the Caribbean were misrepresented in literature by colonial masters.[8] One need not be a literary critic to examine these cultural artifacts and expose their misrepresentations. Sandor Gilman[9] and Roy Porter[10] delve into how people suffering from "mental illness" were represented and treated in the nineteenth and twentieth centuries. Alice Miller[11] and Marcia Bunge[12] explore social and theological representations of childhood and how they influenced child-rearing. And Michel Foucault,[13] a philosopher, turns to the cultural artifacts of the nineteenth century to understand prisons and societal discipline. All of this leads me to say that a pastoral theologian can also turn to literature, assessing and critiquing stories as cultural artifacts revealing various representations embedded in and supported by social, political, and economic systems or

---

6. While I focus on Ahab's masculinity, it is important to note that there were other expressions of masculinity on the *Pequod*, as well as other whaling ships, which I allude to below. That said, Ahab's masculinity is a trope for a kind or type of masculinity.

7. Saïd, *Culture and Imperialism*; Saïd, *Orientalism*.

8. Hall, *Cultural Studies 1983*; Hall, *Representation*.

9. Gilman, *Difference and Pathology*; Gilman, *Inscribing the Other*.

10. Porter, *The Faber Book of Madness*; Porter, *A Social History of Madness*.

11. Miller, *For Your Own Good*.

12. Bunge, *The Child in Christian Thought*.

13. Foucault, *Discipline and Punish*.

apparatuses of the time. What distinguishes a pastoral theologian from those already cited is that a pastoral theologian's critical analysis of a text (1) depends on the interpretive lens of care and faith, (2) aims at identifying sources of pathologies or distortions of care and faith, and (3) offers pastoral interventions to alleviate unnecessary suffering and free individuals and communities from marginalization and oppression.[14]

A second clarification entails the point that Melville was not aiming to portray a pathological type of masculinity linked to liberalism, capitalism, and imperialism. It is more likely that Melville, like other artists before him, was simply writing a tale about human obsession and its tragic results. That said, my premise is that novelists dip their pens in the culture of their time, unconsciously portraying social, economic, and political beliefs of the era.[15] Third, if Melville's depiction of Ahab is consonant with masculine tropes of the time, then this raises a question about a twenty-first-century diagnostic analysis. Don't I as a writer also dip my pen into my culture and, if so, wouldn't it be unseemly to judge Ahab's masculinity by twenty-first-century views? A simple answer to that question is that Melville wrote a tragic story about the mad perversity of Ahab's obsession that led to utter disaster—an obsession that one might find across time and culture. I rush to add that what we have in common with Melville's time is liberalism, capitalism, and a kind of imperialism—a post-imperial imperialism.[16] This suggests that similar pathological types of masculinity are present in our day and culture, though I do not have the time to explore or provide examples of that idea in this article except to identify men such as Martin Shkreli, Donald Trump, Jordan Peterson, Matt Gaetz, and others who, in my view, exemplify pathological masculinity—a pathological masculinity that is dangerous. Fourth, another premise is that care and faith are gendered and that both are shaped by cultural, political, and economic institutions, as well as concomitant disciplinary regimes. So, the dynamics of care and faith in Melville's depiction of Ahab (of his masculinity) are shaped by the cultural, political, and economic forces of his time. Fifth, my overall approach to this novel is analogous to a pastoral psychotherapist who listens to a patient's story with an eye toward raising a person's consciousness in order "to choose an action with respect to the *real source of the conflict,*

---

14. The third aspect is not addressed in this chapter.

15. Some stories seem to transcend time and cultures. Greek myths and the tragedies of Shakespeare are examples. However, these stories still contain representations grounded in the culture and period they originated in. For instance, Oedipus Rex displays a masculinity rooted in unquestioned Greek patriarchy.

16. See Johnson, *Sorrows of Empire*; Klein, *The Shock Doctrine*; Lundestad, *The Rise and Decline*; Rieff, "Liberal Imperialism."

i.e., the social structure."[17] As Frantz Fanon and Ralph Ellison recognized, psychopathologies or psychological suffering are often rooted in social, political, and economic systems of oppression and marginalization, and knowing this can assist one to act toward the real sources of suffering.[18] Thus, we need to pay close attention to how the apparatuses of capitalism, liberalism, and imperialism can distort masculinity and, concomitantly, relations of care and faith. Finally, and relatedly, this chapter reflects my belief that pastoral theologians are also public-political theologians who carefully critique cultural, political, and economic structures and forces that impact human survival and flourishing.[19] For political pastoral theologians, one possibility is to examine critically cultural artifacts, revealing illusions and distorted representations with the aim of constructing pastoral actions that contribute to the flourishing of human beings, other species, and the Earth.

Interpretive Lens of Care and Faith

Pastoral theologians have long been concerned about the foundations and practices of pastoral care,[20] care of children,[21] care of older women,[22] care for the traumatized,[23] care for ostracized persons,[24] care for the grieving,[25] and innumerable other issues of human suffering and need. Recently, care theorists have also sought to explore the notion of care, though with particular focus on care as a political concept.[26] Likewise, some pastoral theologians recognize that care is inextricably connected to political and economic realities.[27] It is neither possible nor necessary to summarize these

17. Fanon, *Black Skin, White Masks*.
18. Fanon, *Alienation and Freedom*; Ellison, *Shadow and Act*.
19. LaMothe, *Care of Souls*.
20. Clebsch and Jaekle, *Pastoral Care in Historical Perspective*; Clinebell, *Basic Types of Pastoral Care*; Doehring, *The Practice of Pastoral Care*; Dykstra, *Images of Pastoral Care*; Gerkin, *An Introduction to Pastoral Care*; Patton, *Pastoral Care in Context*; Scheib, *Pastoral Care*.
21. Flesberg, *The Switching Hour*; Lester, *Pastoral Care*.
22. Scheib, *Challenging Invisibility*.
23. Poling, *Render unto God*; van Deusen Hunsinger, *Bearing the Unbearable*.
24. Marshall, *Counseling Lesbian Partners*; Sanders, *A Brief Guide to Ministry*.
25. Kelley, *Grief*; White, *Saying Goodbye*.
26. Bubeck, *Care, Gender, and Justice*; Gilligan, *In a Different Voice*; Hamington, *Embodied Care*; Robinson, *The Ethics of Care*; Robinson, *Globalizing Care*; Sevenhuijsen, *Citizenship and the Ethics of Care*; Tronto, *Caring Democracy*; Tronto, *Moral Boundaries*.
27. Helsel, *Pastoral Power*; LaMothe, *Care of Souls*; LaMothe, *Pastoral Reflections*;

discourses about care. Instead, my purpose here is to provide a cursory overview of the concept of care (and faith) so that it can serve as an interpretive lens for depicting Ahab's distorted masculinity. To do this, I first turn to Daniel Engster's definition of care before offering an emended version that takes into account pastoral perspectives.[28]

Engster, after surveying care theory literature, offered this definition: care is "everything we do to help individuals meet their vital biological needs, develop or maintain their basic capabilities, and avoid or alleviate unnecessary or unwanted pain and suffering, so that they can survive, develop, and function in society."[29] Since the strengths and limitations of Engster's definition have been addressed elsewhere,[30] let's push ahead to a modified definition that includes core pastoral theological principles. Care is everything we do to help individuals, families, communities, and societies to (1) meet vital biological, psychosocial, and existential or spiritual needs of individuals, families, and communities; (2) develop or maintain basic capabilities with the aim of human flourishing; (3) facilitate participation in the polis; and (4) maintain a habitable environment for the common good of all.[31] I add to this definition that care and pastoral care are political concepts that necessarily involve shared critical[32] and constructive reflection on how the structures (and their accompanying narratives and practices) of the state, governing authorities, and non-state organizations (e.g., businesses, labor unions, religious and secular communities, etc.) and actors meet or fail to meet the four features of this definition of care.

While there are many attributes of care vis-à-vis the polis, I focus on two foundational attributes, namely, personal recognition and knowing[33] and self-limitation for the sake of the Other. The basis of all acts of genuine care is recognizing the Other as a person—a unique, inviolable, valued, and agentic subject. From a theological perspective, recognition of the Other

---

Rogers-Vaughn, *Caring for Souls*; Smith, *The Relational Self*.

28. Engster, *The Heart of Justice*.

29. Engster, *The Heart of Justice*, 28.

30. LaMothe, *Care of Souls*.

31. LaMothe, *Pastoral Reflections*, 8.

32. Max Horkheimer commented that "the future of humanity depends on the existence today of the critical attitude." Horkheimer, as quoted in Wolin, *Politics and Vision*, 231. This critical attitude becomes crucial when cultural critics, such as Henry Giroux and Dany-Robert Dufour, note that with the rise of neoliberal capitalism there has been an increase in the formation of subjects or citizens who are acritical of the systems that contribute to their suffering and the suffering of others, including other species. Giroux, *Disposable Youth*; Dufour, *The Art of Shrinking Heads*.

33. For a more in-depth discussion of personal knowing and the polis, see Macmurray, *Persons in Relation*.

as a person affirms the dictum that human beings are created in the image and likeness of God[34] and, therefore, are due dignity and respect, which are revealed in acts of attending to their needs and emotional experiences, namely, acts of care. I add that personal recognition and knowing creates a communicative space for Others to appear as they are, to express their needs, desires, and experiences, which eventuates in the development of (or sustains) the self-esteem, self-confidence, and self-respect necessary for social agency.[35] The personal recognition in acts of care includes the dialectal tension between likeness in difference and difference in likeness.[36] Put another way, when I recognize Others as persons, there is a moment of identification and disidentification. Identification means the Other is like me qua person. The moment of disidentification (not-me) fosters a space for Others to assert themselves in their singularities, as they are—not as I wish or expect them to be. This disidentification creates a psychic-relational space for me to know the Other as a person in all that person's uniqueness and particularity. Personal knowing, in brief, founds the possibility for me to care for individuals as they are, with their particular experiences and needs.[37]

Personal recognition and knowing are not simply things that found caring relations within families and friendships. There are larger social, cultural, and political realities where personal recognition provides the

---

34. A problem with this phrase is that it is often associated simply with human beings. This means human beings are privileged over other species, which, more often than not, provides the rationale to exploit other species. I contend that the phrase "created in the image and likeness of God" also refers to other species. Let me add here that there is a similar problem with the idea of personal recognition. Being a "person" is typically associated with other human beings, denying personhood to other species. Anthropologists such as Eduardo Kohn, Tim Ingold, and Eduardo Viveiros de Castro have noted that many Indigenous people see other species as persons or potential persons, which is a central feature of their epistemologies. They believe that one can only know another being by seeing that being as a person, which does not mean other species are pseudo human beings. The personhood of an owl is completely distinct from the personhood of a human being. Ingold, *The Perception of the Environment*; Kohn, *How Forests Think*; Viveiros de Castro, *Cannibal Metaphysics*.

35. Honneth, *The Struggle for Recognition*.

36. Benjamin, "Sameness and Difference."

37. William Easterly's work illustrates the problems that arise when personal recognition is abstract and removed from the concrete realities of persons' lives. He documents how caring experts are determined to provide aid for people in need (e.g., Ethiopia). They devise plans and programs to address needs without asking the recipients what they need or their thoughts about how to meet these needs. This is a kind of abstract, distant personal recognition that eschews the particular experiences and ideas of those who receive aid. As Easterly points out, while these experts are well-meaning and somewhat helpful, they often have less than the desired impact because they do not know the people they seek to serve. Easterly, *The Tyranny of Experts*.

basis of social-civic care necessary for the survival and well-being of the community or society.[38] Personal recognitions in these more macro contexts are supported by collective narratives, practices, and institutions that undergird the basic civic care that establishes cooperation and, ideally, the mutual attending to and meeting the needs of other members of society. In other words, mutual-personal recognition is necessary for civic care and cooperation toward realizing the common good. Let me offer a simple example. The mutual-personal recognition that takes place between a shopper and cashier can be said to represent basic civic or social care between strangers who share a common language. At the most basic level, each is meeting the need to be recognized and treated as a person, which founds a cooperation between them toward a shared goal. Shoppers who treat the cashier merely as an object in service of his needs and desires may get their groceries, but they will contribute to the cashier's experience of alienation, hurt, and humiliation.

John Macmurray points out that personal recognition necessarily includes object knowing.[39] Object knowing, which is related to instrumental reasoning, is simply the ability to recognize, categorize, and use objects in space, and this capacity appears first in psychosocial development. The child, in other words, necessarily needs to be able to locate, categorize, evaluate, and engage various objects. The capacity to recognize Others (and other species) as persons develops later. For Macmurray, these two forms of knowing are interrelated, though they can be separated. For instance, to recall Hegel, the master does not recognize the slave as a person but rather as an object to serve and meet the master's self-interests. If personal recognition is even present, it is subordinated to instrumental knowing, dismissing or denying the singularity of the enslaved person. This is an unjust and careless relation.

---

38. Michael Hardt and Antonio Negri, in their book *Commonwealth*, argue that love is an essential concept for politics because it is central in the establishment of what they call the common—the shared material and created resources. Similarly, Martha Nussbaum contends that love is a necessary political concept. I view love and care as related but distinct concepts, but my focus here is on the more general term of care. Briefly, it may be helpful to say a few words about these two terms. Love includes care, but to care does not necessarily include love. I can care about people I have never met while sending them aid. The Samaritan cared for the injured man, but I do not think he loved him. Some might try to make the case that he did love him, but this is love in the abstract. A physician or nurse can care for someone she thinks is despicable. There is care, but no love. Care, then, from my perspective is more a fundamental human reality and a more fundamental political concept. I believe, then, that developing and maintaining caring attitudes and behaviors in society are more realistic goals than love. Care for others, for neighbors, is more likely and more common than love. Hardt and Negri, *Commonwealth*, 179–88. Nussbaum, *Political Emotions*.

39. Macmurray, *Persons in Relation*.

This said, Macmurray also recognizes occasions when personal knowing is subordinate to object knowing, as in the case of a physician diagnosing a patient. This is ethical as long as it is time limited and clearly for the sake of caring for the patient qua person. To return to the grocery store, both the shopper and the cashier are operating out of their respective roles, but ideally in the foreground is mutual-personal recognition, while object knowing remains in the background. If the cashier were to see the shoppers simply and solely in terms of their role as shoppers, then object knowing would be in the foreground. In short, personal recognition and knowing, which depend on object knowing being secondary, found acts of care that involve recognizing and meeting needs. In the social-public realm, mutual-personal recognition is necessary for civic care that leads to an individual and shared sense of self-esteem, self-respect, and self-confidence that are necessary for civic agency and cooperation.[40]

A second crucial aspect of care is the capacity for self-limitation aimed at meeting the Other's needs. There are degrees of self-limitation. On one end of the scale, it can include sacrificing one's life to save the life of another person. On the other is the trivial self-limitation in something like opening a door for a person in need of help. There are also routine examples of good-enough parents who, in caring for the manifold needs of their children, limit themselves for the sake of their children's flourishing. In terms of the social-political realm, the capacity for self-limitation is necessary for civic agency and cooperation. For Hegel, self-limitation includes the realization that "each subject is able to perceive the liberty of the other as the prerequisite of his own self-realization."[41] In other words, individuals eventually realize that the Other constitutes the "condition of their own freedom,"[42] which attends some degree of mutual self-limitation for the sake of each having the freedom to pursue some good. This also means that mutual self-limitation is necessary for social cooperation toward the common good, which means there must be sufficient expression of civic care and agency to achieve some aspects of the common good.

Here we note two types of self limitation vis-à-vis care. The first type of self-limitation relates to the social contract, wherein mutual self-limitation contributes to the exercise of civic agency. Thomas Hobbes, I believe, was skeptical about this, advocating for a leviathan to ensure the social contract of self-limitation. There is an instrumental aspect to this kind of self-limitation. The second type of social self-limitation entails limiting oneself

---

40. See Honneth, *The Struggle for Recognition*.
41. Honneth, *Freedom's Right*, 8.
42. Honneth, *Freedom's Right*, 50.

simply for the sake of the Other's survival and flourishing. Self-limitation in this respect is not "contractual." Neighbors caring for an older person on their street can limit themselves by virtue of meeting the needs of the elderly person.

This said, the capacity for self-limitation is not always or necessarily personal or aimed at care or another's freedom. As Max Weber illustrated, the rise in capitalism in the West could be partly attributed to the spirit of Protestantism and its asceticism or self-limitation.[43] So, wealthy capitalists can exhibit a significant capacity for self-limitation (and instrumental reasoning associated with object knowing) in pursuit of their own ends, while disregarding the agencies, freedoms, and needs of Others. In this context, capitalists "care" for their workers to the extent that the workers cooperate in achieving a profit. This means personal recognition is conditional and instrumental, as well as subordinate to object knowing. Capitalists, in one sense, recognize that their "self-realization" (self-interests) depends on the cooperation of Others, but this is not mutual because the capitalists do not care about the self-realization of their workers, or, if they do care, this care is not essential to the aims of profit.

Closely associated with the notion of care is faith. These concepts are to my mind inextricably related. Faith for Niebuhr is an anthropological concept that entails three interrelated dialectical pairs, namely, belief-disbelief, trust-distrust, and loyalty-disloyalty (I add hope-hopelessness).[44] The dynamics of faith, for Niebuhr, are joined to and contingent on collectively held narratives that inform individuals' decisions about who or what to believe or disbelieve, who to trust or not trust, and to whom one is obliged to be loyal. From a different yet related angle, Roman Catholic theologian Karl Rahner states that faith is "an abiding feature of man's mode of existence as a *person*,"[45] welding the idea of faith to the recognition of Others as persons. Indeed, faith is thus understood as "primarily and properly not a relation of man to things, propositions, or formulas, but a *relation* to persons."[46] The dynamics of faith, then, are related to personal recognition and knowing, which, as noted above, founds all caring acts.

Since I mentioned care in relation to parents, it is notable that Erik Erikson depicts the first developmental task for child and parent as navigating trust and mistrust.[47] The parent's caring attunement to the baby's assertions

43. Weber, *The Protestant Ethic*.
44. Niebuhr, *Faith on Earth*.
45. Rahner, "A Way to Faith," 496.
46. Frei, "Faith and Knowledge," 520.
47. Erikson, *Childhood and Society*.

provide pre-representational experiences of trust, which necessarily accompany cooperation. When there are relational disruptions and a heightening of anxiety and mistrust, the parent's reparative acts of care restore trust and cooperation. In shifting to the social realm, it is difficult to imagine a functioning society without some degree of civic faith, wherein there is sufficient mutual belief, trust, loyalty, and hope necessary for civic cooperation toward a common aim. If we think of a Hobbesian depiction of society that is grounded in the "primal act of recognition as enmity,"[48] we can imagine that it is a society where everybody cares for themselves and no other, and trust and loyalty are enforced by the leviathan—a leviathan that, through political violence or threat of political violence, enforces the social contract of instrumental self-limitation. This might be a stable society, but in my view it would be a dystopian society, one in which personal recognition and knowing would, at best, be subordinate to object knowing or instrumental reasoning. Moreover, self-limitation would be for the sake of one's own self-realization, while trust, loyalty, and cooperation would be contingent and conditional (on achieving one's needs and desires). A dystopian society where care and faith are conditional might survive, but it could not flourish.

There are two more facets of care and faith. Precarity is an existential feature of all living beings. Human beings are not invulnerable; they are vulnerable in the face of the vicissitudes of life. A second aspect of life is its existential insignificance and impermanence. Relations of good-enough care and faith help us face and manage precarity, as well as existential insignificance and impermanence. Parental care, for instance, helps children become resilient in the face of the precarious realities of life. Caring and devotion to a sick friend or relative help manage the precarity of an illness. From a different angle, the care and love we have for people mean they are significant to us and they, hopefully, experience themselves as significant. Care and faith, however, are impermanent, eventually passing in time and memory. It is a mistake to confuse the impermanence of our capacity to assign significance with eternity. Indeed, to do so is a defense against facing precarity, vulnerability, and existential insignificance and impermanence. All we have is now—moments of caring and, if you will, faithing, which will pass out of existence and memory.

In summary, mutual civic care is foundational for any polity if it is to survive and flourish. The core of care is interpersonal recognition, wherein each individual affirms and respects the Other's uniqueness, value, inviolability, and responsiveness, which further establishes an individual's sense of self-esteem, self-respect, and self-confidence—the foundation of political agency.

---

48. Wolin, *Politics and Vision.* 418.

Care, vis-à-vis a polis, is inextricably joined to relational or civic faith—trust, fidelity, and hope. Together, both civic care and trust found spaces of speaking and acting together—political cooperation—wherein actors assert their agency for the survival and flourishing of its members. This care and faith, ideally, help us handle existential precarity and provide experiences of significance in the face of existential insignificance and impermanence.

The *Pequod* as a Floating Polis of Men: Distortions of Care and Faith

To turn briefly to Melville's novel, here we see a society of men, a polis on the sea, comprising men from diverse cultures who are plying the oceans in search of whales to kill for profit. Their cooperation is aimed at survival and wages or profit, and this cooperation suggests a level of mutual personal recognition, trust, and fidelity. The captain of a whaling ship is, in a sense, a leviathan, ensuring there is sufficient cooperation to achieve the crew's mission. Yet in the case of Ahab, we have a captain who is singularly obsessed with ensuring the success of his self-interests alone. Before turning to Melville's novel, it is important to say more about the background systemic sources for Ahab's masculinity, obsession, and attendant distortion of care and faith.

Nineteenth-century Semiotic Systems and *Moby-Dick*

Moby-Dick was published in 1851, not long after the imperialist idea of Manifest Destiny emerged and nearly thirty years after the Monroe Doctrine was established. The idea of Manifest Destiny rationalized and justified ruthless imperialist expansion into and expropriation of Native American lands to the Pacific Ocean (and beyond, e.g., Alaska, Hawaii, the Philippines). At the same time, the Monroe Doctrine justified political, economic, and military control of Central and South American countries. U.S. imperialism, despite its various secular and theological rationalizations of the empire of liberty (Thomas Jefferson) or bringing civilization to Native peoples, was inextricably joined to the proliferation of capitalism, which Major General Smedley Butler poignantly depicted in his work *War Is a Racket*.[49] As the U.S. imperial proclivities emerged, the nineteenth century also saw explosive growth in industrialization in the U.S. and the imperialistic, martial pursuit of other markets in the U.S. and abroad. The incredible

---

49. Butler, *War Is a Racket*.

expansion of capitalism, then, was accompanied by imperialism and liberal philosophy, which Hobbes and Locke had developed in concert with the rise of capitalism in England and its imperialistic ambitions.[50] Liberalism, in the U.S., served to bolster the proliferation in the pursuit of individual self-interests or self-realization, which neatly fit with and supported the growth of capitalism and Western imperial expansion exemplified in the nineteenth-century phrase "Go West young man"—a phrase that masks (mainly male) settler imperialism and the ethnic cleansing of Indigenous peoples. From a different angle, Hobbes's liberal view of freedom sought to guarantee that "individuals are subject to no other vision of the good life than their own,"[51] which, I argue, intersected with Western capitalism and imperialism. In Charles Taylor's words, "Self-determining freedom demands that I break the hold of all . . . external impositions, and decide for myself alone."[52] This liberal view, while bolstering capitalism's focus on property and individual wealth and fueling imperialism's disregard of the self-interests of other peoples (except to the extent one has to limit oneself to, ironically, advance one's self-interests), undermined the idea of "self-realization as an eminently communal, cooperative endeavor."[53]

These semiotic systems are evident in Melville's novel. The whaling ship *Pequod* was a capitalist enterprise. Financed by two local men (Bildad and Captain Peleg), the *Pequod's* mission was to harvest whales (blubber, oil, ivory, etc.) for the sake of profit.[54] Whaling ships were not searching for whales to obtain whale meat to feed people for the sake of their survival. Whales, like other species, were regarded as mere commodities to be exploited, reflecting a capitalist preoccupation with profit and markets.[55] Naturally, by returning to Nantucket with the "product,"[56] the owners would obtain their profit and the sailors would receive their wages. The owners, in financing the ship, were pursuing their self-interests. They elicited

50. Wood, *The Origin of Capitalism*.
51. Robinson, *The Ethics of Care*, 57.
52. Taylor, *The Ethics of Authenticity*, 27. It is important to note that the juxtaposition of capitalism and individual freedom was promulgated by Hayek, Friedman, and others after World War II, and for many people this refers to the rise of neoliberal capitalism. See Hayek, *The Road to Serfdom*; Jones, *Masters of the Universe*; Oreskes and Conway, *The Big Myth*.
53. Honneth, *Freedom's Right*, 139.
54. Melville, *Moby-Dick*, 202–10.
55. See Phillips, *American Theocracy*.
56. I have placed this term in quotes because it exemplifies the depersonalization of whales. Whales, in the capitalistic system, are mere objects to be exploited, denying their singularities.

cooperation from the crew by offering compensation in the form of wages, but the crew, as in any capitalist enterprise, would not share in the profits—especially considering the dangers and difficulties of this endeavor. In one sense, the crewmen, to the extent they were persons, were cogs in the machine. They could lose their lives, but the worse outcome for the owners was simply the loss of their investment. The crew and the captain were to serve the owners' self-realization and were, if necessary, expendable to ensure the success of the voyage—profits.

As captain of the ship, Ahab was the leader of this floating polis of men, and his leadership was shaped and largely determined by capitalist investors. They expected and hired him to return to Nantucket with the goods, but Ahab's obsession with the white whale distracted him from these contractual expectations. At one point, Starbuck, the chief mate, reminded Captain Ahab that this whaling ship's mission or duty was to provide profit to the Nantucket investors,[57] which apparently Ahab dismissed because of his singular pursuit of his self-interest—killing the white whale—suggesting that the crew was there to serve Ahab's self-interests. Of course, Ahab could do this because, in one sense, while at sea, he was the leviathan—not subject to the disciplinary regimes of capitalism. Yet, he still had to enlist the sailors' cooperation (trust) to pursue his self-interest (secondarily the owners'). To increase the sailors' motivation, Ahab, like any capitalist leader on Wall Street, promised a bonus (gold) to the person catching sight of and killing the white whale.[58] Of course, if Ahab's crew had caught and killed the white whale, then Ahab's self-interest and the owners' self-interest in profit would have been satisfied, but that would have been a banal ending—banal because it would simply be a tale of the glories of capitalistic exploitation of other species and the Earth and not a tale of one man's destructive obsession.

Capitalism, to anthropomorphize it, relentlessly and ruthlessly pursues markets and profits wherever they may be. It is, in its essence, both an equal opportunity exploiter (when unregulated) and imperialistic in that it seeks to extend its reach into other countries for the sake of controlling markets and garnering wealth. While the novel has in its background capitalism, the imperialism of the U.S. is less clear but nevertheless present. Indeed, William Bourecht argues that Melville's Ahab represents a masculinity tied to the imperial self, which Melville, he argues, rejects.[59] For instance, Ahab exclaims to Starbuck that he would "chase him (white whale) round Good Hope, and around the Horn, and around the Norway maelstrom, and round perdition's

---

57. Melville, *Moby-Dick*, 378.
58. Melville, *Moby-Dick*, 374.
59. Baurecht, "To Reign Is Worth Ambition."

flames before I give up."⁶⁰ While this certainly reveals Ahab's ruthless obsession, it also can reflect the imperialistic aspect of capitalism and the U.S. of that century. By 1851, the U.S. was well on the way to controlling what would become the continental U.S. and was pursuing markets throughout the Pacific, as well as throughout South and Central America. The *Pequod*, like other American whaling ships, plied the waters of the world in search of whales. There were no boundaries that could not be transgressed, because the ocean was the field in which these ships toiled. They could go anywhere in their relentless search for whales. This paralleled U.S. imperialism (and capitalism) with its transgression of peoples' geographic boundaries, which had its origins in British imperialism of the colonial period. In brief, the mindset associated with the imperialist ideas connected with Manifest Destiny and the Monroe Doctrine—the Continent is under U.S. control and the land we settle is rightfully ours—and capitalism's obsession with profits and markets are, I argue, the backdrop of Melville's novel and Ahab's obsession with killing the white whale.

Let me take an interpretive leap to further highlight the background presence of imperialism and capitalism. The *Pequod* hailed from Nantucket, and the Pequot or Mashantucket Pequot tribe were situated in what is now Connecticut. Perhaps there is a link between the ship's name and this particular Native American tribe. If not, the *Pequod* certainly suggests indigenous roots. I suggest the name itself is a symbolic relic of British and American imperialism—of its "victories" and, at the same time, the tendency to domesticate and screen the ruthless violence used to seize control of lands (and cultures) by naming the apparatuses of colonial capitalism after Native peoples. Put differently, the name not only points to a history of expropriating lands and subjugating Indigenous peoples, it also reflects the seizure and use of their name—in the name of capitalism's exploitation of the ocean's resources for profit. The use of Native American cultures for the purposes of profit or some other gain has a long history in the U.S., and I suggest the ship's name is part of that history—a history rife with imperialistic and capitalistic exploitation of peoples, lands, and waters.

Further evidence of the background of capitalism and imperialism is seen in the objectification and exploitation of whales. As mentioned above, whales are perceived as mere objects to be harvested for profit. This objectification or reification⁶¹ is inextricably yoked to capitalism's instrumental reasoning and corresponding absence of personal knowing.⁶² Moreover,

---

60. Melville, *Moby-Dick*, 378.
61. Lukács, *History and Class Consciousness*.
62. Studying various Indigenous peoples in Central and South America, Eduardo

instrumental, objectifying reasoning is shaped by liberalism with the notion of pursuing one's self-interests with, in this case, little or no consideration of the consequences, such as decimating whale populations. Indeed, the ruthless (care-less) pursuit of whales for profit is connected to the idea that human beings must dominate and subdue nature, which, in turn, fits well with capitalism's objectification and exploitation of nature, including workers. The *Pequod*, in brief, is a society of men who serve and operate out of a capitalist-imperialist ethos. In other words, their subjectivity, their masculinity, is embedded in these intersecting systems.

As indicated above, liberal philosophy's exaltation of individualism and pursuit of one's self-interests fit hand-in-glove with both capitalism and imperialism. Ahab represents individualism on steroids. We could simply focus on his single-minded obsession with the white whale, which would lead us to see Ahab as a tragic figure—a figure who likely transcends cultures and time. This may be true, but I think, given Melville's sociocultural context, Ahab represents excessive individualism inextricably yoked to capitalism and imperialism, wherein he relentlessly pursues his self-interest while finding ways to enlist others to cooperate in achieving his aim. More strongly stated, the self-interests of the crew, such as their survival and later garnering their wages, are of no interest to Ahab unless he secures the white whale. Ahab's self-realization of vengeance is primary, and he believes the crew should be in service to his interests, which means he cares little about his crew members' self-realization or self-interests (or well-being) nor the expectations of capitalist investors. The obvious evidence for this is seen in Ahab's relentless pursuit of the whale that results in the destruction of the ship and the demise of all the crew except one—the narrator, Ishmael (somebody had to survive to tell the story). Ironically, the obsessive-compulsive, imperialistic-capitalistic pursuit of markets and profits through whaling is undermined by Ahab's obsessive self-interest in killing the whale. Herein lies a contradiction of capitalism: capitalism, in the West, depends on the liberal philosophy of individualism, yet individualism taken to its extreme can interfere with the aims of capitalism. Certainly, the owners of the *Pequod* lost their investment (perhaps they had insurance) and their

---

Kohn and Eduardo Viveiros de Castro note that these peoples view other species as persons or potential persons and that for them this personification, if you will, is necessary for gaining knowledge of the other creature, the habitat, and themselves. This does not imply that Indigenous people believe other species qua persons means that other animals are identical to human beings/persons. There is a multiplicity of perspectives and multinaturalism inherent in their personal epistemologies. This kind of thinking and relating is distinctly different from the depersonalization associated with settler colonialism under the sway of capitalism and liberalism. Kohn, *How Forests Think*. Viveiros de Castro, *Cannibal Metaphysics*.

profit. And Ahab's crew, except one, was sacrificed on the altar of Ahab's interests and desires.

There is one other important feature of capitalism and imperialism. At the time Melville was writing, the U.S. considered itself to be a representative democracy. Of course, this democracy excluded African Americans, women, and Indigenous peoples from voting. Moreover, capitalistic entities (corporations) and apparatuses of imperialism are not democratic. Indeed, to this day, corporate leaders eschew democratic organizations within their corporations. Imperialistic apparatuses are hardly democratic when it comes to Indigenous people, whose voices, if they are heard at all, are ignored or dismissed. My point here is that in Melville's society (and presently) there were systems that promoted autocratic rule. This is evident on the *Pequod*. This is a society of men ruled by the captain—the captain is an autocratic sovereign. Ahab may be responsible to his capitalist overlords who own the ship, but at sea Ahab rules. It is precisely this context of autocracy that allows Ahab to live out his obsession. Put another way, despite the crew members' concerns about Ahab, they collude with his obsession because they exist within autocratic polities, namely, settler capitalism and the polities of seamanship.

Let me extend this by saying the crew members are also part of and share in the ethos of autocratic sovereignty. I do not simply mean this is true because they obey and, therefore, collude with Ahab. Rather, I am saying that the ethos of the time was that "men" were meant to dominate nature. The idea that human beings are superior to and given license to have dominion over nature has a long history in Western theologies and philosophies. For Giorgio Agamben, a central theme in Western philosophies (and theologies) is the existence of a "deep ontological rift . . . between animal and human."[63] Agamben writes:

> It is as if determining the border between human and animal were not just one question among many discussed by philosophers and theologians, scientists and politicians, but rather a fundamental metaphysico-political operation in which alone something like 'man' can be decided upon and produced. If animal life and human life could be superimposed perfectly, then neither man nor animal—and, perhaps, not even the divine—would any longer be thinkable.[64]

63. Dickinson, "The 'Absence' of Gender," 173.
64. Agamben, *The Open*. Bruno Latour and Jacques Derrida make similar arguments regarding the ontological rift. Latour, *We Have Never Been Modern*. Derrida, *The Animal*.

This rift is entwined with beliefs that human beings are to have dominion over other species and that other species are inferior to human beings, thus able to be exploited. Not surprisingly, this political and theological worldview fits hand-in-glove with imperialism and capitalism. My point here is the autocratic polity of the *Pequod* is linked to the larger societal and political apparatuses that produce and maintain the beliefs in human dominion and superiority. The crewmen, then, while being "ruled" by Ahab were themselves rulers over nature. This is evident in their collective objectification of other species, in this case whales, for their own benefit. There is no question among the crew as to their right to kill as many whales as possible, and I am arguing that this is connected to the belief that human beings, in this case men, have dominion over other species and the Earth.

Ahab as a Trope of Pathological Masculinity

It is impossible to grow up in a culture and not be formed by the dominant semiotic systems that organize society and relations, which includes how one understands and lives out what it means to be a man. Writing about the changes in pastoral care (and identity) in U.S. history, Brooks Holifield noted that during the mid-nineteenth century there was a "veritable cult of masculinity" that eschewed anything that smacked of "effeminacy." He states further that "the economic consequence of the war [the Civil War] intensified the cult of masculinity by glorifying the barons of industry."[65] Sarah Wilson, from a different perspective, connects Melville's depiction of masculinity to the Antebellum period. Naturally, this "cult of masculinity" is best understood on a continuum, with one end being adaptive and the other pathological.[66] This means that one can find a great diversity of masculine expressions within the culture, and Ahab falls on the extreme side of the continuum representing pathology.[67]

Before I address Ahab's pathological masculinity, let me briefly clear away a psychodynamic rendering of his obsession with the white whale. One might hypothesize that Ahab's obsessions stemmed from the traumatic loss of his leg and his near-death experience, compliments of Moby Dick. This loss may be understood as a blow to Ahab's phallic narcissism, which

---

65. Holifield, A History of *Pastoral Care in America*, 167.

66. Wilson, "Melville."

67. In using the term *pathology*, I am simply referring to those psychological conditions that are consistently self-limiting and destructive to self and others. Moreover, as noted above, psychological illnesses often have etiologies in cultural, political, and economic practices.

is manifested in his preoccupation with the white whale and his unquestioning certainty about pursuing and killing the whale, thus restoring or redeeming his narcissistic invulnerability. But this diagnosis would suggest that the source of Ahab's obsession and his masculinity lies exclusively in his personality and family of origin, as well as in the single traumatic event of losing his leg. Moreover, in the novel we note that another male captain lost a limb to Moby Dick but responded very differently to the loss, suggesting other factors are at play. If Ahab were a real person and we had access to his childhood experiences (Ahab's mother died when he was a year old),[68] the diagnosis might be plausible, but it would still be incomplete because we would be ignoring larger systemic forces shaping his personality. As Frantz Fanon[69] and others have noted, psychological struggles also have their origins in political, economic, and cultural realities. In short, psychodynamic rendering of the sources and features of Ahab's obsession, while important, is insufficient, which is a reason for considering larger systemic apparatuses and how they likely shaped his subjectivity.

There is one other point to be made. As noted above, the *Pequod* is piloted and sailed by men. This masculine environment or society not only provides a laboratory in which to observe the male species; it further highlights what exactly is pathological or destructive. In other words, Melville's story is one that represents a group of men having to cooperate to achieve the ends of survival and profit. We see their struggles and successes as men—the kind of men and type of masculinity attracted to the rigors and dangers of sailing and whaling. This said, cooperation in this male autocratic society, as I note below, requires a kind of care for and fidelity to each other, not simply toward the shared aim of whaling but toward protecting each other from the elements. Put differently, in the pursuit of their individual self-interests, there must also be a mutual care and self-limitation to facilitate their cooperation toward surviving and making a profit. The main point here is that Melville's story provides a tableau in which to observe male interactions and, in so doing, obtain a sense of where they might be on the masculinity continuum of healthy to destructive.

Let's return to Ahab. Ahab is introduced in the story by Captain Peleg (an owner of the *Pequod*), who acknowledges that Ahab was a "queer man" but a good man.[70] True, Ahab lost his leg and lay nearly "dead for 3 days and nights," which he survived because of "his unsurmountable willfulness" and

---

68. Melville, *Moby-Dick*, 232.
69. Fanon, *Black Skin, White Masks*.
70. Melville, *Moby-Dick*, 233.

infinite fortitude.[71] Unlike Jesus, however, Ahab, after three days, returned from the dead "moody and savage"[72] and "a little out of his mind."[73] I suspect "queer" in this context meant Ahab exhibited behavior that would be considered odd by other seafaring men, but, apparently, he retained the confidence of the owners, who hired Ahab to captain the ship and secure a profit.

When Ahab boards the ship, he is aloof, often sequestering himself in his cabin and rarely appearing on deck, which adds to the crew members' perception of his moodiness and oddity.[74] Eventually, this changes as Ahab engages his first mate more frequently, revealing much about his interests and aims. But I suggest that his initial aloofness reflects a coldness or lack of care and interest in and about the crew, either as a whole or as individual crew members. "Lack of care" does not mean that Ahab is completely uninterested in the crew, but this is subordinate to his intentions, to his obsessions. The crewmen are mere instruments in his pursuit of Moby Dick. Ahab tells Starbuck about "the accursed white [whale] that ravaged"[75] him and that Ahab's "vengeance will fetch a great premium" for the crew and the owners, conflating his obsession with the mission of the ship. Shortly after this, Ahab exclaims, "I will wreak hate upon him"[76] and "I am madness maddened."[77] Ahab goes so far to say that "The prophecy was that I should be dismembered . . . I now prophesy that I will dismember my dismemberer."[78] All of this is to reveal not only Ahab's obsession but also to alert the obedient crew members that they exist to serve the interests of Ahab, which means that he recognizes them as objects that function and cooperate to meet his aims. If he cares about the crew, it is an instrumental, objectifying care. We might say that Ahab recognizes individual crew members as persons, but this is subordinate to what John Macmurray calls object knowing.[79] For Macmurray, subordinating personal knowing to object knowing is only ethical if it is time limited and for the sake of the individual, as in the case of a doctor diagnosing a patient. In Ahab's case, he cares only for the crewmen to the extent that they cooperate in fulfilling

71. Melville, *Moby-Dick*, 281. Later in the novel. Ahab's fortitude and passion are emphasized. "The firm tower, that is Ahab; the volcano, that is Ahab; the courageous, the undefeated, and victorious fowl, that, too, is Ahab" (970).

72. Melville, *Moby-Dick*, 233.

73. Melville, *Moby-Dick*, 198.

74. Melville, *Moby-Dick*, 353.

75. Melville, *Moby-Dick*, 377.

76. Melville, *Moby-Dick*, 379.

77. Melville, *Moby-Dick*, 388.

78. Melville, *Moby-Dick*, 389.

79. Macmurray, *Persons in Relation*.

his mission, which is to kill the white whale. This is a kind of instrumental reasoning (objectification) and relating that parallels the capitalist pursuit of profits, all of which undermines genuine care.

Ahab's preoccupation with finding and killing his nemesis accompanies his extraordinary ability for self-limitation, which is joined to profound carelessness. Like Weber's[80] Protestant capitalists who display considerable ascetical self-restraint or self-limitation in the pursuit of profits, Ahab, with his indomitable will, sacrifices a great deal to achieve his aims, yet his ability to limit himself for the sake of others is profoundly distorted, if not absent. As indicated above, Ahab "cares" for the crewmen to the extent they adopt his aims and, in this sense, the autocratic Ahab will limit himself for their sake. Nevertheless, the crew members are mere pawns (or is it prawns?) in his gambit.

Ahab's singular focus is also revealed in his relentless questioning of other captains the *Pequod* encounters on its travels. Bypassing the social rubrics when encountering another ship and its crew,[81] Ahab plunges forward in querying the captains about their sightings of the white whale. In one encounter with the crew of the *Bachelor*, Ahab shows no curiosity about the crew members themselves or interest in their needs or experiences. Other ships' crew members even ask, "Is your captain crazy?"[82] because Ahab was interested only in the whereabouts of the white whale. Melville even has Ahab encounter a British captain who had also lost a limb to the white whale, except this captain had learned his lesson. Indeed, the captain remarks that the whale is welcome to his arm,[83] which suggests that he was able to handle the loss such that he retained a kind of prudential reasoning that Ahab lacked in his obsession with dismembering the whale.

One of the most poignant illustrations of the underlying cruelty or lack of care vis-à-vis Ahab's obsession is seen in the *Pequod*'s encounters with the whaling vessel *Rachel*. When whaling ships meet, there is often talk of news from home, but Ahab immediately asks about the white whale. Instead of speaking from his own ship, as was customary, the *Rachel*'s captain, Gardner, boards the *Pequod*, sparking curiosity among the crew. Gardner tells Ahab and his crew that two days earlier the white whale had attacked one of their boats and since then the *Rachel* has been scouring the sea for survivors. One of the *Pequod*'s crew, Stubb, says to another crewman, Flask, "I will wager something now," he whispered, "that someone in that missing boat wore off

---

80. Weber, *The Protestant Ethic*.
81. Melville, *Moby-Dick*, 912, 983–85, 1104–5.
82. Melville, *Moby-Dick*, 974.
83. Melville, *Moby-Dick*, 389.

that captain's best coat; mayhap, his watch—he's so cursed anxious to get it back. Who ever heard of pious whale-ships cruising after one missing whaleboat in the height of whaling season?"[84] Then Stubb hears the captain of the *Rachel* cry out, "My boy, my own boy is among them. For God's sake—I beg, I conjure" you (Captain Ahab) to help search for the missing crew for a couple of days.[85] Indeed, the captain of the *Rachel* says he will pay any costs incurred, ensuring that the owners and crew of the *Pequod* would be compensated. This desperate plea changes Stubb's view, and he exclaims that they must save the boy.[86] In this moment, we see that care of and for a child takes precedent over the mission of the *Pequod*, at least for Stubb and Flask. They seem to be willing to limit themselves for the sake of aiding the crew of the *Rachel*. As the captain pleads his case, Ahab "stood like an anvil, receiving every shock, but without the least quivering of his own."[87] Captain Gardener believes Ahab will relent and tells the men to "run, run, men, now and stand by to square in the yards." Ahab immediately responds, "Avast." "Captain Gardener, I will not do it. Even now I lose time. Good-bye."[88] Ahab is unmoved by the entreaties of the captain or the possibility of being paid for the inconvenience of a two-day search, revealing a ruthlessness or carelessness in the pursuit of vengeance. In this vignette, we contrast the devotion and care the captain of the *Rachel* and his crew have for the captain's son and the missing crew members with the iciness of Ahab. Indeed, the masculine care and fidelity expressed by the captain and crew of the *Rachel* reveal that the lost boy and men are, in the end, more important than the aim of profits. I add here that this vignette foretells the ending, where Ahab sacrifices his ship and his crew to satisfy his vengeance on the white whale. (Ironically, it is the *Rachel* that comes and rescues the lone survivor of the *Pequod*.) In refusing to relinquish his obsession, Ahab sacrifices others and his ship, not only revealing that he fails to abide by and be faithful to the capitalist aim of profit[89] but also throwing overboard typical masculine care and cooperation needed to survive the perils of the ocean.

84. Melville, *Moby-Dick*, 1180.
85. Melville, *Moby-Dick*, 1180.
86. Melville, *Moby-Dick*, 1180.
87. Melville, *Moby-Dick*, 1183.
88. Melville, *Moby-Dick*, 1183.
89. One might note a possible contradiction here to my earlier reference to capitalism and how it shapes and has shaped masculinity. In other words, we have Ahab who cares less about profit and Gardner who also sets aside profit for the sake of finding his son and missing crew members. Both captains, for different reasons, have subordinated profit to a different goal. One displays a ruthless, care-less desire, while the other is care-full. Also, capitalism as a dominant semiotic system shaping masculinity does not

Ahab's carelessness is connected to a kind of idolatry, a kind of obsessive faith in his self-interested pursuit or vengeance. The crew of the *Pequod* are trusted as long as they serve the commands and aims of Ahab—an instrumental faith. Indeed, Ahab threatens Starbuck, "There is one God that is Lord over the earth, and one Captain that is lord over the *Pequod*."[90] Ahab, like God, is sovereign and, as sovereign, demands the loyalty of the crew vis-à-vis the aims of the captain. Members of the crew are to trust him blindly, like they trust God. Yet this is not a covenant of love and care but rather a contract—a contract motivated, in part, by wages and by winning the gold for spotting and killing the white whale. Ahab's certain belief that the white whale personifies evil is more dogma than mere belief, and it is from this dogma that he demands fealty. It is the crew's duty to pursue and destroy this evil. Moreover, Ahab possesses a self-certainty seen in the form of religious idolatry—a self-certainty that refuses anything and anyone who might raise questions or doubts. Ahab's indomitable belief is connected to his loyalty, which, on the one hand, is instrumental in that he is loyal to the crew to the extent they assist Ahab to achieve his certain vengeance. On the other hand, Ahab is loyal, in one sense, solely to himself and his obsession—an obsession he will not let go of. For his crew to question his goal or fail to pursue the white whale is deemed to be a betrayal.

It is important to mention that idolatry distorts hope, which is evident in Ahab's obsession. His self-certainty or self-righteousness means that hope is reduced to a self-defined future, which is something other than hope. By this I mean that Ahab is not interested in being open to future possibilities, and this means he ignores future dangers as well as present responsibilities to care for, in this case, the needs and concerns of Captain Gardner. Similarly, we see this in his final pursuit of the white whale, where he ignores not only multiple dangers to himself but also mortal dangers to his crew and ship. There is only one possibility, one future, one vision, and that is achieving his vengeance. Genuine hope does not demand the future conform to one's single idea or image of it. But the kind of masculinity portrayed by Ahab reduces hope to a demand for a certain outcome, and everything else is carelessly sacrificed to this future "prophecy." Ahab's shout about losing

---

mean care is absent or necessarily subordinate. It does mean that the goal of profit must be deliberately set aside if one is to care for one's missing crew. In addition, Ahab's ruthlessness and preoccupation with his self-interest to the exclusion of profit parallels the ruthlessness and preoccupation of capitalism with profit and markets. Ahab's neglect of the goals of capitalism is not a contradiction but rather, in my view, a trope of the consequences of obsession with profits to the exclusion of caring about the needs and experiences of the crew, of workers.

90. Melville, *Moby-Dick*, 1064.

time reflects his rush to meet a future that must be so—a future that his crew must be loyal enough to make possible. It is this future, this future satisfaction of vengeance, that spurs Ahab and distorts hope and obliterates care. This kind of masculinity is dangerous not only to Ahab but also to the functioning and survival of this precarious masculine society.

As to this last point, Melville makes clear that the *Pequod*'s society is decidedly different from other ships. Melville writes that the *Pequod* is a melancholic ship,[91] which is directly the result of the moodiness of the captain. A few pages later, the "moody *Pequod*" comes across another whaling ship, the *Bachelor*.[92] Both captains stand on their respective quarterdecks. Ahab is depicted as "shaggy and black, with a stubborn gloom."[93] By contrast, the other captain is presiding over a party. His crew, for reasons unknown, are enjoying some festivities, likely sailing back home. Ahab and his crew are invited (three times) to celebrate with them, but Ahab declines with irritation, if not disgust, predictably focused on asking repeatedly whether the *Bachelor* had come across the white whale. The *Bachelor*'s society, while not all male (some of the crew had brought their Polynesian wives along—another sign of patriarchy and imperialism), displayed masculinity comprised of comradery, perhaps friendship, mutual trust and fidelity, and enjoyment. The captain and the crew apparently care about and for each other, which is the basis of their mutual trust, cooperation, and festivities. Contrast this with the society of men on the *Pequod*. Melville depicts them as serious, dark, moody, and melancholic, though they find ways to cooperate for the sake of pursuing profits and, more specifically, to fulfill Ahab's desire to find and kill the white whale. One masculine society is alive, vital, and hopeful, the other dark, enervating, empty, and tragic. One society displays mutual care that informs their trust, loyalty, and cooperation; the other male society distorts care by a blind obsession that demands autocratic loyalty. We know the other ship and its society sail off to a hopeful future, while the *Pequod* and its society of unwitting men sail to their doom.

The penultimate illustration of Ahab's refusal to let go and his carelessness is seen in the very last pages of the novel in which the *Pequod* pursues the white whale for three days. Each encounter results in the death and destruction of the some of the crew and whaling boats, yet Ahab refuses to give up because he is certain he is destined to kill the whale. After having his ivory peg leg snapped off by the whale, Ahab exclaims, "Nor white whale, nor man, nor friend, can so much as graze old Ahab in his own proper and inaccessible

---

91. Melville, *Moby-Dick*, 1096.
92. Melville, *Moby-Dick*, 1103.
93. Melville, *Moby-Dick*, 1104.

being."[94] Clearly, this exclamation signals not only Ahab's belief in his invulnerability and his obsessive and unquestionable certainty in fulfilling his destructive mission but also his complete lack of care for and fidelity to the vulnerability and needs of the crew. Surveying the damage after two days of pursuit, Starbuck cries out, "Great God! but for one single instant show thyself . . . never, never wilt thou capture him old man—In Jesus' name no more of this, that's worse than the devil's madness. Two days chased; twice stove to splinters; thy very leg once more snatched from under thee."[95] Ahab responds with a lengthy speech to the crew affirming that he is fated to kill the whale, of this there can be no question. The autocratic speech rouses the melancholic crew, and they continue to pursue the whale, ignoring Starbuck's dire warning and plea. When they encounter the whale again, Starbuck tries once more to get Ahab to turn away. "Oh! Ahab," cried Starbuck, "not too late is it, even now, the third day, to desist. See! Moby Dick seeks thee not. It is thou, thou, that madly seekest him."[96] Of course, Ahab orders them on, even though they are surrounded and harassed by sharks.[97]

The carelessness exemplified in Ahab's refusal to let go of his obsession can be further understood in terms of precarity and existential insignificance and impermanence. Above, I indicated that care and faith help human beings face and partially manage the precarities of life. Certainly, the precarities whalers faced were significant, and the mutual care and fidelity of the crewmen were essential for cooperation not simply to secure the product but to survive. The other ships, like the *Rachel*, represent the kind of mutual care and fidelity that placed profit secondary to the well-being of the crew. By contrast, Ahab's obsession, his refusal to let go after repeated pleas, represents a refusal to face, accept, and deal with the realities of existential precarity. It is as if Ahab's belief that he is destined to kill the whale renders him invulnerable. The vulnerabilities of the crew he knows well, but he is indifferent. Put another way, his obsession reveals a dismissal of their vulnerabilities, which, in the end, are sacrificed to his vision of killing the whale—a vision apparently invulnerable to the realities of both the sea and whaling.

There is another facet of Ahab's apparent belief that he will kill the whale. One of the ways human beings deal with the realities of existential insignificance and impermanence is by caring for and trusting in others. To be sure, sometimes we ontologize care, believing that we will continue to care and be cared for by God after death. This functions as a kind of

---

94. Melville, *Moby-Dick*, 1245.
95. Melville, *Moby-Dick*, 1247.
96. Melville, *Moby-Dick*, 1264.
97. Melville, *Moby-Dick*, 1266.

ontological and permanent or eternal sense of our own significance, which denies the realities of existential insignificance and impermanence. In Melville's novel, Ahab's obsession parallels this. His vision of killing the whale reflects his significance, while subordinating, at best, the significance of the crew. In other words, he cares for the crew members not in terms of their singularities (hence their individual significance) but only as mere means to attain his end. Their significance, in other words, is reified. When Starbuck pleads with him, Ahab is impervious. It is only his own vision, his own significance, that matters. Similarly, the white whale possesses significance for Ahab, but only in its dismemberment, only in the realization of Ahab's obsession. It as if Ahab recognizes the precarity and impermanence of the crew and whale yet denies his own precarity and impermanence through his refusal to let go of the significance of his vision. In short, an obsession can function to deflect us from facing and accepting our precarity, as well as our existential insignificance and impermanence. Destruction and tragedy ensue, as we see in the final scenes of the novel where Ahab continuously ignores the entreaties to let go of his obsession, carelessness, and infidelity.

Since Starbuck mentions Jesus in his attempt to deter Ahab from further death and destruction, we recall that after three days Christ rose from the dead. By contrast, after three days of pursuing the white whale, Ahab's prophecy, his fatal obsession, sinks with him as he, his ship, and all but one of his crew come to reside in Davy Jones's locker. This particular society of men, shaped by the apparatuses of capitalism, imperialism, and liberalism and led by a man obsessed with vengeance, manifests distorted and destructive forms of masculine care and faith, which leads to a tragic end. As noted above, it is interesting that another society of men—the crew of the *Rachel*—rescue the lone survivor and display a more life-affirming care and faith, even though the crews of the *Rachel* and the *Pequod* shared a similar mission.[98]

Conclusion

Each era may find different meanings in the story of Moby Dick. To be sure, many would agree that its lasting appeal is related to the portrayal of Ahab

---

98. I am not suggesting that the men of the *Rachel* manifest a healthy masculinity, for they too would have been shaped by the same forces that shaped Ahab and his crew. That said, on the continuum, they are healthier in the sense that they cared for each other, setting aside, when necessary, the mission of killing whales for profit to caring first for the lives of other crew members. Put differently, the captain and crew of the *Rachel* recognized their collective precarity and vulnerability, whereas Ahab did not, and Ahab was able to persuade the crew by his certainty in his quest.

and his tragic obsession with the white whale. No doubt every era also has examples of men who, captive to their desires, are willing to carelessly sacrifice themselves and others in the pursuit of their self-interests. Yet, despite the idea that obsessions cut across eras and, perhaps, cultures, in this chapter I have been interested in framing Ahab's masculinity in light of dominant semiotic systems extant in the nineteenth century, namely, capitalism, liberalism, and imperialism, and to interpret this masculinity in light of care and faith. These systems of meaning that shape behavior and perception were dominant in the time of Melville, as they are today, though in different forms. Today's system of meaning manifests a preoccupation (with profits, expansion) that subordinates, exploits, or denies the needs and experiences of Others, just as Ahab denied and exploited the needs and experiences of others in the service of his singular self-interest. Although Ahab ignored the demands of the ship's owners, this does not mean that capitalism did not shape his masculinity. Indeed, what I have argued is that Ahab's obsession parallels capitalism's and imperialism's preoccupation with the metropole's self-interest—a self-interest that carelessly excludes the interests and needs of Indigenous peoples, workers, other species, etc. It is not an accident that Ahab's masculinity, influenced by these systems of objectification, results in his isolation from other men. A profound loneliness lingers in the depths of his obsession, just as there are a great many lonely men (and women) in market societies. This said, the pathological masculinity of Ahab, while having different sources and aims, parallels the catastrophic loneliness of Victor Frankenstein and the creature. That is, in refusing to let go and attempting to master or control nature in order to avoid existential vulnerability, they foreclose the capacity for love and friendship.

But there is another reason I am interested in Moby Dick and the tragic trajectory of masculine preoccupation shaped by capitalism, liberalism, and imperialism. We are separated from Melville's story by nearly two centuries, yet we have in common a world even more dominated by capitalism (global) and postcolonial imperialism.[99] Is Melville's novel a warning and inadvertent prophecy? What if we were to imagine the Earth as the *Pequod* (made of persons from many nations) led by corporate-political captains (mostly male) who are preoccupied with profit and market share—the white whale. These captains ignore calls and cries for help in their relentless, maniacal pursuit of profits and markets. They objectify nature and workers. They seek to dominate and subdue nature as their right, so they believe. They ignore or deny existential precarity, insignificance, and impermanence while making

---

99. See Klein, *The Shock Doctrine*; Kolbert, *The Sixth Extinction*; Malcolm, *Words for a Dying World*; Wallace-Wells, *The Uninhabitable Earth*.

precarious the putative insignificant and impermanent lives of subjugated Others, which includes other species. Like Ahab, they continually ignore, deny, or dismiss the warning signs of global warming and, as a result, the *Pequod* (the polis of humanity) will be destroyed by nature. In this scenario, however, there will be no survivors or, if there are, there will be no *Rachel* to rescue them and, therefore, no one to tell or anyone to listen to the tale of their—our—demise.

3

Scrooge and the Mammon Complex

The Agony of Loss, Masculine Invulnerability, and the Possibility of Redemption

---

That time is short and it doesn't return again. It is slipping away while I write this and while you read it, and the monosyllable of the clock is Loss, loss, loss, unless you devote your heart to its opposition.[1]

Idolatry is the loss of the sense of the existence of the unmanifest, the loss of the sense of search, the loss of the continuous freshness of the encounter with the unmanifest.[2]

There are no limits to our greed, none to our cruelty.[3]

---

1. "Tennessee Williams, "Quotes," https://www.goodreads.com/quotes/7186621-time-is-short-and-it-doesn-t-return-again-it-is.
2. Bakan, *The Duality of Existence*, 6–7.
3. Seneca the Younger, "Moral Letters to Lucilius/Letter 95," Wikisource, https://en.wikisource.org/wiki/Moral_letters_to_Lucilius/Letter_95.

Mary Shelley's novel *Frankenstein* ends with the creature proclaiming that he will soon be dead, finally freed from his miseries.[4] His despair mingles with the pleasure of triumph over the death of his creator, and, if there is any glimmer of hope or consolation for this creature, it is that his "spirit will sleep in peace."[5] Victor, who sought to score a victory over human finitude by reanimating dead flesh, ends up locked in a vicious battle of mutual deprivation, draining any sense of vitality and hope and leaving a long trail of loss and suffering. Herman Melville's novel *Moby-Dick* similarly ends in a damning tragedy. Like Victor, Ahab exhibits a pathological masculinity. His maniacal pursuit of the white whale mutilates any sense of life and love, leaving only the desiccated desire to dismember the whale. This twisted desire tragically leads to the sinking of the *Pequod* and the watery deaths of Ahab and his crew, save one. Shelley and Melville knew there are many instances in life when tragedy reigns, crowding out any hope for or any glimmer of redemption. Only death ends suffering or, if one is hopeful, brings peace to those caught in the grips of pathological masculinity.

While there is a great deal of pathology, sin, and tragedy in life, there are also times when males, captive to inordinate passions, slip the traces, discovering more life-giving ways of being boys and men. When we observe this, it raises questions about how and why this happens instead of the more common tragic endings of distorted masculinity. Why didn't or couldn't Victor or Ahab change when they were continually confronted with the consequences of their inordinate pursuits? Or why does someone else, in the grip of life-diminishing desire and relations, find a way back to life and love? These questions are often, in the end, unanswerable. Or if we offer answers, we discover the elusiveness of any degree of certainty. This chapter offers partial answers to these questions, drawn from Charles Dickens's *A Christmas Carol*. In this novel, written in the same century as *Frankenstein* and *Moby-Dick*, Ebenezer Scrooge[6] is depicted as an isolated and alienated man bent and crippled by greed, though by the end of the story he is free and alive in his old age. Broadly speaking, it is a story of loss and redemption that does not necessarily need to be framed in Christian terms.

---

4. Shelley, *Frankenstein*, 198.

5. Shelley, *Frankenstein*, 198.

6. Scrooge's name came from a tombstone Dickens had seen on a visit to Edinburgh. The grave was for Ebenezer Lennox Scroggie, whose job was given as a meal man—a corn merchant; Dickens misread the inscription as "mean man." "Ebenezer Scrooge," Wikipedia, https://en.wikipedia.org/wiki/Ebenezer_Scrooge, accessed November 10, 2023.

While almost everyone is familiar with the story, I begin with depicting the tale in terms of grief and mourning. To understand the pathological dimension of grief, I rely on the work of Christopher Bollas, arguing that Scrooge uses money as a negative transformational object, like Victor's use of science. Both were defending against past painful losses, as well as the specter of future grief. Put another way, Scrooge's inordinate attachment to money (mammon complex) emerges within a society wherein capitalist apparatuses shape subjectivities.[7] Scrooge, I argue, uses this system to defend against the reality of existential precarity and impermanence. This mammon complex or defense undermines his capacities to be vulnerable, to be empathic, to care for and to trust in other persons. Scrooge, in short, uses money to defend against human precarity and vulnerability. Only by embracing both can Scrooge mourn and experience love. As in the previous chapter, this chapter suggests that capitalism's ethos has the tendency to distort our relations with other human beings, as well as other species and the Earth. Stated more strongly, capitalism gives rise to and supports a kind of sociopathic cruelty in relation not only to othered human beings but also to other species and the Earth. This is, in my view, the backstory of this short novel. From here, I shift to discussing the process of change in Scrooge's way of being in the world. This process, represented by four ghostly visitations, entails Scrooge's confrontation with and surrender to his past, present, and future, which creates a space for redemption. I also consider Scrooge's change as his exercise of the capacity for impotentiality or inoperativity vis-à-vis the structures of, and his self-imposed captivity to, capitalism. The exercise of impotentiality accompanies a sense of freedom to become vulnerable and accept human precarity and impermanence, making possible masculine love, generosity, and compassion for others.

I offer a few more thoughts before delving into *A Christmas Carol*. First, Dickens's story has obvious references to Christianity, and, to my mind, a more complicated rendering is that Christianity is juxtaposed with the barbarisms associated with capitalism and Western imperialism. Bob Cratchit, a loyal and submissive accountant, attends church and represents a Christlike figure in his willingness to forgive Scrooge for his miserliness in his endless pursuit of profit. The frightening apparition of Marley represents eternal punishment for his sins—sins that emerged out of his capitalist greed. The Ghosts of Christmas Past and Present hearken a kind of Christian cosmology—God's goodness in and above time despite humanity's failings. The Ghost of Christmas Future reveals the end result of Scrooge's

---

7. See for instance, Brown, *Undoing the Demos*; Frank, *One Market under God*; Hochschild, *The Managed Heart*; Illouz, *Cold Intimacies*; Lukács, *History and Class Consciousness*; Silva, *Coming Up Short*.

cruelty and indifference. The grave, Scrooge must have known, awaits him, but the Spirit is pointing to an earlier demise wrought by Scrooge's failure to change, which one might frame in terms of conversion. The story, in brief, represents the idea that Christianity humanizes the ardent capitalist, helping Scrooge to mourn and be freer to care for others.

A more complicated rendering, given the backdrop of the nineteenth century's spread of colonial capitalism by ostensibly Christian nations, is that capitalism and Christianity are deeply intertwined in the West, as Max Weber and others have demonstrated.[8] Indeed, the origins of capitalism are found in emerging Western colonizing states—states whose citizens viewed themselves as Christian.[9] Moreover, many, if not most, Christians, past and present, have defended and promoted capitalism and its inherent vices.[10] While I do believe that the ethos of Christianity, as of other religions, can humanize men (in this case), it is not inevitable and is often more complicated because of their imbrication with capitalism. Sadly, any cursory reading of Christian history reveals a long wake of viciousness, death, and destruction. That said, *I claim that the apparatuses of capitalism foster an ethos that cannot possibly humanize individuals, regardless of gender*. Put differently, capitalism produces the mammon complex—a complex that overlooks or denies care and justice for othered human beings and other species.[11]

A second point is my plan to set aside any claims about Christianity with regard to Scrooge's redemption and to use the term *redemption* in a more humanistic way. There are a few reasons for doing so. Any apology for Christianity runs up against not only other religions but also its history of treatment of women, Indigenous peoples, other species, and the Earth. Put differently, Christianity is no guarantee of conversion or virtue. In addition, like Karen Armstrong, I think the central features of the Abrahamic traditions are "the importance of justice and compassion."[12] This is, broadly speaking, an anthropological claim that can be in dialogue with other spiritual and humanist traditions. In other words, justice, love, and compassion are possible capacities of all human beings, whether they possess religious faith or a humanistic faith. Lastly, expanding our view and given the specter of the

---

8. Weber, *The Protestant Ethic*; Frank, *One Market under God*; Cox, *The Market as God*.

9. Wood, *The Origin of Capitalism*.

10. Novak, *The Spirit of Democratic Capitalism*; Novak, *Toward a Theology*.

11. In the eighteenth century, Bernard Mandeville argued that (Western) society functions well on the basis of private vices. Market societies seemingly function well given the public-private vice of greed, and capitalism and its apparatuses foster this vice (and others, such as lust and pride). Mandeville, *The Fable of the Bees*.

12. Armstrong, *A History of God*, 46.

Anthropocene Age, we might then see Dickens's story as a tale not simply of distorted masculinity but more broadly of relations distorted by cruelty and indifference, whether that is toward othered human beings, othered species, or the Earth. From here, the Ghost of Christmas Future points to the early grave of humanity (extinction) as a result of indifference and cruelty to other species and the Earth, as well as the chance of redemption through care and compassion for all human beings, other species, and the Earth.

Scrooge and Loss:
Masculinity and the Fear of Vulnerability

One of the key tasks in ministry is to do the work of empathically understanding persons, which in cases of difficult people like Scrooge is no easy feat. In this portion of the chapter, I set the scene by depicting Scrooge's initial difficult personality and relationships. From here, I turn to an explanation of the sources of Scrooge's miserliness and acerbity, which provides a foundation for defining what is meant by the mammon complex, its relation to negative transformational objects, and how these objects function to defend against the precarity of life as well as the realities of existential insignificance and impermanence.

The story begins with a death. Jacob Marley, Scrooge's longtime financial partner, was declared dead,[13] though this event was not an occasion of sadness or reflection for Scrooge.[14] Indeed, Scrooge, as "an excellent man of business," had conducted his business on the day of the funeral some seven years earlier, seemingly frustrated by the social conventions of going to a funeral and mourning with others.[15] And yet Scrooge, the narrator tells us, never painted over the name "Marley," and their joint business continued to be known as Scrooge and Marley years later.[16] This is curious, suggesting that while Scrooge never allowed himself to mourn his old partner, his partner remained, to some degree, present in his life. I will return to this curiosity below.

Scrooge is described as "a tight-fisted hand at the grindstone . . . A squeezing, wrenching, grasping, scraping, clutching, covetous old sinner!"[17] The narrator describes him further: "The cold within him froze his old features, nipped his pointed nose, shriveled his cheek, stiffened his gait;

13. Dickens, *A Christmas Carol*, 7.
14. Dickens, *A Christmas Carol*, 8.
15. Dickens, *A Christmas Carol*, 8.
16. Dickens, *A Christmas Carol*, 8.
17. Dickens, *A Christmas Carol*, 8.

made his eyes red, his thin lips blue; and spoke out shrewdly in his grating voice."[18] Not an inviting picture, to be sure. Indeed, Scrooge's physical appearance coincided with his way of being in the world with others—an outward expression of an inward reality. We learn that "nobody stopped him in the street to say with gladsome looks 'My dear Scrooge, how are you? When will you come to see me?' No beggars implore him to bestow a trifle, no children asked him what it was o'clock, no man or woman ever once in all his life inquired the way to such and such place . . . Even the blind men's dogs appeared to know him; and when they saw him coming on, would tug their owners into doorways and up courts."[19] Scrooge was not put off or disturbed in any way by people and pets fleeing his presence. Indeed, "It was the very thing he liked. To edge his way along the crowded paths of life, warning all human sympathy to keep its distance."[20] Scrooge's visage was one of perpetual scowling, thereby frightening or disgusting people who crossed his path. He could not be bothered with the routine social conventions of human caring, and he trusted no one. In other words, Scrooge's miserliness was embodied and relational—a man stingy with his affections, as well as his time and money, all of which were etched in his face and expressed in his behaviors.

Dickens's portrayal of Scrooge indicates that he was ornery and parsimonious long before his business partner died. Yet if Scrooge had nothing to do with grieving the death of his partner, why did he then hold on to Marley's name? Perhaps it was a business decision, but I suggest that Marley and Scrooge were both miserly, which would have provided Scrooge with some degree of connection with Marley—a connection of identification—brothers in greed. They would have been alone in the world together, and the death of Marley would have further isolated Scrooge, though he was apparently oblivious to or dismissive of his loneliness and isolation. Also, Marley must have had some degree of affection for Scrooge because the ghost of Marley appears, seven years later, to warn Scrooge of the consequences of his greed. Scrooge initially rejected this specter, believing it had to do with something he ate.[21] Did Scrooge have some affection for Marley? Was there some small seed of care, or dare we say love, for Marley? The narrator tells us that Scrooge was Marley's "sole executor, his sole assign, his sole residuary legatee, his sole friend and sole mourner."[22] But the narrator does

18. Dickens, *A Christmas Carol*, 9.
19. Dickens, *A Christmas Carol*, 9.
20. Dickens, *A Christmas Carol*, 9–10.
21. Dickens, *A Christmas Carol*, 30.
22. Dickens, *A Christmas Carol*, 8.

not say that Scrooge saw Marley as a friend, except when Scrooge, terrified of Marley's ghost, says, "You were always a good friend to me."[23] If Marley had been a friend, instead of a partner used to create more wealth, Scrooge would have mourned his death, if only a little. It was only out of fear that Scrooge claimed Marley was a friend, and this fear, against the backdrop of everything else, makes it difficult to accept Scrooge's exclamation of friendship. This said, I think we can surmise there was an identification of kindred spirits in the shared pursuit of profits.

Kindred spirits or not, Dickens portrays the utter self-willed isolation of this man. However, one character in the story sought to breach Scrooge's fortress of indifference, acerbity, and disdain. Scrooge's indefatigable nephew was undeterred by his uncle's off-putting demeanor and behavior. When Scrooge was striding down the street, his nephew caught up with his uncle and wished him a Merry Christmas, and Scrooge famously replied, "Bah! Humbug." Scrooge then pointed out that his nephew should not be merry because "You're poor enough." The good-natured nephew quipped that his uncle should be merry because "You're rich enough."[24] Flummoxed, Scrooge could only fall back on his "Bah! Humbug" before he launched into a scathing screed about fools who are merry on Christmas. "Every idiot," Scrooge screeched, "who goes about with 'Merry Christmas' on his lips should be boiled with his own pudding, and buried with a stake of holly through his heart."[25] But it is not simply being merry that was the object of Scrooge's disdain. Later in the conversation, he asked his nephew why he had gotten married. The nephew replied, "Because I fell in love."[26] Scrooge repeated this with derision, ending with "as if that were the only one thing in the world more ridiculous than a Merry Christmas."[27] While surprised by the invective, the nephew[28] nevertheless invited Scrooge for Christmas dinner,[29] which Scrooge forcibly and angrily rejected, preferring to be left alone. This scene between Scrooge and his nephew reinforces Scrooge's willed seclusion from others and his preoccupation with business and wealth. It is inconceivable to Scrooge that a poor person or relatively poor person could be happy or content, though he himself, as his nephew points out, is rich and unhappy. Perhaps this observation is what vexed Scrooge,

---

23. Dickens, *A Christmas Carol*, 36.
24. Dickens, *A Christmas Carol*, 11.
25. Dickens, *A Christmas Carol*, 11.
26. Dickens, *A Christmas Carol*, 14.
27. Dickens, *A Christmas Carol*, 14.
28. We learn later that the nephew's name is Fred.
29. Dickens, *A Christmas Carol*, 12.

resulting in his tirade. Moreover, his scoffing about love reveals that Scrooge believed that good wishes and love are equally ridiculous human activities, perhaps because of their fragility and impermanence—unlike capital or wealth. The business of making money is what was most precious and real to him. He trusted money. If he lost money, he could always make more, which provided him with the illusion of permanence and a reason never to grieve or be vulnerable. As Scrooge saw it, only fools and idiots seek the ephemera of merriment, love, and affection, which are inevitably subject to loss (impermanence) and, therefore, painful mourning. Business and money were the sole focus of his care, trust, and fidelity—the basis of any truth or reality.

Scrooge's vitriol begs the question, "Why doth he protest so much?" What would make a man so disliked, so miserably isolated, so preoccupied by the business of making money, and so clueless about his misery that etches his body and forms his behavior? Before answering this, it is important to say more about Scrooge and his way of being in the world. Bob Cratchit, Scrooge's poor and beleaguered, though sanguine, assistant, involuntarily applauded the nephew's comments about the joys of Christmas. Scrooge heatedly responded, "Let me hear another sound from you . . . and you'll keep your Christmas by losing your situation!"[30] This scene is immediately followed by the entrance of two gentlemen asking if Scrooge would offer some money for the poor who do not have enough to eat.[31] Scrooge responded by inquiring about the existence of debtor prisons and workhouses,[32] suggesting that these institutions, which relied on his paying taxes, were sufficient. The two men indicated that these institutions did not help people and that "many would rather die" than go to prison or the workhouses.[33] Scrooge's response was chillingly cruel, yet, to him, logically capitalistic: "If they would rather die, they had better do it, and decrease the surplus population."[34] While "surplus" suggests an economic calculation, Scrooge here is not quite a competent capitalist, because a surplus population—poor people—serves, as Marx noted, as a reserve army of out-of-work people who keep wages low and profits high. This reserve army of the poor serves to heighten the fear of workers—fearful of losing the meager wages they have. Here, we might surmise that the realities of extreme poverty in that market society was a reason for Bob Cratchit's passive acceptance of

30. Dickens, *A Christmas Carol*, 13.
31. Dickens, *A Christmas Carol*, 16.
32. Dickens, *A Christmas Carol*, 16–17.
33. Dickens, *A Christmas Carol*, 17.
34. Dickens, *A Christmas Carol*, 17.

the scanty wages he received from his miserly employer. That aside, these and other scenes reveal Scrooge to be a deeply miserable man, like Frankenstein's creature, who shared his wretchedness with others while being singularly unaware of and unaccountable for his own misery and the misery of others.

Scrooge's unacknowledged unhappiness and alienation stem from a series of painful losses in childhood. The Ghost of Christmas Past provides clues into the sources of Scrooge's pathological grief. One of the first scenes the Ghost of Christmas Past brings Scrooge to is that of a young boy alone at school during the holidays.[35] When Scrooge sees the boy alone at his desk, "Scrooge sat down . . . and wept to see his poor forgotten self as he used to be."[36] Why is this young lad alone at school during the holidays? The Ghost takes him to another Christmas scene where Scrooge sees Fan, his younger sister, coming into the room and kissing him. "Dear, dear brother," Fan exclaims, "I have come to bring you home."[37] She tells him that their father is kinder of late, and he agreed to Fan's plea to go home with her. This suggests that the father sent Scrooge away to school and subsequently denied his coming home. The father was clearly angry, and that anger appeared to be directed at his son. We do not know why this was so, but the absence of a mother/wife likely means that Scrooge's mother died sometime after Fan's birth. We learn from the Ghost that Fan had a big heart and that she later died in adulthood after having given birth to a boy—Scrooge's nephew who invited him to Christmas dinner. I mention Fan's later death to suggest that Scrooge's mother died as well and that his father took it badly, sending his son away. Moreover, sending Scrooge away would have only exacerbated his loss. In other words, he would have lost not only the love of his mother but the needed support of his father after her death.

These double losses would have interfered with Scrooge experiencing grief and working through the tasks of mourning. Put differently, while admittedly conjecture, if his father sent him away after the death of Scrooge's mother, it would have resulted in the nonrecognition of Scrooge's grief. In cases such as these, a child would learn that grief and mourning are not allowed, which, in turn, would mean learning that vulnerability is taboo, and, for Micheal Cholbi, this would interfere with Scrooge becoming more self-aware.[38] Possible evidence for the terrible pain of a dead mother and being

35. Dickens, *A Christmas Carol*, 47.
36. Dickens, *A Christmas Carol*, 47.
37. Dickens, *A Christmas Carol*, 50.
38. Cholbi argues that grief "is an especially crucial source of self-knowledge." If grief and mourning are not recognized, then, according to Cholbi, self-knowledge is impeded. As portrayed in the initial part of the story, Scrooge lacks self-awareness.

deprived of family is found later in the story. For now, Scrooge is allowed to come home as a young man and not to return to school.

A happier, more joyous scene follows of Scrooge as a young man who is apprenticed to Old Fezziwig. Here is a man who knows how to give a party; he invites many people to take part in the Christmas festivities. Scrooge is caught up in the scene as if he is there. He remarks to the Ghost—with his usual economic calculus—that "the happiness [Fezziwig] gives is quite as great as if it cost a fortune."[39] This is followed by Scrooge's guilt regarding how he treats his own clerk, exclaiming, "I should like to be able to say a word or two to my clerk."[40] In terms of grief, this joyous scene is a reminder of what Scrooge has lost—the joys of friendship. In other words, it is not simply about regret for having treated his clerk poorly; it is also that Scrooge had deliberately missed out on being a part of festive occasions. He could have turned out to be another version of Old Fezziwig, but instead he became a bitter, desiccated, miserly old man. And in the story, we learn another reason why Scrooge is miserly and miserable.

The Ghost of Christmas Past next takes him to a place where a young man and woman sit. He observes his younger self: "His face had not the harsh and rigid lines of later years; but it had begun to wear the sign of care and avarice. There was an eager, greedy, restless motion in the eye, which showed the passion that had taken root, and where the shadow of the growing tree would fall."[41] The young woman, Belle,[42] was, for reasons we do not know, in a mourning dress, though the dress is fitting for the scene. Belle sadly tells Scrooge that she has been displaced by an idol, a golden one.[43] Scrooge testily defends his pursuit of wealth and avoidance of poverty. She responds by saying, "You fear the world too much. All your other hopes have merged into the hope of being beyond the chance of its sordid reproach."[44] Belle can see what Scrooge refuses to acknowledge. His singular pursuit of wealth is based in his fear of past and future losses, which has led Scrooge to build a seemingly impenetrable wall that keeps others at bay, in this case, Belle and her love. In addition, this wall protects him from

---

Cholbi, *Grief*, 85.

39. Dickens, *A Christmas Carol*, 58
40. Dickens, *A Christmas Carol*, 58.
41. Dickens, *A Christmas Carol*, 59.
42. In a later scene, this was the name her husband used to address her. Dickens, *A Christmas Carol*, 65.
43. Dickens, *A Christmas Carol*, 59.
44. Dickens, *A Christmas Carol*, 59–60.

reproaches (shame and guilt), like those of his nephew and the two gentlemen, and further maintains his ignorance of himself.

It is important to point out that, some years earlier, Belle and Ebenezer had made a "contract" to marry later, once their financial situations had changed. Belle observes that when the contract "was made, you were another man." Scrooge retorts, "I was a boy."[45] With gentle firmness, she confronts Scrooge: "That which promised happiness when we were one in heart, is fraught with misery now that we are two. How often and how keenly I have thought of this, I will not say. It is enough that I have thought of it, and can release you."[46] Later she says, "I release you. With a full heart, for the love of him you once were."[47] She stands up and leaves, and we can be assured that Scrooge did not pursue her but rather sought safety in the security of his mistress—his golden barren idol, money.

Viewing this scene was very painful for the older Scrooge. He pleaded several times for the Spirit to stop, but there was one more scene to observe. The young woman in the previous scene is now married with children. The family is raucously enjoying Christmas together. Her husband enters the house with presents, and the children are wild with anticipation and joy.[48] The husband tells his wife, Belle, that he had walked past Scrooge's office and observed that Scrooge was working. What struck him was that Scrooge was working on the day his partner, Marley, was dying. This is too much for Scrooge to recollect. "Spirit!" said Scrooge in a broken voice. "Remove me from this place."[49] The Ghost reminds Scrooge that "these were shadows of the things that have been."[50] "That they are what they are," the Ghost continues, "do not blame me!"[51] Scrooge again pleads, saying he cannot tolerate any more.

We see in these two scenes evidence for Scrooge's handling of loss. Deciding to marry a woman awakens, in part, memories of one's experiences with one's mother. I am not saying that a man marries his mother but that any movement toward deeper intimacy touches on those earlier experiences. My hypothesis is that Scrooge's marriage contract with Belle was a conscious desire to seek intimacy, love, trust, and mutual fidelity with her. As she mentions, the contract represented hope for a life of mutual faith and love. At the

---

45. Dickens, *A Christmas Carol*, 60.
46. Dickens, *A Christmas Carol*, 60.
47. Dickens, *A Christmas Carol*, 61.
48. Dickens, *A Christmas Carol*, 63.
49. Dickens, *A Christmas Carol*, 65.
50. Dickens, *A Christmas Carol*, 65.
51. Dickens, *A Christmas Carol*, 65.

same time, the contract would have evoked Scrooge's unconscious fear and anxiety associated with the absent, dead mother. The closer he came to Belle and the date of fulfilling the contract, the more anxiety and fear he would have experienced. As Belle points out, Scrooge is ruled, unknowingly, by fear, which I am suggesting is fear of loss—the past losses associated with his mother's death and his emotionally absent father. Stated differently, this young woman represents the promise of love and happiness, yet she also represents vulnerability and the impermanence of life. Consciously, but perhaps mostly unconsciously, Scrooge selects a safer mistress to wed—money. One can lose money and replace it with more, but one cannot replace a dead parent, as Victor Frankenstein eventually realized. The loss of money, in other words, will not and cannot evoke the depth of vulnerability associated with the death of a loved one. Belle rightly recognized that Scrooge's decisions to pursue wealth led him to become a changed man, and this changed man was no longer someone who could love, who could surrender to joy and its background of existential impermanence. The present-day Scrooge, crying out in pain, realized the "costs" of those decisions—the loss of Belle's love and the loss in the future of a loving family.

Faith and Anti-Transformational Objects: The Mammon Complex and Frozen Grief

The Ghost of Christmas Past brings Scrooge to previous moments and places of aloneness and love, joy and loss. This first visitation reveals the process of Scrooge's surrender to the mammon complex, which I am going to explicate in terms of the dynamics of faith and Christopher Bollas's notion of transformational object. Recall that Scrooge's first memory is of a lonely boy, living at school far from home. I surmise that Scrooge's father sent him away, which plausibly meant that Scrooge felt displaced, losing the care of his father when he needed it most. The loss of this parental care, both in terms of his mother's death and having been sent away, would have been a profound betrayal, giving rise to distrust. This disruption was not, in my view, repaired by his father, even though Fan, his sister, loved her brother, beseeching her father to let him come home. In other words, there is no evidence that he and his father worked through the loss, betrayal, and distrust.

In my interpretation of the story, Scrooge remains unaware of his suffering associated with the death of his mother and the loss of his father's love. He dutifully goes to school and becomes an apprentice-clerk in Fezziwig's business. At some point, he falls in love with Belle and they make a contract to marry when Scrooge is able to support them financially. It is safe to assume that Scrooge initially had the desire to love Belle, and the contract represents both the present and future mutual trust and fidelity between them. The desire for care and love would have emerged against the background of losses and their attendant vulnerability—a background he was not conscious of. As a child, Scrooge did not have the support to face and work through either the death of his mother or the loss of the affection he needed from his father. Grief, mourning, and attendant vulnerabilities, he would have learned, are managed by way of avoidance through the defenses of denial, rationalization, etc. These defenses would have screened earlier losses, despite his desire, in the beginning, to be with Belle. As mentioned above, the closer he moved toward Belle, the higher his anxiety grew because she represented vulnerability—the vulnerability necessary to give and receive love and mutual faith. This is a type of vulnerability associated with the recognition of the existential impermanence of one's love for and faith in others. Evidence for Scrooge's dogged resistance to vulnerability and love is the very trajectory of Scrooge's life in adulthood. He does not get in touch with his past until invited to do so by the Ghost of Christmas Past. Indeed, the Scrooge of the present, in seeing his past self, is uncharacteristically vulnerable, expressing his anguish at the losses he had experienced and contributed to. Up to this point in his life, he had actively killed off interpersonal care, affection, trust, and fidelity, as well as self-awareness. He had made himself, so he unconsciously believes, invulnerable to desire (for others' love) and loss, as seen in his response to the death of Marley and to his nephew. In other words, Scrooge deemed it safer to distrust and, therefore, not surrender to the impermanence of the fidelity and love of others.

By the time the younger Scrooge sits with Belle, she recognizes that he has changed significantly since they made the contract. Scrooge had entered the field of business, which at the time of Dickens was inextricably tied to laissez-faire capitalism. Businesses were part of the apparatuses of capitalism, which came with an ethos of profit. Scrooge would have absorbed this ethos, and I suggest it functions as an anti-transformational object, which is a key feature of what I call the mammon complex. As noted in chapter 1, Bollas conceptualizes the first transformational "object"[52] in terms of the parent who "alters the infant's environment to meet [the infant's] needs."[53] More precisely, the parent-object is "a process that alters the infant's

---

52. Bollas acknowledges that the infant cannot yet differentiate between this or that object in the earliest phase of infancy. He views the "object" as pertaining to the process of parental caring and the infant's pre-representational organizations of this process.

53. Bollas, *The Shadow of the Object*, 15.

experience" or subjectivity.[54] This "object is 'known' not so much by putting it into an object-representation but as a recurrent *experience of being*."[55] This *experience of being* is contingent on the process of reliable parental care and resulting relational trust, which provides the relationship and process or experiences necessary for infants to surrender—to be vulnerable. Naturally, these experiences are organized pre-symbolically, which means transformational objects lie outside consciousness—consciousness organized in relation to developmentally later symbolic processes.

As noted in chapter 1, transformational objects appear in adulthood. In terms of adult life, a transformational object or process "is pursued in order to surrender to it as a mechanism that alters the self, where the subject-as-supplicant now feels himself to be the recipient of *enviro-somatic caring*,"[56] which accompanies an experience of being. I suggest that Scrooge's experience of the playfulness of Old Fezziwig and his contract to marry Belle represent his desire to surrender to this experience of being. Of course, one cannot have this experience without surrendering to it, which means one must be open to *being moved* by the object—being vulnerable—and this requires trust in the fidelity of the Other's care. Adults who surrender to the music played by an orchestra are able to do so because they had sufficient early embodied semiotic experiences of trust in relation to reliable and faithful parental care. Let's imagine that, as an infant, Scrooge did have these experiences, since his mother lived long enough to give birth to Fan, his younger sister, as well as the fact that, by the end of the story, he does indeed manifest a capacity for trust and vulnerability—for surrendering to the experience of being. To return to the earlier part of the tale, this raises the question of why Scrooge as an adult turns away from these experiences of being—these positive transformational objects. As indicated earlier, the death of his mother followed by his being sent away from his family would have been traumatic for the young Scrooge. It is painful enough to have one's mother die, but being sent away, being abandoned and betrayed, compounded his suffering.

Indeed, these losses can be understood as the opposite of experiences of being associated with enviro-somatic caring, which explains part of Scrooge's intense pain of grief. To explain this further, one's experience of being is relational, becoming a part of one's sense of self-in-relation-to a beloved self. When the beloved person dies, *one's grief and associated pain result from the disruption of the experience of being and one's corresponding*

---

54. Bollas, *The Shadow of the Object*, 13.
55. Bollas, *The Shadow of the Object*, 13; italics mine.
56. Bollas, *The Shadow of the Object*, 14; italics mine.

sense of self. To manage and work through these painful disruptions requires people who not only recognize one's grief but also respond with care so that one can do the work of mourning. This was not the case for young Scrooge. The death of his mother would have painfully disrupted his experiences of being and sense of self, which was quickly followed by a father who sent him away—apparently not recognizing his son's grief. From this, Scrooge learns that intimate relationships are profoundly dangerous. To trust other human beings, to surrender to the desire to love and be loved, to be open to being moved by joy, is foolish, idiotic, and ridiculous, as Scrooge reminds his young nephew, which screens his fear of losses—past and future.

Scrooge, then, faces a dilemma. He has positive memories of Old Fezziwig and has a desire to love Belle, but to surrender to these means he will have to become vulnerable. One cannot have an *experience of being* without becoming vulnerable, which also means that one must trust oneself and the Other. Yet, the closer he moves toward surrendering to experiences of being, the more he feels anxiety and fear associated with the traumas of loss—the death of his mother and the rejection by his father. We might imagine that a part of him unconsciously believes that he cannot bear the pain of the lost experiences of being and, therefore, that vulnerability becomes connected to experiences of unrecognized suffering, distrust, and infidelity. It is simply too emotionally dangerous to become aware of and experience these losses, which is evident in the story where Scrooge repeatedly asks people to leave him alone and begs the Ghost of Christmas Past to take him from familiar scenes of warmth, love, and intimacy.

The scene with Belle encapsulates Scrooge's answer to this dilemma. He chooses to pursue an anti-transformational object, which is money. Capitalism provides him an ethos, a rationale, and an infinitely replaceable object. In brief, money *cannot ever function* as a transformational object since it does not and cannot represent the enviro-somatic caring of early life and, concomitantly, experiences of being. However, money can serve as an anti-transformational object. By anti-transformational, I mean several things. First, the experiences of interpersonal trust and fidelity do not apply to money as an object. One cannot have a personal relationship with money, though one can, like Scrooge, place one's trust and fidelity in an object—a lifeless thing. Second and relatedly, no one can have an experience of being by "surrendering" to money. This does not mean that people cannot try. For instance, the story of the Israelites "surrendering" to the golden calf may represent a desire to collectively experience being, but we know in the story this is a failed project because of their desperate fear and anxiety. Idols, to use this term, are anti-transformational because the experience of being is, in this Israelite story, only possible in relation to God. God represents the source of life and experiences of being rather than a lifeless, human-made object. Scrooge, in one sense, "surrenders" to money, but money is incapable of providing an experience of being. Money is a human fiction and not the source of life. Third, the experience of being is paradoxical in that it cannot be chosen and yet one chooses to surrender to it. Put differently, the transformational object is outside one's ability to control or manipulate it, though one has a choice of whether to surrender to it. By contrast, an anti-transformational object is under one's omnipotent (illusory) control. The Israelites made the golden calf, understandably, out of fear and anxiety. Money is created and destroyed: it is under the control of human beings and, even if one loses money, it is possible to earn it back. God and experiences of being, on the other hand, represent the transcendent, which is not made, controlled, or manipulatable. Scrooge, in having wealth and pursuing profit, controls money. Yes, he could lose money due to market forces or bad decisions, but he can make more. In holding fast to money, Scrooge never has to surrender to singular experiences of being that derive from one's relationship to a singular individual who can die. The singular individual and attendant experiences of being are precarious—impermanent. Money is not singular.

All of this raises a question: If an anti-transformational object cannot provide interpersonal trust and fidelity or experiences of being, then what are its psychosocial functions? In other words, why does someone like Scrooge choose money, and how does it operate in his life? One answer to this question is already depicted above. The anti-transformational object functions to protect Scrooge from the existential precarity and impermanence of love and the associated pains of loss and grief. He builds a fortress that keeps people at bay, and, in his isolation, he need not ever be moved by suffering—his or the sufferings of others. Scrooge, in other words, is incapable of self-empathy or self-compassion, and he has no empathy or compassion for those suffering from capitalism's excesses nor even empathy for the travails of his poor suffering clerk and his family. A related psychological function of the anti-transformational object concerns self-knowledge. In the present, Scrooge has no self-knowledge associated with his past or his present suffering. To be sure, he has memories of the past that the Spirit confronts him with, but in the present these memories are repressed by virtue of his focus on making money—the anti-transformational object. When he encounters past memories, he begins to experience joy and later the pain of knowing what he has done and lost, which I will say more about below. Another psychological "benefit" of the anti-transformational object is the pleasure associated with possessing it, being able to make it (agency), and believing that one's wealth makes one superior to others.

Scrooge's avarice, in other words, is linked to his sense of self (dependent on nonhuman objects) and a corresponding belief in his social superiority—the pleasure of pride. Scrooge disdains poor people and his nephew, believing they are lazy, deluded, or both. To be sure, Scrooge is miserable and spreads his misery, but I suggest the pleasures of greed and pride, which accompany the anti-transformational object, deflect him from encountering and becoming conscious of his misery. Consider Scrooge's response to his nephew's apt quip, "You're rich enough."[57] His nephew is suggesting that, despite his wealth, Scrooge is not merry. Scrooge's response is "Bah! Humbug," which, we recall, is followed by an angry screed about how ridiculous merriment is. His nephew's quip is an invitation for self-awareness, for self-knowledge of his misery, which Scrooge defends against by attacking those who are joyful or who desire joy. With an anti-transformational object, one never has to face, surrender to, or lose the experiences of being. One never has to face the precarity and impermanence of love and the singularity of the beloved. One never has to endure grief or do the work of mourning. The anti-transformational object protects Scrooge from desires for intimacy and shields him from loss, while distracting him with the empty pleasures of greed and pride.

In summary, the seeds of the mammon complex were seen in Scrooge's early adult life when he fell prey to decisions to distrust vulnerability. Instead, he adopted an anti-transformational object that repressed painful experiences and knowledge of love lost while psychologically protecting him from acknowledging and surrendering to the precarity and impermanence of a beloved's singularity and attendant experiences of being. This eclipse of memory and self-knowledge accompanied a lack of empathy and compassion for himself and others. The anti-transformational object can also be understood in terms of Scrooge's belief, trust in, and fidelity to this contingent object—an object that he trusted and controlled, eschewing the existential vulnerabilities and uncertainties of interpersonal relationships. The psychosocial costs of the mammon complex are deflected by the empty pleasures of greed and pride—pleasures that cannot be shared because they are possessed in the isolation of the illusion of invulnerability.

From the Mammon Complex to Merriment: The Process of Grief and Mourning

The previous two chapters focused on the dynamics and pathological consequences of tragic grief. In Dickens's story we have a portrayal not only of

---

57. Dickens, *A Christmas Carol*, 11.

tragic grief but also of a process by which this grief and misery are transformed. In this section, I depict this process and argue that it has implications for understanding the process of change or, dare I say, conversion vis-à-vis the toxic masculinity of the mammon complex, as well as for how we might care for those who are caught in the talons of tragic grief.

The process of change begins with the appearance of Scrooge's long-dead business partner, Jacob Marley. Scrooge is understandably skeptical of this specter but asks Marley, "Why do spirits walk the earth, and why do they come to me?"[58] The ghost of Marley replies that he is "doomed to wander the world—oh, woe is me!—and witness what it cannot share, but might have shared on earth, and turned to happiness!"[59] Scrooge wonders about the chains Marley's ghost carries. The ghost replies, "I wear the chains I forged in life. I made it link by link, and yard by yard; I girded it of my own free will . . . Is its pattern strange to *you*?" Scrooge trembles and the ghost answers the question with another question and observation: "Or would you know the weight and length of the strong coil you bear yourself? It was full as heavy and as long as this, seven Christmas Eves ago." Seeing and disturbed by Marley's oppressive suffering and the agony that awaits him, Scrooge begs Marley to speak words of comfort. Marley replies, "I have none to give."[60] In seeing Marley and hearing his words, Scrooge is confronted with the consequences of the decisions he made in life. Marley was like Scrooge, preoccupied by the business of making money, isolating himself from other people and places, and rejecting the needs of others. The chains or defenses forged in life led to his later torment, remorse, loneliness, unhappiness, and perpetual wandering the earth—alone.

Like anyone confronted by his tragic decisions, Scrooge becomes defensive. "'But you were always a good man of business, Jacob,' faltered Scrooge, who now began to apply this to himself."[61] Marley thunders, "Business! Mankind was my business. The common welfare was my business; charity, mercy, forbearance, and benevolence, were all my business. The dealings of my trade were but a drop of water in the comprehensive ocean of my business!"[62] Marley tells Scrooge he has come to warn him and to give him hope—a hope to escape the fate Marley suffers and a hope for merriment. The ghost of Marley, it appears, cares for Scrooge.

---

58. Dickens, *A Christmas Carol*, 31.
59. Dickens, *A Christmas Carol*, 32.
60. Dickens, *A Christmas Carol*, 32.
61. Dickens, *A Christmas Carol*, 35.
62. Dickens, *A Christmas Carol*, 35.

There are two aspects of this initial encounter. The specter is a spectacle of the consequences that await Scrooge for the decisions he is and has been making. To see and experience the horror that awaits him is a first step toward change. Second, Marley is a friend of sorts that Scrooge twice acknowledges. This "friendship" is a feature of the second step toward the process of change. Scrooge trusted Marley in the past and he trusts the ghost of Marley in the present, though later Scrooge tries to dismiss the ghostly visitation. This trust opens up the possibility of being moved by what Marley has become and to heed what he says. Recall that, in the past, Belle confronted Scrooge, revealing to him the consequences of his decisions, which were already etched in his face and demeanor. Later, his nephew tries to coax his uncle to pursue merriment and family instead of isolation. And shortly after that, two gentlemen try to appeal to Scrooge's empathy for the poor, which Scrooge disdainfully dismisses. The pattern is that Scrooge trusts no one and is unmoved by even the most tender of approaches. Yet, Marley's ghost clearly moves Scrooge emotionally. Scrooge observes the horror of Marley's suffering and chains. I think Scrooge is emotionally moved because Marley was a kind of friend or, at the very least, someone who Scrooge identifies with and, in the past, had trusted. To begin to breach the defenses of the anti-transformational object for the sake of grief and mourning, there must be some semblance of trust and fidelity. Otherwise, Scrooge would have dismissed Marley like he did everyone else. This seed of trust opens the possibility for Scrooge to confront the consequences of his decisions.

Marley tells Scrooge that on the next three nights he will be visited by a different spirit. When Marley departs, Scrooge gazes out the window and sees numerous other tormented spirits, some of whom he once knew. This is yet another experience that moves Scrooge. The specters' miseries are not simply loss of freedom and perpetual alienation but the distress that comes from their inability to intervene when seeing the suffering of those who are alive. For instance, Scrooge espies one spirit "in a white waistcoat, with a monstrous iron safe attached to his ankle, who cried piteously at being unable to assist a wretched woman with an infant, whom it saw below, upon a door-step."[63] Scrooge observes that the suffering of all the ghosts was that they "sought to interfere, for good, in human matters, and they had lost the power to do so."[64] To my mind, their misery stemmed from their empathically recognizing and being vulnerable to the suffering of others yet also being confronted by their powerlessness to act. This implies that, while alive, they did possess some capacity to recognize and be moved by the suffering

63. Dickens, *A Christmas Carol*, 38.
64. Dickens, *A Christmas Carol*, 38.

of others but refused to act, to care for others. The lesson for Scrooge: this is what awaits him. It is an exclamation mark after Marley's visage vanishes.

There are three features of this visitation. The first is that Marley's suffering is the result of decisions he made in life—decisions to focus on profit while ignoring the needs and experiences of those in need. The second aspect of Marley's suffering (and the other ghosts Scrooge recognizes) is that they are able to see and be moved by the suffering of other living human beings but are incapable of helping, which only adds to their suffering. It is interesting, though, that Marley does intervene by warning Scrooge. Perhaps the exquisite empathic sensitivity of the ghosts and of Marley in particular entails recognizing Scrooge's suffering—a suffering that Scrooge is not yet able to recognize or experience. The third feature is that, while Marley is condemned to walk the earth alone, disconnected, and weighed down by the chains he forged in life, redemption and experiencing merriment were still possible for Scrooge.

Exhausted, Scrooge collapses into bed, awakening almost twenty-four hours later. He tries but is unable to dismiss the previous night's experience as a bad dream. One would think that Marley's visit would have been enough for Scrooge, or anyone else for that matter, to change his ways. But it is not enough to breach the defenses of the anti-transformational object because the object is but a symptom of some deeper agony that Marley's ghost does not address. Indeed, while Scrooge is disturbed by Marley's appearance and that of the other ghosts, his suffering remains untouched. All Scrooge is aware of is his fear. Marley, in other words, is only pointing to the horrifying consequences of Scrooge's miserliness and his idolatrous possession of the anti-transformational object. If we were to imagine Scrooge changing at this point of the story, it would not be transformational because Scrooge would have changed only as a result of his fear. To be charitable, to provide alms for the poor out of fear of punishment, is a kind of contractual-conditional faith, which would parallel the contractual faith relations of the market society. We see this when Scrooge tries to bargain—unsuccessfully—with Marley's ghost. Let me come at this another way. Recall that Scrooge called his nephew's love and merriment ridiculous. Both love and merriment are gifts, which require trust enough to be vulnerable to surrender to both. By contrast, contractual faith relations are evident whenever love or merriment is offered for a price. One may do the right thing out of fear, but it is not the same as doing something out of genuine love or care for another person or being. Scrooge's fear demands a contract if he is to change. The mammon complex or anti-transformational object is devoid of love and vulnerability, which means that scaring Scrooge into good behavior is not enough to result in genuine change. The real possibility of transformation arises with the process of three ghostly visitations.

On the next night when the clock chimes 1 a.m., Scrooge is momentarily relieved because there appears to be no ghost. And yet, the bed curtains are suddenly drawn back and Dickens describes the Ghost of Christmas Past—Scrooge's past Christmases. Scrooge asks the Ghost "what business brought him there."[65] The Ghost replies, "Your welfare," and a moment later reiterates, "Your reclamation."[66] Like Marley, the Ghost is concerned about Scrooge's welfare but has an additional another concern, which is his reclamation. This is an interesting term. Instead of conversion or healing, the aim is reclamation. What is it that Scrooge is invited to reclaim regarding his past? In the first scene, Scrooge is brought to where he grew up. With the gentle touch of the Ghost, Scrooge becomes "*conscious* of a thousand odours floating in the air, each one connected with a thousand thoughts. And hopes, and joys, and cares long, long forgotten!"[67] The Ghost observes that Scrooge trembles at the sight and a tear forms. The next scene is of "a solitary child, neglected by his friends."[68] Scrooge, as mentioned above, weeps when he sees the painful aloneness of his child-self—long forgotten or repressed.

Another memory involves his sister Fan, who tells young Scrooge that "we're to be together all the Christmas long, and have the merriest time in all the world."[69] The Ghost remarks that Fan has "a large heart," with which Scrooge readily agrees. Another person with a generous spirit was Old Fezziwig.[70] The Ghost offers a comment about the joyful celebration Fezziwig offers his employees: "A small matter to make these silly folks so full of gratitude."[71] This invites Scrooge to *reflect* and articulate his view—"The happiness he gives is quite as great as if it cost a fortune."[72] It is not the money Old Fezziwig spends to have a party, it is his welcoming, playful, and joyful demeanor that are of inestimable value. Scrooge, in other words, recognizes that Fezziwig's generosity and resulting merriment cannot be monetized (as if it cost a great fortune). The last painful scene of Christmas Past is of Belle, his former betrothed who, remember, told Scrooge that he

---

65. Dickens, *A Christmas Carol*, 44.
66. Dickens, *A Christmas Carol*, 45.
67. Dickens, *A Christmas Carol*, 46; italics mine.
68. Dickens, *A Christmas Carol*, 47.
69. Dickens, *A Christmas Carol*, 50.
70. Dickens, *A Christmas Carol*, 53–57.
71. Dickens, *A Christmas Carol*, 58.
72. Dickens, *A Christmas Carol*, 58.

was afraid of the world, of life. She later happily marries another man. These memories evoke joy and pain for Scrooge. The last two memories awaken in Scrooge a recognition of what he has lost as a result of his pursuit of wealth—his golden idol, he notes.[73]

Before moving to the Ghost of Christmas Present, I linger here to discuss in greater detail the process of "reclamation" and its relation to grief and mourning. Philosopher Michael Cholbi argues that the experience of grief and the process of mourning invite the good of self-knowledge. He writes that while "grief is not the only opportunity in life for substantial self-knowledge . . . it is an especially crucial source of self-knowledge."[74] This is knowledge not simply of one's emotions and thoughts regarding the deceased but also of the memories of one's life with the deceased. Self-knowledge is a good, not simply because of the pleasures and pains of past loves but also in the very process of mourning. That is, the self-knowledge of grief and mourning makes possible future intimacies and joys. Scrooge's adoption of the mammon complex (anti-transformational object) represses his memories of love and their attendant thoughts and feelings. The Ghost of Christmas Past is inviting Scrooge to remember, to *reclaim* these memories, and this process of reclamation invites self-reflection and insight—the empathic self-knowledge of grief. We have moved from the self-knowledge associated with fear to the self-knowledge and insight associated with lost loves and the consequences of defending against precarity and impermanence.

One other point about the Ghost's invitation of reclamation. Clearly, in the story, Scrooge surrenders to the Ghost's invitation. The Ghost "clasped him gently by the arm. 'Rise! And walk with me.'" The Ghost's grasp was "gentle as a woman's hand [and] was not to be resisted." Scrooge, in realizing the Ghost was making for the window, cries, "I am mortal and liable to fall." The Ghost calmly and gently replies, "Bear but touch my hand . . . and you shall be upheld in more than this."[75] The point here is that, unlike succumbing to fear during Marley's visitation, Scrooge, while showing some resistance, surrenders to the Ghost, which suggests trust of the Ghost and the process. Reclamation, in short, cannot be forced but only invited. Belle's previous attempt to invite Scrooge to reclaim love and affection failed because Scrooge was already ensconced in the talons of the anti-transformational object. The Ghost of Christmas Past takes Scrooge to scenes of past Christmas holidays, inviting Scrooge to let go, for a time, of the anti-transformational object

---

73. Dickens, *A Christmas Carol*, 59.
74. Cholbi, *Grief*, 85.
75. Dickens, *A Christmas Carol*, 45.

and reclaim his past. It is Scrooge who must surrender to the feelings and thoughts associated with these memories and, in so doing, he gains the self-knowledge of empathy—empathy primarily in relation to his past selves. This reclamation and resulting empathic knowledge are part of mourning and the initial letting go of the mammon complex, which sets the stage for the next visitation—the next step in the process.

The second night Scrooge was prepared, though the Ghost of Christmas Present did not appear in his bedroom. Scrooge, seeing a strange glow emanating from under the door to the next room, reaches for the door, hearing the command, "Come in! Come in! and know me better, man!"[76] The scene Dickens paints is lush. The Ghost is huge, resplendent in his robes. In the first scene Scrooge is whisked to the town, where he sees much merriment, as well as poor persons. Standing outside the bakery, Scrooge asks the Ghost whether the incense he spreads on the dinners of passersby "would apply to any kind of dinner on this day." The Ghost replies, "To any kindly given. To a poor one most . . . Because it needs it most."[77] Scrooge queries the Ghost about closing the bakeries on Sundays, depriving the poor "of their means of dining every seventh day, often the only day they can be said to dine at all."[78] The Ghost is incensed. "There are some upon this earth of yours who lay claim to know us, and who do their deeds of passion, pride, ill-will, hatred, envy, bigotry, and selfishness in our name, who are as strange to us and all our kith and kin."[79] There are two points to be made here. First, unlike the specter who seeks Scrooge's reclamation, *this ghost wants Scrooge to know him*. This invitation is what gives rise to Scrooge's query, and what he discovers is that many Christians may claim to know a representative of Christ's love and generosity, though their actions reveal that they do not. Second, Scrooge's question emerges from his empathy toward the poor. He sees and is moved by their suffering. This is not the same Scrooge who had disdainfully dismissed the two gentlemen who asked for alms for the poor.

The Ghost's generosity and "sympathy with all poor [persons] . . . led him straight to Scrooge's clerk."[80] It is a raucous happy scene, absent Martha, Bob Cratchit, and his son Tiny Tim. Martha arrives before her father and Tiny Tim, hiding in the closet when she hears them approach. Bob Cratchit and Tiny Tim are coming from church services, and Bob is disappointed not to see Martha there. His joy returns when she surprises him, and they

76. Dickens, *A Christmas Carol*, 70.
77. Dickens, *A Christmas Carol*, 77.
78. Dickens, *A Christmas Carol*, 78.
79. Dickens, *A Christmas Carol*, 78.
80. Dickens, *A Christmas Carol*, 79.

all join in to enjoy the festivities, despite their poverty.[81] Scrooge is emotionally moved by this familial scene and especially by Tiny Tim. Scrooge asks the Ghost, "Tell me if Tiny Tim will live." The Ghost responds, "I see a vacant seat in the poor chimney corner, and crutch without an owner . . . If these shadows remain unaltered by the Future, the child will die." Scrooge cries out "No, no. Oh, no, kind Spirit, say he will be spared." The Ghost reiterates his comment about the future, adding, "If he be like to die, he had better do it, and decrease the surplus population."[82] Scrooge hangs his head in shame, knowing these are the very words he used when talking to the two gentlemen who sought a contribution from him to help the poor—the "surplus population." The old Scrooge would have had no shame. The new Scrooge possesses the empathic knowledge associated with recognizing the sufferings of the poor, which is why he now feels shame and guilt.

There are several other scenes, but the last scene entails a party attended by his nieces, nephew, and their friends. While the nieces express their dislike of their uncle, the nephew says that he cannot be angry with Scrooge. He remarks that, with all of Scrooge's wealth, he is an unhappy man, unwilling to take part in the joys of family and friends. At one point, Scrooge begs the Ghost to stay a little longer, to "play" the new game.[83] Scrooge "had imperceptibly become so gay and light of heart," taking part, in one sense, in the game.[84] I note here that we have moved from empathic knowledge of those who are poor to empathy associated with playful participation, even when only Scrooge and the Ghost can see Scrooge play.

Amid the last scene of this visitation, Scrooge espies something beneath the hem of the Ghost's cloak. In moving the cloak aside, there appears "a boy and girl. Yellow, meager, ragged, scowling, wolfish; but prostrate, too, in their humility."[85] Scrooge wonders if these children are his, but the Ghost quickly corrects him and says they belong to humanity. "This boy, the Ghost adds, is Ignorance. This girl is Want. Beware of them both . . . but most of

---

81. Dickens, *A Christmas Carol*, 81–85. Dickens portrays Bob Cratchit as a loving, gracious, and forgiving man who by all accounts accepts his poverty despite being employed. While Dickens clearly was critical of the conditions that create poverty, he constructs a character who, in my view, passively accepts his poverty and its consequences for his wife and children. Granted, this is a story, but a story may be complicit in capitalistic apparatuses that create an army of the poor—a surplus population, which, for Scrooge, means people who are not contributing to the market society.

82. Dickens, *A Christmas Carol*, 86.

83. Dickens, *A Christmas Carol*, 99.

84. Dickens, *A Christmas Carol*, 100.

85. Dickens, *A Christmas Carol*, 102.

all beware of this boy, for on his brow I see that written which is Doom."[86] Scrooge, again emotionally moved by their suffering, asks, "Have they no refuge or resource?" The Ghost of Christmas Present asks, "Are there no prisons? . . . Are there no workhouses?"[87] recalling the very words the Old Scrooge had said, and then just as quickly the Ghost departs. The last scenes move from the self-knowledge and relational experience associated with joy to the self-knowledge of guilt and shame for having dismissed the needs of the poor. In coming to know the Ghost of Christmas Present, Scrooge gains further knowledge of himself (joy, merriment, guilt, and shame), as well as knowledge of the sufferings and joys of others.

The next ghost appears on the third night. For Scrooge, the Ghost of Christmas Future "seemed to scatter gloom and mystery."[88] Scrooge thought he was afraid when Marley's ghost appeared, but this silent Ghost of Christmas Future downright terrifies him. The first scene is of a dead man, and Scrooge listens and observes, knowing that there was no love for this unnamed man in life or death. Scrooge recognizes the misery of this man and the misery he caused, asking the mute ghost if there is anyone who had a kind word to say about him.[89] Not surprisingly, a couple of people are glad that he is dead because their situation has the possibility of improving, though this is not the case for Tiny Tim, whose death preceded this man's death.[90] The reader knows that the dead person is Scrooge, but it is only later that Scrooge becomes aware that it is indeed him. The self-knowledge obtained here is that, while everyone dies, Scrooge's miserliness, albeit a defense against the pain of loss, leads only to more emptiness and suffering (his and, more importantly, other persons'). This is a "terrible" knowledge in that Scrooge is aware that his decisions to isolate himself, to eschew any empathy toward others, not only keeps him from joy but also creates a meaningless, empty life. The Ghost of Christmas Past brings to him an awareness of the meaninglessness of a life not lived—a life trapped in the fortress of the anti-transformational object.

Scrooge awakens weeping and gripping the bedpost. He realizes he is alive and joyously dances around the house. A changed man inhabits this old bleak house, and he goes about buying a turkey for Bob's family, invites himself to dinner with his nephew (Fred) and his nieces, raises Bob's salary, gives generously to charity, etc. Scrooge vows to "live in the Past, Present,

86. Dickens, *A Christmas Carol*, 103.
87. Dickens, *A Christmas Carol*, 103.
88. Dickens, *A Christmas Carol*, 104.
89. Dickens, *A Christmas Carol*, 117.
90. Dickens, *A Christmas Carol*, 118–20.

and the Future,"⁹¹ and later "it was always said of him, that he knew how to keep Christmas well."⁹² This happy result would not have happened if Scrooge had not trusted the spirits and surrendered to and reclaimed past and present experiences of joy, fear, anxiety, sadness, shame, and guilt. He mourned his past and, in the process, let go of the anti-transformational object, which enabled him to experience the precarity and impermanence of merriment and love in the present. This, in turn, fostered a different future. The anti-transformational object forecloses the future by keeping the past repressed and the present rooted in a self-chosen arid fortress of loveless isolation. With an anti-transformational object, nothing happened, happens, or will happen—except the same lifeless way of being in the world. By letting go of the anti-transformational object, Scrooge is in touch with his past, present to his relationships and experiences in the present, and open to the present's trajectory into an unknown future. All of this means Scrooge embraces the precarity of the impermanence of life while being open to love, joy, and grief.

There remains, however, a question in this happy ending. The new Scrooge is generous to friends, workers, and charitable organizations, yet he continues to run his business. He gives up the anti-transformational object of the mammon complex yet continues to be ensconced in the capitalist enterprise, which suggests that for Dickens one can be a Christian and an unquestioning or acritical capitalist.⁹³ So, how we might account for Scrooge's conversion given he remains CEO of Marley and Scrooge? Giorgio Agamben's notion of *inoperativity* can deepen our appreciation of Scrooge's conversion.

Briefly, for Agamben, inoperativity means deactivating the functioning of apparatuses, but this does not mean that these apparatuses cease operating or do not continue to have effects.⁹⁴ To render an apparatus inoperative means exercising one's capacity for impotentiality, and this capacity is inextricably part of Agamben's view of potentiality and actuality. For Agamben, "The very essence of humanity lies in a potentiality that is expressed when it

---

91. Dickens, *A Christmas Carol*, 127.

92. Dickens, *A Christmas Carol*, 138.

93. Given Dickens's sensitivity to the sufferings of poor people in an industrializing country and no doubt his awareness that some European philosophers and public intellectuals and activists were critical of capitalism, I suspect that he considered it possible to be a capitalist and a Christian. In other words, the avarice that lies at the heart of capitalism remains unquestioned. In saying this, I am not suggesting that one cannot be at the same time a Christian and capitalist, but Dickens's story does not interrogate this relationship.

94. Prozorov, *Agamben and Politics*, 31–34.

does not unfold into actuality."[95] That is, human beings possess the capacity to choose not to actualize what is potential—to make inoperative what an apparatus demands or expects.[96] Agamben writes:

> *Other living beings are capable only of their specific potentiality; they can only do this or that. But human beings are the animals who are capable of their own impotentiality. The greatness of human potentiality is measured by the abyss of human impotentiality.* Here it is possible to see how the root of freedom is to be found in the abyss of potentiality. To be free is not simply to have the power to do this or that thing, nor is it simply to have the power to refuse to do this or that thing. To be free is . . . *to be capable of one's own impotentiality.*[97]

To illustrate this complex discussion, Agamben turns to Herman Melville's *Bartleby, The Scrivener*. When Bartleby is told by his boss to do something, Bartleby replies, "I prefer not to." For Agamben, Bartleby is choosing to *not actualize his potentiality*, which is demanded by his boss who, in my view, represents the demands of the larger capitalist apparatuses that are rendered inoperative by Bartleby's preferring not to actualize what he is, in fact, capable of doing. The moment of impotentiality means, in part, that Bartleby is not determined and cannot be determined (in the sense of being commanded by others) by the political-economic apparatuses that are aimed at defining his subjectivity and requiring him to actualize his potentiality vis-à-vis these apparatuses. Colebrook and Maxwell add that "to have potentiality is to be capable of not becoming what one has the capacity to be" or what one is expected to be or do.[98] Of course, the act of inoperativity does not mean that the apparatuses cease operating or that they no longer have effects.

We can understand Scrooge's conversion in terms of inoperativity or the exercise of his impotentiality with regard to capitalism. He prefers not to be captive to the rubrics of profit and the vice of avarice, though

---

95. Colebrook and Maxwell, *Agamben*, 289.

96. For Agamben, Western philosophical traditions have largely "subordinated potentiality to actuality: so we begin with the actual, speaking humans and their political and artistic productions, and we see potentiality at present as a capacity or skill that is defined by the final action. We see potentiality as secondary or accidental" (as quoted in Colebrook and Maxwell, *Agamben*, 188). This is derived, in part, from Aristotle's notion that "actuality is prior to potentiality" (as quoted in in Ugilt, *Giorgi Agamben*, 26), though this does not mean that Aristotle believed that "potentiality exists only in actuality" (Agamben, *Potentialities*, 180).

97. Agamben, *Potentialities*, 182–83.

98. Colebrook and Maxwell, *Agamben*, 38.

he continues to make use of the apparatuses of capitalism. Indeed, in being so magnanimous and generous, he renders these apparatuses of profit inoperative. He does not pursue more wealth but rather uses his wealth to help others, such as Tiny Tim. Scrooge is free of the mammon complex yet resides inoperatively within the market society. In short, he defects, if you will, in place.

Concluding Thoughts

Dickens's story is obviously about a man and how he changes to keep Christmas, though the story can have meaning and significance for any gender as well as serve as a morality tale for any person of a different religious or humanistic faith. For instance, we observe the misery and attenuation of life when persons fail to recognize and surrender to experiences of grief, thereby foreclosing the tasks of mourning. But misery does not have the last word. The process of change, while painful and arduous, can create a space for embracing the precarity of love and joy. Add to this the idea of framing this story in relation to the past, present, and future realities of climate change, or what many scholars and scientists refer to as the sixth extinction event or the Anthropocene Age.[99] We might imagine that the event of the climate emergency represents the Ghosts of the Past, Present, and Future, haunting and inviting many of us in Western market societies to recognize and surrender to the painful realities that our past and present actions have contributed to the sufferings and the past, present, and future extinctions of other species, the degradation of the Earth, and the present and future sufferings of human beings caught in the grips of climate disasters. The question is not whether, in acting inoperatively vis-à-vis global capitalist, nationalist, and imperialist apparatuses, we will experience merriment and become more generous to our friends and neighbors, but whether our grief and mourning will lead to (1) embracing the precarity and existential impermanence of all life and (2) caring for and about the needs and sufferings

---

99. Over two decades ago, scientists Paul Crutzen and Edward Stoermer argued that the world has entered a new age—the Anthropocene—the sixth extinction event caused by human activity. This is a controversial term because not all human beings and societies have contributed to climate change. Some people, such as Jason Moore, suggest that we call this the Capitalocene Era because capitalism has been the primary culprit in climate change, though this too has its detractors. Other related apparatuses are implicated, such as nationalism and imperialism. Given these controversies, I opt for Anthropocene because capitalism, imperialism, and nationalism are human social imaginaries. Crutzen and Stoermer, "The 'Anthropocene.'" See also Klein, *This Changes Everything*; Moore, "Name the System!"

of not simply other human beings (existing and non-existent), but other species (existing and non-existent) and the Earth. Will we take up some aspect of Scrooge's "Total Abstinence Principle,"[100] making possible more empathic, generous, and sustainable ways of dwelling on this fragile Earth? Or, unmoved by these apparitions, will we continue to be dismissive of and miserly toward othered human beings, other species, and the Earth?

---

100. Dickens, *A Christmas Carol*, 138.

4

Toxic Masculinity and the Resistance of Ungovernable Selves in Daniel Black's Novel *The Coming*

They had bought our flesh but not our souls.[1]

They could buy our bodies but not our resolve.[2]

Our love for one another sustained us.[3]

Silence is the enemy of history.[4]

Victor Frankenstein, Captain Ahab, and Ebenezer Scrooge manifest iterations of toxic masculinity that emerge from failure to grieve—failure to embrace human precarity and vulnerability. Only in Dickens's story do we observe a process wherein a man moves from a poisonous form of masculinity to one that manifests love, compassion, generosity, and humility. In each story, the focus is on the individual and his personal history, though I have argued that other social apparatuses (e.g.,

1. Black, *The Coming*, 93–94.
2. Black, *The Coming*, 209.
3. Black, *The Coming*, 120.
4. Black, *The Coming*, 75.

science, capitalism) are implicated in their defenses against grieving and precarity. Placing the spotlight on individual characters can distract us from how beliefs, meanings, and values associated with political, economic, and social imaginaries and their apparatuses are internalized by boys and men, giving rise to selves that create zones of non-justice wherein horrific acts of violence and exploitation are legitimized, applauded, and rationalized. Toxic masculinity, in other words, does not simply arise in situations in which male individuals fail to grieve and, as a result, manifest a pathological and tragic masculinity. Rather, toxic masculinity can emerge collectively, and, in so doing, it becomes normalized or even idealized by a culture or society.

As in the distorted masculinity of Frankenstein, Ahab, and Scrooge, normalized toxic masculinity leaves a wide, deep, and long wake of exploitation and destruction, which includes not simply other human beings but also other species and the Earth. Put differently, the consequences of social, political, and economic apparatuses that produce and maintain normalized destructive masculinity can be understood in terms of what Giorgio Agamben (and others) call "bare life"[5] or what Frantz Fanon labeled "zone of non-being"[6] and Orlando Patterson termed "social death."[7] The term *bare life* concerns persons "caught up in the sovereign ban . . . stripped of all protections and abandoned to the force of law."[8] Stated more starkly, "The sovereign sphere is the sphere in which it is permitted to kill without committing homicide . . . What is captured in the sovereign ban is a human victim who may be killed but not sacrificed."[9] I will say more about bare life and the zone of non-being, but for now let me say that those who suffer as a result of this manifestation of toxic masculinity find ways, if they are not killed, to resist being captive to zones of non-being and, in some cases, overcome their victimizers. Understanding their resilience and resistance is equally as important as understanding the sources of the emergence and maintenance of pernicious types of masculinity.

In this chapter, I continue to use literature to explore and illustrate collective masculinity gone awry, as well as to understand the resilience and resistance of those who suffer the consequences of toxic masculinity. More particularly, I turn to Daniel Black's novel *The Coming*, which depicts the horrors of the Middle Passage and African women and men who endured and resisted the brutal dehumanization at the hands of their male slavers.

5. Agamben, *Homo Sacer*.
6. Fanon, *Black Skin, White Masks*, xii.
7. Patterson, *Slavery and Social Death*.
8. Prozorov, *Agamben and Politics*, 102.
9. Agamben, *Homo Sacer*, 83.

Before delving into the novel, it is necessary to identify and address the various interlocking social, political, and economic systems implicated in the legitimization, normalization, and formation of male subjectivities capable of unimaginable brutality. In the first part of this chapter, I briefly discuss the intersection of capitalism and imperialism and their apparatuses in producing toxic masculinity. I then use Black's novel to illustrate the features and consequences of this type of masculinity. Specifically, I rely on psychoanalytic, philosophical, and pastoral concepts to analyze and describe the toxic masculinity of the male slavers who were bound up in the machineries of capitalism and imperialism. In brief, I contend that the relentlessness of white male brutality and indifference emerges in the midst of capitalist and imperialist societies. Furthermore, I identify the *interrelated* attributes of this toxic masculinity: (1) depersonalization; (2) dependency of identity, significance, and agency on the illusion of superiority; (3) relations of subjugation; (4) impersonal instrumental care and faith; and (5) unconscious fear and hatred of precarity and vulnerability. In terms of the last attribute, slavers split off and project their anxiety and fear regarding their precarity onto dehumanized subjects, and this accompanies zones of non-being or bare life wherein mutual fidelity, trust, and care are denied othered human beings. Following this discussion, I turn my attention to the resilience and resistance of enslaved persons in the face of routine and repeated assaults on their bodies, minds, and relationships. There is, in bare life, something—an excess—that cannot be extinguished except through death. It is this excess I seek to depict as the presence of ungovernable selves, which are the sources of resistance and resilience to the toxic masculinity that fueled the horrors enslaved persons suffered.

Let me offer a few comments before embarking. Statisticians can provide the numbers. Historians can depict events and identify dates. Witnesses can struggle to tell stories of their experiences. The imaginations of poets, novelists, and other artists can move us toward empathy and compassion. In the end, however, the evils and horrors of slavery's production of bare lives exceed statistics, facts, stories, and art. Nevertheless, these stories and histories must be told, must be remembered, to (1) honor and personalize those who suffered and who resisted incredible humiliation and violence; (2) recognize and seek to understand how human depravity can be legitimized, normalized, and sedimented in a society; and (3) discover ways to move toward life-giving compassionate relations. This said, understanding toxic masculinity is not aimed at some distant past associated with slavocracy, as if the machinations of slavery have somehow disappeared. Rather, we see varied forms of it today in which othered human beings are corralled and callously treated without even a whiff of guilt or shame (e.g., human trafficking, immigration detention centers, exploitation of people who are without documents, child soldiers). Add to this that, while slavery is roundly rejected by most people, the specter of white supremacy, which distorts the subjectivities of any gender, continues to live, spreading its vicious tentacles in numerous corners of society. Indeed, white supremacy seems to be highly resistant to efforts to eradicate it, and, sadly, it is growing in the U.S.[10] Given this, while it is important to attend to and understand the sources of systemic destructive masculinities based on illusions of white supremacy, we also need to listen to and understand the personal stories of survivors (e.g., Frederick Douglass,[11] Sojourner Truth, Fannie Lou Hammer, Malcolm X), as well as novelists/artists such as Daniel Black because they aid us in appreciating the ability of people not only to survive but also to pursue, in whatever ways they can, justice and liberation. If we understand this excess and its sources, we can seek to identify or construct apparatuses that affirm and nurture the excess inherent in persons[12] while undermining sources and expressions of toxic masculinity that deny the personhood of othered individuals. One final thought: while not the focus of the chapter, many of

10. See the Southern Poverty Law Center's report on the growth of white supremacy in the United States: *The Year in Hate and Extremism: 2019* (Montgomery, AL: Southern Poverty Law Center, 2020, https://www.splcenter.org/sites/default/files/yih_2020_final.pdf).

11. Scholar Danjuma Gibson is similarly interested in seeking to understand and explain the resiliency of African Americans who suffered at the hands of slave owners and racists. He has written an interesting and detailed psychosocial analysis of Frederick Douglass, accounting for Douglass's psychological resiliency by creating the term *inner force of being*. While interesting, there are several problems with this. First, the phrase tends to essentialize resiliency, as if some individuals have a greater amount of this inner force of being than others. In other words, it is impossible to measure or quantify the "inner force of being." The term also begs the question of whether this is a spiritual or biological source of resiliency. Additionally, this individualizing resiliency overlooks or minimizes the relational foundation of resistance and resiliency. The concept also fails to explain or help us understand resiliency and its sources. In other words, it is not unlike Freud's concept of the death drive that is used to explain the destructive or asocial aspects of human beings. The term *death drive* is a metaphor masquerading as an empirical model. Gibson, *Frederick Douglass*.

12. Many of us typically associate the idea of personhood with human beings. My view, following the work of anthropologists Eduardo Kohn, Eduardo Viveiros de Castro, and Tim Ingold, is that personalizing epistemologies can also refer to the personhoods of other species. This means that other species are not "persons" in the human sense but rather are persons in their own right—unique, inviolable, valued, and responsive. The implications are that other species have agency and, to use Emmanuel Lévinas's view, therefore demand from us an obligatory response of respect and care. Of course, I cannot develop this idea in this chapter since the focus is on toxic masculinity vis-à-vis othered human beings. See Ingold, *The Perception of the Environment*; Kohn, *How Forests Think*; Lévinas, *Totality and Infinity*; Viveiros de Castro, *Cannibal Metaphysics*.

the attributes associated with toxic masculinity are evident in past and present ways of relating to other species and the Earth, which I return to in the conclusion of this chapter. It is not just other human beings who suffer as a result of poisonous masculinity; other species are similarly objectified, constructed as inferior, and commodified to satisfy human needs and desires.[13]

Sources and Attributes of Toxic Masculinity: Western Apparatuses of Capitalism and Imperialism

Daniel Black's novel neither identifies the sources of slavery nor offers a glimpse into the minds or subjectivities of slavers.[14] Nevertheless, the background of the story is readily knowable, given the history of Western colonization, the rise of capitalism, and Eurocentrism—white supremacy.[15] That is, we can glean from this history an understanding of the apparatuses that produced and normalized the subjectivities and actions of the slavers.[16] In addition, while we do not have details in the novel to understand the minds of the slavers, psychological theories and concepts can help illuminate the sources and dynamics of their brutal behaviors. Before delving into the specifics of toxic masculinity, I briefly identify the apparatuses that

---

13. See Keller, *Political Theology of the Earth*; McCarroll, "Listening for the Cries"; Miller-McLemore, "Climate Violence and Earth Justice"; Nussbaum, *Justice for Animals*; Singer, *Animal Liberation*; Wood, *Reoccupy Earth*.

14. There is a twelve-year-old white child among the crew who is not named and who apparently sees the horrific suffering of enslaved persons and feels compassion, giving rise to his secretly providing the enslaved people water. Nevertheless, the boy understandably fears going against his "fathers" and, in the end, does nothing to secure the freedom of enslaved persons. Here we note that acts of care, compassion, and fear collude with the larger apparatuses of slavery. It is also important to mention that one of the slavers is African and that this is the only place in the novel where we might glimpse the mind of a slaver. I deal with this below. Black, *The Coming*, 71–72.

15. See Kendi and Reynolds, *Stamped from the Beginning*; Mills, *The Racial Contract*; Robinson, *Black Marxism*.

16. The slavers in the novel are not given names (except briefly when the enslaved persons overheard the crew; everywhere else in the novel, the crew are nameless), whereas enslaved persons are named. I understand this in a couple of ways. First, the author is humanizing persons who are being viciously objectified. By not assigning names to the slavers, I think, Black is pointing to their dehumanization. That is, by internalizing the beliefs and values of slavery's apparatuses, the slavers dehumanize themselves, which I intend to make clearer below. Second, the story is told from the perspective of enslaved persons. There exists an ontological rift, if you will, between slavers and enslaved persons. The enslaved person cannot cross this rift, which means, in my view, that the slavers must remain nameless. The rift can only be resisted and dismantled through revolution.

founded, legitimated, and justified colonization and slavery because these apparatuses gave and give rise to forms of malignant masculinity.

Historian Jürgen Kocka notes that mercantilism preceded the emergence of capitalism in the sixteenth century. He writes, "As a rule, a thoroughly capitalistic organization of production did not take place, either in agriculture or in trade and manufacture," before the sixteenth century.[17] Ellen Meiksins Wood, however, points out that in the sixteenth century, the origins of capitalism made their initial appearance in revolutionary changes to agricultural laws and policies in England, which undermined the commons as well as increased poverty and displaced people from their homes. These laws and policies later spread to other sectors of the economy, such as manufacturing and finance.[18] Katharina Pistor notes that changes in the law regarding capital, the commons, and business entailed a great deal of litigation that further elaborated, extended, legitimated, and normalized capitalism in England, which eventually spread to other imperialistic European nations and their colonies.[19] The rubrics and apparatuses of capitalism could not have emerged without political and economic elites (mainly men) who enacted the necessary policies, programs, and legislation (apparatuses of capitalism) to legitimate and further the reach and power of capitalism in their respective countries and elsewhere, eventuating in the market societies we see today.[20] These Western elites were imbricated with the apparatuses of global imperialism and the brutal colonization of other peoples and lands. This was especially evident among powerful imperialistic nations such as Britain, France, and Spain (and eventually the U.S.). As Kocka writes, "The rise of capitalism, the development of powerful territorial states, and the expansion of Europe that led to colonialism were all contingent on each other."[21]

The imbrication of capitalism and colonialism was coupled with Eurocentrism and exceptionalism, which, as Woods contends, accompanied the belief that "Europe deserves credit for lifting barriers to the *natural*

17. Kocka, *Capitalism*, 52–53.
18. Wood, *The Origin of Capitalism*.
19. Pistor, *The Code of Capital*.

20. Cox, *The Market as God*; Dardot and Laval, *The New Way of the World*; Jones, *Masters of the Universe*; Sandel, *What Money Can't Buy*.

21. Kocka, *Capitalism*, 54. It is important to mention that Western Christianity dominated imperialistic European nations, which means that Christian religious and secular leaders were implicated in furthering not only the apparatuses of capitalism and imperialism but also slavery. This continues in the prosperity gospel movement, wherein the exploitative nature of capitalism is omitted by way of apotheosis of the market-God. See Cox, *The Market as God*; MacDonald, *Thieves in the Temple*.

development of capitalism."²² She adds that this "includes racists who insist on the *natural* superiority of Europeans over Asians, Africans, and indigenous Americans; cultural chauvinists who think that, for whatever reason, 'the West' has achieved a higher level of cultural development and 'rationality' that has given it an advantage in every other respect."²³ In a similar way, Cedric Robinson uses the term *racial capitalism* to illustrate the intersection of capitalist and racist (and sexist) apparatuses (secular and theological) that were further intertwined with the apparatuses of nationalism and attendant beliefs in European exceptionalism.²⁴ Although Robinson is primarily referring to the treatment of Africans, Euro-white supremacy and exceptionalist beliefs included (and include) racial animus and hostile behaviors toward Indigenous peoples and Asian persons, as Wood points out. Charles Mills takes this further, arguing that colonizing nations and Eurocentrism (i.e., white supremacy) were inextricably intertwined with a *racial contract* that comprised a "political system, a particular power structure of formal and informal rule, socioeconomic privilege, and norms for the differential distribution of material wealth and opportunities, benefits and burdens, rights and duties."²⁵ Mills points out that this contract was political, moral, and epistemological,²⁶ and it "is clearly historically locatable in a series of events marking the creation of the modern world by European colonialism and the voyages of 'discovery' now increasingly called expeditions of conquest."²⁷ Mills adds, "We live in a world which has been foundationally shaped for the past five hundred years by realities of European domination and the gradual consolidation of global white supremacy."²⁸

The epistemological feature of the racial contract is also disclosed in the conscious and unconscious representations and beliefs European peoples had and have regarding othered peoples. W. E. B. Du Bois was an early sociological researcher who revealed how white people negatively constructed Africans and African Americans.²⁹ Decades later, Edward Saïd demon-

---

22. Wood, *The Origin of Capitalism*, 27; italics mine. The history of capitalism and racism reveals the tendency of capitalists and racists to use terms like nature and *development* to essentialize and normalize capitalism and racism. For many Western Christians, this language shifted to theological frameworks, wherein beliefs (more accurately, illusions) in racial inferiority and white supremacy were ontologized.

23. Wood, *The Origin of Capitalism*, 27; italics mine.

24. Robinson, *Black Marxism*.

25. Mills, *The Racial Contract*, 3.

26. Mills, *The Racial Contract*, 9.

27. Mills, *The Racial Contract*, 20.

28. Mills, *The Racial Contract*, 20.

29. Du Bois, *The Souls of Black Folk*. See also Go, *Postcolonial Thought*.

strated how "Orientals" were/are adversely depicted in Western literature, and Edward Hall similarly addressed Eurocentric cultural representations of colonized peoples in the Caribbean.[30] These and other scholars, from various fields including pastoral theology,[31] have contributed to the rise of postcolonial and decolonial studies, all of which are aimed at dismantling the moral, epistemological, and political apparatuses that produce the racial contract of Eurocentrism and, I would add, capitalism.

The main point here is that the rise of capitalism is inseparable from Western imperial powers, and both relied on the production of racist beliefs, policies, programs, etc., to justify, normalize, and legitimate the brutal exploitation of Indigenous peoples and the extraction of wealth from their lands. Slavery, in brief, emerged in conjunction with capitalism and imperialism with the aim of capturing and selling African persons to create more wealth for white European capitalists, colonists, and imperialists.[32] The apparatuses of capitalism, imperialism, and racism have been, I argue, internalized by (mainly) European boys and men,[33] shaping their masculinity and, consequently, their perceptions and behaviors toward so-called inferior beings of othered peoples. This is the backdrop of Black's novel, wherein the slavers' behaviors included chaining and beating prisoners, cramming them below decks, depriving them of sufficient water and food, denying them even the most basic medical care, and subjecting them to rape, arbitrary brutal punishments, and death.

---

30. Saïd, *Orientalism*; Hall, *Cultural Studies 1983*; Hall, *Representation*; See Go, *Postcolonial Thought*.

31. See Lartey and Moon, *Postcolonial Images of Spiritual Care*; McGarrah Sharp, *Misunderstanding Stories*.

32. In the nineteenth century, Karl Marx confirmed the intersection of slavery/racism, imperialism, and capitalism. He wrote, "Direct slavery is as much the pivot of industrialism today as machinery, credit, etc. Without slavery no cotton; without cotton no modern industry. Slavery has given value to the colonies; the colonies have created world trade . . . Slavery is therefore an economic category of the highest importance." As quoted in Robinson, *Black Marxism*, 81.

33. In the novel, there is one crew member who is African, an Asanti man whom the crew calls "Frank." The narrator remarks, "He'd been with us from the beginning of our journey, and he guarded us until the end. Sometimes, with cat-o-nine-tails. He beat us for no good reason . . . Most painful was that he was one of us. He bore the marks of the Asanti." The narrator later comments, "They couldn't have called him his original name. His spirit wouldn't have supported his despicable behavior. So, as Frank, he separated himself from his purpose and thus became a tool for our destruction." I will say more about this later, but for now it is clear that in serving the capitalist imperial machine, this man was alienated from his spirit and, of course, from his people. Black, *The Coming*, 102, 109.

The apparatuses that shaped the captors' subjectivity and motivated their brutality and indifference can be further understood in terms of the notion of bare life. As mentioned above, bare life concerns persons "caught up in the sovereign ban . . . stripped of all protections and abandoned to the force of law."[34] Stated more starkly, "The sovereign sphere is the sphere in which it is permitted to kill without committing homicide . . . What is captured in the sovereign ban is a human victim who may be killed but not sacrificed."[35] Slavers operated within the laws and policies of Western colonizing, capitalistic nations, which meant they were not held accountable for their behaviors toward enslaved persons. Enslaved persons were like livestock and could legally be beaten or killed. There were absolutely no protections for enslaved persons. Slavers were acting in the place of sovereign authorities—members of the capitalist and political classes/elites. The captors were not sovereigns themselves. They did not directly possess political power and authority to determine who lived or died in the polis, but they had sovereign power over enslaved persons. In a way, a slave ship was a polis wherein the captain and crew were sovereigns over their depersonalized cargo. Like a sovereign who, according to Agamben, "is, at the same time, outside and inside the juridical order,"[36] slavers could act with impunity toward enslaved persons. Of course, the capitalists who owned the ships and cargo could hold the crew accountable if they destroyed the cargo, thereby eliminating any chance of profit. But the crew was also motivated to restrain themselves, at least to some extent, so that enough "cargo" survived so that they could be sold and the slavers could get paid.

Bare life also meant that enslaved persons existed in a zone of non-justice, which means the term *justice* simply did not apply to them. These othered human beings were placed within and existed in a zone of life where justice and injustice had no place—a zone inextricably yoked to and dependent on capitalist and imperial apparatuses. This was a zone of bare existence, constructed by human beings, in which human and divine laws of protection did not apply precisely because the enslaved were not recognized as persons. In short, enslaved persons existed outside of human and divine laws—in bare life and the zone of non-justice—leaving open the door to unimaginable brutality performed by white male slavers.

I am arguing here that the social, political, and economic apparatuses of colonizing nations were internalized by the crew, shaping their subjectivity and behavior, which enacted zones of non-justice and attendant conditions

---

34. Prozorov, *Agamben and Politics*, 102.
35. Agamben, *Homo Sacer*, 83.
36. Agamben, *Homo Sacer*, 15.

of bare life. Put another way, in internalizing the values, meanings, and expectations of capitalism and imperialism, the crew exhibited performances of toxic masculinities—toxic because of their brutality, indifference, perfidy, carelessness, and destructiveness. To develop this further, I depict the *interrelated* attributes of toxic masculinity, namely, (1) depersonalization; (2) dependency of identity, significance, and agency on the illusion of superiority; (3) relations of subjugation; (4) impersonal instrumental care and faith; and (5) unconscious fear and hatred of precarity and vulnerability.

Let me approach the topic of depersonalization by way of Giorgio Agamben, who observed that there is a "deep ontological rift . . . between animal and human,"[37] which I mentioned briefly in chapter 2. This gulf between human animals and other species is a part of the assumptive world of most Western persons.[38] Bruno Latour,[39] Jacques Derrida,[40] and Isabelle Stengers[41] make similar observations, indicating that Western political epistemologies create two "entirely distinct ontological zones: that of human beings on the one hand; that of nonhuman on the other."[42] This deep ontological rift or abyss in Western anthropologies, which creates zones of non-justice and bare life vis-à-vis other-than-human species, means that other-than-human species are constructed as inferior and available for human use. Put another way, as nonpersons, other species are believed not to possess reason and, therefore, have no agency, which, in turn, means they are excluded from the political realm and its protections. If other species appear in the political realm, they appear solely in terms of their use value—how they benefit the existence and flourishing of other human persons. They are believed to lack singularity, inviolableness, inherent value, and agency. In short, at the core of this ontological rift are epistemologies of depersonalization.

Let me add to this view of depersonalization. It is not that other species are not seen as possessing being, since they clearly exist and are part of the created order. They exist like we, as persons, exist. Other species, though, are things, lacking singularity, which in religious parlance means lacking a soul.[43] The rift is not simply that human beings are distinct be-

37. Dickinson, "The 'Absence' of Gender," 173.

38. By "Western," I mean persons who have internalized the narratives and practices of European anthropologies. There are people and groups in the West, such as Indigenous peoples, who possess anthropologies that do not produce the ontological rift.

39. Latour, *We Have Never Been Modern*.

40. Derrida, *The Animal*.

41. Stengers, *Making Sense in Common*.

42. Latour, *We Have Never Been Modern*, 10–11.

43. In the West, philosophers and theologians have long denied the idea that other

cause they have souls and other species do not; it is that other species are not only excluded from the earthly political realm and its protections, they are also denied ontological significance and the possibility of eternity. Lacking personhood, they are existentially insignificant and impermanent, though some may have significance in terms of their use value.

The ontological rift and accompanying depersonalization have included othered human beings, like Plato's and Aristotle's barbarians who existed outside the polis or, if they resided in the polis, like enslaved persons, were denied rights and protections since they were not Athenian persons. Worse, the rift is evident in the slavers' depersonalization of their prisoners. The narrator in *The Coming* begins by affirming the personhood of African peoples and also the spirits of other species.

> Our lives had meaning. Some had completed our initiations, some were beginning our initiations. Through this process, we became students of the universe. We learned the healing herbs of the forest. We learned the activity of ants on the hills . . . Among us lived every spirit conceivable . . . There were people who could read the signs of heaven. People who lived both here and beyond. People who could hear the voice of God. People who understood the makings of the universe. People who interpreted the song of the wind.[44]

In this and other passages, the narrator, in my view, is affirming the plurality of personhood among the various peoples and species of the land. The narrator remarks that "we were people of the same land, but we were not identical . . . We were told to respect all life and all life forms."[45] There is no ontological rift here, and this sets the stage for their shock and horror at being forced into a strange and frightening world of slavers, where the ontological rift's depersonalization marks every aspect of their existence. He writes, "With open arms, we embraced those who looked nothing like us, assuming all life honors life. We were wrong." The narrator adds, "Then came the disaster."[46]

The following pages in the novel detail the disaster—the repeated horrors of being captured, marched to the coast, starved, beaten, and then eventually chained together in the cramped, pestilent holds of a slave

---

species have souls, though Aristotle did believe living beings had souls but that these souls were not eternal. Grayling, *The History of Philosophy*, 89.

44. Black, *The Coming*, 10–12.

45. Black, *The Coming*, 13, 17. The narrator does not idealize African peoples. He praises their strengths and achievements as well as identifies their foibles and failings.

46. Black, *The Coming*, 19.

ship.[47] "On board ships," the narrator writes, "captors did not love us. But they wanted us. For something vile, something wrong, something that would diminish the supplier while exalting the supplied."[48] To the crew of the ship, their captives were not persons or even potential persons. They, like other-than-human species, were believed to be devoid of personhood, which meant they could be used as objects or discarded without a hint of remorse or concern. Similarly, like other-than-human species, the enslaved persons were constructed as possessing no political agency and thus possessing no rights—dwelling in a zone of non-justice. All of this points to the ontological abyss between white slavers and their "cargo."

Depersonalization can be further understood in terms of potentiality and actuality. I will say more about potentiality and actuality and their relation to ungovernable selves later, but for now I briefly note Agamben's view that human beings can be understood in terms of "of pure potentiality."[49] We are not, in other words, "reducible to biology, identity, or vocation."[50] Sergei Prozorov, commenting on Agamben's view of potentiality, carries this further, stating, "There is an excess of living being that can never be subsumed under them" (e.g., apparatuses or disciplinary regimes and their representations).[51] This perspective has implications for ethics and politics, as Adam Kotsko and Carlo Salzani note. For Agamben, "The human experience of potentiality (and impotentiality) is at the root of both politics and ethics"[52]—zones of justice. Another way of saying this is that potentiality and actuality are the basis of human freedom and agency, which are in turn the foundation of personhood. Depersonalization entails acts that deny the potentiality of othered human beings (and othered species).[53] Othered human beings are, for the slavers, reduced to biology, to function, to representations of abject inferiority. This said, to deny othered human beings the existential fact of potentiality requires apparatuses of force and violence to ensure enslaved persons do not actualize their potentiality lest that shatter the fragile assumptive world of the slavers who believe their prisoners are not persons. This is evident throughout the novel when the narrator describes all manner of violence and threats of violence they are continuously

47. Black, *The Coming*, 20–32.
48. Black, *The Coming*, 30.
49. Whyte, *Catastrophe and Redemption*, 110.
50. Whyte, *Catastrophe and Redemption*, 110.
51. Prozorov, *Agamben and Politics*, 24.
52. Kotsko and Salzani, *Agamben's Philosophical Lineage*, 60.
53. William Connolly and others have sought to bridge the ontological rift, arguing that other species possess agency, intentionality, freedom, and creativity. Connolly, *Facing the Planetary*.

subjected to—forms of violence that function to deny personhood or even the prisoners' belief in their own personhood. The violence functions to obliterate enslaved persons actualizing their potentiality, placing them outside of both politics (agency and protections) and ethics (zone of justice). In a slavocracy, women and men are forced to accept their status as property (depersonalized—without potentiality) and their sole function as slaves.

I mentioned abject inferiority above as an aspect of depersonalization. The belief in the inferiority of African individuals attends a complementary belief in the superiority of Euro-male slavers.[54] These beliefs, which are central to toxic masculinity, are part of the identity of the male slavers. In other words, their identity, their sense of who they are and their sense of significance—self-esteem and self-respect—are dependent on these beliefs, which are illusions. They are existential illusions because they do not exist in or are not confirmed by nature, which, in turn, means they must be continually reproduced and enforced by political, economic, and cultural disciplinary regimes—regimes that are manufactured to create an identity based on the illusion of superiority. As Don Cupitt writes, "There is no objective purposiveness built into the world . . . Nor is there any objective and fully-independent foundation for, or endorsement of, our valuations."[55] Put another way, human beings are signifying and valuing animals, but we often make the category mistake of believing that our valuative beliefs—such as in our own superiority—are existential or ontological facts instead of impermanent social constructions. Toxic masculinity, then, is toxic not only because it reveals a foundational existential insecurity, namely, the dependence of one's identity and esteem on a denigrated other, but also because this identity's existence requires perpetual force and violence toward others who are deemed inferior. Any sense of identity that is founded on an illusion and depends on force and violence to maintain that illusion is existentially insecure and fragile. The following scene illustrates this point.

> When the bidding began, he [Atiba] looked among the crowd. They were hungry for obedient black flesh. So he gave it to them. They had scowled at him before, but not this time. He knew

---

54. As noted above, one crew member, Frank, is Asanti. The name Frank suggests that he identified with the white-male slavers and their beliefs in their superiority. For instance, Frank said to the enslaved individuals, "You are nothing but animal guts! If you do not obey me, you're going to die! You're here because you are weak and stupid." The narrator comments that Frank's "pride increased whenever he demeaned us, especially in the presence of crewmen . . . Their affirmation excited him." Clearly, Frank constructs the Others as inferior and insignificant, whereas he is, because of his position, superior. Black, *The Coming*, 102, 103.

55. Cupitt, *Above Us Only Sky*, 74.

what to do. He'd learn what they rejected, what they hated most. So, unlike before, he wore the look of sympathy. That was the submission they had wanted, the surrender they'd been after . . . All they sought was his compliance, his acquiescence. So Atiba yielded . . . He assumed the mask of passivity.[56]

The machinery of slavery demanded obedience and the acceptance of the illusion of African persons' existential inferiority, as well as the concomitant acceptance of the superiority of white people. Atiba's mask and performance quieted the mainly male crowd because they now believed Atiba had accepted his situation, his identity as an inferior being. The apparatuses of force, humiliation, and violence could be set aside, though always available for use in case Atiba or any other enslaved person demonstrated any slight behavior suggesting agency, self-esteem, or self-respect. The "mask" and "performance" represent Atiba's acknowledgment of the pervasiveness of white apparatuses of force, humiliation, and violence and, subsequently, the necessity of hiding his self-esteem, self-respect, and agency for the sake of his survival.

Evident in Atiba's performance is another feature of toxic masculinity, namely, the perpetual production of relations of subordination and subjugation. Slavers continually demanded, through acts of violence and humiliation, the complete subjugation of their captives. When Frank, the Asanti crewmember, yelled at other African persons, "If you don't obey me, you're going to die," he was telling them a foundational truth of this capitalistic enterprise—subjugation was a "fact" they must accept or die. Early in the voyage, some of the Africans were able to escape and many others, still chained, rose up and killed some of the crew. The rebellion was quickly and brutally put down by the white crew.[57] Later, the narrator remarked, "They thought they'd won. They believed they'd finally achieved our submission. They were wrong."[58] Like Atiba, other enslaved persons had to appear to accept subjugation for the sake of their survival. Any further attempt to resist or rebel would be met by humiliation, violence, and deprivation.

The one African who was not subjugated was Frank. He apparently basked in all the privileges the white crew enjoyed. But the narrator knew this to be an illusion, at least with regard to Frank. Frank demanded his fellow Africans submit to their being subjugated. The narrator said that Frank "seemed to believe he wasn't one of us. We were fascinated by his blindness. How did he fail to see that they'd kill him, too, if his allegiance ever

56. Black, *The Coming*, 213–14.
57. Black, *The Coming*, 52–54.
58. Black, *The Coming*, 64.

waned?"⁵⁹ The narrator recognized that Frank's status was very tenuous and deeply contingent, which may have been one of the reasons Frank worked hard to subjugate his fellow Africans, thus further ensuring his status as a "free" man. Frank would never be fully accepted by the crew, and Frank, at some level, knew this because he had to continually prove to himself that he was not "African" by humiliating and subjugating his fellow Africans.

Subjugation as a relation and Frank's allegiance to his white employers manifest another attribute of toxic masculinity, which is the presence of instrumental care and faith. Let me first approach this by way of Agamben and psychosocial development. Agamben, in addressing the relation between potentiality and actuality, points out that the movement from potentiality to actuality necessarily implies undergoing change,⁶⁰ raising the question of *what facilitates a person's actualizing their potentiality*. There may be many possibilities here, but when considering psychosocial development, parents' personalizing care⁶¹ founds children's sense of the parents' fidelity and the attendant trust necessary to actualize their potentiality.⁶² From this perspective, acts of depersonalization, such as deprivation and impingement, represent an absence of fidelity, as well as the absence of care and trust, which undermines children's (and adults') ability to actualize their potentiality. Black's novel illustrates the extremes of denying imprisoned Africans the ability to actualize their potentiality. Indeed, the slavers' brutality represents a dearth of both care and faith—trust, loyalty, and hope.⁶³ In short, the depersonalizing actions of the slavers, which represent the absence of care and faith, signify the presence of toxic masculinity.

59. Black, *The Coming*, 102–3.
60. Agamben, *Potentialities*.
61. The notion of care is central to pastoral theology and pastoral ministry. There is a great deal written regarding care in relation to ministry, politics, etc. A general definition can, nevertheless, be offered. Care is everything we do to help individuals, families, communities, and societies to (1) meet vital biological, psychosocial, and existential or spiritual needs of individuals, families, and communities; (2) develop or maintain basic capabilities with the aim of human flourishing; (3) facilitate participation in the polis' space of appearances; and (4) maintain a habitable environment for all. See LaMothe, *Care of Souls*, 30–64.
62. See LaMothe, *A Political Psychoanalysis*.
63. H. Richard Niebuhr viewed the dynamics of faith as consisting of three dialectical, interrelated pairs—belief-disbelief, trust-distrust, loyalty-disloyalty (I add hope-hopelessness). Erik Erikson argued that the first stage of development involved the parent-child couple managing trust-mistrust, which if successfully navigated leads to the virtue of hope. "Trust" is one feature of Niebuhr's understanding of faith, and, when we consider Erikson, we note that parental care is foundational for the emergence of trust and the possibility of hope. Niebuhr, *Faith on Earth*; Erikson, *Childhood and Society*.

One might point out that the prisoners must have received some degree of care so they could be sold to make a profit. The presence of depersonalization, in this context, includes instrumental care in relations of total subjugation, which represents a kind of instrumental faith. The prisoners did receive food and water, especially before being sold. They received this care not for their sake, not for actualizing their potentiality, but for the profit of capitalists who funded the ship. If the prisoners cooperated, like Atiba, if they accepted their subjugated, depersonalized, inferior status and demonstrated some level of loyalty to their "masters," they were considered relatively trustworthy and would receive enough food and water to sustain themselves. As long as they remain subjugated, an instrumental *racial contract* of care would continue,[64] though this in itself would not stave off the arbitrary punishment or other forms of humiliation, or even death. Nevertheless, failing to comply resulted in further brutality and, in many cases, death. The machinery of a slavocracy never rests.

The final feature of toxic masculinity is unconscious fear and hatred of precarity and vulnerability, both of which are entwined with existential insignificance and impermanence. Recall from chapter 1 that Judith Butler argues that precarity and vulnerability are features of human life,[65] indeed, of all life. A feature of the precarity of life is its existential insignificance and impermanence. The fact of our existence does not confer on us existential significance, any more than the existence of an ant means it possesses existential or ontological significance. To be sure, human beings are valuing and signifying creatures, but we tend to make a category mistake when it comes to what we believe about our significance. The fact that we are able to assign value and meaning does not, therefore, establish the fact that we are ontologically significant or permanent (eternal) while other species are ontologically insignificant and impermanent. We, like all other living creatures, have, for a time, existence, but this does not mean we possess ontological significance.[66] Put another way, existence itself does not confer value or significance; human beings (and other species) do, and this significance is impermanent. Indeed, existence—the cosmos—is impermanent in the sense that, according to astrophysicists, it will eventually cease to exist. Leibniz asked why is there something and not nothing, while John Caputo adds, "Why will there be nothing at all rather than something?"[67]

64. Mills, *The Racial Contract*.
65. Butler, *Precarious Life*.
66. For further explication of this argument, see Caputo, *What to Believe?*; Cupitt, *Radical Theology*.
67. Caputo, *What to Believe?* 103.

The precarity of life heightens our anxieties and fears, and we find all manner of ways to shield ourselves from existential insignificance and impermanence. One way to defer aspects of precarity is to project them onto othered human beings (and othered species). Othered human beings become the repositories of our fears of precarity. Bound in the holds of the ship, enslaved persons were rendered radically, existentially insignificant and impermanent. They existed at the whims of the slavers and their value was solely economic and impermanent. They did not have value in themselves and were easily replaced. The narrator exclaimed, "They had bought our flesh but not our souls."[68] To the slaver, a slave represented or signified monetary value. The narrator used the term *soul* to represent singularity or value that is not reduced to mere use value. But to the slavers, the cargo had only use significance, and the enslaved, therefore, lacked singularity.

The problem with evacuating one's fear and anxiety about precarity onto an Other is that as long as the Other lives, even if it is bare life, the Other embodies the realities of existential insignificance and impermanence. Frank, for instance, despised his fellow Africans because, in my view, he saw his own precarity, though he denied it. Instead of moving toward empathy and compassion, Frank, like the other slavers, sought refuge in the apparatuses of slavery to ward off his precarity and vulnerability by believing in his superiority and their abject inferiority and insignificance. This is a kind of toxic masculinity because it requires constant use or threat of force and violence to make the lives of others radically precarious, insignificant. To care for others, to begin to believe these others are due justice, would only reawaken one's own precarity. But this did not happen.[69] Instead, the crew's hatred and disgust toward their human cargo, which screened their anxiety and fear, were simply part of the poisonous perpetual relation that existed between the slavers' and the enslaved persons' bare lives of existential insignificance and impermanence.

In sum, toxic masculinity emerges from the apparatuses of capitalism and imperialism, which legitimizes and justifies practices of bare life and zones of non-justice. More specifically, the toxic masculinity evident in the novel is characterized by acts of depersonalization, carelessness, and perfidy, which foster relations of abject subjugation. Unconscious fear and

---

68. Black, *The Coming*, 93–94.

69. A child of the slavers demonstrated some degree of empathy, but he did not help the enslaved persons because of his fear of being rejected and harmed by the crew. We might also imagine that Frank was terrified by what he saw, feeling helpless in the face of the power of the slavers. He chose to identify with the aggressors in order to survive. As much as Frank hated and was disgusted by his fellow Africans, the reader can imagine how much he also hated himself. Black, *The Coming*, 71–72.

anxiety underlie the brutality and hatred of the slavers. This fear and anxiety can be understood in terms of existential vulnerability and precarity, which are embodied in the abject lives of enslaved persons and defended against by beliefs in white supremacy/power and black inferiority/powerlessness.

Resistance and Resilience in the Face of Toxic Masculinity

"What happens to the 'life' of a subject," wonders Abdul JanMohamed, "who grows up under the threat of death, a threat that is constant, yet unpredictable?"[70] How does one survive the brutal violence, constant humiliations, and ever-lingering threat of arbitrary death? How do people resist apparatuses of depersonalization? In terms of Black's novel, where men and women who are enslaved faced the brutality and horrors of enslavement, how are we to understand their numerous daily acts of resistance and resiliency? I want to focus on five types of acts, namely, love and care, sadness, choosing death, rebellion, and "murder." All of these acts are features of an existential excess that undergirds ungovernable selves, which, building on the previous chapter's discussion, I explicate in light of Agamben's work regarding the relation between potentiality and actuality. This perspective helps us understand that, in contexts of bare life, human beings who are not killed or do not die of despair will continue to find ways to resist and overcome oppression and marginalization—in this case, toxic masculinity.[71] Before turning to the novel to illustrate this, it is necessary to briefly gain further clarity about the notions of potentiality, actuality, and ungovernable selves.

Agamben's philosophical anthropology is, Rasmus Ugilt argues, "centered on the notion of potentiality," and, since this is central, it is important to expand our grasp of this abstract concept if we are to understand the idea of ungovernable selves.[72] The notion of potentiality stems from Aristotle's work regarding the relation between potentiality (*dynamis*) and

---

70. JanMohamed, *The Death-Bound Subject*, 2.

71. As in the novel, some enslaved people commit suicide and simply give up eating, eventually dying. Writing about his father, James Baldwin offers a personal example of someone succumbing to the violence of racism. He writes that "he was defeated long before he died because, at the bottom of his heart, he really believed what white people said about him." Suicide may be considered an act of resistance or stem from deep despair. While despair is a completely understandable response to the horrors of slavery, it seems to me it is not an act of resistance or resilience. However, as I will argue below, some of the prisoners chose to die. These deaths, in my view, are acts of resistance and not acts of despair. Also, more Africans survived slavery (and Jim Crow) than despaired, testifying to an excess of ungovernable selves—an excess that cannot be extinguished except by death. Baldwin, *The Fire Next Time*, 4.

72. Ugilt, *Giorgio Agamben*, 22.

actualization (*energeia*). We do not need to delve too deeply into the complexities of Aristotle's philosophy to address how Agamben is using this concept.[73] In Agamben's perspective, there are two features of Aristotle's view. The first is that "the very essence of humanity lies in a potentiality that is expressed when it does not unfold into actuality."[74] Here is where Agamben turns to illustrate potentiality in terms of impotentiality. He writes:

> *Other living beings are capable only of their specific potentiality; they can only do this or that. But human beings are the animals who are capable of their own impotentiality. The greatness of human potentiality is measured by the abyss of human impotentiality.* Here it is possible to see how the root of freedom is to be found in the abyss of potentiality. To be free is not simply to have the power to do this or that thing, nor is it simply to have the power to refuse to do this or that thing. To be free is ... *to be capable of one's own impotentiality.*[75]

There are two points here. First, potentiality is a feature of all living beings. Second, what differentiates human animals from other species is the potential capacity for impotentiality.[76] Recall from the previous chapter Agamben's depiction of impotentiality vis-à-vis Herman Melville's *Bartleby, The Scrivener*, wherein Bartleby is asked by his boss to do something and he replies, "I prefer not to."[77] For Agamben, Bartleby is exercising the freedom to not actualize his potentiality as a scrivener, which means, in part, that Bartleby is not determined and cannot be determined (in the sense of being

---

73. For the interested reader, it is important to point out that the Western philosophical tradition has largely "subordinated potentiality to actuality: so, we begin with the actual, speaking humans and their political and artistic productions, and we see potentiality at present as a capacity or skill that is defined by the final action. We see potentiality as secondary or accidental" (Agamben, as quoted in Colebrook and Maxwell, *Agamben*, 188. This is derived, in part, from Aristotle's notion that "actuality is prior to potentiality," though this does not mean that Aristotle believed that "potentiality exists only in actuality." Ugilt, *Giorgio Agamben*, 180.

74. Colebrook and Maxwell, *Agamben*, 289.

75. Agamben, *Potentialities*, 182–83.

76. The capacity for impotentiality does not make human beings higher, more special, or superior to other animals. It is simply a capacity that other animals do not have, like a fish having the capacities to live and breathe underwater. This said, I am convinced that impotentiality also is present in other species. Anecdotal evidence of this is my experience of Grace, our cat.

77. Ross Gay has a humorous example of impotentiality. During a basketball camp, children lined up to "take two dribbles to the basket, then shoot." When a seven-year-old boy was next, he said, "I don't wanna." Ross was perplexed and tried other ways to encourage the boy to take his turn, only to hear, "I don't wanna." This little boy was exercising his capacity for impotentiality. Gay, *Inciting Joy*, 155.

commanded by others) to actualize his potentiality. Colebrook and Maxwell add that "to have potentiality is to be capable of *not* becoming what one has the capacity to be."[78] Human beings, then, are not (and cannot be completely) compelled to actualize their potentiality because they possess the freedom to prefer not to. In this sense, human beings possess an ungovernable self precisely because of their capacity for impotentiality.

Consider the apparatuses of society that facilitate the actualization of particular ends, identities, roles, etc. There are, for instance, social-political expectations regarding gender, which we learn in our families as well as through the media and other social-political apparatuses. These apparatuses define and attempt to determine and actualize specific meanings and ends. Put another way, the apparatuses of society govern us, and we are expected to actualize the meanings, expectations, and values of these apparatuses. And yet, human beings frequently slip the traces. While these apparatuses of society are powerful, they cannot determine us because, from Agamben's perspective, each of us, in varying degrees, possesses the capacity for impotentiality. That is, we possess an ungovernable self.

There are two other points to make. In discussing the concept of potentiality with regard to human beings, Agamben points out that, in the case of infants, actualizing their potentiality means undergoing a change.[79] What Agamben does not explore is what is needed for human beings to actualize their potentiality and their capacity for impotentiality. To answer this question would require at least another chapter, but a partial answer will suit my purposes here. Children's ability to actualize their potentiality, including their capacity for impotentiality, requires caring and reliable, trustworthy adults in their lives. Children are dependent, vulnerable, and in a more precarious state than most adults, precisely because their potentialities have not been actualized. Good-enough parents' reliable attunement to their children's needs and assertions provide the relational space for children to possess enough trust (existential faith) to actualize their potentiality and to exercise their capacity to prefer not. Second, parental attunement carries a recognition, conscious or unconscious, that their children exceed any representations parents have of them. No matter how the parent conceives of their child, the child's potentiality exceeds representation—a key part of parents' personal recognition of the child. This is key because it creates spaces for children to exercise both their potentiality and impotentiality—to exercise their ungovernable selves. All of this also refers to adult relationships, wherein sufficient care or love, personal recognition, and faith

---

78. Colebrook and Maxwell, *Agamben*, 38; italics mine.
79. Agamben, *Potentialities*.

(trust, loyalty) provide the matrix for persons to actualize their potentialities, including impotentiality.

The notion of impotentiality is closely linked to another term Agamben uses, which will add to our discussion. For Agamben, *inoperativity* means deactivating the functioning of the apparatuses, which does not mean that these apparatuses do not continue to operate or do not continue to have effects.[80] Put another way, inoperativity vis-à-vis the subject means that, in rendering the grammar of the apparatuses inoperative, the individual is not captive to the apparatuses, even if these apparatuses continue to have their effects. Bartleby, for instance, in "preferring not" to fulfill the boss's demands, rendered inoperative the capitalistic apparatuses, though these apparatuses continued to operate and have their effects. It is important to stress that inoperativity, for Agamben,[81] is not passive. That is, inoperativity or "preferring not" does not "affirm inertia, inactivity or apraxia . . . but [is] a form of *praxis*."[82] Inoperativity, then, is any action of impotentiality that does not actualize what is expected by a society's (or a religion's) apparatuses. For Agamben, the capacity for potentiality and impotentiality and for rendering apparatuses inoperative points to both excess and human freedom, even in the face of the apparatuses of bare life.

Given this, slavery comprises apparatuses and behaviors that seek to force, through violence and threat of violence, human beings to succumb to the slavers' representations of prisoners' "inferiority" and to actualize their capacity for labor while denying their essential capacities for potentiality and impotentiality. Instrumental "care" and "trust" are present to the degree that enslaved persons submit, thereby denying (or disguising) their capacities for impotentiality. Yet, despite forcing persons to submit, the existential reality of human potentiality and impotentiality remains. It is only through killing enslaved persons that potentiality and impotentiality can be annihilated. In short, the capacity for ungovernable selves remains even in the most extreme situations.

Let me turn to the resilience and resistance of ungovernable selves in Black's novel. The narrator depicts the brutal realities on board the slave ship and, yet, something more:

> On day seven [of being onboard a slave ship] a young man's calm, silent disposition captured our attention. He studied our weary eyes, then nodded slowly as if knowing something we didn't. Distress and trauma had not broken him; he shared our

80. Prozorov, *Agamben and Politics*, 31–34.
81. Agamben, *The Open*, 134.
82. Agamben, *The Open*, 33.

rage, as any man would, but something else occupied his mind. Something deep in the soul that could not be spoken. Something the oppressors could not disturb or destroy. Something unnamable, immeasurable, indestructible . . . He was here, but he was not here . . . The following morning we discovered the source of his fixation . . . the dance of love in their eyes.[83]

The apparatuses of slavery denied the suchness and excess of these human beings and, while extremely destructive physically and psychologically, there remained an excess that could not be determined or captured by the apparatuses. This excess was love between this man and a woman, which reminded those who observed the couple that, while "bound and suffering, we possessed something that could not be taken away . . . They'd taught us that love could never be conquered or possessed."[84] This love, which could only be expressed through the eyes of the enslaved, represents, in my view, an act of impotentiality. They preferred not to succumb to the apparatuses of slavery that denied both their humanity and their capacity to love. They certainly experienced the physical and psychological humiliations. Attempts to enforce the illusion of inferiority were deeply felt. Yet, their love for each other entailed acts of impotentiality.

It is obvious that the love and care of this couple were acts of resistance, but why did the lovers and those who recognized the dance of love in their eyes go to such lengths to hide it? The narrator in Black's book, said, "Had the captors known, they surely would've tried to break this bond, to strip these lovers of the last vestige of joy they knew . . . We tried to distract our captors' attention away from them that they might get a few precious moments of seeing and perhaps even brush each other's flesh."[85] First of all, let me say that the witnesses, out of deep care for the couple, sought to protect their excess, and this act of care manifested resistance and inoperativity. The lovers and the witnesses knew that the slavers would quash any attempts to actualize love among their prisoners. Yet, the question remains, why is love dangerous? Why did the witnesses seek to keep the slavers from recognizing this couple's love? I suggest that their love and the care of the witnesses represent an excess, a kind of limitless potentiality that exceeds any apparatus of enforced debasement or depersonalization. As the narrator said, love cannot be conquered, possessed, or commodified. Love, in the face of slavery's apparatuses, was the quintessential actualization of the

---

83. Black, *The Coming*, 37–38.
84. Black, *The Coming*, 39.
85. Black, *The Coming*, 38.

impotentiality of ungovernable selves, rendering inoperative the apparatuses of slavery.[86] Moreover, love is the actualization of personhood—a constructed significance in the face of existential insignificance and impermanence. Love's manifest expression, then, reveals the lies of inferiority, superiority, and subjugation. It is not an accident that the slavers would have crushed or separated the lovers because love threatened to expose the existential falsehood of African persons' inferiority, as well as the emptiness and insecurity of the slavers' identity and their own existential precarity and impermanence. Put another way, the slavers would have crushed anything that would appear unconquerable, ungovernable, as love does. In brief, care and love, in the face of slavery and other forms of racism, were and are acts of resistance by ungovernable selves.

It is not simply this couple manifesting love that portrayed inoperativity. The narrator remarked, "We took refuge in memory."[87] These were memories of love experienced in their families and in their tribes, which reminded them "that no power on earth could extract love from a person's heart."[88] This is yet another example of ungovernable selves. Enslaved persons relied on their memories of love and being loved—memories that sustained them in the midst of depersonalizing brutalities. Memories and experiences of being loved were outside the slavers' control.

Another illustration of the inoperativity of love and care appears once the slave ship landed and enslaved persons were paraded down the streets and confined in squalid, cramped quarters. The narrator said,

> Sometimes we touched each other lovingly. Such was never rejected. We rubbed hands, heads, feet, arms, and backs until at least some comfort was achieved. We knew only each other's names, but it didn't matter. We shared fates, so other details seemed unimportant. We didn't care about favorite colors or the number of rings in one's ear. What would've been the use of such knowledge? What we knew was that we were alone. We were all we had. So, through touch, nods, and talking eyes we encouraged each other to hold on until we discovered what this life might bring.[89]

---

86. Let me stress that when Agamben addresses inoperativity, he recognizes that the apparatuses continue to have their effects. For the couple, inoperativity of their love meant that the apparatuses of slavery could not define or determine them, though the apparatuses continued to function.

87. Black, *The Coming*, 47.

88. Black, *The Coming*, 49.

89. Black, *The Coming*, 135.

Memories of care and love sustained them and were outside the control of the slavers, but so, too, was the embodied care and love communicated to each other in the present. As the narrator remarked, "Our love for each other sustained us. We felt it, invisible, yet tangible, wounded yet living, hurt but not despairing."[90] This love "continued to reverberate in our souls . . . The knowledge of God and the heavens was still in our spirits."[91] And, "Even in torture," the narrator said, "our souls had not withered. They were buried someplace deep within, in a place where no person could go."[92] There are two important points here. First, expressions of love and care for each other manifest the presence of ungovernable selves. In the midst of the vicious apparatuses of depersonalization and violence, enslaved persons personalized each other through embodied acts of love and care for each other. Second, the use of the term soul suggests an excess that is ungovernable. The idea of souls exceeded and, thus, made inoperative the apparatuses of slavery that commodified black bodies. As the narrator exclaimed, "They had bought our flesh but not our souls."[93]

Let me pause here and offer a wonderful real-life example of this claim found in activist Ruby Sales's recollection of her childhood:

> I grew up in the heart of Southern apartheid. And I'm not saying that I didn't realize that it existed, but our parents were spiritual geniuses who created a world and a language where the notion that I was inadequate or inferior or less-than never touched my consciousness. I grew up believing that I was a first-class human being and a first-class person, and our parents were spiritual geniuses who were able to shape a counterculture of black folk religion that raised us from disposability to being essential players in society.[94]

Ruby and her parents were well aware of the racism and violence produced by the apparatuses of Southern apartheid. The consistent care and love of her parents made the apparatuses of racism inoperative, providing relational spaces for Ruby to actualize her potentiality (personhood/agency, significance, self-esteem) and to exercise her capacity for impotentiality. In other words, her parents' care and love rendered inoperative the apparatuses of Jim Crow and created a space for the emergence of Ruby's ungovernable

---

90. Black, *The Coming*, 120–21.
91. Black, *The Coming*, 121.
92. Black, *The Coming*, 122.
93. Black, *The Coming*, 93–94.
94. "Ruby Sales: Where Does It Hurt"?, On Being with Krista Tippett, September 15, 2016, https://onbeing.org/programs/ruby-sales-where-does-it-hurt/#transcript.

self, even as these apparatuses continued to have deadly effects on the lives of African Americans. The resistance and resilience of ungovernable selves are born in the inoperativity of love and care.

In Black's novel, another instance of the resistance of the prisoners was their collective humming—collective acts of care. Shortly after their captors dragged Abuto's lover away, "We began to create rhythms with our fists and feet. All of us. On one accord. Together . . . The sound was so intimidating they dared not try to stop it. If they'd killed us all, that would've been a blessing. And a deep financial loss."[95] As their rhythmic beats slowed, it was replaced by humming.

> One by one, we joined—some in upper registers, some in the depths of our voices—having found a language that needed no words. We hummed until we knew we'd survive. We hummed until we released mothers and fathers who we'd never see again. We hummed until our love and gratitude for each other was clear. We hummed a celebration for living. For fighting. For refusing to die. For enduring when giving up would've been easier . . . Our only defense was to hum, so we hummed that they might know we were with them. That they might be reminded that captors could mar their bodies but not their spirits.[96]

In the midst of unimaginable suffering and oppression, given the diverse languages and cultures of the prisoners, they found a way to resist together—a form of collective resistance that expressed a deep sense of mutual care and love in the face of the brutal carelessness of the slavers. This humming (care) was a collective "preferring not" to accede to the attempts of the slavers to completely subjugate, humiliate, and isolate them. Even in this abject state, women and men chose to hum in the face of the threat of further violence and death. The narrator recognized this threat ("If they'd killed us all . . ."), but the enslaved persons "preferred not" to let this stop them. They rendered the totalizing apparatuses of slavery inoperative when they hummed, while these apparatuses continued to have their terrible effects. Humming, then, represents collective care and the attendant excess of ungovernable selves in the face of violence and death.

One more point about humming and ungovernable selves. Killing enslaved persons would mean the obliteration of their capacities for potentiality and impotentiality, excess, and ungovernable selves. Yet, prior to the moment of death, their collective decision to hum, regardless of the consequences, represents the affirmation of excess in the face of its possible

---

95. Black, *The Coming*, 42–43.
96. Black, *The Coming*, 43–44.

annihilation. Put differently, like the care of the lovers, the enslaved persons' humming represents a confirmation of their significance (personhood, singularity, agency, incalculable worth), rendering the apparatuses of ontological insignificance inoperative. They took the risk (vulnerability) in the face of substantial precarity to express their care and support for each other, even if they could not express this in a shared language. Humming, in short, was the actualization of their potentiality to care, making inoperative the apparatuses of slavery—a manifestation of ungovernable selves.

Another iteration of resistance was their feelings of sadness. Apparatuses of depersonalization made enslaved people into objects that were not able to be grieved over. One may regret the loss of a valuable object, but one does not grieve it. Grief, with regard to other human beings, indicates the Other is a person—inviolable, valued, etc. To experience sorrow for oneself and others is a confirmation of personhood. Sorrow honors the life of the person. When the narrator says, "Sadness evolved into resistance,"[97] I interpret this as affirming that their lives are worth grieving and that sadness itself is a form of resistance. If we were to imagine an individual who internalized and believed what the apparatuses of slavery communicated, that person would not experience sorrow. He would not be able to grieve, at least not for himself, because he would see himself as lacking any value. This is why I suggest that sorrow is an act of resistance, an act of ungovernable selves who refuse to abide by the rubrics of depersonalization.

An additional manifestation of ungovernable selves is evident when the narrator remarked that "some decided to die,"[98] though "only the most mature among us could do it."[99] "We'd heard," he explains, "from our sages of the power of the mind over the body. It was an issue of consciousness, they'd said, of one mastery of the Will. So, one or two simply closed their eyes and willingly took Death's hand. It was a kind of melancholy of the soul, a choice to exit the flesh and dwell forever in the spirit . . . Captors frowned at perfectly healthy bodies suddenly devoid of life. They didn't know what we knew. They didn't know who we were."[100] For the narrator, this was a spiritual act, requiring significant maturity that only a few achieved—"The rest [of us] had not reached that level of initiation."[101] As the narrator remarks in several places, the slavers could harm their bodies but not their spirits. The apparatuses of capitalism and slavocracy and the attendant toxic

97. Black, *The Coming*, 50.
98. Black, *The Coming*, 50.
99. Black, *The Coming*, 50.
100. Black, *The Coming*, 55.
101. Black, *The Coming*, 55.

masculinity could not control or subjugate the spiritual realm. From an Agambenian perspective, the spirit is a metaphor for excess, for the ungovernable aspect of human life—of life itself. To *choose* death was an ultimate act of inoperativity, of preferring not to be any part of the toxic capitalistic apparatuses of slavery. To choose death was an act of resistance and agency by ungovernable selves.

The last manifestations of the resistance of ungovernable selves are rebellion and "murder." On the twenty-third day of captivity at sea, the prisoners revolted.

> Our women, those without shackles, led the revolt. How they knew the plan we did not know, but we were grateful. And they were fierce in battle. They attacked captors like starving lionesses, gouging eyes and ripping teeth with bare flesh. More pale enemies intervened, but they, too, were made to bear the marks of our women's rage. Sisters, mothers, and daughters fought with the strength and fortitude of elephants . . . Several men were now unbound and added to the destruction of pale faces.[102]

Despite their courage, the rebellion was quickly crushed and the wounded and dead were dumped overboard while the rest of the prisoners were severely beaten and chained below decks. The violence and rage aimed at freeing themselves from their captors were collective expressions of ungovernable selves. While the prisoners, understandably, had no care for their captors, they could not have rebelled if they had not cared about and for each other.

Another act of violence vis-à-vis ungovernable selves is "murder." One of the last prisoners to be sold at the market was Atiba, who is mentioned earlier in this chapter. "Among his people, he'd been a trickster,"[103] performing for his leaders and his people. In the slave market, "Here, in another place and time, in a much more desperate hour, his skill would save again."[104] Atiba performed for the crowd. "He was a thing to them, an object of ownership, and if only he could accept that, they would love him. But he would never accept that."[105] As a trickster and performer, Atiba was using the rules of the marketplace, the rules of his captors, to trick them into believing he was a docile, inferior slave. His aim, his intention, however, was to not submit, to not be subjugated to the human and divine laws of pale people. His performance, then, represents an ungovernable self precisely

102. Black, *The Coming*, 52–53.
103. Black, *The Coming*, 214.
104. Black, *The Coming*, 214.
105. Black, *The Coming*, 215.

because it was a sham—acting *as if* the rules and laws of white people were true. But his performance was not the only manifestation of an ungovernable self.

After his performance, "a tiny pale man with an even more petite wife," convinced that Atiba was properly subjugated, purchased him, believing that he "would do them well. They were wrong. Atiba would take their lives in not so many days. And he would do so with the blessings and authority of Mawu-Lisa, the Supreme Being."[106] The narrator does not tell us what happened to Atiba, but a safe assumption is that he was brutally killed as a result of his actions. Above, I placed the word murder in quotes because homicide is a term linked to the law. Recall that bare life refers to those who are outside the protection of divine and human laws, such that they can be killed without it being considered a homicide. The captors, for instance, killed (not, according to them, murdered) with impunity, and it was only the law of profit that held them back, affording minimal protections for enslaved persons. While the laws of white people were in effect, Atiba's act was murder. For Atiba, however, killing his captors was spiritually condoned and justified by Mawu-Lisa. Mawu-Lisa was not subject to the laws of white people and, therefore, these laws were not operative. Mawu-Lisa was completely ungovernable and, therefore, Atiba was as well. The white couple were under the protection of white laws and no doubt believed they were safe. But Atiba acted under the divine laws of Mawu-Lisa—the ungovernable. In other words, the laws and rules of white people were rendered inoperative. Setting aside religious language, Mawu-Lisa represents the excess of ungovernable selves in the face of systemic brutality and oppression. Atiba's act was not simply "preferring not" to accede to the laws of slavocracy but was also an exercise of his religious beliefs (existential excess) associated with his belief in a God who cared for him. His act was not murder but a just exercise of an ungovernable self.

One might argue that Atiba's act can be seen as a parallel process, whereby the acts of brutality and depersonalization were returned in the act of killing the two white persons. And was his spiritual rationalization mere justification for depriving two people of their lives? If we were to imaginatively engage Atiba about his reasons for killing, we would be affirming his personhood. And, if we, as readers, debate whether the act was justified or not, we are bringing Atiba into the realm of political personhood, though in a slavocracy he would not be considered to be a person, merely property. If we imagine further that Atiba was caught, he would not be tried for murder because the term does not apply to property that is perceived to be dangerous.

106. Black, *The Coming*, 215.

Just as a property owner might "put down" a violent, unreliable horse, Atiba would have been killed because he was a violent and an unreliable "slave." However, Atiba's spiritual beliefs represent a realm of the polis where issues of justice and personhood are sacred, inviolable. The act of killing, in this case, was a political affirmation of his personhood and the personhood of all Africans. Indeed, the narrator confirmed this: "Atiba, the last man standing, discovered the secret of prosperity in the land of bondage. He was the last of our womb. He would plant the seeds of our return. In our souls, we remembered him. In our hearts, we praised him. In our spirits, we thanked him. This was not the end. There would be another day."[107] I do not think it was the act of killing that the narrator praised but the act of resistance that expressed the reality of ungovernable selves. Atiba was not governed by or captive to the laws of colonial capitalism and their attendant white religions. He was governed by the laws of Mawu-Lisa, the Supreme Being, and in this he belonged to a spiritual polis that was ontologically ungovernable.

For those who were sold and survived, survival itself could be an expression of their ungovernable selves. Equally important is that many who survived no doubt exhibited innumerable subtle (and overt) acts of impotentiality in the face of the toxic masculinity of slavocracy's capitalism. Put another way, acts of resilience and resistance reveal the existential excess, the potentiality and impotentiality of human beings. Even in situations of near total subjugation, human beings, in this case Africans from diverse communities, found ways to care for and trust each other in the face of carelessness, to rebel, and to resist—all manifestations of the existential excess of ungovernable selves.

Conclusion

We rightly abhor types of masculinity associated with slavocracy and white supremacy. Indeed, it is difficult to imagine the sufferings of people who underwent the Middle Passage, as well as the sufferings of untold millions of enslaved persons throughout the centuries. In reading Daniel Black's novel, our abhorrence, outrage, and sadness stem from our capacity for empathic identification. I imagine many readers are appalled at similar situations today in which where human beings are objectified, exploited, marginalized, and, in some cases, killed with impunity. This said, can we extend this capacity for empathy to other-than-human species? Philosopher Peter Singer notes that "more than 77 billion mammals and birds are produced for food

---

107. Black, *The Coming*, 215.

each year."[108] Part of this production includes "factory-farmed pigs" wherein "male piglets have their testicles ripped out." "Pregnant sows," he continues, "are essentially breeding machines, confined for months in gestation crates too narrow for them to turn around."[109] It is not only intelligent, sentient pigs who suffer. "Beef cattle spend the last six months of their lives in feedlots, on bare dirt, eating grain that is not suitable for their digestion, and fed steroids to make them put on more muscle and antibiotics to keep them alive."[110] The horrific treatment of other species includes "egg-laying hens . . . crammed into small battery cages" and fish farms where fish crowded together suffer "from diseases, parasites, asphyxiation, and injuries," having a mortality rate anywhere from 30 to 50%."[111] My point here is that the complete lack of empathy and compassion exhibited by slavers in treating African persons as mere property to be exploited for white desires and needs is also evident in our treatment of other species. Even if we do not ever directly subjugate and exploit other species, we collude by purchasing animal products, just as white persons who never saw a slave purchased products that came from enslaved persons' labor. The Anthropocene Age reveals the toxic relations many of us, of any gender, have with other species. The works of novelists like Daniel Black can deepen and broaden our capacity for empathy, which is an antidote for toxic masculinity. Perhaps we can extend this empathy to other species, recognizing their and our own precarity and the reality of the existential insignificance and impermanence of all life.

---

108. Singer, *Ethics in the Real World*, 51. See also Nussbaum, *Justice for Animals*.
109. Singer, *Ethics in the Real World*, 52.
110. Singer, *Ethics in the Real World*, 52.
111. Singer, *Ethics in the Real World*, 53.

5

The Autobiography of Martin Luther King Jr.

Social Death, Sustaining Objects, and Radical Hope

> She taught me that I should feel a sense of "somebodiness"
> but that on the other hand I had to go out and face
> a system that stared me in the face every day saying
> you are "less than," you are "not equal to."[1]

> I had never in my life been abused by whites, but I had
> already become as conditioned to their existence as though
> I had been a victim of a thousand lynchings.[2]

> Having to live under the threat of death every day, sometimes I feel discouraged. Having to take so much abuse and criticism, sometimes from my own people, sometimes I feel discouraged. Having to go to bed so often frustrated with the chilly winds of adversity about to stagger me, sometimes I feel discouraged and feel my work's in vain. But then the holy spirit revives my soul again.[3]

---

1. King, *The Autobiography*, 3.
2. Wright, *Black Boy*, 72.
3. King, *The Autobiography*, 354.

In Daniel Black's novel *The Coming*, the narrator exclaims that "Atiba, the last man standing, discovered the secret of prosperity in the land of bondage ... He would plant the seeds of our return."[4] I have argued that the seeds of ungovernable selves manifest an excess that could only be extinguished through death. These seeds struggled to blossom in the slavocracies of the Americas, evident in uprisings and revolts in South Carolina, Virginia, Haiti, Brazil, etc.[5] Once slavery ended in the U.S., there was a brief moment when the seeds began to flourish, only to face the arid winds of Jim and Jane Crow laws, as well as judicial and extrajudicial violence aimed at subjugating African Americans. Nevertheless, resistance, resilience, and flourishing took place, as evidenced in the lives of Sojourner Truth, Frederick Douglass, W. E. B. Du Bois, George Washington Carver, and artists such as Zora Neale Hurston, Richard Wright. The Civil Rights Movement of the 1960s was instrumental in dismantling Jim and Jane Crow laws and policies that had hampered the flourishing of African Americans, only to be followed by a new Jim Crow era wherein many African Americans (and other people of color) are policed,[6] restricted from educational resources, exploited economically,[7] and made targets of voting suppression laws.[8] The tentacles of racism are insidiously pervasive, embedded in numerous institutions, and seemingly impossible to eradicate from Americans' psyches.

While we can learn a great deal about the impact of and resistance to racism by reading novels and engaging with other artistic works, in this chapter and chapters 6 and 7 I turn to autobiographical works. These stories reveal the pernicious realities of racism and its impact, in these cases, on black boys and men. Because Martin Luther King Jr., Malcom X, and Nelson Mandela were unique men who encountered similar institutions of racism, I consider each using different interpretive frameworks. Approaching the topics of racism and resilience from different angles will deepen and expand our understanding of both as they pertain to the impacts of distorted white masculinities on black boys and men. More particularly, in this chapter, I examine King's autobiography using the lens of sustaining objects—objects that enabled him (and others) to not only resist the evils of racism but also to flourish in the midst of a society of social death. Since the social-political and economic realities of racism undergird each autobiography, it is

4. Black, *The Coming*, 215.
5. Robinson, *Black Marxism*, 142–64.
6. Goldberg, *The Threat of Race*.
7. Soss et al., *Disciplining the Poor*.
8. See Alexander, *The New Jim Crow*. See also Human Rights Watch, *Racial Discrimination in the United States*, August 8, 2022.

necessary to begin this chapter with a relatively lengthy discussion regarding the attributes, dynamics, and psychosocial functions of racism. This will establish the framework for understanding King's, Malcolm X's, and Nelson Mandela's autobiographies. Once this framework is established, I move to King's autobiography and a discussion of sustaining objects.

It is helpful to offer a few clarifications and caveats before beginning. First, if we read autobiographies looking for truths and facts, we will likely encounter contradictions, falsehoods, and errors in memory. Moreover, in telling our own stories, we are likely to embellish some aspects and omit other events (e.g., King's affairs[9]). My interest is not to determine facts or identify embellishments and omissions but rather to explore how each man constructed and understood his experiences in the face of the apparatuses and disciplinary regimes of racism.

Second, while I focus on King in this chapter, it is necessary to stress that numerous other men and women who faced violence and threats of violence found ways to resist and to seek justice, while caring for families, friends, and communities.[10] In other words, my use of King (and Malcolm X and Nelson Mandela) is aimed at representing the resilience and resistance of boys and men during Jim Crow and the New Jim Crow.[11] As James Baldwin writes, "Perhaps we were, all of us—pimps, whores, racketeers, church members, and children—bound together by the nature of our oppression, the specific and peculiar complex of risks we had to run; if so, within these limits we sometimes achieved with each other a freedom that was close to love."[12]

Third and relatedly, highlighting the resilience of King can lead one to overlook the incredible amount of physical, psychosocial, cultural, and spiritual damage perpetrated on African Americans. Recall James Baldwin speaking about his father: "He was defeated long before he died because, at the bottom of his heart, he really believed what white people said about him."[13]

Fourth, as a white male who grew up during the Civil Rights movement and internalized racial biases and privileges that distort white subjectivities, I have long been interested in understanding the complex history of racism and its traumas in the U.S. and concerned with becoming conscious

9. Michaelson, *Martin Luther King, Jr.* See also Frady, *Martin Luther King, Jr.*, 9.

10. McGuire, *At the Dark End*.

11. Scholar Jay-Paul Hinds explores the spiritual lives of African American boys and men, revealing their struggles and resiliencies in the twenty-first century. Hinds, *A Gift Grows in the Ghetto*.

12. Baldwin, *The Fire Next Time*, 41.

13. Baldwin, *The Fire Next Time*, 4.

of my racial biases and privileges. With this acknowledgment, my aims are to (1) appreciate the perseverance, resilience, and flourishing of people of color who face considerable systemic forces that marginalize and oppress them, (2) highlight African Americans' creative construction of apparatuses that sustained (and sustain) them in the desert of racism, and (3) depict distortions of white masculinities that depend on the illusions of white supremacy for a sense of self-esteem, self-respect, and self-confidence. This latter aim includes the desire to dismantle apparatuses that support white male supremacy, whether it is toward women or people of color.

Racism: Definition, Attributes, and Functions

I mentioned racism in the previous chapter, though the focus there was on slavocracy and its wake of traumas.[14] There is no simple, definitive definition of racism, though we can nevertheless provide definitions and discuss the dynamics and attributes of racism with the intention of understanding its complexities and its attendant existential illusions and insecurities. I begin with a couple of definitions before proceeding to describe racism's attributes and psychosocial functions.

David Goldberg argues that the "notion of race . . . was put to work from the fifteenth century on in the Mediterranean countries."[15] As mentioned in chapter 4, the social construct of race attended Western imperialism and capitalism. This construct justified and legitimated the exploitation of untold numbers of Africans and Indigenous peoples, as well as the extraction of wealth from foreign lands and their peoples. As Goldberg notes, "By the late nineteenth century race had assumed throughout the European orbit a sense of naturalness and commitment, a more or less taken-for-granted marking of social arrangements and possibilities."[16] Goldberg differentiates between racialism and racism, though he acknowledges that both are social imaginaries rather than existential facts. Racialism, he argues, refers to "the view that groups of people are marked by generalizable visible and heritable traits. These generalized traits may be physical and psychological, cultural or culturally inscribed on the body . . . Such views, while presumptively mistaken, are not necessarily dangerous or immoral."[17]

By contrast, racism, for Goldberg, produces the conditions, directly and indirectly, that serve to foreshorten life but also foreshorten life's

---

14. See also Kendi and Reynolds, *Stamped from the Beginning*.
15. Goldberg, *The Threat of Race*, 3.
16. Goldberg, *The Threat of Race*, 3.
17. Goldberg, *The Threat of Race*, 5.

opportunities. Racism, of course, includes "delimbing, whipping, hanging, beating, bombing, shooting or gassing. But it is also targeted or collateral malnutrition, stress formation, physical debilitation, humiliation, and degradation."[18] As Orlando Patterson notes, "Racist oppression took many forms and damaged Afro-American men and women in numerous ways, but the single greatest focus of ethnic domination was the relentless effort to emasculate the Afro-American male in every conceivable way and at every turn."[19] It is also important to mention the humiliation of African American girls and women through hypersexualization, rape, and other brutal, depersonalizing behaviors.[20] Forms of humiliation are political tactics to undermine the political, moral,[21] and economic agencies of African Americans while also depriving them of resources needed to flourish in the polis. All of this could not take place without the deliberate collective creation and ongoing deliberate use of social, political, economic, and cultural apparatuses of force and violence by white persons.[22]

Orlando Patterson uses the notion of social death when addressing the topic of racism, which furthers this discussion.[23] Of course, death may be literal, but social death means that racialized others are excluded or marginalized from public and political life.[24] Abdul JanMohamed, examining the works of Richard Wright, argues that social death manifests a kind of symbolic death, which entails the death of the subject's place and participation in the polis.[25] From a similar angle, Achille Mbembe argues that in a racist democratic society, there is "a *community of fellow creatures* governed, at least in principle, by the law of equality, and a *category of nonfellows* . . . that is established by law."[26] For Judith Butler, those who are excluded are denied political and social recognition, which, in terms of social death, means they "cannot be mourned because they are always already lost or, rather, never 'were', and they must be killed, since they seem to live on, stubbornly, in this state of deadness."[27] It is not simply that in racism people of color are not grievable vis-à-vis the larger society; they are also seen as disposable.

18. Goldberg, *The Threat of Race*, 26.
19. Patterson, *Rituals of Blood*, xiii.
20. McGuire, *At the Dark End*.
21. Mbembe, *Necropolitics*, 5.
22. Goldberg, *The Threat of Race*, 54.
23. Patterson, *Slavery and Social Death*.
24. Mbembe, *Necropolitics*, 38.
25. JanMohamed, *The Death-Bound Subject*, 17.
26. Mbembe, *Necropolitics*, 17.
27. Butler, *Precarious Life*, 34.

This accompanies the tendency wherein no white individual "bears the slightest feeling of responsibility or justice toward" people of color.[28] This irresponsibility and exclusion entail a (mis)recognition of people of color as less than (or not even) persons (*nonfellows*), lacking, white people believe, the capacities for reason and agency. Enslaved persons exemplify the extreme end of social-political exclusion and social death.[29] Since the state constructs enslaved persons as mere property, they cannot, therefore, possess political and moral agency. Near that extreme end are Jim and Jane Crow laws and voter suppression laws that were and are institutionalized attempts to exclude or marginalize African Americans from exercising their political agency.

A similar term to social death is the racial contract that undergirds racist societies. In the previous chapter, I noted philosopher Charles Mills's argument that the racial contract comprises a "political system, a particular power structure of formal and informal rule, socioeconomic privilege, and norms for the differential distribution of material wealth and opportunities, benefits and burdens, rights and duties."[30] This contract is further understood as a kind of civic faith wherein black persons are allowed to survive as long as they submit to their racialized social status as "inferior" beings (and accept white supremacy). This includes restricting them from political spheres of action and concomitantly reducing their access to economic resources. As noted in the previous chapter, African Americans are trusted by white persons to the extent African Americans accept their subordinate or subjugated status. This racialized civic faith accompanies a type of civic care. African Americans who are deemed to be trustworthy (because they ostensibly accept the racial contract) are allotted a minimal amount of societal trust and care (e.g., minimal healthcare, degraded access to educational resources, minimum access to legal representation, degraded infrastructures). Care is denied or further undermined when persons of color refuse to accept subordinate or subjugated status. They are deemed to be untrustworthy, meriting not care but humiliation and even death. As historian Carol Anderson points out, every time black persons have resisted

---

28. Mbembe, *Necropolitics*, 38.

29. As I hope to make clear in this chapter, social death and its misrecognitions do not mean that African Americans live a bare life. They, in various ways, have established and are establishing political gatherings that entail mutual personal recognition, fostering self-esteem, self-confidence, and self-respect. They are, in this polis, grievable, although denied this in the larger political realm. As Gediminas Lesutis comments, "Everyday practices of people experiencing heightened precarity are an important means of coping with one's subjection to violence." Lesutis, *The Politics of Precarity*, 44.

30. Mills, *The Racial Contract*, 3.

or rejected the racial contract, there has been a white backlash, which I interpret, in part, as the use or threat of force to enforce the racial contract.[31] Put another way, forms of resistance are seen by white supremacists as a betrayal of white civic faith and care associated with the racial contract.

I will return to the notion of the racial contract below, but for now I turn to Barbara Trepagnier, who highlights the insidiousness of racism today. She argues that "silent racism refers to the negative thoughts and beliefs that fuel everyday racism and other racist action."[32] These thoughts and beliefs (e.g., inferiority of black persons) about persons in the subordinate group also accompany emotions, such as hostility, hatred, and disgust.[33] Today, the term microaggression[34] covers the everyday actions of racial discrimination committed by white people who are often unconscious of their racial animus and their white privileges. It may be something as common as overlooking an individual—as if they are not there or simply too insignificant to be noticed.

Since I have mentioned cognitions and emotions, I want to shift the discussion to a psychosocial view of the dynamics of racism before returning to a political perspective. During the last six decades, some psychoanalysts have attempted to define and account for racism by relying on psychoanalytic theory and concepts.[35] Culling from this literature, I briefly define white racism and identify some of its psychosocial characteristics and dynamics. Farhad Dalal writes that "whatever racism is, it is essentially a dehumanizing process through which an individual is transformed into The Other, from one of us into one of them. The racialized and dehumanized other is positioned outside the moral [and political] universe, with all its attendant requirements and obligations to fellow human beings."[36] From Dalal's perspective, like Trepagnier's, the black other is depersonalized and estranged by white individuals who construct and treat black people as inferior and white people as superior. This is an example of the psychosocial process of disidentification, wherein black persons are othered such that there is no shared identification. To use Jessica Benjamin's notion of the

31. Anderson, *White Rage*.
32. Trepagnier, *Silent Racism*, 15.
33. Trepagnier, *Silent Racism*, 16.

34. This term was originally coined by Harvard psychiatrist Chester Pierce in 1970. This concept refers to everyday discriminatory actions toward black persons but now has application to any minoritized persons.

35. See Altman, "Black and White Thinking"; Altman, "Whiteness Uncovered;" Kovel, *White Racism*.

36. Dalal, "Racism," 158. See also Dalal, *Race, Colour, and the Process of Racialization*.

dialectic of likeness in difference and difference in likeness, disidentification represents a collapse of this dialectic of identification.[37] Put another way, an ontological abyss forms between white people, who hold to the illusion of their supremacy, and black persons, who are constructed as inferior.

Identifications and disidentifications negatively impact both parties. For now, let me illustrate this through the work of James Baldwin, leaving for later the distortion of white subjectivity. James Baldwin wrote that, as "a kind of bastard of the West," "[I] would have to appropriate these white centuries, I would have to make them mine . . . otherwise I would have no place in *any* scheme."[38] This realization accompanied a painful epiphany: "What was the most difficult was the fact that I was forced to admit something I had always hidden from myself, which the American Negro has had to hide from himself as the price of public progress; that I hated and feared white people. This did not mean I loved black people; on the contrary, I despised them, possibly because they failed to produce a Rembrandt. In effect, I hated and feared the world."[39] In this psychic cauldron of identifications and disidentifications, one can see Baldwin's hatred and fear of whites and other blacks, as well as his self-loathing for being black—a self-loathing that, in part, arose with the realization that he could not find a positive or ideal sense of himself in the public realm with which to anchor his identifications. This near total absence of positive ego ideals was the result of racist disciplinary regimes.

This psychosocial abyss accompanies cognitive operations of denial and projection that sustain white racism. First of all, there is a denial of shared likeness (as persons) and a projection of inferiority onto black individuals (nonfellows). That is, this process of depersonalization or dehumanization, Olatokunbo Aralepo contends, is contingent on the forceful and often violent projection of representations wherein whiteness signifies superiority and blackness inferiority.[40] For instance, as James Cone noted, "Lynching was the white community's way of forcibly reminding blacks of their inferiority and powerlessness."[41] Lynching was a public event and was inextricably linked to and supported by white narratives, as well as social, political, and judicial institutions that projected negative representations onto black persons. These representations were embedded in everyday

37. Benjamin, "Sameness and Difference."
38. Baldwin, *Notes of a Native Son*, 7.
39. Baldwin, *Notes of a Native Son*, 7.
40. Aralepo, "The White Male Therapist/Helper."
41. Cone, *The Cross and the Lynching Tree*, 7.

social narratives[42] and rituals, as well as in government policies, laws, and programs,[43] which served to legitimate and justify racial marginalization, oppression, and judicial and extrajudicial killings. In the purportedly post-racial culture in which we now live,[44] representations of inferiority are ensconced in laws, legal procedures, and housing practices that marginalize large numbers of African Americans.[45] These apparatuses represent the daily operations of white denial and projection.

I wish to linger here for a moment to offer four other angles on denial and projection. First, we might wonder about why there is so much animus toward those who are constructed as inferior. In my view, white projections and denials must be continually employed because, at their core, these beliefs (in superiority and inferiority) are mere socially constructed illusions,[46] though, of course, because of the apparatuses that maintain them, they have very real negative consequences.[47] That is, they are experienced as if these illusions are real. Moreover, white social-political senses of self-esteem, self-respect, and self-confidence (social-political agency) are dependent on these socially constructed illusions of the superiority of white people and the inferiority of persons of color. This means that white esteem, respect, and confidence are not authentic but rather are based on illusions that must be continually enforced through violence and the threat of violence to be felt *as if* they are real. Put another way, white identity (and political agency) is dependent on the illusion/delusion of white supremacy. As Mbembe notes, "The bad object and I are never entirely separable. At the same time, we are never entirely together."[48] In my view, the animus of white supremacists toward African Americans functions to deny this dependency, which, in turn, accompanies a denial of the perennial insecurity of white identity.

Another function of projection and denial is exclusion that serves as a source of social-political belonging for white people while creating an internal enemy.[49] By projecting inferiority onto African Americans, white racists obtain a sense of belonging by way of excluding this group—thus creating

42. See Saïd, *Culture and Imperialism*; Saïd, *Orientalism*.
43. West, *Race Matters*.
44. Wise, *Color-Blind*.
45. Alexander, *The New Jim Crow*.
46. Achille Mbembe, discussing Frantz Fanon, indicates that racism is "in league with delusion." This collective delusion is what I am arguing are the illusions of superiority and inferiority. Mbembe, *Necro-Politics*, 131.
47. See Porter, *American Poison*.
48. Mbembe, *Necropolitics*, 47.
49. Mbembe, *Necropolitics*, 131.

a society of enmity.⁵⁰ This sense of belonging depends on the exclusion or marginalization of "inferior" others. This is a weak form of social-political belonging. I say weak for two reasons. First, this political belonging is weak because it is based on the *illusions* of inferiority and superiority. Second, violence and the threat of violence toward, as well as the humiliation of, black persons serve as the basis of belonging. There is nothing life-giving about this political arrangement. Put another way, a racist democratic society is founded on a life-denying racial contract.

A third aspect of this dynamic of projection and denial has to do with pleasure.[51] There is a conscious and unconscious experience of pleasure that comes from believing *as if* one is superior to others. Yet, in a racist society, even with all the disciplinary regimes, this pleasure is tenuous because (1) it depends on illusions and the continual enforcement of these illusions and (2) black persons cannot be completely constructed as inferior since they possess inherent potentiality or excess—they are ungovernable selves. There are also the attendant pleasures derived from humiliating and, worse, killing African Americans who resist or rebel. Peruse the many pictures of the lynchings of African Americans and observe the arrogant, narcissistic pleasure that attends collective white hatred.

In my view, pleasure derived from humiliating others is hollow. Aristotle argued that the end of human life is *eudaimonia*, which can be translated as flourishing or happiness. This aim is, for Aristotle, achieved through the exercise of political-social virtues.[52] Pleasure that is derived from racialized forms of social, political, and economic humiliation are empty because they depend on projection and the exercise of the political vices of white arrogance, pride, and cowardliness. I would carry this further and argue that the emptiness at the core of this kind of pleasure reveals white persons' bondage to hatred and fear. More concisely, political emptiness or hollowness is evident in that flourishing cannot take place in political-social relations between those constructed as superior and those constructed as inferior. What exists is enmity, wherein the racist "never lets himself be touched by the speech of his subject."[53] It is also empty in an ostensibly democratic polis because "freedom" depends on continually humiliating a group within the polis, which means that freedom itself is an illusion since white racists are in bondage to their projected illusions and the opiates of projection and denial.

50. Mbembe, *Necropolitics*, 141.
51. For a more detailed analysis, see Gay, *American Slavery*.
52. See Barker, *The Politics of Aristotle*, 105.
53. Mbembe, *Necropolitics*, 153.

David Keen's book on the political and social aspects of shame points to a fourth psychosocial feature of white projections and denials. Keen mentions Sigmund Freud's idea that paranoia involves a projection that wards off an idea and experience that are intolerable for the ego.[54] I have already mentioned dependency and insecurity, which are two possible ideas and experiences white supremacists would wish to deny by way of hatred. A more potent and deeper issue is their fear of existential insignificance and impermanence.[55] Let me approach this by way of noting that white supremacy entails omnipotent thinking, which is itself captive to the idea of eternity, timelessness, or permanence. White supremacists do not believe that their superiority is socially constructed. Nor do they believe their superiority is in the past or time limited. They believe it is an ontological or existential fact, and this provides white persons with a sense of significance and permanence—ontological continuity. They project onto black persons not simply inferiority but also existential insignificance and impermanence. This can be further understood in terms of Lynne Layton's notion of the "normative unconscious" and Timothy Zeddies's notion of the "historical unconscious."[56] African Americans, constructed as inferior, are not "normative" in a racist society. What is considered consciously normative in a racist society are white people and their values, beliefs, etc. To return to Keen's book, the non-normative are shamed—deemed to be insignificant (though unconsciously necessary for white identities). For Judith Butler, they are also ungrievable.[57] Evidence of this is the long history of pathologizing and criminalizing black persons.

Speaking of history, the historical unconscious refers to non-normative insignificant others who are not part of the dominant histories of white people. These histories elide countless African American achievements and contributions to society, while at the same time whitewashing (denying) slavery. This is currently evident in reactionary states like Florida. It is not simply that African Americans are excluded or marginalized from social, political, and economic spaces. They are excluded from history. Both the normative and historical unconscious, from my perspective, represent the

---

54. Keen, *Shame*, 169.

55. Writing in the eighteenth century, philosopher David Hume made note of human beings' tendency to desire to be ontologically special or significant. "But the life of a man," he wrote, "is of no greater importance to the universe than that of an oyster." Racism is an attempt to secure significance at the expense of other human beings while also denying the existential truth Hume was pointing to. Hume, *On Suicide*, 16.

56. Layton, *Toward a Social Psychoanalysis*; Zeddies, "Behind, Beneath, Above, and Beyond."

57. Butler, *Precarious Life*.

warding off of the fear, if not the terror, of white existential insignificance and impermanence. This explains, in part, white racists' motivations to retain their beliefs in their putative existential significance and permanence, as well as to nurture conscious and unconscious hatred of African Americans who embody, by way of disciplinary apparatuses, existential, if not ontological, insignificance and impermanence. Put differently, the "black other" is a constant reminder of the reality of existential insignificance and impermanence, which is a reason for white hatred of people of color.

Racism entails the defenses of projection and denial, which raises a question regarding how people adopt these illusions and defenses. How, in other words, are subjectivities formed since racism is not an existential fact? One way to understand this is through the psychoanalytic concept of internalization. Psychoanalyst Roy Schafer realized that the concept of internalization is useful not only for understanding psychosocial development but also for explicating the process of accepting an ideology,[58] such as the ideologies associated with racism. Indeed, Schafer believed the concept used in social theory can account for how the "oppressed and exploited [come] to accept and even idealize the socioeconomic and ideological system in which they and their oppressors are serving as participant-victims."[59] Internalization, for Schafer, refers to "all those processes by which the subject transforms real or imagined regulatory interactions with his environment, and real or imagined characteristics of his environment, into inner regulations and characteristics."[60] These processes of taking in the world as one constructs experience begin in infancy, long before a child is conscious, and continue throughout life. In terms of racism, we can understand this to mean that young children are already internalizing the negative projections of a racist ethos and its attendant racial contract. The thousands of overt and covert messages that black people are worthless, less than human, are unconsciously internalized. James Baldwin and Richard Wright illustrate this process. As Baldwin notes, "Long before the Negro child perceives this difference [white superiority], and even longer before he understands it, he has begun to react to it, he has begun to be controlled by it."[61] Wright said much the same thing, writing, "I had never in my life been abused by whites, but I had already become conditioned to their existence as though I had been a victim of a thousand lynchings."[62]

58. Schafer, *Aspects of Internalization*, xi.
59. Schafer, *Aspects of Internalization*, xi–xii.
60. Schafer, *Aspects of Internalization*, 15.
61. Baldwin, *Notes of a Native Son*, 26.
62. Wright, *Black Boy*, 72.

Internalization is especially complicated for African American boys and men. Children (and adults) need to discover and identify with positive or idealized cultural representations.[63] In a society founded on racism, African American children often unwittingly identify with white "normative" values. This is perhaps most starkly evident in Malcolm X's text describing how, as a young child, he identified with his white classmates, trying to be like them.[64] Even after Malcolm was conscious of racism and even after he deliberately rejected white people, he unwittingly identified with white values by straightening his hair and dating white women.[65] Remembering this period of his life, Malcolm X writes that he "had joined that multitude of Negro men and women in America who are brainwashed into believing that the black people are 'inferior'—and white people 'superior'—that they will even violate and mutilate their God-created bodies to try to look 'pretty' by white standards."[66] This unwitting identification with and internalization of white norms included his father, who actively campaigned against white supremacy. Malcolm X wrote, "I actually believe that as anti-white as my father was, he was subconsciously so afflicted with the white man's brainwashing of Negroes that he inclined to favor the light ones, and I was his lightest child. Most Negro parents in those days would almost instinctively treat any lighter children better than darker ones."[67] Malcolm X was pointing to the conscious and unconscious intertwining and internalization of negative and positive identifications associated with racist beliefs in white superiority and black inferiority.

White children, by contrast, internalize the beliefs in their superiority and their attendant social, political, and economic privileges. At the same time, they internalize the collective cognitive operations of projection and denial, which become foundational for their subjectivity. This suggests that any form of black resistance to, rebellion against, or transgression of white dominance threatens the identity and subjectivity they have internalized. Again, because of the conscious or unconscious belief in the existential facticity and permanence of white superiority, white rage, hostility, and violence toward persons of color function to re-establish or shore up white social-political subjectivities that are dependent on racist illusions.

The psychosocial dynamics of racism described above are clearly rooted in the racial contract Charles Mills discusses. This said, let me add

63. Lee and Martin, *Psychotherapy after Kohut*.
64. Haley, *The Autobiography of Malcolm X*, 26–32.
65. Haley, *The Autobiography of Malcolm X*, 54–55.
66. Haley, *The Autobiography of Malcolm X*, 56–57.
67. Haley, *The Autobiography of Malcolm X*, 4.

four further thoughts regarding racism, the racial contract, and political power. The racial contract can be understood in terms of Hannah Arendt's notion of the *space of appearances*.[68] Arendt uses this term to refer to the public-political space of speaking and acting together vis-à-vis the polis. To speak and act together entails mutual personal recognition,[69] which creates a space for others to appear and to exercise their political agency and freedom.[70] A decent polis possesses sufficient interpersonal recognitions among residents wherein there is the shared esteem, respect, and confidence necessary for the political agency to speak and act together.[71] An illustration of this is seen in the nineteenth-century work of Alexis de Tocqueville. In commenting on the plight of freed African Americans, he writes:

> It is true, that in the North of the Union, marriages may be legally contracted between negroes and whites; but public opinion would stigmatize a man who should connect himself with a negress as infamous ... The electoral franchise has been conferred upon negroes in almost all the States in which slavery has been abolished; but if they come forward to vote, their lives are in danger. If oppressed, they may bring an action at law, but they will find none but whites amongst their judges; and although they may legally serve as jurors, prejudice repulses them from office. The same schools do not receive the child of the black and of the European. In theatres, gold cannot procure a seat for the servile race beside their former masters; in hospitals they lie apart; and although they are allowed to invoke the same Divinity as whites, it must be a different altar, and in their own churches, with their own clergy. The gates of Heaven are not closed against these unhappy beings; but their inferiority is continued to the very confines of the other world ... The negro is free, but he can share neither the rights, nor the pleasures, nor the labor, nor the afflictions, nor the tomb of him who equal he has been declared to be; and he cannot meet him upon fair terms in life or death.[72]

68. Arendt, *The Human Condition*.

69. See Macmurray, *Persons in Relation*.

70. John Macmurray argued that "the primary condition of relative freedom ... consists in the quality of our interpersonal relationships," which necessarily is founded on a social contract of mutual civic care and trust or faith. Macmurray, *Conditions of Freedom*, xv.

71. Margalit, *The Decent Society*.

72. Tocqueville, *Democracy in America*, 416–17. It is important to mention that Tocqueville was also racist. Achille Mbembe writes that "from a Tocquevillian perspective, the freedom of the 'white race' is both absolute and indivisible. It cannot be shared with any nonwhite entity." Mbembe, *Necropolitics*, 162.

What is evident here is the lack of mutual personal recognition of black citizens, which accompanies their marginalization and exclusion from public and political spaces of appearances. Put another way, in terms of the racial contract, their political agency is restricted or denied. They were, as Tocqueville observed, free in name only, not in practice.

A second feature of Arendt's space of appearances is her notion of political power.[73] Arendt views political power in terms of people communicating and cooperating, while force and violence in the political sphere signify the absence or attenuation of political power and the space of appearances. To add to this, I suggest that *mutual personal recognition, which founds civic care and civic faith, is the basis not only for freedom but also for the exercise of political power.* By contrast, the racial contract is founded on misrecognition, force, and violence, which, as we see in Tocqueville's observations above, undermines the exercise of political power by black persons—at least with regard to white-dominated public and political spaces.

A third and related feature of an attenuation of the space of appearances vis-à-vis the racial contract is the creation of zones of injustice or non-justice. A decent society and its attendant spaces of appearances also deal with transgressions of laws. That is, the polis itself is a zone of justice wherein injustices are addressed and repaired.[74] The other side of the coin of civic care is civic justice and, in a decent polis, citizens trust that the notion of justice applies to them. Moreover, in a good-enough society, residents take responsibility for injustices or are held accountable. In terms of the racial contract, justice is, at best, distorted by racial prejudices and lack of legal resources. At worst, the notion simply does not apply—it is a zone of non-justice. As mentioned in the previous chapter, enslaved persons were constructed as property, having no political rights. These persons were denied access to the polis' space of appearances and similarly existed in zones of non-justice. In other words, the very idea of justice did not apply and, therefore, white people neither felt responsible to nor were held accountable for their actions toward slaves. After slavery, during Jim Crow, the idea of justice technically applied, as Tocqueville noted, but in practice it was rarely enforced (e.g., in cases of extrajudicial killings, rape, public humiliations). When it comes to the present day, clearly the notion of justice applies to all African Americans, but given the realities of the criminal justice system and unequal access to education, jobs, healthcare, etc., many African Americans live in zones of injustice.[75] These are zones wherein the notion of justice

---

73. Arendt, *The Human Condition*, 200.
74. See Arendt, *The Promise of Politics*.
75. See Anderson, *White Rage*; Kendi and Reynolds, *Stamped from the Beginning*;

applies but is distorted. Black Lives Matter and other groups have arisen out of the failures of the justice system, and their members seek to obtain recognition and justice.

It is important to note that zones of injustice or non-justice are also connected to the maldistribution of social, political, and economic resources, as Nancy Fraser points out.[76] A decent polis would seek a relatively just distribution of resources so residents could not only survive but also thrive. This implies that the notion of justice applies to all residents and thus that all residents are due the material resources necessary for their well-being— necessary for caring for themselves and others. The racial contract, past and present, means that many African Americans, especially those living at or below the poverty line, have limited access to resources needed for living well. Food deserts, lack of infrastructure, few local medical resources, and minimal public transportation are examples of the problems impeding the just distribution of resources.[77]

Here I want to turn to the fourth feature of the racial contract, namely, white sovereignty, which undergirds every aspect of the discussion above. The notion of sovereignty is deeply complex, but let me briefly summarize its features. Jean Bodin (1530–596), a French jurist and political philosopher, identified four essential features of sovereignty: supreme power (no superior), absolute, indivisible, and perpetual.[78] In the twentieth century, Carl Schmitt argued further that a "sovereign produces and guarantees the situation in its totality. He has a monopoly over this last decision. Therein resides the essence of the state's sovereignty, which may be juristically defined correctly, not as a monopoly to coerce or to rule, but as a monopoly to decide."[79] The monopoly over the decision can be understood as "The sovereign is he who decides on the state of exception."[80] Schmitt adds, "What characterizes an exception is principally unlimited authority, which means the suspension of the entire existing order. In such a situation, it is clear that the state remains, whereas the law recedes."[81] The law and the state, in other words, are subordinate to the absolute authority of the sovereign. The state

---

Porter, *American Poison*.
76. Fraser and Honneth, *Redistribution or Recognition?*
77. See Soss et al., *Disciplining the Poor*; Wacquant, *Punishing the Poor*.
78. Bodin, *On Sovereignty*.
79. Schmitt, *Political Theology*, 13.
80. Schmitt, *Political Theology*, 5.
81. Schmitt, *Political Theology*, 12.

of exception means the sovereign "has the power to decide which life may be killed without the commission of a homicide."[82]

But it is not simply the sovereign who has the power of the state of exception.[83] Giorgio Agamben points out that "the police are always operating within a similar state of exception."[84] That is, the "perpetrator" can be killed without it being considered a homicide (or sacrifice)—Agamben's term *homo sacer* fits here.[85] In terms of a democracy and its attendant racial contract, white sovereignty, not democracy, is the prevailing organizing principle of the polis. To return to Tocqueville's observations, there are obvious laws and policies, constructed by whites, that marginalize black citizens from public and political spaces. Moreover, white police and attendant judicial systems can exonerate police who kill black persons—a state of exception. But it is not only officials; white citizens who use varied forms of violence toward black persons can also be said to operate out of the state of exception. Any cursory reading of U.S. history and South African apartheid illustrates innumerable examples of white citizens' exercise of sovereignty's state of exception and its attendant judicial and extra-judicial violence.

While this perspective on the attributes of racism is not exhaustive, it is necessary to establish a framework for this chapter and the next two chapters. Before moving to King's biography, let me sum up the major points. Racism entails social-political forms of recognition wherein those who are othered are constructed as inferior, while white individuals believe themselves to be superior. These beliefs—more accurately, illusions—are embedded in and produced by apparatuses and disciplinary regimes that aim to shorten and restrict the social, political, and cultural lives of African Americans—social death. In a society imbued with racism, in this case the U.S., African Americans are coerced into accepting a racial contract, which involves accepting and living out their subordinate and subjugated status if they are to obtain a minimal amount of conditional civic care and faith. Failure to abide by this contract leads to white rage and the exercise of judicial and extra-judicial violence and deprivation. This racial contract, I argue, is rooted in the notion of white sovereignty and its state of exception, which restricts social-political spaces of appearances by denying or undermining the political and moral agencies of African Americans. In addition, white sovereignty and the racial contract create zones of injustice and non-justice,

---

82. Schmitt, *Political Theology*, 142.

83. A sovereign does not and cannot exist without sovereign classes and those who operate the social-political apparatuses to ensure the sovereign's power (e.g., police, army, lawyers, judges, business elites).

84. Agamben, *State of Exception*, 103.

85. Agamben, *Homo Sacer*, 42.

limiting or denying social, political, and cultural goods necessary for survival and flourishing. From a psychological perspective, I argue that the dependence of white racists on the illusions of superiority and inferiority for identity and belonging reveals an existential insecurity, which explains, in part, why racists must continually produce (through projection) subjugated others. Alongside this is the psychosocial defense of denial—of existential insignificance and impermanence, as well as denial of responsibility for harming African Americans. The defenses of denial and projection accompany the pleasure of subjugating and humiliating African Americans; obstacles to obtaining this pleasure give rise to white hatred and hostility, which screens from consciousness white existential insecurity. In addition, I have argued that the psychosocial process of internalization explains how men and boys come to adopt these beliefs and defenses. Although I am focusing on masculinity, racism and its distortion of subjectivity pertain to any gender who depends on the illusion.

Martin Luther King Jr.

To withstand the force of social death, to render inoperative the coercive violence of the racial contract, to avoid being captive to machinery that distorts masculinity, and to not be defined and determined by the apparatuses of racism is to overcome bare life. All of this requires individual-collective[86] resiliency, resistance, fortitude, endurance, and the capacity for and exercise of impotentiality.[87] To understand this resiliency and flourishing in the midst of a racist society, I first delve into King's life. From here I turn to the notion of sustaining objects and their attributes.

Martin (originally Michael) Luther King Jr. was born on January 15, 1929, in the heart of Southern apartheid, Atlanta, Georgia.[88] King's father was a prominent preacher at Ebenezer Baptist Church who, from his son's

---

86. While I am focusing on an individual in this chapter, I want to stress that the resiliency of King, as an individual, cannot be understood outside the relationships and communities that sustained him and others.

87. Recall Agamben's depiction of impotentiality. He writes: "*Other living beings are capable only of their specific potentiality; they can only do this or that. But human beings are the animals who are capable of their own impotentiality. The greatness of human potentiality is measured by the abyss of human impotentiality.* Here it is possible to see how the root of freedom is to be found in the abyss of potentiality. To be free is not simply to have the power to do this or that thing, nor is it simply to have the power to refuse to do this or that thing. To be free is ... *to be capable of one's own impotentiality.*" Agamben, *Potentialities*, 182–83.

88. King, *The Autobiography*, 1.

perspective, was a man "strong in his will."[89] He writes further that his father "has always been a very strong and confident person. I have rarely ever met a person more fearless and courageous."[90] Martin must have heard the stories his father told about how he came to live in Atlanta, having grown up working on a plantation. Refusing to succumb to the humiliations of the white owners, his father left for the city and for education. Another illustration of his father's courage and iron will is King's memory of being pulled over by a white policeman, who addressed King's father as "boy." Rev. King Sr. "instantly retorted: 'Let me make it clear to you that you are not talking to a boy. If you persist in referring to me as boy, I will be forced to act *as if* I don't hear a word you are saying.'"[91] This memory, I suggest, revealed a moment of courageous self-preservation (positive political agency, self-esteem, self-respect, and self-confidence) in the face of racist humiliation. I add that the memories functioned to preserve (and consolidate) King's self-esteem and agency.

King's mother was an equally important figure in his life. King describes his mother as "a very devout person with a deep commitment to the Christian faith."[92] Unlike her husband's precarious upbringing, Alberta Williams King, a daughter of a successful minister, grew "up in comparative comfort" and "was provided with all the conveniences that any high school and college student could expect."[93] This privileged upbringing must be understood within the context of segregation. King writes, "In spite of her comfortable circumstances, my mother never complacently adjusted herself to the system of segregation."[94]

Like his mother, King's childhood was, in comparison to other African American children, fairly comfortable, at least with regard to family finances and marital stability.[95] Peniel Joseph notes, while King grew up in the midst of the Jim Crow South, he was "ensconced in the world of black

---

89. King, *The Autobiography*, 4.

90. King, *The Autobiography*, 4.

91. King, *The Autobiography*, 8; italics mine. I will return to the phrase "as if" when addressing the resiliency of exercising one's capacity for impotentiality.

92. King, *The Autobiography*, 1.

93. King, *The Autobiography*, 3.

94. King, *The Autobiography*, 3.

95. King's portrayal of his father and mother, who were both alive at the time he was writing, is a bit idealistic. There is, however, a hint of conflict between Martin and his iron-willed father. While Martin's story is more complex than his portrayal of his parents, his idealization of them manifests their importance and the importance of their ideals in living his life.

elite."[96] Evidence for his more privileged position is noted in King's early childhood awareness of numerous "people standing in breadlines,"[97] something his parents never had to do. Later, King admits he "never experienced the feeling of not having the basic necessities of life."[98]

It is important to stress that King's parents were deeply involved in the church community. He recalls joining "the church at the age of five," following his sister's baptism. He recognized that this was based "out of a childhood desire to keep up with my sister."[99] Nevertheless, he continues, "The church has always been a second home for me. As far back as I can remember I was in church every Sunday. My best friends were in Sunday school, and it was Sunday school that helped me to build the capacity for getting along with people."[100] This second home would follow him into adulthood when he became a pastor.[101]

Having a loving home, both in his family and the church, did not protect King from experiencing the daily humiliations, deprivations, and threats of violence in the Jim Crow South. When King was five or six, he played with a white child who was the same age. "He did not," King remembers, "live in our community, but he was usually around every day; his father owned a store across the street from our house."[102] When they entered different schools, "our friendship began to break . . . The climax came when he told me one day that his father demanded that he would play with me no more."[103] This was deeply disturbing to young Martin: "I will never forget what a great shock this was to me."[104] This incident was brought up at the dinner table that evening and King learned his parents had experienced similar situations of rejection and humiliation. King was aghast, and "from that moment on I was determined to hate every white person. As I grew older and older this

96. Joseph, *The Sword and the Shield*, 55.
97. King, *The Autobiography*, 2.
98. King, *The Autobiography*, 5.
99. King, *The Autobiography*, 6.
100. King, *The Autobiography*, 6.
101. It is interesting that at the very beginning of his autobiography King states, "Of course I was religious. I grew up in the church. My father is a preacher, my grandfather was a preacher, my great-grandfather was a preacher, my only brother is a preacher, my daddy's brother is a preacher. So I didn't have much choice." This can come across as King believing he was destined or even determined by the past to become a preacher, but there are many opportunities in growing up to choose other paths. Moreover, later he felt called by God to be a pastor, which suggests a choice to accept and not something where he had little freedom. King, *The Autobiography*, 1.
102. King, *The Autobiography*, 7.
103. King, *The Autobiography*, 7.
104. King, *The Autobiography*, 7.

feeling continued to grow."[105] This understandable hatred was countered by his parents' Christian injunction to love, but King wondered, "How could I love a race of people who hated me?"[106]

While we can be sure there were many similar incidents of racism in his childhood, three other events are worth mentioning. On a trip to downtown Atlanta to buy shoes, King and his father found "the first empty seats at the front of the store." The store clerk said they needed to move to the back of the store. King's father refused and left, muttering, "I don't care how long I have to live with this system [Jim Crow], I will never accept it."[107] Another memory: When Martin was eight years old, he was in a store when a white woman slapped him, saying, "You are that nigger that stepped on my foot."[108] King did not retaliate because he knew how dangerous it would be. Then, when King was fourteen, he and his beloved teacher, Mrs. Bradley, traveled to Dublin, Georgia, to participate in an oratorical contest. On the bus trip back home, after winning the contest, the white driver forcefully demanded that they give up their seats to white people. When they "didn't move fast enough to suit him . . . he began cursing us."[109] They had to stand in the aisle for the remainder of the trip. King recalls, "It was the angriest I have ever been in my life."[110]

As a child, King experienced the racial contract of segregation and its innumerable "oppressive and barbarous acts."[111] He remembers police brutality and blatant injustices in the courts. He knew of the Ku Klux Klan and their violent attempts to enforce the racial contract, including witnessing the Klan viciously beat an African American. King recalls passing by "spots where Negroes had been savagely lynched."[112] Moreover, while he "came from a home of economic security and relative comfort," he could not forget "the economic insecurity of many of my playmates and the tragic poverty of those living around me."[113] He adds that economic injustice and exploitation also fell on poor white people, though white people retained the social-political privileges that come from a racist polis.[114]

105. King, *The Autobiography*, 7.
106. King, *The Autobiography*, 7.
107. King, *The Autobiography*, 8.
108. King, *The Autobiography*, 9.
109. King, *The Autobiography*, 10.
110. King, *The Autobiography*, 10.
111. King, *The Autobiography*, 10.
112. King, *The Autobiography*, 10.
113. King, *The Autobiography*, 10.
114. King, *The Autobiography*, 11.

After obtaining his degree from Morehouse College in Atlanta, King traveled to Pennsylvania to attend Crozer Seminary and then later to Boston to acquire his doctorate. While the North was not as segregated as the South, racism and the racial contract nevertheless existed in various ways (redlining, fewer economic opportunities, more incarcerations), though it was not as imbued with overt violence as it was in the South. At Boston University, King met and later married Coretta Scott, who hailed from Marion, Alabama. They faced a difficult decision as they finished their degrees. King had opportunities to pastor churches in the North, as well as teaching positions.[115] For Coretta, "A Northern city would afford greater opportunity for continued study than any city in the deep South." They knew they "had a chance to escape from the long night of segregation," wondering, could we "return to a society that condoned a system that I had abhorred since childhood?" Together they anguished over the decision, finally believing that they had "a moral obligation to return."[116]

By returning to the South, King would continue to face the humiliations and violence (and threats of violence). Marshall Frady notes that King was under "the constant shadow of bomb and assassination threats."[117] While on a plane, "a white passenger fell on him with milling fists." In Selma, a racist youth walloped him in the temple, dropping King to the floor, where the youth kicked him savagely."[118] At a conference in Birmingham, a white youth, a member of the American Nazi Party, leapt on the stage and slugged him on his right cheek."[119] Racist autocrat J. Edgar Hoover ordered the FBI to surveil King.[120] In an effort to destroy King, Hoover directed some of the tape transcripts to be released to various news outlets.[121] One package was sent to Coretta, and in it a note "urged King to commit suicide rather than risk public shame."[122] King was also jailed and, as we all know, eventually murdered by a white supremacist.[123] I mention these incidents to highlight the racial humiliations, acts of violence, and threats of violence King (and his family and numerous African Americans) experienced. I also want to

---

115. King, *The Autobiography*, 44.
116. King, *The Autobiography*, 44.
117. Frady, *Martin Luther King, Jr.*, 51.
118. Frady, *Martin Luther King, Jr.*, 51.
119. Frady, *Martin Luther King, Jr.*, 51.
120. Frady, *Martin Luther King, Jr.*, 86.
121. Frady, *Martin Luther King, Jr.*, 131–32.
122. Joseph, *The Sword and the Shield*, 208.

123. See Smiley and Ritz for a depiction of King's last year of life and all of his struggles. Smiley and Ritz, *Death of a King*.

make clear that while the South had Jim Crow, the North also possessed apparatuses to enforce the racial contract.

King and Sustaining Objects

Given innumerable humiliations, direct violence, and threats of violence, how do boys and men develop the resiliencies to resist and even rebel against the apparatuses of the racial contract? What sustains people in the midst of political, economic, and cultural oppression and marginalization? In this section, I explore these questions by first explaining what I mean by sustaining and objects. From there, I turn to the notion of sustaining objects, relying on a psychoanalytic developmental perspective inflected by Giorgio Agamben's notion of impotentiality, which I addressed in chapters 3 and 4.

William Clebsch and Charles Jaekle posit four pastoral functions evident in Christian history, namely, healing, guiding, reconciling, and sustaining. Sustaining,[124] they argued, arose out of the growing realization among early Christians that Christ would not return during their lifetime.[125] They needed to find ways to sustain themselves and their communities into the future. In addition, sustaining is also applicable to pastoral situations where there is no realistic hope for cure or healing or when a person, family, or community is facing an irretrievable loss. In these and other situations, Clebsch and Jaekle argue that sustaining comprises four tasks:

> The first task of *preservation* sought to maintain the troubled person's situation with as little loss as possible. Second, this function offered *consolation* that actual losses could not nullify the person's opportunity to achieve his destiny under God. Third, *consolidation* of the remaining resources available to the sufferer built a platform from which to face up to a deprived life. Finally came *redemption*, by embracing the loss and by setting out to achieve whatever historical fulfillment might be wrested from life in the face of irretrievable deprivation.[126]

Leaving aside the notion of redemption, I will consider sustaining primarily in terms of preservation, consolation, and consolidation. This said, let me stress that sustaining does not imply colluding with the disciplinary regimes that produce and enforce the racial contract and social death.

---

124. The pastoral function of sustaining was first discussed in Seward Hiltner's work, *Preface to Pastoral Theology*.

125. Clebsch and Jaekle, *Pastoral Care in Historical Perspective*, 42–43.

126. Clebsch and Jaekle, *Pastoral Care in Historical Perspective*, 43.

Rather, sustaining, in the context of a racialized polis, entails preservation, consolation, and consolidation in the sense of resistance and resiliency in relation to the racial contract. Moreover, while Clebsch and Jaekle focus on the individual, I view sustaining as a corporate, embodied enterprise.

The notion of objects is an umbrella term. It refers to (1) self-other representations (e.g., conscious and unconscious memories), (2) animate and inanimate objects (e.g., animals, toys, talismans), (3) ideas (e.g., God, U.S. Constitution), (4) narratives, (5) practices (e.g., rituals—religious and otherwise), and (6) cultural[127] activities (e.g., art, music). Given these depictions of the terms sustaining and objects, let me turn to King's early life.

Above, I mentioned King's early painful epiphany on the racial contract when his friend was not allowed to play with him. In reflecting on this incident, King writes:

> She [Martin's mother] taught me that I should feel a sense of "somebodiness" but that on the other hand I had to go out and face a system that stared me in the face every day saying you are "less than," you are "not equal to." She told me about slavery and how it ended with the Civil War. She tried to explain the divided system of the South—the segregated schools, restaurants, theaters, housing; the white and colored sign on drinking fountains, waiting rooms, lavatories—as a social condition rather than a natural order. She made it clear that she opposed this system and that I must never allow it to make me feel inferior.[128]

King remembered what his mother said to him about the Jim Crow society, but we can expand this by considering what his parents "taught" him long before he was able to understand the term *somebodiness*. In chapter 4, I mentioned Ruby Sales and her belief that her "parents were spiritual geniuses who created a world and a language where the notion that I was inadequate or inferior or less-than never touched my consciousness."[129] I suggest that both King and Sales had parents whose consistent personal attunement and relational repairs vis-à-vis their infants created spaces of appearances wherein pre-symbolic embodied senses of self-esteem, self-confidence, and self-respect developed—senses of self that necessarily found the agency to assert themselves in relational spaces. It is important to stress that these presymbolic representations of self include representations of the Other (mother/father) and that both are linked to interpersonal processes of care.

127. I am including religion under the term cultural.
128. King, *The Autobiography*, 3–4.
129. "Ruby Sales: Where Does It Hurt"?, On Being with Krista Tippett, September 15, 2016, https://onbeing.org/programs/ruby-sales-where-does-it-hurt/#transcript.

I suggest that these early presymbolic organizations of experience were present in King's understanding of his mother's comment about somebodiness. In other words, the idea and experience of somebodiness functions, in part, as a transformational object. Recall that Christopher Bollas wrote that a transformational object "is 'known' not so much by putting it into an object-representation, but as a recurrent *experience of being*."[130] This experience of "being," in my view, is the presymbolic, embodied senses of self-esteem, self-respect, and self-confidence that undergirds agency. An example of this is King's belief that God was his companion in the struggles he faced and that the universe was fundamentally good.[131]

But the notion of "God" is linked to narratives and rituals, all of which stem from a capacity for symbolization, which is a later development. To link these early presymbolic experiences of *being* sustained by his parents to King's later experiences of being sustained and to his use of objects to sustain himself, I turn to Donald Winnicott's notion of transitional objects and phenomena.

Winnicott writes that transitional phenomena represent "separation that is not separation but a form of union."[132] The infant is beginning to further differentiate between self, parent, and other objects. The first transitional object, let's say a cherished blanket, represents the parent-infant caring process.[133] The earliest selection of a transitional object, in other words, is in "accordance with its consistency, texture, size, volume, shape, and odor,"[134] as well as the parent's "technique of mothering"—the caregiver's handling, holding, comforting, and consoling the infant.[135] That is, the object, because it represents the parent-infant caring interactions, provides the solace to manage the task of differentiation—separation as the infant becomes more distinct from the parent-object[136] and begins to engage with other objects in the environment. For Winnicott, in possessing this object, the infant both retains and partially hands over his or her belief in omnipotence in the act of recognition and use of external objects.[137] There is, for Winnicott, a paradoxical interplay of the internal and external. The transitional object is "not

---

130. Bollas, *The Shadow of the Object*, 13; italics mine.
131. King, *The Autobiography*, 118–19.
132. Winnicott, *Playing and Reality*, 98.
133. This early transitional object is analogous to Bollas's notion of transformational objects.
134. Kestenberg and Weinstein, "Transitional Objects," 89.
135. Winnicott, *Playing and Reality*, 11.
136. Winnicott, *Playing and Reality*, 3–4.
137. Winnicott, *Playing and Reality*, 9–11.

an internal object—it is a possession. Yet it is not (for the infant) an external object either."[138]

It is clear that Winnicott, at times, is referring to early pre-symbolic experiences. In other words, this early transitional object (e.g., a blanket) precedes the infant's capacity to organize experience by way of cultural symbols. This said, the object represents not only the technique or process of parental care but also the embodied-embedded semiotic senses of self-esteem, self-respect, and self-confidence. The transition, then, represents the infant's developing ability to differentiate while also being able to link these senses of self with other "chosen" objects, such as the blanket. The blanket then can function as a sustaining object that preserves and consolidates the child's experiences of esteem, confidence, and respect.

I add here another idea. This early period and object signify the nascent capacity for impotentiality. Put differently, the selection of a transitional object not only provides solace in the face of separation; it also allows infants to exercise their burgeoning capacity to "prefer not" to engage with their parents. With regard to Martin's experience of somebodiness, I am suggesting that early parental personal recognitions and care created a space for Martin to assert his nascent agency, which was connected to presymbolic organizations of self-esteem, self-respect, and self-confidence. "God," then, represents, in part, these early experiences and senses of self that sustained him later in life.[139] In addition, this care provided Martin opportunities to exercise his capacity for impotentiality, which would become crucial in sustaining how he related to racism. An early manifestation of Martin's exercise of impotentiality was his refusal to care for or to love white people.[140] Remember, this exercise of impotentiality was in contradiction to his parents' exercise of impotentiality, which entailed loving white people while resisting the apparatuses of Jim Crow.

To further understand sustaining vis-à-vis psychosocial development, I continue with Winnicott's notion of transitional objects. Winnicott did not clearly differentiate between the transitional objects that precede symbolization and those that he viewed as part of adult life, but clearly there are significant cognitive and relational differences between a transitional object of early childhood and one taken from and representing the cultural field

---

138. Winnicott, *Playing and Reality*, 9.

139. For a detailed study of the correlation between early organizations and of experience and God objects, see Rizzuto, *The Birth of the Living God*.

140. I wish to stress that this early attempt to prefer not only partially rendered racial apparatuses inoperative. In other words, hatred of white people, however understandable, kept Martin captive to the grammar of racism. His parents' encouragement to resist through love represents a freer expression of inoperativity.

in adulthood.[141] This secondary transitional object entails a child's selection and use of cultural objects to organize experience. The cultural object selected by a child not only represents the technique of parental care; it also represents the child's entry into and use of the cultural-symbolic world. As Paul Pruyser posited, "The [secondary] transitional object may be the first means for articulating that aspect of selfhood that is social and public."[142] Stated differently, the second transitional object functions as a bridge from the idiosyncratic world of parent-infant interactions to the more expansive sociocultural world. By bridge, I mean the child is learning to incorporate and make use of shared language, narratives, and practices to organize experience, communicate, and construct self-other narratives. The object, then, provides a safe place (because it is under the child's belief in his or her omnipotent control) for the child to assimilate, accommodate, and use these larger shared cultural meanings, values, etc., albeit with the child's unique constructions. This process includes exercising the capacity for impotentiality, rendering inoperative aspects of the parents' care and story, which creates spaces for the child's unique constructions.

Before turning to King as an adult, I want to shift to the parents' exercise of care, especially with regard to Martin's parents and a racist society. Martin's parents (like Ruby's parents) in caring for Martin and his siblings, rendered inoperative the machinery of racism with its illusions of inferiority and superiority. Their care created a space of appearances wherein Martin was recognized and treated as a person—unique, inviolable, valued, and responsive subject. When his parents encouraged Martin to love his enemies, they were inviting him to exercise his capacity for impotentiality, rendering the apparatuses of racism inoperative. Recall that young Martin rejected this teaching, vowing to hate white people. In so doing, his exercise of inoperativity left him trapped in the machinery of racism and its dynamics. By contrast, his parents' religious beliefs and practices vis-à-vis love sustained them because, in part, they were not captive to the hatred that racism produces. Of course, making racism inoperative did not, of course, shield his father or mother from the humiliations of racism, but they were not captive to or controlled by its apparatuses. I suggest that, like Ruby Sales's parents, they were spiritual geniuses because they exercised this capacity for inoperativity, which sustained them in the midst of social death.

There is another part of this story of transitional objects, sustaining, and racism. Transitional objects also facilitate a person's transition to the

---

141. For a critique of Winnicott's view of transitional objects see, Brody, "Transitional Objects"; Litt, "Theories of Transitional Object Attachment."

142. Pruyser, *The Play of the Imagination*, 59.

wider social-cultural world. Martin's parents were obviously deeply involved in the church (and wider community), with its Christian beliefs, values, expectations, and rituals. The church itself functioned as a polis wherein mutual-interpersonal recognition created spaces of appearances among members, such that they experienced an individual and collective sense of esteem, respect, and confidence—all foundational to their exercise of political and ecclesial agency. The space the church created made inoperative the apparatuses of racism, which explains Martin's shock when he learned that his white friend could no longer play with him. I think he had grown up in a church community that sustained his sense of self-esteem, self-respect, and self-confidence. He naturally would have extended this to other areas of life, like playing with the white boy. This early humiliation would contradict all that he had tacitly internalized. Martin's understandable hatred reflects a profound experience of existential injustice, which was initially inconceivable given his five years of being sustained in a religious community that created and maintained spaces of appearances—spaces that represent the possibility of caring and just relations.[143]

Once King left to attend Morehouse College and later Crozer Seminary and Boston University, he struggled to construct a political theology and philosophy that incorporated the teachings of his parents and that would sustain him in politically resisting racism (and classism).[144] His theology and philosophy entailed nonviolent resistance, which epitomizes the individual and collective exercise of impotentiality. King and many others, within and outside of his church, developed nonviolent direct actions, rendering inoperative Jim Crow laws. Naturally, rendering these unjust laws inoperative did not protect King and others from being beaten, threatened, killed, or jailed. This said, King exclaimed, "We will meet the forces of hate with the power of love . . . We must say to our white brothers all over the South, We will match your capacity to inflict suffering with our capacity to endure suffering . . . Bomb our homes and we will still love you . . . We will so appeal to your heart and conscience that we will win you in the process."[145] The "we" here is crucially important. This was a corporate effort

---

143. I am not idealizing Martin's parents, family, or their religious community. Every family and community has disruptions, conflicts, etc. That said, his parents (and his community), under considerable challenges due to living in a racist society, were clearly good enough.

144. For a more in-depth examination of King's political philosophy, see Shelby and Terry, *To Shape a New World*.

145. Frady, *Martin Luther King, Jr.*, 5.

at impotentiality, which meant that the collective effort sustained each other by way of mutual interpersonal recognition and care.[146]

King's political philosophy and theology of love and nonviolent resistance included rendering inoperative Jim Crow laws (indeed, any law that results in injustice). "Any law," King wrote, "that degrades human personality is unjust. All segregation statutes are unjust because segregation distorts the soul and damages the personality. It gives the segregator a false sense of superiority and the segregated a false sense of inferiority. Segregation substitutes . . . an 'I-It' relationship for an 'I-Thou' relationship and ends up relegating persons to the status of things."[147] I-Thou relations reflect the beloved community (polis), manifesting spaces of appearances and zones of care and justice, while I-It relations embodied in the racial contract restrict or deny the space of appearances and foster a zone of non-justice. The beloved community represents an ideal and reality wherein care and justice are exercised and unjust laws are made corporately inoperative.

It is important to mention that the inoperativity of love and nonviolent resistance did not mean that King and others did not struggle with their own hatred. Love may render hate inoperative, but it does not magically mean that hatred (or despair) is then absent. In January of 1956, while away from home, King's house was bombed. Thankfully, Corretta and their child survived. That night, Martin, lying awake, "began to think of the viciousness of other people who would bomb my home. I could feel the anger rising when I realized that my wife and baby could have been killed . . . I was once more on the verge of corroding hatred. And once more I caught myself and said: 'You must not allow yourself to become bitter.'"[148] Understandably, King struggled with anger, hatred, and bitterness throughout his adult life, largely rendering these inoperative.[149] Preceding the bombing, King recalled an evening when he lay his head on the kitchen table, psychologically and physically weary. He confessed to God his weakness, lack of courage, and fear. In response to his pleas, King heard a quiet, assuring voice say: "Martin Luther, stand up for righteousness. Stand up for justice. Stand up for truth.

---

146. This does not mean there were not conflicts, tensions, and rejections in the Civil Rights Movement and its varied organizations and communities. Indeed, as Smiley and Ritz note, during the last year of King's life he faced defections and criticisms from African American religious and political leaders. Smiley and Ritz, *The Death of a King*.

147. King, *The Autobiography*, 193.

148. King, *The Autobiography*, 80.

149. The bombing at Birmingham's Sixteenth Street Baptist Church, which killed four girls, was another occasion for bitterness and despair. King, *The Autobiography*, 230–31.

And lo, I will be with you. Even until the end of the world."[150] King recalled, "At that moment I experienced the Divine as I had never experienced Him before. Almost at once my fears began to go. My uncertainty disappeared. I was ready to face anything."[151] God, in these and numerous other instances, functioned to sustain King—consoling him, preserving his capacities for impotentiality (love), and consolidating his motivation for nonviolent resistance. This said, let me stress that "God" as a sustaining object could not have been fully grasped without the religious communities that held and tried to live out the theological beliefs and values linked to love and nonviolent activism.

Let me add that we can understand King's (and others') actualizing his capacity for inoperativity, vis-à-vis the grammar of racism, as a spiritual practice and virtue that emerge from and are sustained by the community of faith and ancillary organizations (e.g., the Student Nonviolent Coordinating Committee). Like any practice or virtue, the capacity of inoperativity must be exercised and sustained in the face of racism lest it devolve into hatred, anger, bitterness, and despair.

There is one other crucial point to make about sustaining objects in the midst of the prevalence and persistence of racism. Jonathan Lear explores the notion of radical hope as it pertains to the Crow people.[152] The Crow people, like other Indigenous groups, experienced and suffered from the racism and ethnic cleansing of Euro-American settlers. Removed from their lands and deprived of their rituals, the Crow people mourned these losses while they simultaneously developed sustaining practices in the face of racist apparatuses that were not going away and could not be defeated. Lear, with a sense of awe and respect, recognizes Crow chief Plenty Coups's "daunting form of commitment to a goodness in the world that transcends one's current ability to grasp it."[153] Lear concludes that Plenty Coups's (and his people's) radical hope was not mere optimism, which would be a turning away from the bleak reality his people confronted. Instead, Plenty Coups's actions signified a radical and courageous stance of hope in the face of anxiety and uncertainty. I would add that the Crow people's radical hope could not have survived without the sustaining objects that they held on to.

King's autobiography also reveals a kind of radical hope in the face of rampant oppression. King retained his commitment to goodness in the

---

150. King, *The Autobiography*, 77–78.
151. King, *The Autobiography*, 78.
152. Lear, *Radical Hope*.
153. Lear, *Radical Hope*, 100.

world, despite setbacks and his acts not seeming to bear fruit. In his last speech, King said:

> And each of you in some way is building some kind of temple. The struggle is always there. It gets discouraging sometimes. It gets very disenchanting sometimes. Some of us are trying to build a temple of peace. We speak out against the war, we protest, but it seems that your head is going against a concrete wall. It seems to mean nothing. And so often as you set out to build a temple of peace you are left lonesome; you are left discouraged; you are left bewildered. Well, that is the story of life. And the thing that makes me happy is that I can hear a voice crying through the vista of time, saying: "It may not come today or it may not come tomorrow, but it is well that it is within thine heart. It's well that you are trying."[154]

Toward the end of his speech, King exclaimed that God "allowed me to go up to the mountain. And I've looked over, and I've seen the promised land. I may not get there with you. But I want you to know tonight, that we as a people, will get to the promised land. And I'm happy tonight. I'm not worried about anything. I'm not fearing any man. Mine eyes have seen the glory of the coming Lord."[155] King was murdered the next day.

In exercising his capacity for inoperativity vis-à-vis the machinery of racism, King manifested a kind or radical hope.[156] It was radical in the sense that realizing a vision of freedom, while desirable, was not contingent on his being free today. It was contingent on his resistance to racism in the present. It was sufficient that care and freedom were in his heart and that he and numerous others were trying despite great odds. I add that his hope was radical because his care for all people was not contingent on white people reciprocating recognition and care. King's radical care and hope could not have emerged or been able to endure without the sustaining objects of his communities of faith.

---

154. Lear, *Radical Hope*, 157.

155. Lear, *Radical Hope*, 365.

156. Miguel De La Torre is deeply critical of Christian hope, radical or otherwise. He writes that Christian hope was and is imbricated with the oppressive structures of Western conquering and colonization. His critique is important to keep in mind when writing about hope in the context of racism. See De La Torre, *Embracing Hopelessness*.

Conclusion

Racism and other forms of oppression and marginalization harm individuals' subjectivities (in this book, boys' and men's) and their communities. Nevertheless, these individuals and their families and communities create practices, narratives, and objects that sustain them. Their resiliencies, in other words, are manifested in creating spaces of appearances wherein persons obtain the self-esteem, self-confidence, and self-respect that are necessary for exercising agency and inoperativity in the face of the apparatuses of racism. Martin Luther King Jr.'s life also demonstrates how resiliencies and inoperativity lead to forms of resistance that are not captive to the hatred, mendacity, and despair racism produces. Indeed, resiliency and resistance are the soil from which revolutions blossom.

6

The Autobiography of Malcolm X
Being Aggrieved and the Emergence of an Anarchic Self

> It is because of you, the men that created white supremacy, that this man [Malcolm X] is dead.[1]

> This innocent country set you down in a ghetto in which, in fact, it intended that you should perish. Let me spell out precisely what I mean by that, for the heart of the matter is here, and the root of my dispute with my country. You were born where you were born and faced the future that you faced because you were black and for no other reason. The limits of your ambition were, thus, expected to be set forever.[2]

> These [black] bodies have been conditioned, through coercion, to consider the self and find the self to be in a condition of *lack* and in this deficit to find something that can at best be called self-hatred: *I think, therefore I hate myself.*[3]

> I am not against using violence in self-defense. I don't even call it violence when it's self-defense. I call it intelligence.[4]

1. James Baldwin as quoted in Kendi. *Stamped from the Beginning*, 389.
2. Baldwin, *The Fire Next Time*, 7.
3. Sawyer, *Black Minded*, 23.
4. Malcolm X as quoted in Sawyer, *Black Minded*, 18–19.

Malcolm X was a contemporary of Martin Luther King Jr. and while, as adults, they were both ministers in their respective religious communities, they had decidedly different upbringings and views and methods regarding how to resist racism and seek political change.[5] Martin was born and raised in the heart of southern apartheid, while Malcolm, born in Omaha, Nebraska, and grew up in Lansing, Michigan—a northern state ostensibly free of Jim Crow laws but not of vicious, virulent racism. Martin grew up in a middle-class family, while Malcolm's family struggled with deep poverty—a poverty produced by the intersection of capitalism and racism. As an adult, Martin, as a Christian pastor, influenced by the teachings of Gandhi,[6] advocated for nonviolent resistance, while Malcolm, as a minister for the Nation of Islam, was not opposed to the use of political violence for self-defense,[7] nor to the threat of political violence to obtain voting rights—ballot (freedom) or bullet.[8] Notwithstanding these differences, both men had painful early epiphanies of the oppression and marginalization stemming from pervasive racism, and both men, in light of these epiphanies, ended up as revolutionary exemplars whose lives were brutally cut short.[9]

As with King, one can consider Malcom X's life from the perspective of sustaining objects. However, in this chapter, I twist the kaleidoscope's lens to highlight another way to understand racism and black persons' (in this case, boys' and men's) resiliency and resistance to being aggrieved. In brief, I use the term *being aggrieved* to portray the impacts of the apparatuses of racism on African American individuals and communities. In addition, I consider Malcolm X's resiliency and forms of resistance to racism in terms of the notion of the anarchic self—the self that emerges in the matrix of loving relationships that do not succumb to the sovereignty of white racism but rather, despite being aggrieved, seek to secure the individual and communal self-esteem, self-confidence, and self-respect that found political agency. I begin by discussing what I mean by being aggrieved, providing illustrations from Malcolm X's autobiography and other sources. This establishes the foundation for defining the anarchic self and describing its sources and attributes.

A few clarifications are necessary before beginning. First, racism and its impacts on the lives of millions of people are deeply complex, which indicates, in my view, that we need to approach both with multiple interpretive

5. See Joseph, *The Sword and the Shield*.
6. See Mantena, "Showdown for Nonviolence."
7. See Sawyer, *Black Minded*.
8. Breitman, *Malcom X Speaks*, 30.
9. Marable, *Malcolm X*, 479–87.

frameworks. This is the reason I spend three chapters on racism and its influence on boys and men. Second, I have had a strong preference for Malcolm X since I first read his autobiography decades ago. Given the family's poverty, the murder of his father, and the government's persistent intrusion in his family's life, Malcolm X's story is remarkable for manifesting a series of conversions—religious and secular—throughout his life, which, to my mind, makes him a more compelling figure than King. I wish to stress that I am not idealizing Malcolm X (or King) and, while I am aware of his flaws and foibles,[10] these do not concern me here. Instead, I am interested in understanding his resiliency and revolutionary resistance in relation to racism, as well as his later rejection of the Nation of Islam. Third and relatedly, I do not think that Malcolm X is a singular figure. In other words, there are and were many people who exercised their anarchic selves in the face of systemic racism. This chapter, then, is a testament to the resiliencies and resistances of African American individuals and communities. Fourth, in chapter 4 I used Agamben's term ungovernable selves to depict the resistance and resiliency enslaved persons in Daniel Black's novel. The term anarchic self has affinities with Agamben's notion, but it differs in that it refers to particular political arrangements, namely, a polis without a sovereign and the attendant apparatuses of sovereignty. As I will explain in greater detail below, good-enough parental care is fundamentally anarchic, which gives birth to anarchic selves that are the seeds of resiliency, resistance, and revolution vis-à-vis the sovereignty of white supremacy. This said, I will claim that at the end of Malcolm X's short life, the seeds of his anarchic self were beginning to bloom.

Let me offer some further clarifications regarding my use of the term being aggrieved. A friendly critic may wonder why I use this term instead of the notions of trauma and soul murder, which would seem more applicable from a psychology of religion perspective. My first response is that not all experiences of racism are traumatic, yet I claim that experiences of racism fall under the category of being aggrieved and necessarily involve the dynamics of faith. Consider the recent book by Ta-Nahisi Coates, wherein he writes to his son about his struggles as an African American male growing up and living in a racist country. In my view, this is not a letter of traumatic experiences, though clearly there were a few. Rather, it is a letter, like that by James Baldwin,[11] about the pervasiveness of *being* aggrieved by the daily routine humiliations of racism, which breed distrust, betrayal, and hopelessness between persons deemed to be superior and those constructed as

---

10. See Marable, *Malcolm X*; Payne and Payne, *The Dead Are Arising*.
11. Baldwin, *Notes of a Native Son*.

inferior. Thus, *the notion of being aggrieved has broader implications than psychology of religion's focus on trauma and its relation to faith.* Let me add that the notion of being aggrieved vis-à-vis the psychology of religion relies on a philosophical-theological psychology that undermines the narrow attempt to simply pathologize the victims of racism or the victimizers. Relatedly, my use of this term moves away from an exclusive, if not reductionistic, psychological focus to a more existential and ontological framework. In short, the existential or ontological features of being aggrieved indicate that racism and its consequences cannot be adequately understood when relying primarily on a psychosocial perspective.

One could argue that the evocative term *soul murder* similarly points to the ontological consequences of some forms of trauma. But this term, unlike being aggrieved, is problematic for a number of reasons. Soul murder implies intention, perhaps the intention of one or more people. When we consider systemic racism, it becomes clear that many white people, for example, may not have any intention of harming black persons, yet they participate in various ways in the system and structures of racism that oppress and marginalize African Americans, while privileging, directly and indirectly, white people. Second, despite the evocativeness of the notion of soul murder, it is questionable, from a theological perspective, whether human beings have the power to destroy souls, though severe trauma at the hands of other human beings certainly impacts one's soul. Soul murder also overlooks the power in persons' (souls') resistance to being victimized. There were and are numerous ways people resist racism, indicating a liveliness of souls despite the apparatuses that aim to diminish persons and communities of color. Finally, the notion of soul murder tends to individualize trauma. One would hardly think of an entire group of people whose souls were murdered. The concept of being aggrieved, by contrast, does not hint at individual murder, as if racists can destroy a soul or a victim of racism has little power to resist. That is, being aggrieved can refer to an entire community without implying that everyone is traumatized and without implying that victims of racism do not have the power to resist.

Racism, Being Aggrieved, and Malcolm Little

The term *aggrieved* comes from the Middle English *agreven*, which has its roots in the Latin *aggravāre*—to make heavy or worsen. The concept means to oppress or wrong grievously, to injure by injustice. The Middle English *agreven* is related to *greven* and *grieven*, meaning to feel sorrow, to experience, consciously or unconsciously, mental and physical distress. In general, the term aggrieve means that there is injustice and carelessness that have led to injury and that this injury in turn has led to sorrow, mental distress, and other losses.

Given this general perspective, let me depict some of the features of being aggrieved as it pertains to racism and the racial contract.[12] I want to begin with Aristotle's view of human beings as political animals.[13] Human beings, for Aristotle, are also understood in terms of the notions of potentiality and actuality. As mentioned in chapter 3, Agamben[14] contends that potentiality and actuality pertain to all species, though, for Agamben, human animals are distinct from other species in that humans "*are . . . capable of their own impotentiality. The greatness of human potentiality is measured by the abyss of human impotentiality.*"[15] Simply put, "to *be* alive," to exist, means having the attributes of potentiality and actuality. For human beings, this means possessing the capacity for impotentiality—a capacity necessary to exercise and experience freedom. As a political animal, human beings are, ideally, able to actualize their potentiality and impotentiality in the context of a good-enough polis or community of mutual care and faith. This political philosophy is an ontological perspective that situates the actualization of potentiality in human political relations.

In chapter 4, I noted that Agamben does not elaborate on what actually is required for human animals to actualize their potentialities and impotentiality. Moreover, he does not inform us about what actualization means with regard to the polis, except to note that *to be* free is . . . *to be capable of one's own impotentiality.*[16] With regard to the first lacuna, I argued that parents' personalizing reliable care (including repair) vis-à-vis children is necessary for children to experience sufficient trust to risk acting

---

12. Mills, *The Racial Contract*.
13. See Lane, *The Birth of Politics*.
14. To remind the reader, Agamben argues that Western philosophical traditions have largely "subordinated potentiality to actuality: so we begin with the actual, speaking humans and their political and artistic productions, and we see potentiality at present as a capacity or skill that is defined by the final action. We see potentiality as secondary or accidental" (as quoted in Colebrook and Maxwell, *Agamben*, 188). This is derived, in part, from Aristotle's notion that "actuality is prior to potentiality" (in Ugilt, *Giorgi Agamben: Political Philosophy*, 26), though this does not mean that Aristotle believed that "potentiality exists only in actuality" (Agamben, *Potentialities*, 180).
15. Recall that the exercise of impotentiality means preferring not to act on the expectations and demands of another person or system. Malcolm provides numerous examples from childhood of his rebelling or subverting his mother's demands. In my view, these actions can be understood as exercising his capacity for impotentiality. Haley, *The Autobiography of Malcolm X*, 8–9.
16. Agamben, *Potentialities*, 182–83.

toward exercising their capacities of potentiality and impotentiality—toward preferring not. More broadly, parents' personal recognitions, which are the epistemological foundation for caring relations, foster experiences of trust and a relational space of appearances wherein children actualize their potentialities and begin to exercise their capacity for impotentiality. Parent-children interactions are already situated in the polis, which suggests that parents require a polis wherein they are recognized and treated as persons to actualize their potentiality to care for their children. This means that they must receive sufficient political, social, and economic care for their and their children's survival and flourishing.[17] In short, civic care and civic faith (trust, loyalty) are foundational for persons actualizing their potentialities and impotentiality, and actualization is *to become and to be*.

As noted, Agamben's focus with regard to actualizing potentiality and impotentiality is human freedom. I am suggesting that this particular feature of being human depends on good-enough civic care and civic faith. More can be said about *being* free in relation to actualizing potentiality and impotentiality in the polis. In previous chapters, I also noted that good-enough parental personalizing care is necessary for children to develop senses of self-esteem, self-confidence, and self-respect—key features of the experience and exercise of freedom. Political philosopher Axel Honneth notes that these senses of self are foundational for civic or political agency and cooperation.[18] Granted, infants and young children lack political agency, though it is potential. Actualizing political agency requires not only the care of parents but also the personalizing of civic care and civic faith. In brief, to *be* (to survive and flourish), as a human animal, depends on reliable caring relationships wherein one is recognized and treated as a person, which fosters relational trust and a space of appearances. These spaces or relationships support the experiences of self-esteem, self-confidence, and self-respect that are necessary for the political agency to actualize one's potentialities and impotentiality—to be free in the midst of finitude and precarity.

Given the context of human finitude and my repeated mentions of existential insignificance and impermanence, it is important to say more with regard to *being* human. Parents' personalizing care, which carries the message "We want you to be,"[19] accompanies valuation. Good-enough par-

17. Donald Winnicott made a similar claim, contending that for parents to be able to hold and handle their children, the parents must be held by the larger community/polis. Winnicott, *Playing and Reality*.

18. See Honneth, *The Struggle for Recognition*.

19. Below, I mention Hannah Arendt and her use of the phrase *volo ut sis* (I want you to be). This phrase represents loving or caring relations that are absent in the racial contract of white sovereignty.

ents view their children as inestimably valuable, and this undergirds and accompanies their emotional and material care for their children. As noted earlier, this communicates to children that they are valuable in themselves—*to be* is to be and experience *being* valuable, which founds experiences and subsequent (presymbolic and later symbolic) organizations of self-esteem, self-confidence, and self-respect. A sense of being valuable can be momentary, but children have a sense of their *being valued* and valuable over time—continuity as going on being significant. So, children's agency, exercise, and experience of freedom, their senses of self-esteem, self-confidence, and self-respect, are inextricably tied to embodied caring relations where they are constructed as valuable over time. Later, children can use the symbols of religion and culture to construct their experience of being valued. For instance, the Christian notions of *imago dei* and the kingdom of God represent this experience of being valued over time (and outside of time). There are psychosocial benefits to anchoring value ontologically, though as I noted in chapter 4, this is a category mistake. Human beings, like all living beings, are existentially insignificant and impermanent. That said, it is in light of this existential reality that parents construct their children as being of value and children experience *being valued*.

It is necessary to stress a number of points here. First, the experience of freedom precedes and founds the polis. By this I mean, in good-enough parent care, an infant or young child is already exercising (nascent) agency and experiencing a sense of freedom, though these experiences are organized pre-symbolically. Second, the experience of freedom and senses of self-esteem, self-confidence, and self-respect are dependent on materiality. That is, *to be* is embodied in relation to a caregiver who, along with personal recognition, provides the necessary material necessities (food, clothing, housing) for infants to actualize their potentialities and impotentiality. Third, implicit in the parents' caring personal recognitions is the categorical demand to care for their children's *well-being*, which includes nurturing their capacities for actualizing potentialities and impotentiality.[20] Fourth, personal recognition and care, whether we are talking about parents and children or members of a good-enough polis,[21] necessarily imply just relations. Care and justice are two sides of the same relational coin. Justice without care is desiccated and impersonal. Care without justice is sentimental and can easily collude with systems of oppression and marginalization.[22] Fifth, many of us are likely to

---

20. This view emerges from my reading of Emmanuel Lévinas. He uses the metaphor of face to argue that there is, in the encounter with the Other, an infinite obligation to care, to treat the Other justly. Lévinas, *Totality and Infinity*.

21. See Margalit, *The Decent Society*.

22. See LaMothe, *Care of Souls*.

consider *being* vis-à-vis an individual. Yet, human *being* cannot be abstracted from the web of human relationships—relationships are inextricably tied to the polis, which is dependent on a biodiverse Earth. Sixth, *being* is not a state. It is dynamic because of the realities of existence, namely, existential precarity, insignificance, and impermanence. Relatedly, the experience of beingness and freedom exist on a continuum, with one end being abject slavery (bare life) and torture and the other end love and joy.

Given this, being aggrieved entails any political, social, cultural, and religious actions and apparatuses that undermine civic care and justice such that individuals and communities encounter obstacles in actualizing their potentialities and exercising their impotentiality. The diminution of civic care and justice accompanies varying degrees of depersonalization (devaluation) vis-à-vis othered persons and communities, which attends a reduction of the space of appearances. This reduction, in turn, means that apparatuses that fuel social-political depersonalization seek to undermine othered individuals' and communities' senses of self-esteem, self-confidence, and self-respect—political agency and experiences of freedom—their sense of *being*. That is, a racist society and attendant apparatuses of the racial contract aim to diminish, deny, and even obliterate racialized persons' experiences of singularity and experiences of being valued in themselves. Put another way, the apparatuses of the racial contract, which are founded in the notion of white supremacy and sovereignty, undermine or obliterate civic care, civic faith, and the space of appearances vis-à-vis persons of color. The racial contract, at its core, communicates to othered persons that they are to be subordinate and subjugated, which is inimical to relations that entail actualizing potentialities. These experiences of being aggrieved, then, occur in relation to human beings who rely on the apparatuses of the racial contract to (1) curtail othered persons' potentialities and exercise of impotentiality, (2) privilege the "becomings" of white persons, and (3) eschew accountability or experiences of remorse for individual and collective actions that depersonalize othered individuals and communities.

With this framework regarding being aggrieved, let me turn to Malcolm X. The very beginning of Malcolm's autobiography highlights the toxic racist precarity that preceded his birth.[23] No doubt Malcolm was told the

---

23. Manning Marable notes that the "apex of Klan activity in Nebraska came in the mid-1920s. By then the Klan numbered tens of thousands, drawn from every social class. In 1925, a women's branch was established . . . [and] white children were mobilized, boys joining the Junior Klan and girls the TriK club . . . That same year, 1925, the KKK's annual state convention was staged to coincide with the Nebraska State Fair." My point here is that this night of white racist intimidation was routine and pervasive in Nebraska. Marable, *Malcolm X*, 23.

story, perhaps by his mother or older siblings, that "hooded Ku Klux Klan riders galloped up to our home in Omaha, Nebraska."[24] At night, they surrounded the house, "brandishing their shotguns and rifles" and shouting for Malcolm's father to come out.[25] His mother stood in the doorway and said that the only people in the house were her three children. Infuriated, Klan members, who represented and operated to make real the illusions of white supremacy and sovereignty, told her that she and her husband "had better get out of town, because 'the good Christian white people' were not going to stand for my father's 'spreading trouble' among 'good' Negroes of Omaha with the 'back to Africa' preachings of Marcus Garvey."[26] After uttering more threats and shattering a window, they rode away.[27]

I start with this vignette because it powerfully manifests aspects of being aggrieved that were occurring long before Malcolm drew his first breath. The Klan was an extra-judicial white political apparatus that sought to enforce the subordination and subjugation of black persons and communities through acts of intimidation and terror—acts that were aimed at denying black persons political agency, justice, and experiences of being valued members of the polis. Apparently, the "good Negroes of Omaha" were those African Americans who accepted white sovereignty and, in return, were, to an extent, trusted by racists and afforded some meager portion of civic care. In this story, the Klan was especially exercised by Malcolm's father, Earl Little Sr., who preached the philosophy of Marcus Garvey—black economic success, independence (economic and political), self-respect, self-worth, and freedom.[28] Perhaps worse for "good Christian white" people of Omaha was Garvey's belief "that people of African descent had to embrace a black God and a black theology of liberation,"[29] which represents the desire for political freedom in a society of white sovereignty that denies both the freedom of and respect for black persons. Earl Little and Marcus Garvey, in other words, were attempting to counter the pervasive white supremacy and sovereignty that aimed to undermine or deny the political, social, and economic agency of black men and women, as well as destroy black persons' self-esteem, self-confidence, and self-respect, through acts of terror and

24. Haley, *The Autobiography of Malcolm X*, 1.
25. Haley, *The Autobiography of Malcolm X*, 1.
26. Haley, *The Autobiography of Malcolm X*, 1.
27. An expanded version of this story comes from a 1991 interview with Malcolm's older brother Wilfred. Wilfred would later have "flashbacks of the terror," keeping him awake at night. Payne, *The Dead Are Arising*, 4–5.
28. Marable, *Malcolm X*, 18–20.
29. Marable, *Malcolm X*, 19.

daily humiliations.[30] In this sense, Earl Little represented a threat to white supremacy and sovereignty.

As Les Payne points out, it was not only Earl Little's preaching that infuriated racists. Earl and Louise Little "moved away from their first cramped quarters on the northern strip of city blocks designated for Negroes" to "a rented farmhouse—among white neighbors."[31] Payne indicates that in the 1920s the "exercise of open housing was a civil right reserved for Caucasians; however, violating this policy was in keeping with the rebellious spirit of the pioneering, young Negro couple."[32] There are several points here. First, laws protecting the political and economic rights of white Americans did not apply to African Americans and thus the exercise of those rights by African Americans would result in a backlash—legal, extra-legal forms of violence and intimidation.[33] Second, being aggrieved is pervasive, not simply political but also economical, extending, in this case, to the very impoverished dwellings and neighborhoods where people were forced to reside. Third, Earl and Louise demonstrated extraordinary courage in deciding to rent a house in a white area, and their courage was an integral part of Malcolm's story. Indeed, their courage presaged Malcolm's bravery in fighting for justice for African Americans. They were, in other words, significant figures in Malcolm's early life who represented and modeled not simply resistance to white supremacy and sovereignty but also rebelliousness toward racism in all its varied and insidious manifestations.

After this incident, Earl and Louise decided to move away after Malcolm was born,[34] eventually ending up in Lansing, Michigan, after short sojourns in Milwaukee, Wisconsin, and later East Chicago, Indiana.[35] In Michigan, Earl Little continued his preaching in Baptist churches to earn money for a store he hoped to open, and he continued advocating for the principles espoused by Marcus Garvey. Again, and not surprisingly, his activism ran afoul of white racists, though this took the form of "a local hate

---

30. At first blush it may appear odd or contradictory that white racists wanted to get rid of Black people who advocated returning to Africa or who wished to segregate themselves from White people, as Malcolm X advocated for a time. White racists do not want to get rid of all Black people because to do so would mean they would not have an "inferior" class of people to bolster their fragile or tenuous political agency and esteem, which are dependent on the illusions of white superiority and inferiority of people of color. If there were no black people, white racists would have to create them to shore up their fragile political agency.

31. Payne, *The Dead Are Arising*, 5.

32. Payne, *The Dead Are Arising*, 5.

33. See Alexander, *The New Jim Crow*; Anderson, *White Rage*.

34. Haley, *The Autobiography of Malcolm X*, 1.

35. Marable, *Malcolm X*, 24–25.

society called The Black Legion."[36] The "Black Legionnaires," Malcolm continued, "were reviling [his father] as an 'uppity nigger' for wanting to own a store, for living outside the Lansing Negro district, for spreading unrest and dissention among 'the good niggers.'"[37] During this time, late at night, two white men set fire to the Littles' home, and white policemen and firemen stood around watching their home burn to the ground.[38] The family moved again only to experience further harassment by white people, forcing them to move to the outskirts of East Lansing.[39] Even here, the police followed, frequently questioning and searching their home for the gun Earl Little used to protect his family against the two white men who set fire to their home. The gun was never found.

The daily humiliations, threats, and stressors that come from living under the sovereignty of the racial contract impacted his parents' interactions with each other and the children. Malcolm recalls his father beating his wife, usually, from Malcolm's vantage point, because she corrected his use of English.[40] In other words, we might surmise that Earl became enraged as a result of feeling humiliated,[41] suggesting further the expectation of patriarchal subservience of women, which remained part of Malcolm's religious beliefs. Louise would fight back, and Malcolm remembered those fights, especially the last fight before his father's likely murder. Living in a society that seeks to humiliate and subjugate a group of people and resisting and rebelling within this society leads to even greater humiliation and terror, which would negatively impact any marital relationship. Earl and Louise were proud people, and this pride shielded the underlying racist humiliations they experienced throughout their lives and that were part of the enormous stressors placed on their marriage.

In terms of their relationships with their children, Malcolm recalled that racism shaped their interactions. "I actually believe," Malcom remarked, "that as anti-white as my father was, he was subconsciously so afflicted with the white man's brain washing of Negroes that he was inclined to favor the

---

36. Haley, *The Autobiography of Malcolm X*, 3.
37. Haley, *The Autobiography of Malcolm X*, 3.
38. Marable points out that a detective was assigned to the case, and he suspected Earl Little for starting the fire in order to collect insurance. Earl was arrested but not indicted. Pursuing Earl served to deflect the investigation from pursuing the racists who started the fire. Marable, *Malcolm X*, 26.
39. Haley, *The Autobiography of Malcolm X*, 4.
40. Haley, *The Autobiography of Malcolm X*, 4.
41. One might suspect that experiencing daily humiliations outside the home would make one sensitive to humiliations at home, which, in my view, would be the case for both Earl and Louise Little.

light ones [children], and I was his lightest child."[42] Earl favored this child, taking Malcolm along to meetings.[43] While Malcolm was preferred by his father because he was lighter skinned, his lighter-skinned mother, Macolm remembered, "gave me more hell for the same reason."[44] Perhaps the motive, Malcolm mused, was she did not want Malcolm "to become afflicted with a sense of color-superiority."[45] In my view, she did not want him to anchor his sense of self-esteem, self-confidence, and self-respect on looking more white than black—on the illusions of superiority and inferiority.

Let me spend a bit more time on parent-child relations vis-à-vis being aggrieved by turning briefly to Ta-Nehisi Coates memoir, as well as other authors who inform Coates's memoir. Coates writes, "My father was so very afraid. I felt it in the sting of his black leather belt, which he applied with more anxiety than anger."[46] His father's physical discipline, like that of Earl and Louise, took place against the background of pervasive violence and threat of violence—rooted in the sociopolitical machinery of the racial contract—and was aimed at protecting his son. As Richard Wright wrote, "I had never in my life been abused by whites, but I had already become conditioned to their existence as though I had been a victim of a thousand lynchings."[47] Fathers and mothers caring for their children in a racist society would know these dangers well. As Coates writes, "Everyone has lost a child, somehow to the streets, to jail, to drugs, to guns."[48] Recalling his dad's voice, "Either I can beat him, or the police,"[49] Coates struggles with whether or not it saved him. "All I know," he writes, "is the violence rose from the fear like smoke from a fire, and I cannot say whether that violence, even administered in fear and love, sounded the alarm or choked us at the exit."[50] Nevertheless, despite the fear and anxiety, "It was a loving house even as it was besieged by its country, but it *was* hard."[51]

Coates's remarks fit, in part, with Malcolm's recollections. Parents, in loving their children, prepare them to survive being aggrieved by the racial contract. As James Baldwin knew well, "Long before the Negro child

---

42. Haley, *The Autobiography of Malcolm X*, 4.
43. Haley, *The Autobiography of Malcolm X*, 6–7.
44. Haley, *The Autobiography of Malcolm X*, 8.
45. Haley, *The Autobiography of Malcolm X*, 8.
46. Coates, *Between the World and Me*, 15.
47. Wright, *Black Boy*, 72.
48. Coates, *Between the World and Me*, 16.
49. Coates, *Between the World and Me*, 16.
50. Coates, *Between the World and Me*, 17.
51. Coates, *Between the World and Me*, 126.

perceives this difference [white superiority], and even longer before he understands it, he has begun to react to it, he has begun to be controlled by it."[52] Baldwin also notes that, "Negroes in this country—and Negroes do not, strictly or legally speaking, exist in any other—are really taught to despise themselves from the moment their eyes open on the world. This world is white and they are black. White people hold power, which means they are superior to blacks ... and the world has innumerable ways of making this difference known and felt and feared."[53] Nevertheless, parents try to help their children navigate the perils of white racism. That is, parents, in caring for their children, consciously and unconsciously prepare them to withstand being aggrieved.

When a tragedy strikes, we often remember what took place before it occurred. Malcolm remembered his mother and father fighting and his father storming off. Earl did not return that night, heightening his mother's anxiety and distress.[54] In the early hours of the morning, the police showed up, taking his mother to the hospital to identify Earl's body.[55] The circumstances of Earl's death were shrouded in mystery. The coroner and police said it was accidental, but there were rumors suggesting murder. While never proven, Marable Manning writes that "a forensic reconstruction of Earl Little's death suggests that the story Philbert had heard may have been true."[56] Malcolm's brother Philbert had heard that his Dad had been hit from behind and shoved onto the streetcar tracks. Given the numerous threats and attempts on Earl's life (and the lives of his family), murder, which is the ultimate act of being aggrieved, was more likely than accidentally getting run over by a streetcar. Moreover, the police and other authorities were probably not motivated to investigate someone they considered uppity. Recall that the police[57] and firefighters had watched while the Littles' house burned down.

Earl died in the midst of the Depression, leaving two insurance policies, one of which was denied because the company said, without evidence, that

52. Baldwin, *Notes of a Native Son*, 26.
53. Baldwin, *The Fire Next Time*, 25–26.
54. Haley, *The Autobiography of Malcolm X*, 10.
55. Haley, *The Autobiography of Malcolm X*, 10.
56. Marable, *Malcolm X*, 31.
57. It is important to mention that in an interview decades later with Wilfred Little, he recalled the police had found Earl Little alive, and while Earl was being taken to the hospital, the police sped toward the Little home in hopes of Louise being able to see her husband before he died. Wilfred found the officer to be sincere. This said, it is a safe bet that white officers would not vigorously pursue an investigation into Earl Little's death. Payne, *The Dead Are Arising*, 82–87.

Earl had committed suicide.[58] The other insurance company paid, which helped, for a time, this family of nine people. Marable writes that after Earl's untimely death, "Louise desperately continued to seek ways to keep her family afloat. She was careful to maintain a household routine that would nurture order and a sense of family."[59] But despite her attempts, Louise and her eight children faced substantial headwinds. In the midst of an economic depression that disproportionately impacted African Americans,[60] Louise also encountered sexism. She struggled to find work, taking up various menial jobs and later being let go because white employers heard that she was black and a widow.[61]

Because this was during the Great Depression, the state had programs to help poor families. Malcolm recalled numerous visits by state welfare people "asking a thousand questions."[62] The family did receive a monthly welfare check, but their financial situation continued to be precarious, placing great stress on Louise. This stress was exacerbated by the numerous intrusions by ostensibly caring state welfare people.[63] The shame of being dependent on the state, along with the shame evoked by the state apparatuses that labeled all welfare food "Not To Be Sold,"[64] undermined his mother's physical and mental well-being. After being jilted by a man who Malcolm believed feared taking on the responsibility for eight children,[65] Louise began to decompensate under all of these systems of oppression. The state became involved, and Malcolm, by court order, was placed in the care of well-meaning white people. Decades later, one can sense the hurt and rage Malcolm carried from these events. He wrote, "I truly believe that if ever a state social agency destroyed a family, it destroyed ours. We wanted and tried to stay together. Our home didn't have to be destroyed. But Welfare, the courts, and their doctor, gave us the one-two-three punch ... I have rarely talked about my mother, for I believe that I am capable of killing a person, without hesitation, who happened to make the wrong kind of remark about my mother."[66] He wrote further, "I have no mercy or compassion in me for a society that will crush people, and then penalize them for

58. Haley, *The Autobiography of Malcolm X*, 11.
59. Marable, *Malcolm X*, 33.
60. See Klein, "Last Hired."
61. Haley, *The Autobiography of Malcolm X*, 12.
62. Haley, *The Autobiography of Malcolm X*, 12.
63. Haley, *The Autobiography of Malcolm X*, 17.
64. Haley, *The Autobiography of Malcolm X*, 14.
65. Haley, *The Autobiography of Malcolm X*, 19.
66. Haley, *The Autobiography of Malcolm X*, 22.

not being able to stand up under the weight."[67] The pain in this statement reveals the experience of being aggrieved.

It is understandable that a young boy, taken from his family and placed with a white family, would try to adapt by conforming to his white peers and adults. Malcolm remembered that he "soon became accepted by them—as a mascot."[68] While being "accepted,"[69] he found that "they would even talk about me, or about 'niggers,' as though I wasn't there . . . A hundred times a day, they used the word 'nigger.'"[70] He added that "it just never dawned upon them that I could understand, that I wasn't a pet, but a human being."[71] Nevertheless, Malcolm overlooked these negative appellations and his treatment as a mascot or pet until a deeply painful epiphany in eighth grade. After class one afternoon, Mr. Ostrowski,[72] Malcolm's teacher, under the guise of caring about Malcolm, asked if he had considered a career. "The truth is I hadn't," Malcolm recalled. "I never have figured out why I told him, 'Well, yes sir, I've been thinking I'd like to be a lawyer.'"[73] Here we see a young boy aspiring to reach for a socially and (ideally) politically esteemed profession against the background of constant messages regarding black inferiority. His teacher replied, "Malcolm, one of life's first needs is for us to be realistic. Don't misunderstand me, now. We all here like you, you know that. But you've got to be realistic about being a nigger. A lawyer—that's no realistic goal for a nigger. You need to think about something you can be. You're good with your hands—making things. Everyone admires your carpentry shop work. Why don't you plan on carpentry?"[74] Malcolm said, "It was then I began to change—inside I drew away from white people . . . Where 'nigger' had slipped off my back before, wherever I heard it now, I stopped and looked at whoever said it."[75]

67. Haley, *The Autobiography of Malcolm X*, 22.
68. Haley, *The Autobiography of Malcolm X*, 29.
69. Being "accepted" by white racists meant accepting subordinate and subjugated status. Being accepted represents the racial contract wherein Black persons are allowed to live as long as they do not transgress the illusions of white sovereignty.
70. Haley, *The Autobiography of Malcolm X*, 28.
71. Haley, *The Autobiography of Malcolm X*, 28.
72. Biographer Manning Marable indicates that the teacher's name was Richard Kaminska. Malcolm may have misremembered or altered the name, possibly for legal reasons. Since the autobiography uses a different name, I have decided to retain Malcolm's version. Marable, *Malcolm X*, 38.
73. Haley, *The Autobiography of Malcolm X*, 38.
74. Haley, *The Autobiography of Malcolm X*, 38.
75. Haley, *The Autobiography of Malcolm X*, 38.

To be threatened before one is born, to move frequently as a result of racial harassment and threats, to have one's home burned to the ground while police and firemen watch, to experience the untimely death of one's father under suspicious circumstances, to receive assistance from the state at the cost of being surveilled and humiliated, to see one's remaining parent buckle under the weight of racism and sexism, to be taken from one's brothers and sisters and placed in white homes, to be treated like a pet, to be called and seen as a "nigger," are events that give rise to experiences of being aggrieved. Social, political, and economic apparatuses of the racial contract of white sovereignty, in other words, operate assiduously to chip away at individual and shared embodied senses of self-esteem, self-confidence, and self-respect with the aim of undermining social, political, and economic agency. The racial contract seeks to undermine spaces of appearances, diminish the polis' mutual care and trust necessary to actualize one's potentialities, and weaken one's sense of being valued as a singular being. As Coates states, "Racism is a visceral experience . . . it dislodges brains, blocks airways, rips muscle, extracts organs, cracks bones, breaks teeth."[76] For Coates, the reality of racism evokes "the sheer terror of disembodiment,"[77] which has its roots in the violent commodification of black bodies—"they transfigured our very bodies into sugar, tobacco, cotton, and gold."[78] "Disembodiment," he writes, "is a kind of terrorism, and the threat of it alters the orbit of all our lives and, like terrorism, this distortion is intentional."[79] Malcolm's childhood experiences parallel Coates's use of the terms nakedness and disembodiment—experiences of being aggrieved.

Before turning to Malcolm's resistance to the racial contract, it is important to say a bit more about his experiences of being aggrieved. When Malcolm moved to Boston to live with Ella,[80] his older half-sister, he became increasingly involved in the "'valley' below the Hill among the pool sharks, pimps, hustlers, and plain old hardworking Negroes, all pinching a bit of weekend escapism from the rigors of menial-class strivings at such

---

76. Coates, *Between the World and Me*, 10.
77. Coates, *Between the World and Me*, 12.
78. Coates, *Between the World and Me*, 71.
79. Coates, *Between the World and Me*, 114.

80. Marable notes that Ella had numerous encounters with the court system, which is not mentioned in Malcolm's autobiography. Marable writes that Ella's middle-class existence hid an erratic lifestyle supported by petty crime. In temperament, Ella turned out to be neither a stable parent figure nor a particularly pleasant house-mate." Payne portrays a more positive picture of Ella, indicating that "Ella was turning increasingly respectable," which took place before Malcolm arrived in Boston. Marable, *Malcolm X*, 40; Payne, *The Dead Are Arising*, 147.

places as the Hi-Hat, the Savoy, and Wally's Paradise."[81] Malcolm, eschewing the middle-class ethos of Ella's neighborhood, found a sense of belonging and esteem in the black culture and underground economy of Boston's poor black residents.[82] Reflecting later on these early experiences and, in particular, the pain of straightening his hair (conking), Malcolm wrote, "This was my first really big step toward self-degradation . . . I had joined that multitude of Negro men and women in America who are [so] brainwashed into believing that black people are 'inferior'—and white people 'superior'—that they will violate and mutilate their God-given bodies to try to look 'pretty' by white standards."[83]

Malcolm, with the aid of Ella's contacts, was able to obtain a job with the railroad, which would enable him to travel to New York City. He was excited because "even as far back as Lansing, I had been hearing about how fabulous New York was, and especially Harlem."[84] Malcolm sank deeper into the problems associated with an underground economy, which eventually led to his arrest for carrying a concealed weapon and larceny.[85] Once arrested, Malcolm gave up the other members of his gang.[86] He and Shorty, a black friend, received the harshest sentences that could be imposed, while the two white women received much lighter sentences, with Bea serving only five months of a five year sentence.[87] Shorty recalled that before he was sentenced, the judge had told him that he "had had no business associating with white women."[88] Malcolm's memory was that he turned to his defense lawyer, saying, "We seem to be getting sentenced because of those girls." The lawyer "got red from the neck up and shuffled his papers: 'You had no business with white girls.'"[89]

Manning writes, "Prison life can shatter the soul and will of anyone who experiences it."[90] While not shattering Malcolm's soul, prison life was particularly grievous in that people who are incarcerated are depersonalized

81. Payne, *The Dead Are Arising*, 152.
82. Haley, *The Autobiography of Malcolm X*, 48–58.
83. Haley, *The Autobiography of Malcolm X*, 56–57.
84. Haley, *The Autobiography of Malcolm X*, 73.
85. Marable, *Malcolm X*, 67–68.

86. Malcolm omits the fact that he told the police who the other members of the gang were. Manning comments that "Malcolm rarely examined his own behavior—his broken relationship with Gloria Strother, his physical abuse of Bea Caragulian—let alone his betrayal of his partners." Marable, *Malcolm X*, 69.

87. Marable, *Malcolm X*, 68.
88. Marable, *Malcolm X*, 68.
89. Haley, *The Autobiography of Malcolm X*, 153.
90. Marable, *Malcolm X*, 90.

and humiliated in countless ways. For instance, Malcolm was, like other inmates, given a prison number, which became a part of him. Malcolm wrote, "You never heard your name, only your number. On all your clothing, every item was your number, stenciled. It grew stenciled on your brain."[91] "Any person," Malcolm remarked, "who claims to have deep feeling for other human beings should think a long, long time before he votes to have other men kept behind bars—caged . . . Behind bars, a man never reforms. He will never forget. He never will get completely over the memory of bars."[92] He will be aggrieved.

Disparities in arrests and sentencing were and are produced by political, legal, economic, and social apparatuses linked to racism and classism.[93] The routine humiliations of racism, the constant drumbeat of black "inferiority," and economic and physical segregation are exacerbated when one is caught up in the carceral state.[94] Malcolm's experiences of the "justice" system, which was and is an apparatus of the racial contract, and his experiences of prison life fall under the category of being aggrieved—physical, psychological, political, and spiritual degradation.

In summary, Malcolm's autobiography begins with a scene of being aggrieved.[95] White racists of Omaha, Nebraska, threatened Louise Little, who was pregnant with Malcolm. Long before his painful epiphany of the racial contract in eighth grade, Malcolm was born into and grew up in a racist society that produced apparatuses that undermined the civic care and justice and civic faith needed to facilitate the actualization of the political, social, and economic senses of self-esteem, self-respect, and self-confidence that found social and political agency. The exclusion or marginalization of African Americans from the space of appearances, which is evident throughout Malcolm X's autobiography, only occurs by apparatuses of the racial contract that deny the singularities of African Americans—a denial evident in systemic and pervasive political, social, and economic humiliations.

91. Haley, *The Autobiography of Malcolm X*, 155.
92. Haley, *The Autobiography of Malcolm X*, 155.
93. See Alexander, *The New Jim Crow*; Wacquant, *Punishing the Poor*.
94. Taylor, *The Executed God*.
95. I have not mentioned Malcolm's experiences of being aggrieved associated with his time in the Nation of Islam. Malcolm, toward the end of his life, was threatened by members of the Nation of Islam, especially when he decided to part ways. The founding myths of the Nation of Islam retained the illusions of superiority and inferiority, reversing them, as well as hierarchical ways of ordering the religion. Malcolm's conversion to Islam was seen to undermine the Nation of Islam. While Malcolm X, in my view, experienced being aggrieved by members of the Nation of Islam, the focus in this chapter is on experiences of being aggrieved due to the racial contract.

The Birth and Development of Malcolm X's Anarchic Self

In this section, I turn to the ways Malcolm and members of his family (and community) fostered resiliencies and resistances to the racial contract of white sovereignty and supremacy and its manifold ways of aggrieving black persons. It is important to begin with the totalitarianism of the racial contract and its relation to what I describe as "anarchic selves."[96] From here, I connect the concept to Malcolm's story.

Hannah Arendt, in trying to understand the rise of the Nazi regime, authored a book on totalitarianism that continues to be studied and discussed.[97] Briefly, the term *totalitarianism* refers to an iteration of sovereignty wherein political systems dominate all sectors of social, political, and economic life. This domination succeeds by virtue of apparatuses of constant and pervasive terror, coercion, and intimidation.[98] Arendt would not have considered a democratic nation like the U.S. to be totalitarian,[99] and, while I agree, in part, there has always been a totalitarian strain in U.S. politics, even before the Revolutionary War. Let me explain. British (and French) colonization of what we now call the U.S. (and Canada) represents a totalitarian political system in relation to Native peoples who were brutalized, ethnically cleansed, and systematically denied political recognition—or if recognized, they were demeaned, exploited, and betrayed.[100] Totalitarian genocidal practices toward Native peoples continued after the U.S. freed itself from the British Commonwealth. Native peoples who survived colonization were forcibly removed to other areas of the country and their cultures undermined.[101] Alongside the colonization of Native peoples was systematic

---

96. The term *anarchy* carries a great deal of emotional freight, as well as a complex history. Anarchy simply means "without rulers" or without a sovereign in relation to organizing a society. Thomas Hobbes, who associated anarchy with chaos and mob rule (which is not, by definition, anarchy), left a legacy of social-political opprobrium toward anarchy and anyone who called themselves anarchists. Not surprisingly, Hobbes was part of and served the sovereign class. In the nineteenth century, Pierre-Joseph Proudhon embraced the idea of anarchy, though it continues today to be associated with the chaos and violence of mob rule. I am using *anarchy* to refer to relations where sovereignty and its apparatuses do not operate or do not dominate social relations. See Bookchin, *Post-Scarcity Anarchism*; Prichard, *Anarchism*; Sheehan, *Anarchism*.

97. Arendt, *The Origins of Totalitarianism*. Simona Forti provides a history of the concept of totalitarianism, indicating changes in meaning. For my purposes, I will use the brief definition above. See Forti, *Totalitarianism*.

98. Forti, *Totalitarianism*, 3.

99. See Stonebridge, *We Are Free*, 141–42.

100. Over three hundred treaties were made between Native peoples and the U.S. government. All of them were violated by the United States. See Welch, *After Empire*.

101. See Lear, *Radical Hope*; Neihardt, *Black Elk Speaks*.

brutalization and exploitation of Africans for capitalistic economic wealth. Even after the so-called emancipation, African Americans continued to be exploited, humiliated, and brutalized (lynchings, rapes, incarceration).[102]

There are three points here. First, the exploitation of Native peoples and Africans reflects a totalitarian system based on white sovereignty and supremacy. Second, white sovereignty is supported by apparatuses that systematically occlude political, social, economic, and cultural spaces of appearances, while also undermining, denying, or negating the political agencies (and sense of self-esteem, self-respect, and self-confidence) of Native peoples and African Americans. Third, a group of people can live in a democratic society, but aspects of this society and political system can resemble a totalitarian system. Malcolm X's autobiography is an illustration of a family surviving in the midst of a totalitarian system of white sovereignty and superiority—white rule and dominance of nearly all aspects of life.[103]

There is one area of life that totalitarian systems such as white sovereignty struggle to control, and that is parents' care for their children.[104] As mentioned above, the interactions between Earl and Louise and their children *were shaped but not determined* by the racism of white sovereignty. Moreover, I noted that the intimidation and terror used by white racists was present while Louise was pregnant with Malcolm. Even with all of these stressors on his parents, Malcolm felt loved by them, and this love, I contend, was anarchic vis-à-vis white sovereignty.

Before turning to Malcolm X's autobiography to depict this further, let me return to Ruby Sales's recollection of her childhood growing up in the midst of white sovereignty and its racial contract.

---

102. See Kendi and Reynolds, *Stamped from the Beginning*; McGuire, *At the Dark End*.

103. The reader may counter this by saying that Malcolm X's father and Malcolm X himself engaged in free speech, challenging white sovereignty. Does this not indicate a democracy and not a totalitarian system? Time does not allow me to make an extended argument defending my claim. What is clear in the U.S., especially during Malcolm's short life, is that U.S. democracy entailed white sovereignty in nearly all levels of political and economic life. I would add that the rise of white supremacy groups in the U.S. since the presidential election of Barack Obama indicates the persistent desire of many white people to maintain white dominance in political and economic life. See Anderson, *White Rage*.

104. I need to qualify this. During slavery, the children born of enslaved persons were considered the property of slave owners. There are innumerable instances of parents being separated from their children as a result of the parents' being sold or killed. Frederick Douglass was born into slavery and had no memory of his mother. This said, when parents and children were kept together, then enslaved parents had more opportunities to care for their children despite the horrible conditions of slavery. Douglass, *Narrative*.

> I grew up in the heart of Southern apartheid. And I'm not saying that I didn't realize that it existed, but our parents were spiritual geniuses who created a world and a language where the notion that I was inadequate or inferior or less-than never touched my consciousness. I grew up believing that I was a first-class human being and a first-class person, and our parents were spiritual geniuses who were able to shape a counterculture of black folk religion that raised us from disposability to being essential players in society.[105]

The fundamental aim of Ruby's parents' care was *volo ut sis*—I want you to be.[106] This type of care created spaces for Ruby to experience enough trust to exercise and actualize her potentialities—to be. More specifically, innumerable acts of caring for her and her siblings represented the exercise of her parents' capacity to render inoperative the totalitarian apparatuses of white supremacy, creating spaces for Ruby to actualize her potentialities (and impotentiality). Put differently, their acts of recognizing and treating Ruby as a person—a unique, valued, inviolable, responsive subject—founded the conditions for Ruby to develop social (and later, political) agency—agency rooted in her experiences and senses of self-esteem, self-confidence, and self-respect.

To be sure, Ruby's parents exercised considerable power in relation to her (it was an asymmetrical relationship), but this power was one of caring for her well-being. This caring power was devoid of any kind of "ruling" power, especially white rule, and this was, in my view, countercultural (or better, counter-political vis-à-vis white rule). Put another way, her parents' reliable care rendered inoperative any apparatus associated with sovereignty, especially white sovereignty. In chapter 4, I suggested that caring for Ruby led to an ungovernable self. Another way of framing this is that innumerable acts of parental love and care give rise to an anarchic self—a self that emerges from and is rooted in caring relations wherein there is no sovereign, especially no white sovereignty and its totalitarian apparatuses. It is a self without a ruler—a self in relation to the caring power of good-enough parents.

Let me elaborate further. Ruby's anarchic self, which has its roots in early infant-parent interactions, represents experiences of freedom wherein Ruby exercises her sense of agency in relation to powerful parents who care

---

105. "Ruby Sales: Where Does It Hurt"?, On Being with Krista Tippett, September 15, 2016, https://onbeing.org/programs/ruby-sales-where-does-it-hurt/#transcript.

106. This phrase is taken from Hannah Arendt's work. Lyndsey Stonebridge contends, "*I want you to be* remains one of the most powerful statements of her thought." Stonebridge, *We Are Free*, 119.

for her. There is, in other words, no apparatuses of sovereignty in which agency and freedom are contingent. Of course, Ruby, like Malcolm and Marrtin Luther King, became acutely aware of the machinations of white supremacy and sovereignty—a sovereignty that worked to subjugate the agency of African Americans, undermining political, social, and economic freedom. However, this painful awareness did not, for Ruby, undermine her anarchic self. Indeed, her anarchic self, in my view, served as a foundation for her activism and resistance to white supremacy and sovereignty.

Before turning to Malcolm, it is important to mention Earl Little's rebellions against white supremacy. Earl's advocating for black economic and political independence represented a desire for black political agency and, concomitantly, liberation from white rule and its racial contract. His attraction to Marcus Garvey and the idea of an independent black nation further illustrates the desire to render inoperative the apparatuses of white supremacy and sovereignty. Indeed, the vitriol and violence directed at Earl and Louise by racists serve as clear evidence of white persons' dependence on white supremacy and sovereignty for a sense of esteem and political agency. White racists, in other words, feared (and fear) the rise of African American political agency and freedom because black freedom and agency threatened (and threatens) to expose the illusions of white supremacy and attendant fragile self-esteem, confidence, and respect that depended on these illusions. While we do not know much about Earl Little's early life, my thought is that his resistance to and rebellion toward white rule stemmed from his anarchic self.

To shift to Malcolm, his parents, like Ruby's, faced the totalitarian headwinds of racism, all the while seeking to care for their many children. Malcolm recalled his father driving "his old black touring car, sometimes taking me to meeting places all round Lansing,"[107] which likely provided a sense of intimacy and belonging with his father.[108] He also remembered his mother "always working—cooking, washing, ironing, cleaning, and fussing over eight children."[109] Louise's domestic work and "fussing" to my mind points to her devotion to and care for her children. Another special memory was Malcolm's mother giving him a small garden plot to tend and grow his own vegetables, which he loved.[110] This special memory, I suggest, screens other memories of feeling special or valued by his mother (and father). After

---

107. Haley, *The Autobiography of Malcolm X*, 7.

108. Marable points out that by age five Malcolm was becoming his father's favorite. Marable, *Malcolm X*, 27.

109. Haley, *The Autobiography of Malcolm X*, 7.

110. Haley, *The Autobiography of Malcolm X*, 8–9.

Earl's death, Louise struggled mightily to care for her eight children against significant odds. The other older kids, like Wilfred and Hilda, began to care for the younger children as the family struggled to survive.[111] The fact that his siblings fought to stay together and remain connected throughout his life indicates that they cared deeply for each other and that this care developed in relation to the care they had received from their parents.

What I am suggesting here is that their parental care, while shaped by racism's white sovereignty, was founded on *we want you to be*, which fostered senses of self-esteem, self-confidence, and self-respect that were not linked to or dependent on white supremacy and sovereignty. Malcolm's parents' caring actions, in other words, created spaces where Malcolm (and his siblings) could actualize (agency) their potentiality (and impotentiality),[112] which accompanied a sense of freedom—freedom outside the confines of white sovereignty. The power of his parents' care was not based or dependent on white supremacy and sovereignty, and this caring power gave rise to Malcolm's anarchic self.

Where, in his story, do we note the emergence of Malcolm's anarchic self vis-à-vis white supremacy and sovereignty? The first conscious awareness of an attempt to reject and render inoperative white rule was Malcolm's response to his teacher, Mr. Ostrowski. Malcolm began to reject and rebel against derogatory appellations, as well as being constructed as a mascot of white people. His dive into Boston's and New York's black cultural and economic life was an attempt to render inoperative the dominance of white rule, though Malcolm later recognizes the insidious nature of the totalitarian tendency of the apparatuses of white supremacy evident in the ways white values of beauty seeped into decisions he made, whether they involved conking or dating white women.

Of course, all of this comes with qualifications that raise further questions that must be addressed. First, there is plenty of evidence that Malcolm's father grew up in a patriarchal religious and political milieu, and while Louise at times asserted her own authority, patriarchy was an unquestioned organizing feature of family life. Moreover, this political philosophy and theology would continue to be a part of Malcolm X's adult religious life and was also unquestioned. In this case, while one could argue that white sovereignty was rendered inoperative in Malcolm's family, but patriarchy remained a central organizing feature of the Nation of Islam and Islam.[113]

---

111. Haley, *The Autobiography of Malcolm X*, 11–12.

112. Malcolm provides numerous childhood examples of his rebelling against or subverting his mother's demands. In my view, these actions can be understood as his exercising his capacity for impotentiality. Haley, *The Autobiography of Malcolm X*, 8–9.

113. Michael Sawyer addresses the changes Malcolm made regarding his early

This would seem to negate the premise that parental care gives rise to an anarchic self. Second, Malcolm's initial conversion involved believing the Nation of Islam's founding myths, wherein white supremacy and sovereignty was rejected and replaced by the original supremacy and sovereignty of black (male) persons. Malcolm's conversion in prison would appear, then, to operate out of sovereignty—black sovereignty. While this represents a rejection of white sovereignty, it does not appear to be an exercise of an anarchic self.

My response to this requires first attending to a couple of Malcolm's conversions. When Malcolm was in prison, his brother Philbert wrote him a letter, indicating that he had "discovered the 'natural religion for the black man.'"[114] A later letter from his younger brother Reginald entreated Malcolm to stop eating pork and smoking cigarettes, which were taboo in the Nation of Islam, but Malcolm did not know this at the time.[115] Malcolm initially began to receive the teachings of the Nation of Islam through his brothers. One such teaching entailed an origin myth of Africans, which was proposed as "true knowledge." In this founding myth, "The black man, original man, built great empires and civilizations and cultures while the white man was still living on all fours in caves."[116] Later, the "devil white man . . . pillaged, murdered, raped, and exploited every race of man not white."[117] The story continues with the brainwashing of black people by whites and the false religion (Christianity) taught to black people.[118] While this myth and other teachings provided Malcolm and other believers with senses of self-esteem, self-confidence, and self-respect (political agency), it simply reverses the existing racial hierarchy and sovereignty. Originally, Africans (ostensibly men) ruled over the world before they were betrayed by a race of inferior white people, upending "a peaceful heaven on earth into a hell torn by quarrelling and fighting."[119] Malcolm's initial conversion included this catechism from the Nation of Islam, which itself was organized in terms of the rule of black men.

Because of Elijah Muhammad's consistent attention to Malcolm inside and, later, after prison, Malcolm expressed deep admiration for and

---

misogynistic treatment of women and his later respecting and accepting women in the revolution. Regardless, Sawyer points out, Malcolm X retained a paternalism toward African American women. Sawyer, *Black Minded*, 70–73.

114. Haley, *The Autobiography of Malcolm X*, 158.
115. Haley, *The Autobiography of Malcolm X*, 158.
116. Haley, *The Autobiography of Malcolm X*, 165.
117. Haley, *The Autobiography of Malcolm X*, 165.
118. Haley, *The Autobiography of Malcolm X*, 166.
119. Haley, *The Autobiography of Malcolm X*, 169.

devotion to Muhammad, which were evident in his ministry. This lasted until Malcolm could no longer deny the rumors of Muhammad's philandering. Another seed of difficulty for Malcolm began when he was silenced by Muhammad for remarks made after John F. Kennedy's assassination.[120] Not long after, Malcolm heard of a death order given by the man he had so long admired.[121] This knowledge propelled his exit from the Nation of Islam and the establishment of his own mosque.[122] His leaving the Nation of Islam also followed a pilgrimage to Mecca, which included visiting some African nations.[123] This pilgrimage accompanied other conversions. Malcolm X noted that Islam embraced people of all races and cultures, which lessened his tendency to see all white people as "devils."[124] At the same time, Malcolm accepted Allah as sovereign, suggesting that he no longer accepted the sovereignty of black people or a black man, like Elijah Muhammad. Allah's sovereignty was the only true sovereignty, relativizing any human iteration of sovereignty.

Malcolm X was murdered not long after his pilgrimages, so he was denied the chance to make further changes. This said, I argue that even before his conversion to the National of Islam, he was consistently rebelling against white sovereignty and supremacy. After his conversion, he accepted the Nation of Islam's belief in the past sovereignty of black people, which is another form of rejecting white sovereignty. Malcolm's last conversion to Islam resulted in his jettisoning the Nation of Islam's origin story and accepting the sovereignty of Allah, who accepted and cared for all human believers regardless of color or geography. All of this appears to belie the idea of the presence of an anarchic self, but I contend that it was present and might have emerged more clearly later if Malcolm had lived.

Let me explain. The anarchic self arises in the presence of the care of parents who are not operating out of the apparatuses of sovereignty, whether this entails patriarchy or white sovereignty. This care gives rise to senses of self-esteem, self-respect, and self-confidence that found the agentic freedom to actualize one's potentiality's (and impotentiality). Good-enough parental care, then, renders inoperative the apparatuses of sovereignty, though, as seen in Malcom's autobiography, the apparatuses of white supremacy continue to have their effects. Naturally, children internalize the narratives and beliefs that attend society's ideas about organizing society. In the West, the

120. Haley, *The Autobiography of Malcolm X*, 308–9.
121. Haley, *The Autobiography of Malcolm X*, 315.
122. Haley, *The Autobiography of Malcolm X*, 322–23.
123. Haley, *The Autobiography of Malcolm X*, 325.
124. See Haley, *The Autobiography of Malcolm X*, 370.

idea of sovereignty as existentially necessary for ordering social-political life has been produced and supported by the religious and secular apparatuses. The very idea of sovereignty's existential, if not ontological, facticity, becomes internalized. Malcolm initially did not question but later rejected white sovereignty. It was replaced, in part, by black sovereignty and patriarchy, which means that sovereignty remained unquestioned. All of this said, I suggest that Malcolm's original rejections in eighth grade, his dives into black culture, his conversion to the Nation of Islam, and his later conversion to Islam reveal the underlying seed of the anarchic self. The anarchic self is the burr in the saddle of every form of sovereignty, and this burr is especially evident in totalitarian forms of sovereignty such as white supremacy. The early pre-symbolic and later early symbolic organizations of the anarchic self are not lost when individuals adopt the beliefs of their religion, culture, and society. In other words, caring actions that do not stem from or are not conditioned by sovereignty's apparatuses are tacitly present throughout persons' lives, and, in political situations of oppression and marginalization, this early self, I argue, provides the foundation for resiliency and acts of resistance, rebellion, revolution, etc.

Toward the end of his short life, Malcolm gave a number of speeches that reflected radical changes in his outlook.

> True Islam taught me that it takes *all* of the religious, political, economic, psychological, and racial ingredients, or characteristics, to make the Human Family and the Human Society complete. Since I learned the *truth* in Mecca, my dearest friends have come to include *all* kinds—some Christians, Jews, Buddhists, Hindus, agnostics, and even atheists! I have friends who are called capitalists, Socialists, and Communists! Some of my friends are moderates, conservatives, extremists—some are even Uncle Toms. My friends today are black, brown, red, yellow, and *white*."[125]

This is an inclusive, pluralistic experience and vision of an anarchic self. Sovereignty of whatever kind constructs boundaries, divisions, and classes. Sovereignty is only tentatively and conditionally inclusive. In these speeches, Malcolm articulated a type of belonging that is not dependent on religion or political ideology linked to sovereignty. The "Human Family," in other words, is a metaphor that embraces all and represents a type of belonging where the organizing power in relationships is one of mutual personal recognition, acceptance, and care—an anarchic care rising from and creating anarchic selves.

125. Haley, *The Autobiography of Malcolm X*, 382.

In my imagination, if Malcolm had lived longer or if he had been born today, this inclusive vision would extend to other species. In the vision above, the Human Family is confined, understandably, to human beings. Malcolm X's conversion, I believe, entailed a recognition of all human beings and the understanding that we are all dependent on each other. The exclusion of other species from the political, as Agamben notes, has long been a Western political and religious project linked to beliefs in the necessity of human sovereignty.[126] But, as the climate crisis has shown time and again, the exclusion of other species from the Human Family has resulted in great harm to human beings, other species, and the Earth. The Human Family, in other words, depends on the well-being of our animal brothers and sisters—more broadly, our siblings. The destructive and divisive attributes of white sovereignty parallel human sovereignty over other species. I like to think that Malcolm X, because he had "a wide-open mind"[127] and an anarchic self, would have included other species as part of the family and society.

Conclusion

In the midst of all kinds of precarity, human beings are resilient, even as they suffer the slings and arrows of totalitarian systems such as the racial contract. It is important to explore and understand these resiliencies and resistances, regardless of gender. For Malcolm X and countless others, the racial contract of white supremacy and sovereignty led to various experiences of being aggrieved. I argued that being aggrieved cannot completely undo (except in death) the seed of an anarchic self that emerged from the caring ministrations of parents who make inoperative the apparatuses of white supremacy and sovereignty. This nascent anarchic self is the seed that gives rise to resiliencies, forms of resistance, and types of disobedience and rebellion. At its root, as was evident in the last months of Malcolm's life, is an inclusive vision of a human family and human society that thrives due to mutual interpersonal recognition, respect, and care—a vision and social contract where the foundation of care is *volo ut sis*.

---

126. Agamben, *The Open*.
127. Haley, *The Autobiography of Malcolm X*, 388.

7

Nelson Mandela, Transgression, and the Beauty of Becoming

> A hero is a man who believes in something, who is courageous, who may risk his life for the good of the community.[1]

> A work of art makes me feel alive because it reveals new linkages between myself and others and myself and the world.[2]

> I know this sounds as if I'm a cranky art teacher . . . But the thing is, in all my experience as an artist, I have found that there are some people who want to destroy beauty.[3]

> A man who takes away another man's freedom is a prisoner of hatred.[4]

The white faces fill the picture and in the middle of the photo is a teenage black girl, wearing a dress, looking determined, as she makes her way through the crowd. I will always remember seeing

---

1. Mandela as quoted in Stengel, *Mandela's Way*, 234.
2. Gay, *Freud on Sublimation*, 40.
3. Winspear, *Leaving Everything Most Loved*, 180.
4. Mandela, *Long Walk to Freedom*, 642.

photographs taken in Little Rock, Arkansas, during desegregation. The rage, hatred, hostility, and sheer mendacity are forever captured in the faces of white men and women, hurling insults and threats at this child. This photo depicts the utter ugliness of racism. The white people in this photo can only be described as hideous, their faces twisted and deformed by hatred. In this sea of malice, this black teenager walks resolutely, courageously, though I suspect with understandable fear. There is, when contrasted with the ugliness of the white racists, an understated beauty that emanates from her—a beauty that cannot be suborned by the narcissistic racial animosity that surrounds her.

The previous two chapters focused on understanding what sustains people in the midst of oppression, as well as how we might comprehend the rise and persistent appearance of anarchic or ungovernable selves who resist and seek to liberate themselves from the shackles of racism. In this chapter, I want to pursue a different line of argument. Martin Luther King Jr., Malcolm X, and Nelson Mandela (as well as innumerable women activists and revolutionaries) manifest a kind of aesthetics and beauty in their transgressing the apparatuses of racism. I am not necessarily suggesting that they were physically beautiful but rather that their way of being in a polis riven by racism manifested an aesthetics that was beautiful in the sense of being attractive. To make my case, I begin by explicating how I am using the terms *aesthetics* and *beauty*. More specifically, relying on Giorgio Agamben, Alfred North Whitehead, and Hannah Arendt, I situate aesthetics and its attributes in psychosocial development and the polis, which means there is a relation between aesthetics, care, and freedom. Once this is accomplished, I use Nelson Mandela's life story to illustrate a political aesthetics and beauty that were apparent in his transgressing the racist political ethos of South Africa. Aesthetics and beauty, with regard to care and justice, are not confined to people resisting racism, which is why I conclude the chapter with a brief discussion of the implications of this view with regard to the beauty of other species and climate activists. In other words, the aesthetics and beauty of other species are forms of existential transgression in the face of the ugliness of the ontological rift and its varied forms of objectification of other species and the Earth. Climate activists, at their best, find ways to transgress the ugliness of global capitalism, imperialism, etc., with the aim of preserving the manifold expressions of the lived and living beauty of all species.

I would like to offer a few clarifications before starting this journey. Readers may wonder why I take this approach when discussing racism and its relation, in this book, to men and boys. Racism entails valuations, which mean that standards of beauty, art, and aesthetics privilege white people and their works—art, literature, film, etc. I remember growing up in the 1960s when the refrain "Black is beautiful" made its way into public-political life. Like any slogan, it is both literal and metaphorical. "Black," as a color, is not in itself beautiful, but people who are constructed as "black" and their cultures are beautiful—physically, politically, etc. The slogan transgressed white standards of beauty and aesthetics. ("White" is also not in itself beautiful.) This is why I am interested in framing transgressions in terms of aesthetics and beauty. That said, I have long been *attracted* to writings about King, Malcolm X, Mandela and others (women and men) who have grown up in the midst of the pervasive ugliness of racism (and other forms of oppression) and yet have managed to exercise political virtues of courage, humility, hospitality, and generosity. It is clear that they attract a lot of people, and this chapter is my way of understanding and appreciating this attraction in terms of political aesthetics and beauty. Of course, I must rush to admit I am not an expert on the topics of aesthetics and beauty, and I am certainly not an expert on Nelson Mandela and South Africa. Nevertheless, connecting the ideas of beauty, aesthetics, politics, and transgression can offer a different perspective when encountering the ugliness and vices of the varied realities of political violence, hostility, and hatred endemic in the U.S. and elsewhere.

Aesthetics, Beauty, and the Polis

To situate aesthetics and beauty and their attributes in psychosocial development and the polis, I need to first offer some brief explanation of these two terms. From here, I turn first to how these terms apply to psychosocial development—potentiality to actuality—and to the polis and the exercise of political agency/freedom and virtues. Establishing this framework sets the stage for turning to the life of Nelson Mandela.

The idea of aesthetics, in the West, goes back to Plato and Aristotle. The term is derived from the Greek *aisthētikós*, which refers to sensory perception. The exploration of sensory perception, in part, led to a branch of philosophy concerned with notions of beauty and art, which has a long history into which we need not delve. For my purposes, however, it is important to point out that, for Aristotle, aesthetics and art are inextricably features of the polis. In his *Politics*, Aristotle argued that "when there are many [who contribute to the process of deliberation], each can bring his share of goodness and moral prudence; and when all meet together the people may thus become something in the nature of a single person, who—as he has many feet, many hands, and many senses—may also have many qualities of character and intelligence. This is the reason why the many are also better judges of music and the writings of poets."[5] Here we note that the sensory perception of collective deliberation can lead to better political and aesthetic judgments. Also implied here is the relation between aesthetics, beauty, and (political) virtues, which I will say more about later.

Aesthetics is an integral feature of life, and not just political life. In commenting on the philosophy of Alfred North Whitehead, Roland Faber writes, "There is never just an abstract world of logical relations, but always primarily an aesthetic world that also exhibits logical relations."[6] This aesthetic world, for Whitehead, is one of togetherness or belonging (not simply or solely deliberation), which Faber argues "is the most profound intuition of Whitehead's philosophy."[7] This world, in other words, "is not a plurality of isolated objects or particles or merely abstract ideas and forms or categories, but a togetherness of a becoming multiplicity of experiences."[8] This "becoming of togetherness is one of creativity and decay, of movements of change and novelty, of perishing and recreation, advancement and decadence."[9] In addition to togetherness and plurality, for Whitehead, "All experience is fundamentally aesthetic," though there are perversions that undermine the aesthetics of belongingness.[10] Racism (and other forms of oppression and exploitation) is an obvious perversion, producing an aesthetics of ugliness. It is important to mention that the aesthetics of belongingness is not, for Whitehead, to be confused with unity. Faber writes, "There is always something that escapes unity and unification."[11] What remains, even in moments or states of disjunction, is a dynamic and aesthetic multiplicity "always engaged in a process of mutuality and togetherness."[12]

Before elaborating further on aesthetics, I want to stress that, for Whitehead and psychoanalysts such as Christopher Bollas, aesthetics is not confined to symbolization or reason. It is an existential reality of experience.

5. Barker, *The Politics of Aristotle*, 123. Of course, Aristotle's "Many" vis-à-vis political deliberation does not include women and children.

6. Faber, *The Mind of Whitehead*, 479.

7. Faber, *The Mind of Whitehead*, 13. Faber points out the Whitehead sees hate, war, jealousy, greed (political vices) "as nothing but the perversion of togetherness." Racism, then, would clearly be a perversion of belongingness and not aesthetic or capable of beauty.

8. Faber, *The Mind of Whitehead*, 18.

9. Faber, *The Mind of Whitehead*, 20.

10. It is important to mention that "belongingness" does not simply refer to human beings. It entails all life and matter. Faber, *The Mind of Whitehead*, 186. Below, I address belongingness in terms of parent-children relations, which means that the aesthetics of care is embodied and relational.

11. Faber, *The Mind of Whitehead*, 151.

12. Faber, *The Mind of Whitehead*, 151.

In terms of human beings, aesthetics vis-à-vis experience pertains to infants' presymbolic organizations of experience—organizations that entail varied moments of belongingness, which can include disjunctions. There is, in brief, an aesthetics of semiosis. As mentioned in previous chapters, the parents' care for infants facilitates infants' nascent agentic capacities to actualize their potentiality, and this care is part of infants' organization of aesthetic experience—presymbolic semiosis. Eventually, the capacities for symbolization and reason are actualized, which can deepen and broaden children's and adults' aesthetic experiences of belongingness. As Whitehead notes, "The function of Reason is to promote the art of life" and "the Art of Life is the reason of Reason."[13]

Since I mentioned art, let me say a bit about aesthetics, art, and beauty before returning to aesthetics and politics. For Aristotle, while connected to the political, aesthetics is also related to the arts, and the arts have particular ends associated with beauty.[14] Leaping to the twentieth century, philosopher John Dewey remarked that art vis-à-vis beauty is "assumed to be the especial theme of aesthetics"[15] and "art . . . is a product of inspiration and skill."[16] When we listen to and observe a production of art, we know that which we deem to be beautiful requires considerable skills and creativity. This said, we do not need to confine aesthetics, beauty, and creativity to the most skilled among us. Children who draw, paint, sing, etc., are engaged in the practice of creating art. There is an aesthetics among the most "primitive" of artistic creations, revealing connections of multiplicity and belongingness. There is a hallway at the school where I teach that has numerous framed drawings by children and, while they will never be considered great works of art, they are clearly artistic creations exhibiting varying degrees of skill and inspiration. In other words, these drawings, these works of art, draw my attention and attraction. They are, for all practical purposes, works of beauty.

There is another important feature regarding aesthetics, art, and beauty. Psychoanalyst Volney Gay contends that a "work of art makes me feel alive because it reveals new linkages between myself and others and myself and the world."[17] Christopher Bollas has a similar view of art. He argues that art can serve as a transformational object,[18] wherein we experience a sense of being and rapport with the object—a sense that is attended

---

13. Whitehead, quoted in Faber, *The Mind of Whitehead*, 184, 197.
14. Barker, *The Politics of Aristotle*, 354.
15. Dewey, *Art as Experience*, 129.
16. Kris, *Psychoanalytic Explorations in Art*, 253.
17. Gay, *Freud on Sublimation*, 40.
18. Bollas, *The Shadow of the Object*, 13, 28.

by being with, which is analogous to Martin Buber's I-Thou experience[19] and Whitehead's notion of belongingness. The aesthetic inspiration of the artist, in other words, can evoke in the viewer (and artist) experiences of feeling alive and a sense of rapport with the object. It is not simply an object we see. We can hear and feel things that bring us to a space of connection that we did not experience before. There are aesthetics and beauty in a symphony, as well as in a caress. Put another way, art, in all its diverse forms, manifests beauty that attracts us and moves us to see or hear and experience something new, as well as an experience of being alive with the object (and others). Even if we return again and again to a painting in a museum, our musings may help us to see what we had not seen or experienced before. Or it may simply be that a work of art moves us to experience awe in the presence of beauty—beauty that was produced through incredible imagination and skill.

Beneath or behind our experiences of beauty are existential impermanence and insignificance. Aesthetics and beauty are part and parcel of life's precarity. Still life paintings represent, for instance, fruit long since gone—eaten or rotted—perhaps even before the painting was finished. Sculptures of famous figures memorialize people who died decades or centuries ago, many long forgotten. Origami is an art form that embraces impermanence. Beautiful works of paper art represent skill, inspiration, and impermanence. Ironically, art, in my view, is an attempt to capture beauty in the moment, recognizing that all art will succumb to the realities of time—existential transience. I add that part of our experience of beauty and aliveness is inextricably linked to and depends on the reality of existential impermanence. All life, all experience is transient, and this transience creates a space to savor moments of beauty, of aliveness, of rapport. When we try to hold on to permanence, beauty slips from our fingers, leaving only the ugliness of human grasping.

I mentioned existential insignificance vis-à-vis aesthetics and art. Human beings are valuing creatures. We assign significance, and our experiences of art, rapport, and aliveness indicate why and to what degree something is significant. Whatever we believe to be significant takes place against the background of existential impermanence. Go to any large art museum and you will view beautiful paintings of people from the past, people you do not know and who hold no significance for you. The painting may be significant, and this significance may be monetized. Yet, the painting itself is not permanent and is, in the end, existentially insignificant, as is the person depicted in the painting. Of course, the aesthetic experience of beauty is

---

19. Buber, *I and Thou*.

personally (and maybe socially) significant, but this experience is transient and insignificant, which is why experiences of aliveness, rapport, and beauty are sweet, if you will. The harder we try to hold on to significance, like King Laius and Shelley's Frankenstein did, tragedy results. In short, accepting existential insignificance and impermanence creates a space for experiencing the beauty of works of art.

I want to circle back to the relation between aesthetics and the political. Jim Josefson points out that Hannah Arendt, like Aristotle and Whitehead, contends that aesthetics and the beautiful are features of politics.[20] In his *Politics*, Aristotle mentions the aesthetics of political deliberation, which Arendt argues discloses a "common world."[21] These deliberations are founded on "an open deliberative community of plural equals that *may* reach enough consensus to act in concert."[22] There are a number of key points in Arendt's position. First, Arendt's space of appearances, which is the foundation of the polis, requires individuals who recognize and treat each other as persons—unique, inviolable, valued, responsive subjects. Second, treating others as unique means caring for them, which is why I have repeatedly mentioned the necessity of civic care (and faith) for a viable polis. This civic care enables individuals to actualize their potentialities (becoming), including their capacity for impotentiality—political freedom. It is necessary to stress that recognition of the singularity of others means acceptance of multiplicity or, in Arendt's term, plurality—echoing Whitehead. In short, the aesthetics of political deliberation is founded on interpersonal recognition[23] and civic care, which together are the basis for the very emergence and exercise of the political agencies of plural others.

A third aspect of Arendt's political philosophy and aesthetics is the necessity of forgiveness. For Arendt, included in the polis' civic faith is "the faculty to make and to keep promises."[24] Political agency and freedom means we make and keep promises, Arendt argues, and these promises are necessary given the uncertainties and insecurities of the future, as well as the reality of relational disjunctions due to broken promises.[25] Broken promises, in other words, disrupt the aesthetics of political deliberation and the creation

20. Josefson, *Hannah Arendt's Aesthetic Politics*.
21. Josefson, *Hannah Arendt's Aesthetic Politics*, 77.
22. Josefson, *Hannah Arendt's Aesthetic Politics*, 77.
23. For a discussion on the importance of personal recognition within the polis, see Honneth, *The Struggle for Recognition*; Macmurray, *Persons in Relation*.
24. Arendt, *The Human Condition*, 237.
25. Arendt, *The Human Condition*, 237. I would add that we make and keep promises because of our existential precarity, which includes the realities of existential insignificance and impermanence.

of a common world. We are faithful and, at times, faithless creatures, which, if the polis is to survive and thrive, requires the faculty of forgiveness. Arendt writes, "It is rather that forgiving attempts the seemingly impossible, to undo what has been done, and that it succeeds in making a new beginning where beginnings seemed to have become no longer possible."[26] In short, a decent aesthetics of a polis would entail customs and institutions that would facilitate relational repairs due to the broken promises that disrupt deliberations.

Naturally, we can imagine situations in which people make promises that are destructive to others. A polis may, like Plato and Aristotle's city-state, restrict promise-making and keeping to a particular class, ignoring the voices of others, like women. Or in a kleptocracy, such as Russia, promise-making and promise-keeping are distorted by dishonesty, corruption, and the use of coercion and violence to enforce the rule of kleptocrats. Kleptocrats, plutocrats, and other iterations of political elites reserve promise-making, promise-keeping, and forgiveness primarily for themselves, which accompanies the rejection of plurality or multiplicity in political life. In other words, as Whitehead and Arendt note, where promise-making and—keeping are corrupted by hierarchy, privilege, and force, multiplicity and plurality are diminished. This is a significant problem because, for Whitehead, multiplicity, which is "itself an abstraction from the aesthetics of experience," is a key feature of the very foundation of existence, including political existence.[27] There is multiplicity in becoming,[28] the arts,[29] modes of beauty,[30] consciousness,[31] etc. Multiplicity, for Whitehead, is a foundational feature of the belongingness of all creation, which means, in part, the existential uniqueness of all beings. Perversions of promise-making and—keeping undermine belongingness and multiplicity while producing an aesthetics of ugliness in the polis.

Similarly, for Arendt, political action ideally "must express a love of the world and commitment to actualizing the plurality within it."[32] Arendt notes, "In man, otherness, which he shares with everything that is, and distinctness, which he shares with everything alive, becomes uniqueness, and human plurality is the paradoxical plurality of unique beings."[33] What

---

26. Arendt, *The Promise of Politics*, 58.
27. Whitehead, quoted in in Faber, *The Mind of Whitehead*, 182.
28. Faber, *The Mind of Whitehead*, 188.
29. Faber, *The Mind of Whitehead*, 446.
30. Faber, *The Mind of Whitehead*, 470.
31. Faber, *The Mind of Whitehead*, 282.
32. Josefson, *Hannah Arendt's Aesthetic Politics*, 60.
33. Arendt, *The Human Condition*, 176.

we can glean from all of this is that the aesthetics of making and keeping promises in the polis, as well as of repairing broken promises, has the ends of political deliberation, a common pluralistic world, and the flourishing of members who, as a result of mutual personal recognition and care, actualize their potentialities. Actualization of the potentialities of singular beings, by definition, denotes multiplicity or plurality. Any political system that denies or undermines the existential political reality of multiplicity is not only an indecent society;[34] it is an ugly or unattractive society. A slavocracy or an apartheid society of white supremacy, wherein white racists make promises contingent on maintaining white superiority and black inferiority, is an indecent and despicable polis. In other words, these white promises of superiority are, in truth, perfidious, producing ugliness, as evident in the photos of Little Rock, Arkansas, and, I would add, the images of the near complete destruction of Gaza.

Connected to making and keeping promises and the capacity to forgive is the fourth feature of aesthetics and the polis, namely, political virtues.[35] Whitehead mentions nobility as a political virtue,[36] but I would prefer the virtue of integrity in relation to making and keeping promises. Nobility implies social class hierarchies, while the virtue of integrity can refer to any person in making and keeping promises. Integrity accompanies the virtue of honesty.[37] We make good faith pledges to each other as we deliberate in making decisions for the common good of all. Self-deception, deception of others, and lying are political vices that undermine civic faith. In short, a person who is dishonest or who accepts the repeated lies of political leaders is someone who has no or little integrity.[38]

---

34. See Margalit, *The Decent Society*.

35. The notion of "virtue" has a long history into which I need not delve. That said, let me briefly turn to Alasdair MacIntyre, who states that virtue is "an acquired human quality the possession and exercise of which tends to enable us to achieve goods which are internal to practices and the lack of which prevents us from achieving any such goods." Virtue is something that someone possesses and exercises, which, of course, is linked to knowledge, skills, and motivation. Political virtues entail the qualities and exercise of skills and practices that have as their ends the plurality, mutual personal recognition and care, deliberation in common, and repair. MacIntyre, *After Virtue*, 191.

36. Whitehead as cited in Faber, *The Mind of Whitehead*, 244.

37. See Arendt, *On Lying and Politics*.

38. Granted, there is a certain "art" to lying, which is especially evident in those politicians who can tell a good story. Also, we have seen how inveterate liars can attract many adherents who blindly follow, deceiving themselves about the truth. In Whitehead's schema, this kind of art and attraction are perversions because, in my view, the results are political polarization and destruction.

In addition to the virtue of honesty, the art of forgiving requires the political virtues of humility, prudence, patience, and generosity. One must have the humility to recognize and take accountability for one's failures, whether that is breaking promises or failing to recognize and respect the singularities of others. The virtues of prudence and patience involve recognizing when, where, and how to repair disjunctions (the art of repair), as well as realizing that repair may take a long time and a lot of work. There is also a virtue of courage, which is needed at times to risk repair or risk recognizing and caring for people who are excluded. Courage can also be exercised in the midst of political failures, critiquing unjust political situations and calling into account political leaders.

Of course, the virtues of courage, prudence, patience, and generosity can be manifested in acts of political violence, such as revolutions, rebellions, and protests. Similarly, those who wield political power may use the apparatuses of the state to commit violence in keeping people in check. Hobbes's leviathan is an example, and we might imagine those of the dominant political class exercising virtues of courage as they use political violence to maintain public order. How then are we to discern aesthetics and beauty given the realities of political violence and the presence of political virtues?

First of all, I agree with Arendt's[39] view that political violence is a failure of politics (collapse of the space of appearances and a common world or belongingness) and for Whitehead a perversion of aesthetics.[40] A failure of politics does not mean political violence is unjustified. The violent rebellions of enslaved persons, overthrowing of dictators, and violent protests seeking economic relief are just some examples where political violence may be justified, but engaging in justified acts of political violence does not mean one is innocent or unaccountable for destruction. However, political violence, while having, in these cases, the aims of justice, represent a failure of politics in that violence would not have been chosen if people had not been oppressed, marginalized, or excluded from political mutual personal recognition and deliberation. Let me add that political violence also is, in the act itself, anti-political, whether it is just or unjust.[41] By this I mean there can be no deliberation with the enemy and, therefore, the space of appearances, along with civic care and civic faith, does not exist between political enemies. In terms of aesthetics and beauty, there is never any beauty in political violence, even when justified. It is not and cannot be beautiful because in the moment of political violence the aesthetics of belongingness is abandoned.

---

39. Arendt, *The Human Condition*, 202.
40. Faber, *The Mind of Whitehead*, 438.
41. LaMothe, "Pastoral Theology."

The fifth and sixth attributes of aesthetics and politics are creativity and freedom, and both are connected to beauty. While the notions of creativity and freedom are deeply complex and contested, a brief depiction is sufficient for my purposes in constructing a framework to connect aesthetics and beauty to the political transgressions of Mandela. For Arendt, freedom is the condition of thought,[42] and thought necessarily implies the capacities for imagination and creativity.[43] Similarly, Whitehead links creativity with freedom, and both are essential to actual and potential experiences of togetherness.[44] In the previous two chapters, I discussed how there are nascent imagination, creativity, and freedom in early childhood, all of which are dependent on parents' reliable caring actions, which include repairs. There is an aesthetics and creativity in good-enough parents caring for their children, and this aesthetics entails parental imagination, freedom, and the resulting beauty of caring interactions. For instance, there are numerous paintings and photographs of parents caressing, cuddling, kissing, and feeding their children. A painting of a parent and child can by itself be judged by its aesthetics, creativity, and beauty, but the painting represents an aesthetic, creative moment of beauty between a caring parent and child. The beauty of this interaction is represented in the painting, but the painting can only point to and not capture the beauty of this aesthetic, embodied caring moment between parent and child.

Let me add to this by focusing on the child. In Agambenian terms, children's nascent agency and freedom are evident when they actualize their potentialities, as well as exercise their capacity for impotentiality—by preferring not. The actualization of potentiality includes aesthetics, in the sense of organizing experience and accompanying agentic action. There is, in other words, a nascent freedom or agency present—a freedom that attends nascent imagination. The beauty and aesthetics we observe in the parent-child creative, caring interaction includes beauty vis-à-vis the infant. The infant, then, is participating in an embodied, relational moment of aesthetic beauty, though the infant cannot construct conceptually the experience and

---

42. Arendt's notion of thinking is not mere cognition. It is clear in her book on Adolf Eichmann that genuine thought entails self-reflection, critical thinking, and imagination. Eichmann was thoughtless (but not stupid) in the sense of his lack of imagination, critical thinking, or self-reflection. Eichmann was a banal, boring, insipid man, like political leaders who also demonstrate a lack of imagination, critical thinking, and self-reflection. And we have mountains of evidence how dangerous these men are and how hideous their machinations. Arendt, *Eichmann in Jerusalem*.

43. Arendt, *The Human Condition*, 324.

44. Faber, *The Mind of Whitehead*, 303.

relation as beautiful. A key point is that beauty and aesthetics here are embodied, presymbolic, and relational.

It is important to extend this idea to the context of the polis. Parents, in exercising their capacities to care for children, are themselves situated in a polis, and it is, for Arendt, the polis that is the proper sphere of freedom.[45] For the polis to serve as a sphere of freedom, the space of appearances must include mutual personal recognition (singularities amid plurality), mutual care, and institutions and practices of repair (justice). As Donald Winnicott notes,[46] for parents to actualize the freedom and creativity in handling, holding, and caring for their children, they must be held and cared for by the larger polis. The care of the larger polis is instrumental in contributing to the freedom and creativity of parents in caring for their children.

We can understand how the polis' space of appearances and apparatuses can be crucial to parents' creativity, imagination, and freedom to care for their children and to children's nascent freedom and creative imagination, but what do the polis and political life itself have to do with beauty? Can the polis ever be beautiful? There is a good amount of literature that depicts varied kinds of utopias, and these utopias are creative, imaginative leaps representing the possibility of beauty vis-à-vis the polis. In Christian terms, the kingdom of God is represented as the penultimate beautiful polis. These imaginative creations point not only to how far the human polis is from a utopia but also to the possibility of the polis being, in its own way, beautiful. Utopian depictions of the polis may be dismissed, but they, in my view, point to the possibility of creating something beautiful, something aesthetically pleasing and moving, as a political community. More specifically, to act together, to deliberate together, vis-à-vis the polis' space of appearances requires mutual personal recognition, civic care, and civic trust, which found the individual and shared senses of self-esteem, self-confidence, and self-respect that are essential to political agency in the actualization of individual and shared potentialities. There is, then, an aesthetic to people exercising their freedom and creativity together, which is attractive and, perhaps, at times, beautiful. We do not have to aspire to a utopia to see and experience this. There is, for instance, something beautiful about people acting and deliberating together in caring for each other and others in the midst of a disaster like a tornado.

The implication of all this is that a polis may be ugly. There is an ugliness or lack of beauty in regimes that undermine the freedom and creativity of their citizens. In graphic novels, a corrupt city is portrayed as decrepit,

---

45. Arendt, *The Human Condition*, 30–31.
46. Winnicott, *Playing and Reality*.

chaotic, dingy, etc. Tolkien's *Lord of the Rings* portrays Mordor as filthy, disgusting, and noxious. In the real world, to return to the photographs of Little Rock, there is an embodied, relational ugliness in the politics of racism. Racism produces apparatuses that seek to undermine the esteem, confidence, respect, agency, and freedom of those it oppresses and marginalizes. The polis is not simply indecent, as Avishai Margalit notes;[47] it is, in my view, an embodiment of political ugliness.

This does not mean that imagination and creativity are absent in racist societies. Nor does it mean that there is no beauty in racist societies. Let me come at this in several ways. First, racists can exercise agency, freedom, and creativity in their shared deliberation and action. The Dred Scott decision represents a quite imaginative or creative piece of racist deliberation. There was a great deal of political agency manifested in the consistent creation of Jim and Jane Crow laws, as well as apartheid laws and policies. One might even argue that these examples represent a kind of aesthetics, but there is nothing beautiful or approximating the ideal of beauty in any of these or other examples. They are indeed all perversions of aesthetics. I would also mention that there is creativity, imagination, and freedom in designing and constructing weapons of mass destruction, but the use and ends of these weapons are ugly, not only because these weapons are aimed at destroying human beings but also because they destroy other species and their environment. Racism and war may exhibit a kind of aesthetics, but they are never beautiful. They are perversions and a failure of politics.

If racist societies are not beautiful, this does not mean that those who are oppressed are ugly or incapable of being beautiful or constructing beautiful objects. There can, in an indecent polis, be creativity, imagination, and freedom that are beautiful in spite of oppression and marginalization. In the previous two chapters, I indicated that King and Malcolm X engaged in their respective religious communities, wherein members deliberated together and used their imaginations and freedoms to resist the machinations of a racist society. The slogan "Black is beautiful" accompanies a communal and societal effort to celebrate and affirm the esteem, respect, confidence, agency, creativity, and freedom of African Americans. Even in the midst of Jim and Jane Crow laws and policies, African Americans manifested creativity and freedom in the maintenance of social-communal communication, care, and the arts—music, painting, sculpture, literature.

There is another important point to make. Above, I indicated that parents' care is situated within the context of the polis and the polis ideally cares for parents so they can care for their children. But, as demonstrated in the

---

47. Margalit, *The Decent Society*.

previous two chapters, a racist society finds innumerable ways to not care for parents of color. Nevertheless, good-enough parents, like Ruby Sales's, are able to render inoperative the apparatuses of racism in caring for their children. In so doing, they foster a space for their children to actualize their imagination, creativity, and freedom, which represents something beautiful in the midst of the ugliness of racism. This is why, in my view, Ruby calls her parents spiritual geniuses. She could have called them artists as well because they created a space for their children to flourish amid the ugliness of a racist society. Put differently, parents who render the apparatuses of racism inoperative manifest political virtues that make possible an aesthetic and experience that cannot be controlled, undermined, or destroyed (except through death) by racism. Beauty—embodied and relational—is, in these cases, politically transgressive and subversive because it reveals a freedom and creative imagination that exceed all attempts to undermine African Americans.

It is helpful to summarize the main points before turning to Mandela, political transgressions, and beauty. In general, aesthetics and beauty, existentially, reflect a belongingness or togetherness of a polis that is founded in embodied, relational care and mutual personal recognition, which, in turn, make possible aesthetic experiences of being alive. What we call beautiful takes inspiration and skill, whether we are talking about objects of beauty or practices seen and experienced as beautiful. Overall, aesthetics and beauty, I argue, are inextricably part of existential impermanence and insignificance. That is, our desire to create and experience beauty emerges from the reality of existential impermanence and insignificance, even as we are saying in the present that what is beautiful is significant. The relation between politics and aesthetics is more complicated, though clearly connected to belongingness, inspiration, skills, and impermanence. I noted that Aristotle, Whitehead, and Arendt linked beauty and aesthetics to politics. Deliberation in common is the foundation of beauty and aesthetics, and this deliberation entails the creation of spaces of appearances wherein there is sufficient mutual personal recognition, civic care, and civic faith amidst diverse (but equal) members who are actualizing their potentialities and capacity for impotentiality—freedom, agency, and flourishing. Personal recognition and actualization of potentialities necessarily mean a multiplicity of plural equals in this space of appearances. This common space of deliberation, of promise-making and promise-keeping, also requires practices of forgiveness, repairing moments of political disjunction that can threaten the aesthetics of political belongingness. Promise making and repair vis-à-vis the space of appearances and deliberation require the political virtues of integrity, honesty, humility, hospitality, patience, generosity, courage, and prudence. In other words, the practice of these virtues undergirds the aesthetics of political belongingness and deliberation of plural others. Two other features of the relation between politics and beauty are creativity and freedom, which have their origin in the good-enough care of parents for their children. While I argue that this care is dependent on the larger polis' civic care, it is not determined by this care. Parents, exercising political virtues and freedom, can render inoperative apparatuses of oppression, creating aesthetic spaces for their infants and children to actualize their potentialities (have agency) in the midst of embodied belongingness.

Mandela, Transgressions, and Political Beauty

Nelson Rolihlahla Mandela (Rolihlahla means Tree Shaker in Xhosa[48]—an apt name) was born into the Xhosa tribe July 18, 1918, in the small village of Mvezo.[49] Some of his earliest memories involve his father telling "stories of historic battles and heroic Xhosa warriors" and his mother recalling "Xhosa legends and fables that had come down from numberless generations."[50] While his father was a hereditary chief[51] and "an unofficial priest" of the Xhosa religion, Mandela's mother was a Methodist Christian. Initially, religion, Mandela writes, "was a ritual that I indulged in for my mother's sake and to which I attached no meaning."[52] Later, when Mandela went to a missionary school, "Religion was a part of the fabric of life and I attended each Sunday."[53] Mandela identified two central factors in his life, namely, "chieftaincy (Xhosa leadership) and the church."[54] Both significantly

48. Stengel, *Mandela's Way*, 227.
49. Sampson, *Mandela*, 5.
50. Mandela, *Long Walk to Freedom*, 11.
51. Sampson, *Mandela*, 5.
52. Mandela, *Long Walk to Freedom*, 20.
53. Mandela, *Long Walk to Freedom*, 20.
54. Mandela, *Long Walk to Freedom*, 20. Nelson Mandela, unlike Martin Luther King Jr., understood his desire for and commitment to freedom and justice for black people mainly in political, not religious, terms. While the political framework was dominant, Mandela's religious views and experiences were present, though much further in the background. While Mandela's religious experience and commitments took a back seat to his political obligations and self-understanding, they were not completely absent. He plainly states twice in his autobiography that Christianity was a key influence in his life, though it is difficult to be clear about how his religious experiences and values shaped his political experiences and commitments. This said, when Mandela was forty-two, he addressed a meeting of ministers in Cape Town. The meeting began with a minister's prayer that "stayed with me over these many years and was a source of strength at a difficult time." The prayer exemplifies the intersection of the political and religious aspects of his life. The minister "thanked the Lord for His bounty and

shaped Mandela's early experiences and commitments. It is apparent, in his autobiography, that political leadership or chieftaincy was in the foreground and the church in the background of his concerns, self-understanding, and motivations. Put differently, what becomes clear in his autobiography is the prevalence and importance of African culture in forming and framing his experience and views of the world. Since African culture for centuries intersected with Christian missionaries, Mandela's religious experience as a child was both Xhosan and Christian—with Xhosan culture and chieftaincy being the most prominent.[55]

Let me linger for a moment on Mandela's childhood. His father had four wives who each lived in their own *kraal*,[56] though these families were tightly connected, sharing meals, duties, etc. While close to his mother, Mandela, recalling his childhood, said, "I had mothers who were very supportive and regarded me as their son. Not as a stepson or half-son, as you would say in the culture amongst whites. They were mothers in the proper sense of the word."[57] The closeness to these mothers extended to their offspring as well.[58] There was, in brief, a sense of togetherness in this extended family—a togetherness that I contend emerged from mutual personal recognition and care that gave rise to shared experiences of being alive.

While Mandela's mother was a Christian, his father was not, though according to Anthony Sampson, his father had Christian friends and was respectful of Christians.[59] Sampson goes on to say that Mandela's father was strict, a believer in African religion, and a man "with no sense of inferiority toward whites."[60] When Mandela was nine, his father died, apparently from a lung condition from which he had suffered for some time. After his father died, Mandela and his mother left on "a long journey by foot from Qunu to the 'Great Place' of Mqhekezweni."[61] Jongintaba, leader of the Madiba

---

goodness, for His mercy and His concern for all men. But then he took the liberty of reminding the Lord that some of His subjects were more downtrodden than others, and that it sometimes seemed as though He was not paying attention. The minister then said that if the Lord did not show a little more initiative in leading the black man to salvation, the black man would have to take matters into his own two hands." Mandela, *Long Walk to Freedom*, 265.

55. Mandela noted that "The two principles that governed my life at Mqhekezweni were chieftaincy and the Church." Mandela, *Long Walk to Freedom*, 19.

56. Sampson, *Mandela*, 6.

57. Sampson, *Mandela*, 7.

58. Sampson, *Mandela*, 7.

59. Sampson, *Mandela*, 6–7.

60. Sampson, *Mandela*, 6.

61. Sampson, *Mandela*, 9.

clan, "readily agreed to adopt Mandela as if he were his own son."[62] But it is important to stress Mandela's experiences of Xhosa belonging prior to his father's death and the journey to the Madiba tribe.

The importance of Xhosan traditions is evident in one of the key turning points in Mandela's life—his initiation into adulthood, which was a cultural, spiritual, and I would add, political experience.[63] Also, during his teen years, two experiences seemed to awaken Mandela's political consciousness, moving him slowly down the road to political chieftaincy instead of the religious chieftaincy as embodied in the life of fellow South African Archbishop Tutu. Mandela had a passion for learning about African history, and he set out to listen to the "most ancient of chiefs," Zwelibhangile Joyi.[64] From Chief Joyi, he learned how the white man came to Africa with "fire-breathing weapons," shattering "the fellowship of the various tribes."[65] He listened to heroic tales of Xhosa warriors and learned about the dignity and courage of his people. After his initiation into adulthood at age sixteen, Mandela listened to Chief Meligqili tell the audience that Xhosas "are slaves in our own country. We are tenants on our own soil."[66] Mandela initially rejected these words, because, at that age, he did not perceive or experience the white man as an oppressor. His response was to become angry at the chief, only later realizing that "his words soon began to work in me."[67] Both chiefs initiated a gradual turn or conversion in Mandela's political views and experience. Paulo Freire's concept of conscientization fits here.[68] As he grew older and encountered the white South African world, Mandela gradually became increasingly aware of the pervasive racism and oppression in South Africa.

Childhood lays the foundation for adult life and, here, for Mandela's adult political life with its transgressions and beauty.[69] In other words, I argue that Mandela's early life exhibits a political aesthetics that would remain central to the rest of his life and activism. Let me approach this by

62. Sampson, *Mandela*, 9.
63. Mandela, *Long Walk to Freedom*, 11, 25–29.
64. Mandela, *Long Walk to Freedom*, 23.
65. Mandela, *Long Walk to Freedom*, 23.
66. Mandela, *Long Walk to Freedom*, 30.
67. Mandela, *Long Walk to Freedom*, 30.
68. Freire, "Conscientisation."
69. Lest we think that Mandela's childhood had little to do with his later political life, Mandela himself said, "To be an African in South Africa means one is politicized from the moment of one's birth, whether one acknowledges it or not. An African child is born in an African Only hospital, taken home in an African Only bus, lives in an African Only area, and attends African Only schools, if he attends at all." Mandela, *Long Walk to Freedom*, 95.

first noting that parental care, in this case primarily maternal, entailed four mothers and, later, surrogate fathers. The *kraals*, in other words, were a type of polis, existing within the larger tribal polis. In this *kraal* polis, while patriarchal, a sense of belongingness, linked to parental care,[70] shared trust, and mutual personal recognition, founded his sense of being alive with plural others—siblings, half-siblings, etc. Mandela said that the underlying premise of African family and tribal existence is *Umuntu ngumuntu ngabantu*, "A person is a person through other people."[71] This premise of political life founds the aesthetics of togetherness, as well as the inherent dignity or integrity of each person, which, in turn, demands mutual respect and affirms the necessity of plurality or multiplicity of life and agency.

While his father was not nearly as present as his mothers,[72] Mandela would have observed his father's courage in his dealing with white people, as well as listened to the stories of the courage of past and present Xhosa heroes.[73] Clearly, he was learning that courage is a political virtue, exercised on behalf of protecting and liberating members of the tribe. When Mandela was attending school, an African poet, Krune Mqhayi, said, "The assegai stands for what is glorious and true in African history; it is a symbol of the African as warrior and the African as artist."[74] The virtue of courage, given this, is aesthetic and situated firmly in the political—in belongingness. He would have many occasions in adulthood when this virtue was tested in the fires of South African racist political and economic oppression of Indigenous Africans.

The virtue of courage Mandela observed in his father and in other leaders accompanied other virtues that would shape his adult life. After Mandela's father died, the acting regent, Jongintaba Dalindyebo—a leader who would teach Mandela a great deal about political leadership—generously adopted him.[75] The assembly, where the regent presided, "was a democracy in its purest form. There may have been a hierarchy of importance among speakers, but everyone was heard."[76] Despite the often-obstreperous

70. Mandela uses the term *love*, saying that it was the most important thing to him. I use the more general term of care to expand the frame to the polis. Stengel, *Mandela's Way*, 181.

71. Stengel, *Mandela's Way*, 231.

72. Mandela asserted that while "my mother was the center of my existence, I defined myself through my father." Mandela, *Long Walk to Freedom*, 14–15.

73. Mandela, *Long Walk to Freedom*, 12–13.

74. Mandela, *Long Walk to Freedom*, 41.

75. Mandela, *Long Walk to Freedom*, 20.

76. Mandela, *Long Walk to Freedom*, 21. Mandela knew well that the women of the tribe were deemed second-class citizens, a fact that the adult Mandela worked hard to change.

conversations in these political deliberations, the regent "simply listened, not defending himself."[77] Mandela continues, "As a leader, I have always followed the principles I first saw demonstrated by the regent at the Great Palace. I have always endeavored to listen to what each and every person in a discussion had to say before venturing my own opinion."[78] In my view, the regent, and later Mandela, manifested several political virtues, namely, patience, respect, generosity, humility, and prudence. While Mandela admitted he was stubborn, he, like the regent, demonstrated a significant amount of patience in listening to diverse views, whether in the African National Congress, in prison, or as president of South Africa. To genuinely listen in contentious deliberations also requires generosity and respect for the speaker, as well as prudence regarding when and when not to speak. And note that Mandela said at the end of the deliberations with the regent, he offered his own "opinion," which suggests a kind of humility. The regent, and later Mandela, had a voice and an opinion like other members of the community. The regent, in other words, exercised an art that Mandela carefully observed and remembered, and this art is situated in the aesthetics of togetherness—a togetherness founded on mutual personal recognition and respect, as well as civic care and trust.

The aesthetics of deliberation included two other lessons Mandela learned as a child. One day, playing with his friends, Mandela jumped onto the back of a donkey. The donkey "bolted into a nearby thornbush,"[79] trying to unseat him. Mandela was indeed thrown, and he rose with scratches on his face and body and felt humiliated in front of his friends. "I had lost face," Mandela states, "among my friends. Even though it was a donkey that unseated me, I learned that to humiliate another person is to make him suffer an unnecessarily cruel fate. Even as a boy, I defeated my opponents without dishonoring them."[80] This painful lesson not only fostered a deep empathy for people being humiliated (innumerable Indigenous people); it also led to his exercising the virtue of respecting others, even when they were racists. I suggest that this respect is integral to the aesthetics of political life in that it manifests a fundamental principle of political life, namely, belongingness, as well as the potential for belongingness. Put differently, humiliating people involves misrecognition, a reduction of the space of appearances, and an exclusion from experiences of togetherness (e.g., social and political alienation). By contrast, exercising the virtue of respect keeps open the possibility

77. Mandela, *Long Walk to Freedom*, 21.
78. Mandela, *Long Walk to Freedom*, 21.
79. Mandela, *Long Walk to Freedom*, 10.
80. Mandela, *Long Walk to Freedom*, 10.

of togetherness in situations where there is alienation, such as racist humiliations. To exercise this virtue requires the virtues of courage, generosity, and patience, as we will see when I shift to Mandela's adult life.

Two more features of Mandela's childhood are worth mentioning, namely, freedom and creativity, because they were central to his political life and liberative transgressions as an adult. Mandela recalled that "from an early age, I spent most of my free time in the veld playing and fighting with other boys of the village ... At night I shared my food and blanket with these same boys. I was no more than five when I became a herd-boy, looking after sheep and calves in the fields."[81] Within the confines of village and family life with its duties and responsibilities, Mandela, as a child, experienced a sense of freedom. At this early age, he did not yet consciously experience the oppressive policies and laws that restricted African freedoms with regard to association and movement. I suggest that Mandela's experience of freedom was rooted in the care he experienced in his family (with four mothers and their children) and in his village, wherein mutual personal recognition created spaces of appearances for Mandela and others to actualize their potentialities, including their potentiality to exercise impotentiality.

Note that part of the playing (freedom) in the veld included fighting other boys. Mandela said that it was in the veld, playing with other boys, that he "learned to stick fight."[82] Two ideas come to mind about this. The first is that Mandela had a number of friends he fought with, which suggests developing the ability to repair relationships. The capacity to repair is an essential element of political freedom and togetherness, which for Arendt entails the capacity to forgive.[83] Another interesting feature of this part of his story is that the sentence on stick fighting was followed by this: "From these days I date my love of the veld, of open spaces, the simple beauties of nature, the clean line of the horizon."[84] There is an intersection here of polis, freedom, nature, and beauty. In other words, the beauty of the veld is inextricably tied to the experience and exercise of freedom in Mandela's playing with friends.

Closely associated with freedom in childhood is creativity. Mandela writes, "As boys, we were mostly left to our own devices [freedom]. We played with toys we made ourselves. We molded animals and birds out of clay. We made ox-driven sleighs out of branches. Nature was our playground."[85] A

---

81. Mandela, *Long Walk to Freedom*, 9.
82. Mandela, *Long Walk to Freedom*, 9.
83. Arendt, *The Promise of Politics*.
84. Mandela, *Long Walk to Freedom*, 9.
85. Mandela, *Long Walk to Freedom*, 9.

great deal of creativity was part of their play, and it is important to stress that this play entailed the aesthetics of togetherness. In other words, creating objects to play requires skills and inspiration. While the primary function of these objects was communal play, they were, nevertheless, works of art. The lesson here, in my view, is that play and creativity are central to experiences of togetherness and aliveness. The racist policies of South African governments denied and restricted creative play and the aesthetics of togetherness between white people and Indigenous people. I suggest that Mandela's childhood experiences of freedom and creativity vis-à-vis the aesthetic of togetherness and aliveness would serve as impetus and hope in his political transgressions. By this I mean that Mandela, in exercising his impotentiality in preferring not to abide by racist policies and laws, held out the potential for working with and among whites in creating a new South Africa. But I am getting ahead of myself.

Let me summarize what I have gleaned regarding Mandela's formative years vis-à-vis aesthetics, beauty, and the polis. In his family, Mandela experienced the care and trust of his mothers, which was founded on mutual personal recognition (*Umuntu ngumuntu ngabantu*) and which created spaces for Mandela to actualize his potentialities and experience a sense of aliveness with others. There was, in this, an aesthetic of belongingness. During this time, he heard stories about the family's past political and religious leaders. In addition, he had opportunities to observe leaders like his father and, later, the regent who adopted him as his son. He learned, from them, the importance of courage, respect, generosity, and patience with regard to the diverse voices of others.

Childhood provided the foundation for Mandela's adult political activism and leadership, but his experiences in adulthood also deepened and expanded the beauty of his political life. Unlike King and Malcolm X, as a child Mandela did not have a singular epiphany regarding the ugliness of racism and its pervasiveness in political and economic life in South Africa. Mandela writes, "I had no epiphany, no singular revelation, no moment of truth, but a steady accumulation of a thousand slights, a thousand unremembered moments, produced in me anger, a rebelliousness, a desire to fight the system that imprisoned my people."[86] While Mandela was at university, he had numerous friends who were actively engaged in political organizations, protests, etc.[87] Mandela had not yet taken this road, despite the thousand slights. Nevertheless, in the political community of the university, Mandela's anger and political rebelliousness against the injustices of

---

86. Mandela, *Long Walk to Freedom*, 95.
87. Sampson, *Mandela*, 25–28.

racism were manifested. Anthony Sampson writes that Mandela was elected to be on the Students' Representative Council at Fort Hare, a well-regarded university. Only a quarter of the students voted in protest of the conditions black students faced. Mandela and others on the council resigned in protest because of the terrible food served to the black students.[88] The election was held again, and the same six students were elected. After this election, the other five elected representatives "agreed to stay on the council, but Mandela felt he could not ignore the views of the majority, and he resigned."[89] Mandela was warned by the administration that if he did not serve on the council, he would be expelled. He continued to refuse, and he was expelled. Sampson writes that "Mandela's stubbornness came to the fore."[90]

While this rebellion or transgression did not occur in the larger political arena, it was, in part, a political action against the systemic realities of racism. Also, while I can certainly understand why Mandela would be seen as obstinate or stubborn, in this and other transgressions, I would see this act as an exercise of the political virtues of integrity and courage. Mandela knew that the consequences of this act would anger and disappoint the regent, who had treated him as a son and sent him to university. It took courage and integrity to stand up to the administration and others who were putting pressure on Mandela to stay on the council. I add here that Mandela's exercise of freedom does not quite fit Agamben's idea of impotentiality—preferring not. To "prefer not" is in the subjunctive mood, implying the possibility of a discussion that may result in the task being carried out. There is no subjunctive mood in Mandela's decision to refuse the demands of the administration to sit on the council. Simply, his exercise of freedom was "I will not serve. End of discussion." "I will not" and the virtues of integrity and courage appeared in this political sphere.

A more complicated exercise of freedom took place when he arrived back home and faced the wrath of the regent. The regent demanded that Mandela apologize, which he refused to do, displaying not simply stubbornness but integrity. Not long after this incident, the regent called Mandela and Justice (a son of the regent) and said that, because he was not long for this world, he had "arranged unions for both of you."[91] They left feeling dejected. "At the time," Mandela writes, "I was more advanced socially than politically. While I would not have considered fighting the political system

---

88. The African students learned "that the white students at Rhodes University... were much better fed." Sampson, *Mandela*, 28.

89. Sampson, *Mandela*, 28.

90. Sampson, *Mandela*, 29.

91. Mandela, *Long Walk to Freedom*, 53.

of the white man, I was quite prepared to rebel against the social system of my own people."[92] The social system he was intending to transgress was arranged marriages. Mandela and Justice concocted a plan to escape to Johannesburg, the consequences being that they would be on their own, losing the social and economic resources of the regent. This time, "I will not" led not to expulsion but rather to self-expulsion. In my view, this refusal and transgression required a great deal of courage, as well as integrity.

Anyone who has read Mandela's autobiography will recognize that Mandela, in response to the regent, attempted to manipulate the system through half-truths and lies. This continued in Johannesburg when he and Justice sought help from leaders who knew the regent, as well as when a friend of Mandela was arrested for possessing a gun.[93] Lying is not a virtue, but the situations Mandela faced were complicated. In relation to the regent and his friends, Mandela had little social or political power to exercise his freedom, his capacity to prefer or will not. He was in a vulnerable position, having to rely on any available talents and resources to "will not." Moreover, in relation to the prevalence of racist apparatuses, the situation was even more precarious. Why would honesty be due to oppressors? I argue that what was integral to Mandela at this stage of his political and social transgression was the issue of fairness. What happened at university regarding the treatment of African students was unfair, and being expected to obey the regent to marry was similarly unfair. In both instances, Mandela's agency and freedom were overlooked or denied. The decision to rebel was a sign of his integrity to the principle of fairness due to him and to others. Put differently, to prefer not, to will not, was an exercise of courageous freedom based on what he saw as an injustice or unfairness. As Mandela aged, he was more honest and forthright, but this did not mean he was transparent with his oppressors. In addition, the machinations he learned in transgressing the regent's demands would serve him well in navigating the political labyrinths of white political supremacy and its institutions.

While Mandela was not ready to rebel against the white man, he would soon find himself in situations where he was offered many opportunities to do so. "In 1946," Mandela writes, "a number of critical events occurred that shaped my political development and the direction of the struggle."[94] There was a massive strike by African miners, which led to the arrests and political prosecutions of fifty-two men.[95] Later that year, "The Smuts govern-

---

92. Mandela, *Long Walk to Freedom*, 54.
93. Mandela, *Long Walk to Freedom*, 67.
94. Mandela, *Long Walk to Freedom*, 101.
95. Mandela, *Long Walk to Freedom*, 102–3.

ment passed the Asiatic Land Tenure Act," which Mandela said changed his approach to political work.[96] The Indian protests against this act "became a model for the type of protests that we in the Youth League were calling for. It instilled a spirit of defiance and radicalism among the people,"[97] which included Mandela. One example of this was the Defiance Campaign of 1952, which involved protests against six unjust laws.[98] In July of that year, Mandela, along with other leaders, was arrested. "The charge was violation of the Suppression of Communism Act."[99] This campaign was pivotal in Mandela's political development and leadership. He writes,

> The campaign freed me from any lingering sense of doubt or inferiority I might still have felt; it liberated me from feeling overwhelmed by the power and seeming invincibility of the white man and his institutions. But now the white man had felt the power of my punches and I could walk upright like a man, and look everyone in the eye with dignity that comes from not having succumbed to oppression and fear. I had come of age as a freedom fighter.[100]

This statement reflects, in my view, the aesthetics of dignity and transgressive political agency.

Being a freedom fighter could be construed to refer to black South Africans only, but this was not the case. In 1954, the National Action Council invited diverse organizations to convene to establish a freedom charter.[101] One of the leaflets read:

> We call the people of South Africa black and white—let us speak of freedom! . . . Let the voices of all people be heard. And let the demands of all the people for the things that will make us free be recorded. Let the demands be gathered together in a great charter of freedom.[102]

Mandela and others, as freedom fighters, were fighting for the freedoms of all people. Implicit in this aim is the belief that racism, while severely

---

96. Mandela, *Long Walk to Freedom*, 103. This act restricted Indians from the right to buy property, which galvanized the Indian community.

97. Mandela, *Long Walk to Freedom*, 104. The Youth League was part of African National Congress, which Mandela had joined.

98. Sampson, *Mandela*, 67.

99. Mandela, *Long Walk to Freedom*, 136.

100. Mandela, *Long Walk to Freedom*, 140.

101. Mandela, *Long Walk to Freedom*, 171.

102. Mandela, *Long Walk to Freedom*, 172.

impacting black South Africans, also undermined the freedom of white South Africans. In addition, there is the belief that all people, white and all people of color, belong in the South African polis and that this belonging required political agency, mutual personal care, civic faith and trust, and justice, all of which were undermined by political, economic, and societal racist apparatuses. This charter and Mandela's embrace of it are illustrations of the aesthetics of the possibility of political belonging, which may be said to be beautiful while its achievement is even more so.

Of course, to be a freedom fighter implies the thorny issue of the use of political violence. Mandela advocated for nonviolent resistance until such time that state-sanctioned violence against Africans could no longer be tolerated.[103] "I myself," Mandela writes, "believed . . . that nonviolence was a tactic that should be abandoned when it no longer worked."[104] At an African National Congress meeting, Mandela "explained why I believed we had no choice but to turn to violence."[105] Naturally, there was a choice, but Mandela firmly believed that nonviolence was not working and, more importantly, that it was unethical to promote nonviolence when people were being brutalized and killed by state apparatuses. This said, Mandela (and others), recognizing the dangers and ethical issues of political violence, wished "to guide this violence . . . according to the principles where we save lives by attacking symbols of oppression, and not people."[106] Not long after this change in African National Congress policy, an arrest warrant was issued for Mandela and he went underground to continue the struggle that was his life.[107]

In 1962, Mandela was arrested by South African police and placed on trial.[108] "Prison," Mandela contends, "not only robs you of your freedom, it attempts to take away your identity. Everyone wears the same uniform, eats the same food, follows the same schedule. It is by definition a purely authoritarian state that tolerates no independence or individuality."[109] Prison would become another arena where Mandela would continue his struggle for freedom. Early on, Mandela refused (willed not) to wear shorts (a form of degradation to black Africans), and he refused to eat the food

103. Sampson, *Mandela*, 145–46.
104. Mandela, *Long Walk to Freedom*, 272.
105. Mandela, *Long Walk to Freedom*, 271.
106. Mandela, *Long Walk to Freedom*, 272.
107. Mandela, *Long Walk to Freedom*, 276.
108. Mandela, *Long Walk to Freedom*, 314.
109. Mandela, *Long Walk to Freedom*, 333.

given to him.[110] This first protest was followed by numerous others once he was transferred to Robben Island. Mandela's militancy in prison was guided by the principles of dignity (self and other), freedom, and justice/fairness. Even given the degrading and humiliating practices of prison life, Mandela treated the guards and the wardens with respect—respect for them as persons who thus merited a basic level of respect.

To continue to stand up and transgress the rules of prison life, where the guards held all the power and prisoners were in even more precarious situations than they were in an apartheid society, took a considerable amount of courage. Mandela is candid about the times he was afraid when confronting the guards or prison authorities, yet he acted on behalf of himself and other prisoners for twenty-seven years. The virtue of courage is a virtue precisely because one acts despite one's fear. This virtue was accompanied by his integrity in holding to the values of resistance in the pursuit of freedom and justice. This integrity and pursuit, like the leaflet quoted above, meant not denying freedom and justice to white South Africans. Mandela writes, "It was during those long, lonely years that my hunger for the freedom of my own people became a hunger for the freedom of all people . . . I knew as well as I knew anything that the oppressor must be liberated just as surely as the oppressed. A man who takes away another man's freedom is a prisoner of hatred."[111] Care, freedom, and justice for all necessarily embraces diversity—diversity of opinions, lifestyles, persons, groups, etc.[112] There is, in all this, a tapestry of political aesthetics and beauty, which Mandela would carry into his political life after prison.

Before Mandela was released from prison, he was in talks with South African government leaders who were under increasing political and economic pressure from the international community. Even though he could have worked out a deal for his release, Mandela told President de Klerk that he would continue his work with the African National Congress once released. The struggle was his life, both in prison and in the larger society, and he would not succumb to the temptation to be freed from prison at the cost of his political vocation. This reveals his commitment to the cause of freedom, as well as his courage and integrity. On February 11, 1990, Mandela, on his own terms, walked out of prison a free man.[113] "My ten thousand days of imprisonment were over," he exclaimed. But his work had only begun in earnest since he had to continue to negotiate with President de Klerk

---

110. Mandela, *Long Walk to Freedom*, 561.
111. Mandela, *Long Walk to Freedom*, 642.
112. See Sampson, *Mandela*, 512–13.
113. Mandela, *Long Walk to Freedom*, 265.

and others in his own organization on a transition to democratic rule.[114] In 1994, Mandela was elected president of South Africa, and the "generals and police chiefs saluted him and pledged loyalty." Mandela, reflecting on this moment, writes that a "few years before they would not have saluted but arrested me."[115] Once elected, Mandela would continue his struggle, though in the form of governing. In this struggle, he relied on his integrity, courage, and humility—virtues forged in the fires of apartheid and prison.

Let me add here that Mandela, in his dealings with prison guards and officials, white government officials, and others, also demonstrated the (political) virtues of hospitality and generosity. Warrant Officer Swart was assigned to Mandela and told him, sheepishly, that when driving prisoners to work sites, he used to deliberately hit bumps to make the ride more unpleasant for the prisoners. Mandela laughed and later wrote that Swart "became like a younger brother to me."[116] White author Richard Stengel recalls Mandela telling Stengel's future wife, "I give you my blessing [for their marriage] because Richard is my son."[117] It is not an accident that Stengel's memory is at the very end of his book, in the chapter titled "The Gift." Mandela's hospitality and generosity extended to black *and* white persons. In addition, even his enemies were recipients of his generosity and hospitality. Even as he pushed for freedoms, Mandela was respectful (and firm) in his meetings with Presidents Botha and de Klerk. In his generosity and hospitality, Mandela demonstrated respect for them as persons even though they had participated in policies and practices that led to the eclipse of political and economic freedoms of millions of native South Africans. I would add that these political virtues commanded respect from white officers and officials.

The virtues of courage, humility, hospitality, and generosity were also evident in Mandela's forgiving his enemies.[118] Above, I mentioned that political aesthetics require promise-making and forgiveness. As Arendt stated, a thriving polis depends on practices of forgiveness because human beings are also promise-breaking creatures. Anthony Sampson points out that forgiveness "was not an obvious role for him to play. In his years before jail he had been quite aggressive ... The younger Mandela enjoyed confronting his enemies."[119] This does not mean that age and maturity softened or weakened

114. Sampson, *Mandela*, 424–68.
115. Sampson, *Mandela*, 485.
116. Mandela, *Long Walk to Freedom*, 265.
117. Stengel, *Mandela's Way*, 239.
118. I wish to stress that forgiveness and reconciliation were central to many Black South Africans, perhaps the most famous being Desmund Tutu. Tutu, *No Future without Forgiveness*.
119. Sampson, *Mandela*, 512.

Mandela's pursuit of justice. Rather, Mandela continued to push, confront, etc., but he did so by exercising his political virtues toward all, including his enemies. I think he, and other leaders, such as Desmond Tutu, recognized that the future of South Africa depended on working together for the common good, which required the hard work of forgiveness and reconciliation. The political practice of forgiveness and reconciliation founds, in many ways, the aesthetics of politics and, when we observe and experience the result, there is beauty.

A Brief Word on Political Aesthetics and Beauty in the Anthropocene Age

I have been focusing on beauty in relation to acts of political transgression toward racist apparatuses. Shifting to the climate emergency may come across as abrupt, as having little or nothing to do with Mandela and transgressions. But I would argue that the ugliness of racism parallels the political ugliness of rampant neoliberal capitalism, imperialism, and colonization of nature. Other species and the Earth are objectified, depersonalized, exist outside the zones of care and justice—outside the zone of the political. When other species are cared about and for, by and large, this care falls under the heading of instrumental epistemology, which includes the construction of other species as inferior—the ontological rift between humans and other species. Consider the profound and horrific ugliness of factory farms, industrial slaughterhouses (untold billions of sentient beings), and laboratory experimentations. Observe the environmental devastation of mountaintop removal mining. Ponder the likelihood that half of the known species will become extinct by the end of this century.[120] Just as racism is a constant threat to the flourishing of the polis because its apparatuses produce an ontological rift between white and black persons, so too are the apparatuses of capitalism, imperialism, and the colonization that produce and maintain an ontological rift between human beings and other species, leading to an environmental catastrophe that will destroy the very foundation of political life, namely, a habitable Earth.

The aesthetics and beauty of politics in the climate crisis entail rendering inoperative apparatuses of the ontological rift, and rendering inoperative necessarily means transgression. These transgressions include recognition of the singularities of other species, which, in turn, accompanies including them in the polis' space of appearances. To recognize the singularity of other species is not based on the fact that we need a biodiverse Earth to survive

120. See Wilson, *The Future of Life*.

and thrive as human beings. That is true, but recognition of the singularities of other species and the Earth accompanies the categorical command to respect and care for these species, which also means that other species and the Earth are included in the zone of justice. To be sure, the aesthetics of political deliberation does not directly apply to other species, but our deliberations must include their needs, their flourishing. This may take the form of recognizing the personhood of other species, of rivers, of lands, etc., which is happening in New Zealand and elsewhere.[121] An ecological politics, then, requires an aesthetics and beauty that seeks to render inoperative Western political-economic apparatuses that produce the ontological rift and the accompanying ugliness of wanton exploitation of other species and the Earth.

Conclusion

We tend to think of aesthetics and beauty in terms of art and not politics and transgression. Yet, most people can agree that racism in the body politic is ugly. There is an ugliness in racism—an ugliness born of vices of hatred, arrogance/pride, bitterness, fear masquerading as bravado, and rancorous divisions. The ugliness of racism is evident in its soullessness in that it cannot give rise to the political mutual personal recognition and care necessary for the flourishing of all. In this chapter, I have highlighted the aesthetics and beauty of political transgressions vis-à-vis racist state(s) apparatuses that functioned to oppress and marginalize Indigenous South Africans and other communities of color. Even in the midst of political oppression and violence, glimmers of political aesthetics and beauty gathered strength and eventually flourished—a flourishing that was transgressive and revolutionary. The beauty and aesthetics of political belonging and deliberation, I argued, depend on embodied, relational care and mutual personal recognition, which, in turn, make possible deliberative agencies and attendant experiences of being alive together. In addition, aesthetics and beauty require skills and practices, which I suggested fall under the category of political virtues—courage, humility, hospitality, and generosity. These virtues found the practices of forgiveness and reconciliation, which are necessary to mend the fabric of political deliberation. These are the ingredients that make politics an art—a beautiful work of art in a process that Mandela and others struggled to create. We can extend this political aesthetics and beauty to exercising the virtues

---

121. A quick internet search will reveal the growing movement to declare rivers, lakes, etc., persons. The notion of person then means that rivers have political rights. While this is important, the use of "rights" language tends to overlook the categorical existential command to care for the Earth and other species.

of courage, humility, hospitality, and generosity toward the singularities of other species and the Earth. These virtues will include practices of reconciliation with other species—our siblings—and the Earth as the material, living source of all beings who reside on and in this precious planet.

8

Western Men, the Ontological Rift, and Opportunities for Repair in Jack London's Call of the Wild

---

Man is the only creature who has been able, until now, to step out of line and get away with it. As the only being with the gall to consider himself Lord of Creation, Man is only too capable of not recognizing himself in the beings subject to his dominion.[1]

> Any physical object which by its influence deteriorates its environment, commits suicide.[2]

> It has been the custom of the land-robbing and sea-robbing Anglo Saxon to give the law to conquered peoples, and ofttimes this law is harsh.[3]

It be true, we ate flour, and salt pork, and drank tea which was a great delight; only, when we could not get tea, it was very bad and we became short of speech and quick of anger. So we grew to hunger for the things the white men brought in trade. Trade! Trade! All the time it was trade![4]

1. Kovel, *The Radical Spirit*, 288.
2. Alfred North Whitehead, quoted in Wood, *Reoccupy Earth*, 65.
3. London, "The League of the Old Men," 368.
4. London, "The League of the Old Men," 377.

In several of the previous chapters, I made brief comments regarding how the discussion connects to the climate emergency or the Anthropocene Age. This highlights my concern with what most Western persons have done and are doing to the Earth and other species. The climate crisis reveals that we and millions of other species are in danger of extinction. It is an age of great existential precarity. At the same time, the climate crisis reveals how we conceptualize and relate to "nature"[5] and, more specifically, to other species. These conceptualizations can be found in literature, science, philosophies, and theologies. A century ago, we might have taken these ideas or abstractions of nature and other species as relatively benign or, in some cases, destructive, but we (at least most Western human beings) had no clue just how globally destructive our conceptualizations were.[6] How we relate to nature and how we behave are inextricably tied to the stories we tell about ourselves and the world. And many of our stories, whether we are referring to literature, philosophy, theology, or science, often hide premises that serve to justify, rationalize, or ignore our narcissistic, exploitative cruelties to other species, othered human beings, and the Earth. Indeed, our stories frequently elide the lives and singularities of other species, relegating them to our collective normative and historical unconscious.[7]

Our abstractions, our conceptualizations, as Edward Saïd convincingly demonstrated decades ago, shape our beliefs, values, and behaviors toward other human beings. Saïd argued, for instance, that Western literature portrayed so-called Orientals in deeply distorted ways.[8] Western conceptualizations of "Orientals" were tied to Western apparatuses of imperialism, capitalism, and racism. In a similar way, we can examine Western novels (and other media, such as movies) and glean how nature and other

---

5. I use quotation marks because the idea of nature, in the West, tends to be seen as something other than human. Nature can be personified, such as Mother Nature, but it nevertheless remains something Western human beings stand apart from. "Nature" is an abstraction that often screens human anxieties and fears. Human beings often take their abstractions to be real, existent, rather than merely a convenient or conventional abstraction that communicates and, at times, justifies our relations to other species and the Earth. In reality, there is no "nature." All living beings are dependent on this sphere we call Earth. Human beings, like all species, are part of this world, this Earth. We are not distinct from nature, just as ants are not distinct from nature. As Albert Camus wrote, "When an abstraction starts to kill you, you have to get to work on it." Camus, *The Plague*, 69.

6. It is important to point out that there were a few Cassandras who observed and spoke about environmental destruction wrought by the excesses of capitalism. London was not one of those. See Foster, *The Return of Nature*; Wulf, *The Invention of Nature*.

7. Layton, *Toward a Social Psychoanalysis*; Zeddies, "Behind, Beneath, Above, and Beyond."

8. Saïd, *Culture and Imperialism*; Saïd, *Orientalism*.

species are represented. Indeed, I have already considered Captain Ahab and humans' capitalistic-imperialistic, exploitative, objectifying relations with whales. Ahab and other whaling captains were not interested in killing whales to provide needed food for their people. Rather, they and their capitalist sponsors relentlessly, ruthlessly, and perversely pursued profits. As Jack London writes in one of his short stories: "And yet they [Western men] grow fat on their many ills, and prosper, and lay a heavy hand over all the world and tread mightily upon its peoples."[9] To return to Melville's story, the white whale represents nature, something other-than-human to be controlled and a thing that exists to serve the interests, desires, and needs of human beings. Put another way, the underlying thrust of the novel is human attempts to dominate nature. In this and the next chapter, I turn to novelist Jack London and his short novels *Call of the Wild* and *White Fang* to portray further how Western men (and women) construct and relate to other species and nature.

I have chosen these stories of Alaska for several interrelated reasons. First, these two novels represent the collision between U.S. capitalistic imperialism and Indigenous peoples who are represented as primitive—closer to nature. In other words, London portrays the Territory of Alaska as wild, dangerous, yet virginal, open to be tamed, controlled, subjugated, and exploited by white men viciously seeking profit and riches. Alaska, in other words, represents how Western human beings have treated other species and the Earth, which has led to the current climate crisis. Second and relatedly, London demonstrates the imaginative empathic ability to depict the inner lives of Buck, a domesticated dog, and White Fang, a wolf. Indeed, their inner lives, their subjectivities, are impacted by white colonization of what we now call the State of Alaska. While probably not his intent, London's empathic imagination is itself an attempt to recognize and respect the singularities of other species—an empathic imagination that bridges the ontological rift created and maintained by the apparatuses of human sovereignty, imperialism, and capitalism. Third and relatedly, in these stories, there are hints of the possibility of repairs between human beings and other animals. These repairs result from rendering inoperative the apparatuses of colonization and capitalism that create the ontological rift and its attendant instrumental epistemologies. In rendering these inoperative, spaces are created for people to recognize and respect the singularities of other species and the land (Earth).

In this chapter, I begin by setting the stage for *Call of the Wild*, which starts in California and ends in the Alaskan Territory. From here I return

---

9. London, "The League of the Old Men," 378.

to the notion of the ontological rift and its attributes, as well as the notions of impotentiality and freedom, which I use as an interpretive framework for explicating this story of brutal exploitation and moments of repair. I end with a few brief thoughts about the climate crisis and reimagining our conceptualizations and treatment of other species and the Earth.

It is necessary to offer a few comments and clarifications before beginning. Anthropologists Eduardo Kohn, Tim Ingold, and Eduardo Viveiros de Castro note that some Indigenous peoples view other species as persons or potential persons.[10] This personification, if you will, is, for them, necessary for gaining knowledge of the other creature, the habitat, and themselves. These Indigenous people do not believe other species qua persons are identical to human beings qua persons. Rather, personification gives way to the idea of multinaturalism inherent in their personal epistemologies. London's stories of Buck and White Fang follow this. London personifies these and other dogs, acknowledging their subjectivity. Some might argue that London anthropomorphizes these dogs; however, it is clear in these stories that these dogs have a unique dog subjectivity and are not human beings. This ability to empathize also suggests the possibility or strain of multinaturalism in these stories. This said, these stories take place against Western epistemologies that foster the ontological rift between human animals and other animals. London's stories, in other words, represent a complex and ambiguous intersection between the ontological rift and the epistemological capacity of multinaturalism.

Another comment clarifies my use of these stories. I am not an expert on literature or, more particularly, Jack London. My approach is to examine these stories from the perspective of men's relationships to other species in general and dogs in particular. Whether London intended it or not, these stories reveal the distorted ways men relate to other species but also the glimmer of more constructive, reparative relations—relations that render inoperative apparatuses that produce the ontological rift between human beings and other species. This becomes increasingly paramount in an age where we are experiencing the disastrous results of Western philosophies, theologies, and science with regard to the climate crisis and the sixth extinction event. While I refrain from using theology in this and the last chapter, there is something redemptive or salvific in Buck and John Thornton's relationship. What is interesting here is that John, because of his care, "saved" Buck from death, a favor Buck would return months later. What was salvific or redemptive was the relationship—a relationship characterized by mutual

---

10. Ingold, *The Perception of the Environment*; Kohn, *How Forests Think*; Viveiros de Castro, *Cannibal Metaphysics*.

love. Redemption exists in relationships of love, which we need more of in the climate crisis.

Buck, Santa Clara, and the "Wilds" of Alaska

The novel begins with Buck living with Judge Miller in Santa Clara Valley, California. It is a bucolic, peaceful setting. "Buck," London writes, "was neither house-dog nor kennel-dog. The whole realm was his."[11] Buck would hunt with the judge's sons, escort the judge's daughters to school, and "lay at the Judge's feet before a roaring library fire."[12] During the four years since his puppyhood, Buck "had lived the life of a sated aristocrat; he had a fine pride in himself, was even a trifle egotistical, as country gentlemen sometimes become because of their insular situation."[13] In this putative Edenic setting, dark clouds hovered in the distance.

London writes that "Buck did not read the newspapers, or he would have known that trouble was brewing, not alone for himself, but for every tide-water dog, strong of muscle and with warm long hair, from Puget Sound to San Diego."[14] In the far north, "Men, groping in the Arctic darkness, had found a yellow metal, and because steamship and transportation companies were booming the find, thousands of men were rushing into Northland. These men wanted dogs, with strong muscles by which to toil, and furry coats to protect them from the frost."[15] The "Klondike strike dragged men from all the world,"[16] and some of these men sought profit not from gold but from stealing dogs and selling them to prospectors and others seeking their fortunes in the Alaskan territory.

Since Buck was treated well by the judge and his family, he naturally expected similar treatment from those who worked for the judge. As a result, Buck trusted everyone who lived and worked on the property, believing, naively, that they would care for him. Manuel was one of the gardener's helpers, and he "had one besetting sin. He loved to play Chinese lottery."[17] Unfortunately, "The wages of a gardener's helper do not lap over the needs of a wife and numerous progeny,"[18] which, in short, meant he needed easy cash. The

---

11. London, *Call of the Wild*, 762.
12. London, *Call of the Wild*, 762.
13. London, *Call of the Wild*, 762.
14. London, *Call of the Wild*, 761.
15. London, *Call of the Wild*, 761.
16. London, *Call of the Wild*, 763.
17. London, *Call of the Wild*, 763.
18. London, *Call of the Wild*, 763.

judge and the family were gone for the day, and Manuel took Buck on what he thought was a stroll. Buck, recognizing but not knowing Manuel, trusted him because he worked for the judge. To Buck's surprise, Manuel put a rope around his neck, which Buck "accepted . . . with quiet dignity."[19] When the money was exchanged, the rope was handed over and Buck growled and "struggled in a fury." The buyer choked and beat Buck. "Never in all of his life had he been so vilely treated," and he was thrown unconscious into a baggage car.[20] This marked only the beginning of his travails.

The long journey to Alaska was filled with the torment of frequent beatings and lack of water and food. Handed over to a dog-breaker,[21] Buck repeatedly attacked him, only to be knocked senseless. When he came to, the man said, "You've learned your place, and I know mine. Be a good dog and all 'll go well . . . Be a bad dog, and I'll whale the stuff-in' outa you. Understand?"[22] The man then gave Buck water and meat. Buck knew he was beaten, "but he was not broken."[23] There were many more days to endure in the bowels of the ship while he and other captives sailed to Alaska.

The ship docked on Dyea beach, which was, for Buck, "like a nightmare. Every hour was filled with shock and surprise. He had suddenly been jerked from the heart of civilization and flung into the primordial."[24] The men and dogs "were not town dogs and men. They were savages, all of them, who knew no law but the law of club and fang."[25] Buck and other dogs were first purchased by two French Canadians, Francois and Perrault. Placed in a harness, Buck began his education as a sled dog. Buck, no longer living the life of a country squire, "swiftly lost the fastidiousness which had characterized his old life. A dainty eater, he found that his mates, finishing first, robbed him of his unfinished rations. There was no defending it. While he was fighting off two or three, it was disappearing down the throats of others. To remedy this he ate as fast as they."[26] "The completeness of his decivilization was now evidenced by his ability to flee from the defense of a moral consideration and so to save his hide."[27]

19. London, *Call of the Wild*, 763.
20. London, *Call of the Wild*, 762.
21. London, *Call of the Wild*, 766.
22. London, *Call of the Wild*, 767.
23. London, *Call of the Wild*, 767.
24. London, *Call of the Wild*, 770. Dyea is north of Juneau, Alaska, and was a key disembarking point during the gold rush in the late nineteenth century.
25. London, *Call of the Wild*, 770.
26. London, *Call of the Wild*, 775.
27. London, *Call of the Wild*, 776.

The conditions of trail life were rough. While Buck and the other dogs received beatings, this was usually because they had transgressed a command. Francois and Perrault would not beat the dogs arbitrarily. But this would change. When Francois and Perrault had arrived in Skagway, Buck was exchanged to other owners. Charles, Hal, and Mercedes, Hal's sister and Charles's wife,[28] were Americans bent on pursuing their fortune in the Alaskan territory. Hal was merciless in exploiting the dogs, whipping them frequently. Mercedes, after observing the brutality, cried out to Hall, "'You mustn't,' as she caught hold of the whip and wrenched it from him."[29] Even though the sled was overloaded, Hal was having none of this, yelling at Mercedes that she did not know anything about dogs and that the dogs were lazy and, therefore, required the whip. Mercedes, because she was "a clannish creature,"[30] backed down. She was not unlike a slave owner's wife who laments at enslaved persons being whipped, saying, "You poor, poor dears, why don't you pull hard?—then you wouldn't be whipped."[31] And clearly what was happening to Buck and other dogs was a form of slavery.

It was not only that Buck and the other dogs were being beaten and stressed beyond measure in their traces. It was the lack of food. Hal "cut down even the orthodox ration and tried to increase the day's travel."[32] To her credit, Mercedes, "unable to cajole him into giving the dogs still more . . . stole from the fish-sacks and fed them slyly,"[33] which kept Buck and the other dogs barely alive. After a brutal trek to reach Dawson City, Hal, Mercedes, and Charles stumbled into John Thornton's camp on the White River. The dogs collapsed as "though they had been struck dead."[34] John warned them that continuing to Dawson City across the ice was foolish, but this warning was ignored. Hal picked up the whip and yelled at Buck, who was the leader, to get up and move. Buck tried several times, but he had no energy left after being beaten and starved for days. This enraged Hal, and he "exchanged the whip for the customary club."[35] John, who had watched all of this with growing unease, finally "sprang upon the man who wielded the club. Hal was hurled backward, as though struck by a falling tree." Enraged,

28. London, *Call of the Wild*, 797.
29. London, *Call of the Wild*, 798.
30. London, *Call of the Wild*, 798.
31. London, *Call of the Wild*, 799.
32. London, *Call of the Wild*, 801.
33. London, *Call of the Wild*, 801.
34. London, *Call of the Wild*, 805.
35. London, *Call of the Wild*, 806.

John said, "If you strike that dog again, I will kill you."[36] Hal protested that he owned the dog, but John persisted. Hal reached for his knife, which John batted away with an axe handle. Picking up the knife, John cut Buck from the traces. Hal, Charles, and Mercedes, failing to heed John's warning, left the camp, crossing the ice on a sled. When they were a quarter mile out on the ice, Buck and John watched the sled "crawling along over the ice. Suddenly, they saw its back end drop down, as into a rut, and the gee-pole, with Hal clinging to it, jerk into the air. Mercedes's scream came to their ears. They saw Charles turn and make one step to run back, and then a whole section of ice give way and the dogs and humans disappeared."[37]

This is where the story takes another dramatic turn, but before continuing with Buck's travails, it is important to analyze this story to portray the ontological rift and its attributes. At the time London was writing, it was common in the West to juxtapose civilization and nature, as if there were a gulf between the two. Instead of seeing them as distinct interconnected abstractions, they were taken to refer to different and separate realities. In addition, human animals that lived outside of civilization—Native peoples—were constructed as primitive or savage (decivilized, lacking morality),[38] which is evident in this and other London stories, which I will come to later. Chapters 2 and 4 both mention the ontological chasm between human beings and other species, but it may be helpful to recall some of the main points. Western political philosophies and theologies possess apparatuses that produce and maintain a "deep ontological rift . . . between animal and human."[39] Agamben writes:

> It is as if determining the border between human and animal were not just one question among many discussed by philosophers and theologians, scientists and politicians, but rather a fundamental metaphysico-political operation in which alone something like 'man' can be decided upon and produced. If animal life and human life could be superimposed perfectly, then neither man nor animal—and, perhaps, not even the divine—would any longer be thinkable.[40]

36. London, *Call of the Wild*, 806.

37. London, *Call of the Wild*, 807.

38. *Decivilization* is the term London uses, which reflects the juxtaposition of civilization and that which exists outside of it. It is also important to note that he associates civilization with morality and decivilization with its absence. This is interesting because there does not seem to be much if any morality in rapacious capitalism, which is a product of civilization. London, *Call of the Wild*, 776.

39. Dickinson, "The Absence of Gender," 173.

40. Agamben, *The Open*. Bruno Latour and Jacques Derrida make similar

This gulf between human animals and other species is a part of the assumptive world of most Western persons.[41] Bruno Latour,[42] Jacques Derrida,[43] and Isabelle Stengers[44] make similar observations; as Latour puts it, Western political epistemologies create two "entirely distinct ontological zones: that of human beings on the one hand; that of nonhuman on the other."[45] There are several interrelated features of the abyss. The first is the belief that human beings have dominion over other species because other species are constructed as inferior to human beings. Any inferior beings are thus able to be exploited.[46] Put another way, human dominion is justified and legitimated by beliefs in human superiority over inferior animals, such as dogs. This is evident in the very beginning of London's novel when Buck is captured and sold into slavery. The capitalist-imperialist mindset that engulfed the lower U.S. extended into Alaska, where Western human dominion and superiority are evident in the exploitation of other species, Native peoples, and the appropriation of land—white, Eurocentric notions of property that legitimated taking land from Indigenous peoples. More particularly, we see the rift when the "dog-breaker" viciously beat Buck to instill the superiority of the master/owner and the inferiority of dogs—a command and obedience relationship. It was also evident in Hal's claim of ownership and thus the right to beat or kill Buck or any other dog that Hal considered to be his property.

Second and relatedly, the beliefs in inferiority and superiority undergird a type of recognition that denies the singularity of another animal.[47]

---

arguments regarding the ontological rift. Latour, *We Have Never Been Modern*; Derrida, *The Animal*.

41. By "Western" I mean persons who have internalized the narratives and practices of European anthropologies. There are people and groups in the West, such as Indigenous peoples, who possess anthropologies that do not produce the ontological rift.

42. Latour, *We Have Never Been Modern*.

43. Derrida, *The Animal*.

44. Stengers, *Making Sense in Common*.

45. Latour, *We Have Never Been Modern*, 10–11.

46. I have mentioned in previous chapters that constructing other species as inferior can also occur between human beings. Whenever this occurs, othered or depersonalized human beings are exploited or killed with impunity.

47. The idea that individual species possess singularity does not mean that that all species are equal. When we consider a single species, such as human beings, equality does not follow the idea of their individual singularity. There are all kinds of inequalities, but inequality does not mean inferior or superior. If someone who is clearly smarter than others, that does not mean that person is superior and the others are inferior. To indicate that an individual possesses singularity means that the values of inferiority and superiority do not apply.

Only the superior human being is singular and thus merits respect and inherent dignity. Native peoples, who are "closer to nature" and not civilized, like other species, do not merit respect. In terms of Buck, he possesses no inherent singularity and, therefore, he is not due dignity or respect from his owners.[48] This does not mean that animals like Buck have no value. They certainly have use value, given the capitalistic system that fuels greed and lust for more and more profits. However, once this use value passes because of illness, disease, or incapacity of some sort, the dog is left to die or is killed. These dogs are, in short, expendable, meriting care only to the degree they fulfill their function. Buck, like his comrades, then, has no inherent existential singularity that would command respect and care, though he receives care as long as he holds use value. His value is merely contingent, a transient use value that is yoked to instrumental capitalistic epistemology.

Let me add that care vis-à-vis use value is also connected to a kind of trust that exists in spaces where the ontological rift dominates. When the dog-breaker beat Buck into submission, he was establishing a contract. If Buck accepted his subordinate and subjugated role of obeying his master, the master would trust him. Buck could trust the owner to provide some degree of care as long as Buck performed his duties. This type of contract parallels the racial contract, wherein enslaved persons, lacking singularity and possessing inferiority in the eyes of slavers, were trusted to the extent they accepted their subjugated status and performed their roles to the satisfaction of the slavers. Buck experienced this animal contract with Francois and Perrault, though with Hal this contract was repeatedly broken. However, as in slavery, there was no one to hold Hal accountable because capitalistic animal contracts favor only the owner since, in this case, Buck is a mere dog lacking singularity. Mercedes's attempts to stop Hal from beating and starving the dogs were not based on any law. Similarly, John's intervention was not based on the law. Indeed, one could argue that John broke the law of property by taking Buck into his camp. Hal was right, according to the capitalistic contract. He owned Buck and could do with him as he wished.

Connected to the belief in the inferiority of other species and instrumental epistemology is the zone of non-justice, which is the third feature of the rift. If a man is beaten or killed by another man, this act usually falls within the sphere of injustice,[49] even if it happened in a territory like Alaska. This is because an individual human being is ideally believed to be singular, possessing inherent existential dignity and value. Individual human

---

48. His first French Canadian owners did respect Buck, but it was an instrumental respect for Buck's capacities to survive and lead the other dogs.

49. See Nussbaum, *Justice for Animals*.

beings are due recognition of their singularity and value or significance, which means they are afforded protections under the law. But Buck, from the moment of his abduction, falls into a zone of non-justice where there are no protections and no rights. Justice simply does not apply to him or any other animal. This means that the "superior" human being, like Hal, who exercises the law of the club, cannot be held accountable for beating or killing an animal he owns. Like the racial contract, Hal can dominate Buck with impunity because justice does not apply.

The rift's belief in the inferiority of other species and the attendant zone of non-justice can be understood further in terms of the notions of potentiality and actuality. In terms of human beings, ideally, we believe that they are not "reducible to biology, identity, or vocation."[50] Sergei Prozorov, commenting on Agamben's view of potentiality, carries this further, stating, "there is an excess of living being that can never be subsumed under them" (e.g., apparatuses or disciplinary regimes and their representations).[51] This perspective has implications for ethics and politics, as Adam Kotsko and Carlo Salzani note. For Agamben, "The human experience of potentiality (and impotentiality) is at the root of both politics and ethics"[52]—zones of justice. Another way of saying this is that potentiality and actuality are the basis of human freedom and agency. We believe that to be a singular human being is to have agency and freedom—the capacity to actualize our potentialities. With regard to the ontological rift, this is decidedly not the case for inferior animals. Other species may actualize their potentialities, but they are determined by their biology. They do not have political agency or freedom.[53] Buck is construed by Hal and others as a mere animal, lacking agency and freedom. However, London's story about Buck belies this by giving Buck thoughts, agency, will, desire, freedom, and potentiality. Indeed, the fact that Buck had to be beaten (but not broken) and subjugated indicates that he had agency and a sense of freedom, which can only be denied through death.

I want to linger here a moment to consider the attributes of the ontological rift from a psychosocial perspective because this helps explain, in part, the perennial desire to dominate (the pleasure of dominating) and its underlying insecurity, anxiety, and rage. To construct another human being or other animal as existentially inferior accompanies a sense of superiority.

50. Whyte, *Catastrophe and Redemption*, 110.
51. Prozorov, *Agamben and Politics*, 24.
52. Kotsko and Salzani, *Agamben's Philosophical Lineage*, 60.
53. William Connolly and others have sought to bridge the ontological rift by arguing that other species possess agency, intentionality, freedom, and creativity. Connolly, *Facing the Planetary*.

This means one's existential significance is tied to and dependent on a belief in one's superiority, while other species are deemed to be insignificant, except, in some cases, in terms of their transient use value, but even that is contingent and impermanent. Hal and others believe their superiority and significance are existential facts, but all of this rested on the reality that human-created beliefs are impermanent. In other words, there is nothing in nature that confirms the superiority of human beings—it is a mere, though profoundly destructive, belief—a belief that is not universal and is impermanent. Moreover, holding this belief depends on enforcing inferiority on other beings. What Hal and other human beings get wrong is that their felt sense of significance is contingent on the *illusions* of superiority and inferiority—illusions felt to be real or factual as a result of human-constructed apparatuses that produce and maintain them. This dependence reveals an existential insecurity and anxiety about their own existential insignificance and impermanence. Buck and these other dogs, for Hal and other exploiters, are insignificant and exist at the whim of their owners who are, at their core, insecure because of their dependence on illusions for a sense of their worth. Put differently, Hal splits off his fear and anxiety regarding the facticity of existential insignificance and impermanence and projects them onto Buck and other species. Splitting and projection provides him with a sense of his own existential significance, which is based on illusions.

I regard this existential insecurity as unstable because it must continually be propped up by apparatuses of domination, which we note in the centuries-long enforcement of the racial contract. Moreover, this insecurity is noted in the unsettledness and rage of people like Hal. Hal became enraged whenever he believed the dogs were not performing to his expectations. That is, he believed they were transgressing his rule and power, which was integral to his sense of self. Any transgression, real or imagined, evoked insecurity related to existential significance contingent on the illusions of superiority. This is evident from another angle. Recall Buck's experience from the very beginning of the novel when he was abducted. He was enraged at his treatment, at being treated as a mere object to be dominated and constantly threatened with beatings and death. Buck was beaten into submission but not broken. He continued to feel rage but feared expressing or acting on it lest he be killed. His rage, in one sense, revealed his experience of the existential lie being forced on him—that he and other animals were inferior, lacking singularity.

Hal and other colonizers (and dominators) were involved in a category mistake of the ontological rift—a mistake that many of us in the West fall into. It is existentially true that human beings are signifying and valuing creatures (as are other species, but not in the same way). The capacities for signifying and valuing, though, are impermanent (not eternal) and do not mark us as being superior—only human beings believe this. These capacities arise as a result of our existence and will end when we pass out of existence. Instead of facing this, we mistakenly think that our capacities for signifying and valuing make us existentially superior and ontologically valuable. And we elevate all this to permanence (e.g., the kingdom of God). The cosmos, however, does not afford human beings or any other species significance, ontological or otherwise, which means that in light of the cosmos we, like other species, are existentially insignificant and impermanent. To counter this, we assign significance, and then, anxious about the existential realities of insignificance and impermanence, we construct ourselves as superior and eternal. Buck and other dogs are subjected to human creations of significance and insignificance with their attendant objectifications, carelessness, and zones of injustice constructed and maintained by the apparatuses of the ontological rift. It is a contract made in hell.

Love, Repair, and the Abeyance of the Ontological Rift

Buck's rescue by John dramatically shifts the trajectory of the story. The men Buck encountered in the Alaskan Territory were, at best, fair in meting out punishment and, at worse, cruel, like Hal. What they possessed in common was the idea that Buck and other dogs were inferior to human beings and could be used for any human need or desire. Dogs, these white men believed, lacked singularity, which opened spaces for dogs like Buck to be used, and when their use value diminished or was absent, they could be killed with impunity. This cruel reality of the men Buck encountered would recede as a result of John's love and his recognition of the existential singularity of Buck, rendering inoperative the machinations of the ontological rift. John's love entailed acceptance of the realities of impermanence and the shared precarity of all living beings. Depicting and analyzing this shift are the focus of this section.

Once Hal and company slid into the icy waters of the White River, John turned his attention to Buck. John "knelt beside him and with rough, kindly hands, searched for broken bones," revealing not broken bones but "many bruises and a state of terrible starvation."[54] Under John's care, "Buck waxed lazy as his wounds healed, his muscles swelled out, and flesh came back to cover his bones."[55] John had two other dogs in the camp, Skeet and Nig, who were also involved in Buck's recovery. Skeet, every morning,

54. London, *Call of the Wild*, 807.
55. London, *Call of the Wild*, 808.

would wash and cleanse Buck's wounds. Nig was "equally friendly, though less demonstrative."[56] John's care and respect, as well as Skeet's and Nig's ministrations and friendship, were unlike anything Buck had encountered before. There was no competition or jealousy between the dogs. Indeed, there was a playfulness, "in which Thornton himself could not forbear to join; and in this fashion Buck romped through convalescence and into a new existence."[57]

Buck had an epiphany one day when he was with John, Nig, and Skeet. He realized that "love, genuine passionate love, was his for the first time. This he had never experienced at Judge Miller's down in the sun-kissed Santa Clara Valley. With the Judge's sons, hunting and tramping, it had been a working partnership ... But love that was feverish and burning, that was adoration, that was *madness*, it had taken John Thornton to arouse."[58] Buck was grateful that John had saved him, but there was more. Unlike other men who "saw to the welfare of their dogs from a sense of duty and business expediency ... [John] saw to the welfare of his as if they were his own children."[59] Buck, understandably given his horrific treatment at the hands of Hal, adored John, and "for a long time after his rescue, Buck did not like Thornton to get out of his sight."[60] No doubt Buck feared losing the love that John had shown—a loss that might send him back to the cruelties of men like Hal.

This fear, however, abated, and "in spite of this great love he bore John Thornton" Buck began to feel the pull of what London calls the primitive or wild. "Deep in the forest," London writes, "a call was sounding, and as often as he heard this call, mysteriously thrilling and luring, he felt compelled to turn his back upon the fire and the beaten earth around it, and plunge into the forest ... But as often as he gained the unbroken earth and the green shade, the love for John Thornton drew him back to the fire again."[61] Here we note the juxtaposition of the primitive or wild and the love ensconced in John—a civilized man.[62]

---

56. London, *Call of the Wild*, 808.
57. London, *Call of the Wild*, 808.
58. London, *Call of the Wild*, 808; italics mine.
59. London, *Call of the Wild*, 809.
60. London, *Call of the Wild*, 809.
61. London, *Call of the Wild*, 811.
62. At least with regard to this story, one wonders if London viewed love as arising only in civilization, despite its brutalities. London's portrayal of Native peoples in this story leaves the impression that he viewed them as primitive, lacking civilization and perhaps love, like John.

Before continuing with the story, let me pause to explain how I understand this love and its connection to madness. John's love for Buck (and his other companions) certainly healed Buck's physical and psychological wounds received at the hands of other men. More importantly, John's love for Buck and Buck's love for John represent a bridging of the ontological rift between human beings and other species. In loving Buck, John rendered inoperative the capitalistic-imperialistic apparatuses that produced the ontological rift and its attributes. Buck was seen and treated as a singular being, absent of any illusory notions of superiority or inferiority and absent of instrumental epistemologies. I would suggest that John's love reflected a personalizing epistemology, wherein Buck was recognized and treated as a person—a unique, valued, inviolable, and responsive subject. Personal recognition did not mean that Buck was a human person—remember, John treated the dogs *as if* they were his own children.[63] John recognized the personhood of Buck qua dog. Put differently, John recognized Buck's singularity. This loving personal recognition created spaces for Buck to experience and actualize his senses of self-esteem, self-respect, and self-confidence—to be himself, to be an agent. Previously, even at the judge's home, Buck had been treated in terms of his use value. With John, love, in countless ways, communicated *volo ut sis* (I want you to be).

John's love rendered the animal contract void. He cared for Buck as he was and not because of what Buck could do for him. Buck was free to roam the camp and to leave, suggesting a kind of care and trust that had no strings. Buck, in other words, was not constructed in terms of his use value but rather in terms of his singularity.

Above, London uses the term "madness" in connection with this passionate love. In my estimation, John's love was madness in the sense that it contradicted social conventions and demands connected to the ontological rift, which included rejection of the rubrics of capitalism. In terms of the ontological rift, it is crazy to see and treat other species in terms of their singularity. It is madness or folly to treat other species, such as dogs, either in terms of their singularities or as if they have agency or freedom.

Let me turn to Agamben, who recognizes the ontological rift but overlooks freedom and agency when it comes to other species. Human beings, and only human beings, for Agamben, are capable of the capacity for exercising impotentiality—for preferring not. He writes:

---

63. See anthropologists Eduardo Kohn and Eduardo Viveiros de Castro for a discussion on how some Native peoples recognize the personhood of other species—a personhood that does not mean other species are human or like humans. Kohn, *How Forests Think*; Viveiros de Castro, *Cannibal Metaphysics*.

> *Other living beings are capable only of their specific potentiality; they can only do this or that. But human beings are the animals who are capable of their own impotentiality. The greatness of human potentiality is measured by the abyss of human impotentiality.* Here it is possible to see how the root of freedom is to be found in the abyss of potentiality. To be free is not simply to have the power to do this or that thing, nor is it simply to have the power to refuse to do this or that thing. To be free is . . . *to be capable of one's own impotentiality.*[64]

To illustrate this complex discussion, Agamben turns to Herman Melville's *Bartleby, the Scrivener*. Bartleby is told by his boss to do something, and Bartleby replies, "I prefer not to." For Agamben, Bartleby is choosing to *not actualize his potentiality*, which is demanded by his boss who, in my view, represents the demands of larger capitalist apparatuses. The moment of impotentiality means, in part, that Bartleby is not determined and cannot be determined (in the sense of being commanded by others) by the political-economic apparatuses that are aimed at defining his subjectivity and requiring him to actualize his potentiality. Colebrook and Maxwell add that "to have potentiality is to be capable of not becoming what one has the capacity to be" or what one is expected to be.[65]

This perspective is not the case for London. For London, Buck, Skeet, and Nig exercise their impotentiality by way of playing. In his previous experiences at the hands of men caught in the grips of capitalism, Buck was constructed as having no agency, no freedom. He was forced to live out the demands of men and beaten severely for refusing, for preferring not to, for rebelling. For those adhering to the ontological rifts and its apparatuses, it is indeed madness, the height of irrationality, or simply naivete to treat Buck and other dogs as if they have the capacity to exercise freedom (impotentiality) and agency. This is madness given the epistemologies linked to capitalism, imperialism, and other Western isms that produce and maintain civilization's ontological rift.

It was John's love that fostered a space for Buck to exercise his freedom, his capacity to prefer not or will not. John made no demands on Buck to toil in the traces. Buck had free reign of the camp, and later, when the call of the wild became too strong to ignore, Buck would spend days away from the camp.[66] Even when Buck worked for John, it was always something he

---

64. Agamben, *Potentialities*, 182–83.
65. Colebrook and Maxwell. *Agamben*, 38.
66. London, *Call of the Wild*, 819–23.

chose to do because he loved John.[67] His agency and freedom were also evident in his choosing to save John's life at great personal risk.[68] To be sure, one could argue that Buck felt compelled to save John, but we would not say another human being saving another human being acted without freedom. To be sure, human beings may feel compelled to save someone they love, but this love is not a signifier of bondage but of freedom. I am sure that if Hal had been caught up in the river, Buck would have preferred not to respond.

There is a complication to be addressed before continuing with the story. London repeatedly juxtaposes civilization and the primitive in this story, which was typical of his time. The primitive was associated with wildness (hence the title of the story), nature, and the law of "kill or be killed, eat or be eaten."[69] Civilization was associated with the lure of fire, roof, softness,[70] and perhaps the possibility of love. Both the primitive and civilization were part of Buck's struggle. Indeed, for Buck, John's love is linked to civilization, though interestingly enough this very civilization was allied to the brutality and viciousness of those who stole Buck, his subsequent "owners," and the other dogs he vied with in order to survive. It is difficult to know whether London would have seen the "primitive" or "primordial" in the ruthlessness of "civilized" capitalists pursuing prurient profit at any cost. But I am more of the mind that London was juxtaposing these two terms, associating primitiveness with violence outside "civilized" law, as demonstrated in the killings of John, Pete (John's companion), Skeet, and Nig by members of the Yeehat tribe.[71] The problem with this is twofold. First, the term *primitive* becomes associated with Native peoples such as the Yeehat. They would, according to London's schema, exist outside of civilization and its putative morality, thus operating according to the "laws" of nature—tooth and claw. That said, we can easily imagine that the Yeehat, like many other Indigenous peoples who experienced the vicious, rapacious colonization of their lands, were enraged at white settlers and miners and sought to defend their lands. Second and relatedly, the portrayal of civilization as one of roof, fire, and softness (love) obviously screens the brutal frenzy of so-called civilized white men who sought to pursue profits in Alaska. Buck certainly would have experienced this side of civilization at the hands of Hal and others. In short, London does appear to separate civilization and nature, demonstrating less

---

67. London, *Call of the Wild*, 813.
68. London, *Call of the Wild*, 814.
69. London, *Call of the Wild*, 810.
70. London, *Call of the Wild*, 810.
71. London, *Call of the Wild*, 829.

empathic imagination for Native peoples than he had for Buck and civilized men like John and Pete.

I have already given away another key part of the story—the killing of John, Pete, Skeet, and Nig. Buck was increasingly away from camp when the Yeehats attacked. After taking down a "great moose . . . he turned his face toward camp and John Thornton."[72] As he made his way, Buck "was oppressed with a sense of calamity happening, if it were not calamity already happened."[73] Some miles from camp, Buck "came upon a fresh trail that sent his neck hair rippling and bristling."[74] Scattered around the camp were the bodies of Nig, Skeet, Pete, and John. "A gust of overpowering rage swept over him . . . For the last time in his life he allowed passion to usurp cunning and reason, and it was because of his great love for John Thornton that he lost his head."[75] Buck attacked the Yeehats, who were shocked at the ferocity of this dog. Those who survived fled, and some of them were hunted down and killed by Buck over a period of a week. The "survivors gathered together in the lower valley and counted their losses."[76] Buck, "wearying of the pursuit . . . returned to the desolate camp." There he "brooded by the pool or roamed restlessly about the camp." Buck felt "a great void in him, somewhat akin to hunger, but a void which ached and ached, and which food could not fill."[77] During the night, Buck heard the yelps of a pack of wolves hunting. The sound "was the call, the many-noted call, sounding more luringly and compellingly than ever before. And as never before, he was ready to obey. John Thornton was dead. The last tie was broken. Man and the claims of man no longer bound him."[78] Buck, in his grief, turned away from the camp and, after a series of fights, joined and then led the pack of timber wolves. He had finally heeded the call of the wild after losing the love of John.

Creating Spaces of Inoperative Love in the Anthropocene Age

This story represents, in my view, relationships marred by alienation. In the beginning, Buck experienced being at home with the judge and his family, though later he recognized that these relationships were instrumental in

72. London, *Call of the Wild*, 827.
73. London, *Call of the Wild*, 828.
74. London, *Call of the Wild*, 828.
75. London, *Call of the Wild*, 828.
76. London, *Call of the Wild*, 829.
77. London, *Call of the Wild*, 829.
78. London, *Call of the Wild*, 830.

nature. This initial idyllic scene was followed by an experience of betrayal when Manuel sold Buck. From here Buck experienced the brutal instrumental relations fostered by predatory colonial capitalism. Buck was alienated from and by men but also from his fellow dogs, who were also striving to survive. Alienation exists in the ways "civilized" men treat each other, Indigenous people, and the land (exploitation and extraction of resources). Indeed, the juxtaposition between "civilized" and "primitive" in the text reveals a kind of alienation. The civilization that London writes from was one dominated by capitalistic and imperialistic apparatuses—apparatuses that foster instrumental epistemologies and relations of exploitation and extraction. Finally, we see this alienation between the Yeehats and white people, such as Pete and John.

Diverse forms of alienation are evident in our current environmental crisis. London, of course, was writing long before people became aware of how environmentally alienating and destructive market-colonial "civilization" was and is. Many of us today, however, living in an era of global capitalism, market societies, and petrocultures, experience, in varying degrees, the realities of the climate emergency—an emergency that was and is caused by capitalism's and Western political philosophies (and theologies), apparatuses that produce and maintain the ontological rift between human beings and other species.[79] Whether London was cognizant of this or not, his story of the love between John and Buck offers hints at how we might reimagine living in the Anthropocene with other species.

Above, I indicated that John's care and, later, love for Buck could be understood as rendering inoperative the apparatuses of imperialism and capitalism. When John recognized Buck's singularity, even as Buck was on his last legs, he demonstrated an empathic care for Buck as a singular being. John, then, intervened to protect Buck from Hal's brutality. His care and later love created spaces for John, as a human animal, and Buck, as a dog animal, to move from alienation to belongingness—an I-Thou relationship, to use Martin Buber's notion.[80] It was a relationship in which the singularities of each being were recognized, respected, and cared for. In fact, John had already crossed this rift with his two other dogs, and these dogs, Skeet and Nig, likewise, were able to care for and join with Buck. Previously, Buck had been alienated from other dogs because they competed with him for survival. With Skeet and Nig, as well as with John, they cooperated, which

---

79. For further explanation of this rift and its apparatuses vis-à-vis the climate emergency, see LaMothe, *The Coming Jesus*; LaMothe, *A Radical Political Theology*.

80. Buber, *I and Thou*.

included playing together. This was a belongingness that was free of instrumental epistemologies of exploitation endemic to the ontological rift.

I want to tease out other points with regard to inoperative care or love and its implications for living in the climate crisis. John, living in the Alaskan territory, knew well the precarity of life. With obvious care, he warned Hal, Charles, and Mercedes that to continue their journey would be perilous—and it was. I think John's restraint in handling Hal also demonstrated his care not to increase Hal's precarity. By all rights, he could have killed Hal because Hal had attacked him with a knife. To return to Buck, the base of John's empathy for Buck's condition was that John knew well the precarity of the lives of dogs. His care for Buck represents helping Buck's resilience in the face of life's precariousness. I add that John himself was recovering from falling into the icy waters and was later saved by Buck from the river. John, then, experienced the precarity of life for human beings and for dogs, and this fueled his motivation to care, even for a person like Hal. All this suggests the absence of the ontological rift because the presence of the rift tends to project precarity and insignificance onto other species. For instance, dogs, like Buck, were instrumentally exploited not only to satisfy human desires and needs but also were sacrificed when the well-being, real or imagined, of human beings was at stake. Precarity was exacerbated for these enslaved dogs, while men were allowed to overlook their own precarity as a result of their putative superiority. John, by contrast, recognized the precarity of both human beings and dogs, which motivated him to care for dogs in his charge to the point of letting Buck choose to stay and help in the camp or leave and roam the forests.

Two interrelated features of precarity require explanation vis-à-vis bridging the ontological rift. Embracing our shared precarity founds the recognition of the singularities of other species, which includes accepting our shared existential insignificance and impermanence. It is important to linger here so that greater clarity is established. Human beings and other species are semiotic creatures who have the capacity to assign value or significance to ourselves, other species, and objects. These valuations (and disvaluations) shape our epistemologies and relations to other human beings, other species, and the Earth. In other words, to recognize the singularity of another human being or another animal is to assign positive value, which gives rise to and founds respect and care. This other animal, for us, is existentially valuable, but all valuations are existentially impermanent. As noted above, we make a category mistake when we think that our valuations are ontological and eternal—a mistake that involves assigning ontological significance to ourselves while assigning existential insignificance to other species. Put another way, the cosmos, the universe, does not assign significance, which is why I use the terms existential insignificance and impermanence in referring to all life. In the story, Buck and other dogs are existentially insignificant—retaining, for a time, mere use value. Hal and other men see themselves as existentially significant and not subject to question. John's care and later love for Buck, in my estimation, meant he assigned existential significance to Buck in the midst of the realities of existential precarity. Indeed, London's story itself represents the significance of a dog's subjective existence. Yet, all of this takes place against existential insignificance and impermanence. Imagine Buck is a real creature. He, like John, dies, and his death is the eclipse of his experiences of being significant in the eyes of John. London's story highlights the significance of Buck and John, yet this story is itself impermanent.

To embrace precarity and attendant existential insignificance and impermanence does not lead to nihilism or despair but rather emphasizes the importance of our present actions in recognizing, respecting, and caring for the singularities of all species. In my interpretation, John's care for Buck was founded on John's acceptance of precarity, as well as the existential insignificance and impermanence of other human beings and other species. The times when Buck played with Skeet, Nig, and John represent their being in the moment of shared significance, which was itself impermanent. When Buck found John, Pete, Skeet, and Nig murdered, he went into a rage, killing numerous men from the Yeehat tribe. Buck was not unfamiliar with death before he encountered John, but this moment evoked a frenzied rage, which I understand as the horror and profound sadness upon confronting the realities of the existential impermanence of love. Buck's killing the Yeehat men was projecting onto them what they had projected onto John, Pete, Skeet, and Nig, which was the denial of singularity, significance, and the enforcement of impermanence. In those murderous moments, the Yeehats were existentially insignificant to Buck, and the murders enforced their impermanence. More positively, John's and Buck's mutual care and love took place against the background of existential insignificance and impermanence. Accepting this makes possible acts that bridge the ontological rift, and these acts reflect the absence of nihilism or despair.

There is one more point to be made here. Above, I noted that London's story juxtaposes civilization and the primitive or wild. When Buck lived in Santa Clara, the "primitive" part of himself was suppressed. After being captured and beaten, the primitive was repressed in relation to his "owners" but was present when Buck had to live by the law of fang and claw to survive. John's love for Buck was paradoxical. Buck was drawn to remain in civilization (John's camp), but the call of the wild began to take on a life of its own.

John's love, in other words, created a space for Buck to listen to his "primal" nature and, with John's death, Buck left civilization and returned to the wild.

Civilization, while having the benefits of fire and roof, contains its own capitalistic and imperialistic brutality in its exploitation of other species (and some human beings) and ruthless extraction of resources. Civilization, with its capitalistic and imperialistic apparatuses, creates an ontological rift. Hal and Charles, for instance, wanted to get rich, and they ruthlessly exploited their dogs to attain this aim. Indeed, in my view, Hal and Charles represent the anxious, insecure, and manic striving of civilized people caught in the grips of capitalistic imperialism. Their striving is a symptom of an existential dis-ease of carelessness, which includes the ongoing repression of the realities of existential precarity, as well as human existential insignificance and impermanence. Their aggression reveals men who live lives of not-so-quiet desperation in the face of precarity. Put differently, the repetitive narratives linked to capitalism and imperialism foster individual and collective self-deception regarding the realities of existential insignificance and impermanence. By contrast, John's care for Buck renders inoperative the apparatuses of civilization that separate civilization from the so-called primitive. John's love is absent of the anxious striving associated with maintaining the ontological rift. Indeed, he does not have to bridge this rift because in his care there is no rift.

In the current climate crisis caused by human-made apparatuses that produce the ontological rift, recognition of the singularities of other human beings, other species, and the Earth founds relations of care, value, and respect for the diversity or multiplicity of forms of life. This care requires accepting our collective precarity and vulnerability, as well as the attendant realities of our own (and other species' and the Earth's) existential insignificance and impermanence. The forms of living that accompany care for other species and the Earth mean rejecting those self-deceptions ensconced in narratives and abstractions that promulgate the rift between humanity and nature. Care does not so much bridge the rift between human animals and other species as it denies that there is any rift at all. This rift is a fabricated illusion that has had and is still having terrible effects, evident in the slaughtering of billions of animals every year,[81] as well as the destructive realities of the climate crisis. Remember, to render inoperative the apparatuses of civilization and the ontological rift does not mean these do not continue to have their destructive effects. John's love of Buck, for instance, did not undo the apparatuses of imperialistic capitalism, though it created transient spaces where the rift was nonexistent.

81. Singer, *Ethics in the Real World*, 51.

All of this may come across as a return to romanticizing "nature" or as quasi-mystical naturalism. There is nothing mystical or romantic about the hard work of John caring for Buck, Skeet, and Nig. To recognize and respect the singularities of other species is hard work, requiring us to set aside our instrumental epistemologies that privilege our existence at the cost of the existence of other species. This hard work demands deconstructing zones of non-justice where other species are objectified and slaughtered by the billions every year. This is psychological, physical, political, and spiritual work because it requires confronting ourselves and changing how we relate to other species and the Earth.

Recall in chapter 4 my mention of Ruby Sales's comments about her parents and their community of faith. For Ruby, they were spiritual geniuses because they created a language and a world where white sovereignty and its ontological rift between white people and black people were rendered inoperative by her parents' reliable anarchic care for their children. Their care was against the backdrop of Southern apartheid, and this care took a great deal of labor. There is nothing romantic, mystical, or idealistic about Ruby's depiction of her early life and her parents as spiritual geniuses, just as there was nothing romantic, mystical, or idealistic about the mutual care and love between John and Buck. All of that took work, day in and day out. We are invited to do the same.

Conclusion

Literature, as Edward Saïd demonstrated,[82] reveals and conceals the premises that shape how we recognize and treat other human beings and, in London's story, other species. It is not usually the intent of the novelist to expose or mine the depths of their representations of others, but their stories inevitably make use of and show these representations. If we take the time to critically analyze stories, we can begin to hold a mirror up to our society or our religion since religions are comprised of stories as well. Indeed, the Abrahamic traditions are replete with representations that parallel London's story. Other species, if they are represented, are seen as inferior, possessing, if anything, only use value. They lack souls and agency and are condemned to existential impermanence, while some human beings enjoy the possibility of eternity with the sovereign God. A critical exploration of the stories we tell and live out of becomes increasingly important when we face the existential precarity of the climate crisis. In doing this work, in painfully facing our destructive delusions and illusions, we can render inoperative

---

82. Saïd, *Culture and Imperialism*; Saïd, *Orientalism*.

these stories and attendant apparatuses, which creates space for authoring new stories and living out new ways of being and relating to other species and the Earth.

9

Men and the Silence of Other Species
Traumatic Encounters and the Possibilities of Healing

> A vast silence reigned over the land. The land itself was desolation, lifeless, without movement, so lone and cold that the spirit of it was not even that of sadness. There was a hint in it of laughter, but a laughter more terrible than sadness . . . a laughter cold as the frost partaking of the grimness of infallibility. It was the masterful and incommunicable wisdom of eternity laughing at the futility of life and the effort of life . . . But there was life, abroad in the land and defiant.[1]

> Soul blindness [the inability to see beyond oneself or one's kind] is not just a human problem; it is a cosmic one.[2]

> Nonhuman selves . . . have ontologically unique properties associated with their constitutively semiotic nature.[3]

> All life is semiotic and all semiosis is alive.[4]

---

1. London, *White Fang*, 385.
2. Kohn, *How Forests Think*, 117.
3. Kohn, *How Forests Think*, 91.
4. Kohn, *How Forests Think*, 117.

When I was living in Germany four decades ago, I moved to a village on the outskirts of Würzburg. Early in the morning, I would head off for a six-mile run. One morning, I took a different route that took me to another part of the suburbs. Never will I forget the eerie sounds emanating from a large plant, corralled by high fences. Several days later, I learned that this was an industrial slaughterhouse and what I had heard was the not-so-silent cries of the collective trauma of thousands of cattle.[5] From that day forward, I vowed not to eat meat, though there have been some rare lapses (*mea culpa, mea culpa*).

In truth, it is not that other species are silent.[6] Most of us have simply found ways not to hear or not to listen to the diverse communications of other species and their sufferings and traumas.[7] I recall a philosopher saying that several friends urged her to read a book about other species because it would turn her toward vegetarianism. When asked about this, the philosopher laughed and admitted she had not read it because she did not want to stop eating meat. This is understandable, but it shows how dearly we hold on to our privileges—privileges that depend on the silencing of other species, denying their singularities. It is easier to deny, rationalize, ignore, or cultivate indifference than it is to do the emotional and spiritual labor of listening compassionately—to be moved by the voices and cries of other species. As Gemma Corradi Fiumara argues, "Unless we are ready, receptive—and also, possibly, vulnerable—the experience of listening appears to be impossible."[8]

In this last chapter, I use Jack London's tale of White Fang to explore the traumatic relations between men and other species, in this story a wolf. Included in this short novel is also an example of how relationships of care

---

5. Peter Singer notes that "more than 77 billion mammals and birds are produced for food each year. If we include fish farming, the number of vertebrate animals we raise more than doubles, and if we add wild fish, the total number killed may be more than a trillion. Most of this unimaginable suffering that we inflict on these animals in raising and killing them is unnecessary." Singer, *Ethics in the Real World*, 51.

6. Zoë Schlanger's recent book explores the lives and communications of plant species. In the last forty years, botanists are beginning to understand the behaviors and communications of plants, which raises a host of complicated issues about intelligence, consciousness, and ethics. The focus of this chapter, however, is on the silencing of other-than-human animals. Schlanger, *The Light Eaters*.

7. The title is partially taken from scholar Gayatri Chakravorty Spivak's work, "Can the Subaltern Speak?" This paper, like the works of Edward Saïd, had a significant impact on postcolonial studies. Those of us in the West, instead of listening to the voices of so-called subalterns, projected onto them representations that distorted their experiences and served to rationalize the West's colonial and postcolonial exploitation of other states and peoples. Spivak, "Can the Subaltern Speak?"

8. Corradi Fiumara, *The Other Side of Language*, 119.

and love can foster sufficient relational trust to heal the wounds of trauma, though the traumas are never forgotten. These are relationships that entail listening and being moved by, in this story, the subjectivity of White Fang—a listening that dismantles the colonizing apparatuses of the ontological rift that are the source of so much unnecessary suffering perpetrated by men (and women) on other species. I begin with a discussion about the meaning of the term *trauma* and address its characteristics and applicability to other species. I then turn to London's novel to depict White Fang's traumatic experiences and his resulting silence.[9] From there I shift to the last part of the story, wherein Weedon Scott rescues White Fang from certain death, beginning the long laborious trek to forming a relationship of profound mutual trust, care, and love. I end this chapter with a brief return to the realities of climate change and the need to radically alter our relationships with other species (including trees, other plants, etc.). The dire revelations of climate change, in other words, invites us not only to listen to the sufferings of other species but also to accept and live out the categorical ecological command to care for other species and the Earth.

Before returning to the wilds of the Alaskan Territory, let me offer some clarifications. A reader of London's works will notice the parallels between *White Fang* and *Call of the Wild*. Both stories are about men's relationships with dogs, the rescuing of these dogs, and the relationships that develop between the men and the dogs. Each story juxtaposes civilization and nature or the wild, though in *Call of the Wild* we have a dog taken from civilization while *White Fang* is a story of a wolf taken from nature, eventually arriving in California—civilization. In the previous chapter, I did not focus on Buck's trauma, though it is implicit in the presence of the ontological rift and its attributes. Buck, like White Fang, was repeatedly traumatized by men, and then two men, possessing a depth of compassion, cared for Buck and were foundational to his healing. So, in this chapter, I want to expand the focus to trauma and healing, mainly because nearly all of the trauma literature refers to human beings and not other species. Perhaps this absence is yet another symptom of the apparatuses of the ontological rift that foster relations of domination, which function to silence other species. Second, it is important to mention that in Western history there have been philosophers and others who have advocated for including other species in our discussions

---

9. The approach I am taking in this chapter is not novel. Anastassiya Andrianova, for instance, examines the works of Tolstoy and Bulgakov from the perspective of animal studies and trauma theory. These celebrated authors narrate the traumatic suffering of animals, much as Jack London does. Similarly, Tony Vinci examines various modern novelists and their depictions of animal suffering. Andrianova, "Narrating Animal Trauma"; Vinci, *Ghost, Android, Animal*.

about ethics and justice. Stephen Newmyer addresses the work of Plutarch and his argument about the rights of animals.[10] A couple of centuries after Plutarch, Neoplatonic scholar Porphyry, writing in the third century, argued it was our moral duty to extend justice to other animals.[11] Centuries later, Jeremy Bentham, Johannes Kniess writes, argued for the welfare of animals. Also, Stephen Puryear explores the nineteenth-century work of Arthur Schopenhauer and his concern for the rights of animals. More recently, philosophers such as Peter Singer, Andrew Linzey, and Martha Nussbaum have explored the thorny ethical issues regarding human beings' treatment of other species.[12] In the Christian tradition, Francis of Assisi also seemed to have had profound empathy and compassion for other species. These writers are rare exceptions to the rule—the rule being human dominion over and instrumental use of other species and the Earth.

A third clarification entails the implicit premise of the subjectivity of other species. In other words, to consider the sufferings of other species implies that other species possess a subjectivity or self. As anthropologist Eduardo Kohn notes, "What we call mind, or self, is a product of semiosis . . . Selves, human or nonhuman, simple or complex, are the outcomes of semiosis . . . They are waypoints in a semiotic process."[13] Jack London's stories about Buck and White Fang, while imaginative, nevertheless reveal the existential fact that many Western human beings find innumerable ways to deny the selfhood and intelligence of other species. Lastly, the silence of other species is meant to convey hearing but not caring enough to listen or be moved by the communications of other species. When we hear but do not listen, we are ostensibly saying that other species have no singular significance, no selfhood, no subjectivity, no intelligence. The belief in the insignificance of other species is the first step toward acts that lead to trauma. We see this frequently among human animals. Consider any marginalized group and note the lack or absence of the dominant group's willingness to listen, understand, and be moved by the sufferings of marginalized and oppressed persons. Slavery, marginalization of women, the treatment of LGBTQI persons, South African and U.S. apartheid vis-à-vis black persons, and conservative Israelis' oppression of Palestinians are just some examples of assigning insignificance to the voices of othered persons and groups. Of

10. Newmyer, *Animals, Rights, and Reasons*.

11. Porphyry, "On Abstinence from Animal Food," book 1, pp. 11–44. The Tertullian Project, https://www.tertullian.org/fathers/porphyry_abstinence_01_book1.htm.

12. Kniess, "Bentham on Animal Welfare"; Puryear, "Schopenhauer on the Rights of Animals"; Linzey, *Why Animal Suffering Matters*; Nussbaum, *Justice for Animals*; Singer, *Animal Liberation*; Singer, *Ethics in the Real World*.

13. Kohn, *How Forests Think*, 117.

course, we are rightly horrified by these injustices, but when we turn to the lives of other species, a similar dynamic takes place in manifold ways. Most of us have simply become inured to the injustices toward other species. To cross the divide or ontological abyss, to become more empathic and compassionate, to listen to the singularities of other species, means doing the psychological and spiritual work of letting go of our illusions of superiority so that we recognize the singularities of not only other human beings but also other species. This is the first step toward acts of care—acts that render inoperative trauma-inducing apparatuses and, as a result, create possibilities of healing.

Trauma and Other Species

The idea of mental suffering goes back to the ancient Greeks, who offered varied explanations and remedies. In the nineteenth century, the term *psychological trauma* was a technical concept used mainly by physicians treating patients. For instance, French physician Jean-Martin Charcot sought to examine, list, and treat symptoms of "hysteria," which was associated with women's psychological suffering.[14] It was Sigmund Freud who initially argued that the source of these symptoms were childhood experiences of psychological trauma, a view he later discarded.[15] Otto Rank, an early disciple of Freud, posited that birth itself was a source of trauma and not simply childhood experiences of impingement and deprivation.[16] An existential implication of this view is that to be human means beginning life with trauma, which is arguable. Before Rank's proposal, William James viewed an infant's entry into the world not as trauma but as "one great blooming buzzing confusion."[17]

The search for the sources of trauma also led to questions about how individuals psychologically cope with trauma, as well as what treatment modalities can help heal the traumas. Pierre Janet's notion of dissociation and Freud's notion of repression are concepts used to depict how unbearable experiences are psychically managed.[18] World War I sparked greater interest in understanding traumatic experiences. Psychological responses of soldiers (shell shock), followed by World War II, Vietnam War, and

14. Gay, *Freud: A Life*, 48–53.
15. Freud, "The Aetiology of Hysteria." See Fassin and Rechtman, *The Empire of Trauma*, 30–39; Herman, *Trauma and Recovery*, 10–14.
16. Rank, *The Trauma of Birth*.
17. James, *The Principles of Psychology*, 488.
18. See Gay, *Freud: A Life*.

other recent American wars, furthered the clinical research on traumatic experiences—post-traumatic stress and moral injury.[19] Questions about treatment protocols continue to be part of the discourse regarding trauma. Protocols vary from various talking cures to the use of psilocybin and other mind-altering medications.

Use of the concept of trauma has shifted dramatically in the last fifty years. Didier Fassin and Richard Rechtman[20] note that the notion of trauma became unmoored from its clinical location and began to be used in the larger society to refer to any painful and disturbing experience.[21] The concept, then, became pervasive in social discourses, which has had political implications.[22] While social-political aspects of the common use of the notion of trauma are important, they is not my focus here. Instead, I provide some general comments about the meanings of trauma as they refer to human beings before using the term in light of the suffering of other-than-human species.

Decades ago, Hanna Segal understood trauma to comprise the loss of symbolic function, which means that an experience associated with a traumatic event is organized semiotically, not semantically.[23] A child, for instance, who is traumatized is not able to organize the experience through symbolization, though the experience is organized semiotically.[24] When this occurs, experiences of trauma often remain outside of symbolic and autobiographical meaning systems. Today we use the term post-traumatic stress to refer, in part, to experiences that remain largely outside autobiographical or semantic memory systems,[25] though they continue to be part of eidetic memory. In one sense, this is a fancy way of saying that experiences of past traumas continue to haunt persons in the present.

Using different language, Cathy Caruth argues that trauma is identified as horrific events or crises in a person's life that are unassimilated

---

19. See Graham, *Moral Injury*; Gray, *The Warriors*; Hillman, *A Terrible Love of War*; Moon, *Coming Home*; Moon, *Warriors between Worlds*; Morris, *Moral Injury*; Ramsay and Doehring, *Military Moral Injury*.

20. Fassin and Rechtman, *The Empire of Trauma*.

21. Will Self and Parul Sehgal have recently addressed how the notion of trauma has become a trope in the literary world and the problems associated with its ubiquity. Self, "A Posthumous Shock"; Sehgal, "The Case against the Trauma Plot."

22. Fassin and Rechtman, *The Empire of Trauma*, 27–30.

23. Segal, "Notes on Symbol Formation."

24. LaMothe, "The Absence of Cure."

25. van der Kolk et al., "History of Trauma in Psychiatry"; van der Kolk et al., "Dissociation and Information Processing."

with that person's consciousness and narrative constructions.[26] Caruth contends these are "unclaimed experiences."[27] Unclaimed experiences is another way to conceptualize semiotically versus semantically organized experiences. But it is not simply how trauma is organized that is important. Caruth adds that the core of trauma is "the lack of support, of help, of comfort; being utterly left alone with the experience and having no one to listen."[28] Sue Grand holds a similar view, calling trauma an experience of catastrophic loneliness.[29] Connected to this catastrophic loneliness is the concomitant shattering of one's assumptive world,[30] creating a sense of the non-reparability of relationships, which Ronnie Jan-Bulman notes.[31] Like Janoff-Bulman, Fred Alford argues that "trauma takes away our confidence in the existence of a stable, ordered, and meaningful existence."[32] The shattering of one's assumptive world of trust and a corresponding belief in the non-reparability of relationships are attended by profound distrust, helplessness, and hopelessness,[33] which undermines persons' capacity for intimate relationships.

Developmentally, the capacities for and use of language and symbols to organize experience depend on relations of trust wherein persons can be vulnerable to caring adults. Attachment theorists have long observed that trauma disrupts children's capacities for relational trust, which, in turn, undermines their capacities for self-reflexivity and organizing coherent narratives.[34] Trauma, in other words, shatters their assumptive world of trust, leaving experience unclaimed. Put differently, when trauma occurs at the point of extreme vulnerability, vulnerability becomes linked to distrust, intolerable anxiety, powerlessness, and catastrophic, existential loneliness. The experience is unclaimed because vulnerability is required to do the work of processing the trauma with another person, but any movement toward vulnerability heightens anxiety and distrust.

Let me complicate this further. It is not that semiotic and symbolic capacities in organizing experience are two radically separate systems

26. Caruth, *Listening to Trauma*; Caruth, *Unclaimed Experience*.
27. Caruth, *Unclaimed Experience*, 4.
28. Caruth, *Unclaimed Experience*, 202.
29. Grand, *The Reproduction of Evil*.
30. Janoff-Bulman, *Shattered Assumptions*.
31. See Bromberg, "Treating Patients with Symptoms," 902.
32. Alford, *Trauma and Forgiveness*, 10.
33. Freyd, *Betrayal Trauma*.
34. See Fonagy, *Attachment Theory and Psychoanalysis*; Fonagy and Target, "Attachment and Reflective Function"; Gergley and Unoka, "Attachment and Mentalization in Infants"; Holmes, *Attachment, Intimacy, Autonomy*.

vis-à-vis one's assumptive world. Long before symbolization is taking place, infants organize experience semiotically. Relying on the work of Merleau-Ponty and Fanon, Athena Colman argues that infants first develop a corporeal schema that "can be understood as having to do with [the] pre-representational [semiotic] mode of experience through which we continually, but without conscious effort, dynamically orient and restructure our body in the world according to our projects."[35] Similarly, philosopher Mark Johnson contends that embodied constitutional structures exist "pre-conceptually and non-propositionally in our ongoing meaningful organization of our experience, understanding, and reasoning."[36] Semiotically organized embodied schemas become intertwined with more complex symbolic-semiotic organizations of our assumptive world, and both are contingent on consistent relations of care and trust. Trauma undermines embodied pre-representational and symbolic modes of organizing experience. Put another way, *trauma is disorienting and painful because it is in radical opposition to the foundations that make organizing experience possible*, leaving victims struggling to find ways to make sense of what happened.

An illustration can be helpful. Jean Améry, a French journalist and resistance fighter, was bound and beaten by the Gestapo during World War II. Some years later, he wrote of his experience of torture:

> The first blow brings home to the prisoner that he is helpless . . . Yet I am certain that with the very first blow that descends on him he loses something we will perhaps call "trust in the world." Trust in the world includes all sorts of things . . . the certainty that by reason of written or unwritten social contracts the other person will respect my physical, and with it also my metaphysical being. The boundaries of my body are also the boundaries of my self. My skin surface shields me against the external world. If I am to have trust, I must feel on it only what I *want* to feel . . . The expectation of help, the certainty of help, is indeed one of the fundamental experiences of human beings . . . The expectation of help is as much a constitutional psychic element as is the struggle for existence . . . But with the first blow of the policeman's fist, against which there can be no defense and which no helping hand will ward off, a part of our life ends and it can never again be revived . . . Whoever has succumbed to torture can no longer feel at home in the world.[37]

35. Colman, "Corporeal Schemas and Body Images," 128.

36. Johnson, *The Body in the Mind*, 40. See also Lakoff and Johnson, *Philosophy in the Flesh*.

37. Améry, "Torture," 126, 127, 136.

The first blow of the policeman occurred at the point where Jean Améry was at his most vulnerable, shattering his assumptive world—a world of embodied self integrity, of trust vis-à-vis the expectation of help and care, of ownership of his body, and of caring repair. Put differently, Améry's assumptive world was grounded in his experience of early life, wherein he could trust and be vulnerable to caring parents. These semiotic organizations of experience were grounded in and connected to his ability to make use of cultural symbols to organize and relationally process experience—to make sense of the world. When he was tortured, this assumptive world of existential trust and fidelity no longer made sense, leaving unbearable experiences of torture unassimilable.

One may immediately question this, noting that Améry later wrote about his experience, suggesting that he was able to assimilate the experience into symbols and autobiographical memory. This is true, but only to an extent. Many people who have been traumatized can, in time, talk about their experiences, but this does not mean that these unbearable experiences are entirely claimed. In one sense, they cannot be claimed because trauma, especially trauma at the hands of other human beings, is completely and radically at odds with the assumptive embodied, pre-representational world of trust and vulnerability. Put another way, experiences associated with severe trauma essentially lie outside human capacity for symbolization because *the very capacity for symbolization is existentially dependent on care, trust, and vulnerability—the openness to receive care.*[38] Trauma is antithetical to care and trust, which means vulnerability becomes equated with terrifying powerlessness. Améry never fully recovered from his experiences of being tortured. He survived, for a time, and narrated his experience, but he lived in a world where he was alienated and isolated from routine meanings, purposes, and intimacies. He was not at home in the world. As Fassin and Rechtman note, "Trauma . . . is not simply the consequence of unbearable experiences, but [is] also in itself a testimony." And the testimony of Améry "is both the product of an experience of inhumanity and the proof of the humanity of those who have endured it."[39]

So far, I have been discussing trauma as it relates to individuals. There is also trauma experienced by groups or communities. Primo Levi, a Holocaust survivor, poignantly narrated his traumatic experiences and their close connection between personal and cultural-religious objects and a sense of self. He wrote,

---

38. See LaMothe, "The Absence of Cure"; Strozier and Flynn, *Trauma and Self*.
39. Fassin and Rechtman. *The Empire of Trauma*, 20.

> But consider what value, what meaning is enclosed even in the smallest of our daily habits, in the hundred possessions which even the poorest beggar owns: a handkerchief, an old letter, the photo of a cherished person. These things are part of us, almost like *limbs of our body* ... Imagine now a man who is deprived of everyone he loves, and at the same time of his house, his habits, his clothes, in short everything he possesses: he will be a *hollow* man ... for he who loses all often easily loses himself.[40]

Levi is obviously talking about himself, but the backdrop of this is the brutal deprivation of Jewish cultural symbols and practices that provided shared meanings and purposes necessary for mutual intimacies. Stripping these away is to deprive individuals and a people of their sense of self and their shared making sense of the world.

Another illustration of this is the treatment of Native peoples by white European colonizers. Jonathan Lear describes how Plenty Coups, the Crow chief, led his people through a period of cultural devastation.[41] For Lear, cultural devastation involves the traumatic loss of narratives and rituals that a group of people uses to interpret current and past events, thus gaining intersubjective meaning and purpose. These narratives and rituals make it possible to assimilate past and present experiences. When these narratives and rituals are stripped away, making sense of the world and experience is radically undermined. For the Crow community, cultural devastation involved the violent and traumatic incursion of white Europeans, the dominance of white European narratives, and the corresponding loss of Crow cultural rituals and narratives that had provided meaning, a sense of hope, purpose, and direction vis-à-vis a Crow future. As Terrence Des Pres writes, "Gone were the myths and institutions, the symbols and technologies which in normal times allow the self [and community] to transcend and lose sight of its actual situation."[42]

The cumulative traumas experienced by European Jews as well as the Crow and other Indigenous communities obviously impact their lives in the present and will do so for the remainder of their existence. Yet, the trauma they experienced and endured has also shaped the lives of subsequent generations—generations that may not have experienced collective trauma. For instance, Hellen Epstein wondered why she and other children of parents who had endured, but never spoke about, the horrors of Nazi concentration

---

40. Levi, *Survival in Auschwitz*, 27 (italics are mine).

41. Lear, *Radical Hope*. See also Strozier and Flynn, *Genocide, War, and Human Survival*.

42. Des Pres, *The Survivor*, 188.

camps had anxieties, paranoia, and nightmares.[43] Interviewing other children of Holocaust survivors, she discovered that trauma can be passed down the generations, even if parents never speak about their sufferings. Her research has been confirmed by numerous studies.[44] Trauma has legs across generations.

Individual or communal victims of trauma find various ways to survive. To be sure, some people may, like Jean Améry, eventually succumb to the unassimilable. Yet most individuals or communities manifest considerable resiliencies, developing psychosocial defenses to survive what is unassimilable. Victims of trauma may survive by way of psychological defense mechanisms such as dissociation, de-symbolization, denial, rationalization, reaction formation, and splitting.[45] They may isolate themselves from any situation that they perceive, consciously or unconsciously, will expose them or make them more vulnerable. Some communities, such as the Crow people, may construct new narratives that help them find paths forward in spite of the traumas. Similarly, African Americans during Jim Crow formed religious communities that sustained them in the midst of the societal traumas of racism. These communities developed and used narratives and relations of mutual personal recognition, trust, and fidelity in the face of political-social violence. Naturally, individual and collective psychosocial responses to trauma, while aimed at survival, range from being constructively adaptive to destructive or unhealthy. For instance, as noted in chapter 5, James Baldwin wrote that his father "was defeated long before he died because, at the bottom of his heart, he really believed what white people said about him."[46] On a larger scale, the years of Israeli persecution of Palestinians and the recent military war and occupation of Gaza represent, in part, the failure of many Israelis to work through the traumas of the Holocaust. As Arwa Damon notes, a vicious, tragic cycle of mutual traumatizing takes place between Israelis and Palestinians.[47]

This brief dive into the notion of trauma highlights trauma's key features as it relates to human beings, namely, unbearable and unclaimed

---

43. Epstein, *Children of the Holocaust*.

44. See Doucet and Rovers, "Generational Trauma"; Krippner and Barrett, "Transgenerational Trauma"; Lev-Wiesel, "Intergenerational Transmission of Trauma."

45. van der Kolk et al., "History of Trauma in Psychiatry"; van der Kolk et al., "Dissociation and Information Processing."

46. Baldwin, *The Fire Next Time*, 4.

47. Michael Levitt et al., "How Generational Trauma among Israelis and Palestinians Fuels the Cycles of Violence," NPR, October 14, 2023, https://www.npr.org/2023/10/14/1205987068/how-generational-trauma-among-israelis-and-palestinians-fuels-the-cycles-of-viol.

experience, shattering of persons' assumptive world, initiation of psychological defenses for survival, and isolation and alienation—resulting from a profound fear of vulnerability and a deep distrust of other human beings. When using the notion of trauma in relation to more-than-human species, a question immediately comes to the fore: Is it possible to use the concept of trauma when it has been developed by studying human beings? Other species do have complex semiotic capacities for communicating[48] and, no doubt, for organizing their experiences, but it is not clear that these species are capable of symbolization. Do other species have an assumptive world that can be shattered? Do they have a culture that can be destroyed? I think it is fair to say that when it comes to trauma, we know a great deal about human beings but we know very little (and care less) about trauma as it pertains to other species—assuming we can apply this concept to the suffering of more-than-human species.[49] Acknowledging this limitation means the following is speculative, though I think it is a necessary speculation if we are to acknowledge and begin to learn more about the suffering of more-than-human species so that we can begin to be more empathic and compassionate toward other species.

Charles Sanders Peirce argued that all living beings, from the "lowly" amoeba to apes and human beings,[50] have varying semiotic capacities that are necessary to move about, engage, and survive in the world.[51] A century later, anthropologist Eduardo Kohn notes, "What we call mind, or self, is a product of semiosis ... Selves, human or nonhuman, simple or complex, are the outcomes of semiosis ... They are waypoints in a semiotic process."[52] It is, of course, easier for us to take note of the semiotic communications of mammals such as dolphins, whales, and chimpanzees, though we are a long way from understanding them. Given this, it is not a stretch to consider that other species have varied, complex assumptive worlds linked to their semiotic capacities, which we largely do not comprehend. And if they have assumptive semiotic worlds, these worlds can be disrupted or shattered. Let

---

48. Let me stress that our scientific understanding of the communications of more-than-human species is limited. We are only beginning to understand their communications. It is also worth mentioning again Schlanger's book *The Light Eaters*. Interviewing numerous botanists and other scientists, she describes the burgeoning and exciting research on communication vis-à-vis plants.

49. Ferdowsian and Merskin, "Parallels in Sources of Trauma."

50. See Peirce, *Peirce on Signs*.

51. Barry Stampfl also uses Peirce and semiotics to argue for post-traumatic stress disorder in referring to canine suffering. I am extending the use of semiotics to living beings because Peirce does as well. Stampfl, "Theorizing Canine PTSD."

52. Kohn, *How Forests Think*, 117.

me return to Jack London's imaginative stories to offer an unscientific illustration from the previous chapter.[53] Buck was a large dog who "lived at a big house in the sun-kissed Santa Clara Valley . . . And over this great demesne, here he was born and here he had lived the four years of his life."[54] London depicted Buck's early assumptive world, which was severely disrupted. Recall that the gardener, who Buck trusted, took him for a walk with the aim of selling Buck to a stranger, who subsequently tied a rope to Buck's collar. "Buck had accepted the rope with quiet dignity. To be sure, it was an unwonted performance: but he had learned to trust in men he knew."[55] When Buck resisted, the man brutally beat him, shattering Buck's world wherein he could trust men because they had been loyal to him and cared for and about him. This was the beginning of a series of traumas that would lead him to being sold in Alaska. London wrote, "Buck's first day on the Dyea beach was like a nightmare. Every hour was filled with shock and surprise. He had been suddenly jerked from the heart of civilization and flung into the heart of things primordial."[56] London's empathic imagination gives voice to the shattering of Buck's assumptive world.

While it is seemingly a large claim to suggest that the concept of trauma applies to other-than-human species, I believe most readers would agree that sentient beings suffer, sometimes intensely. Above, I mentioned hearing the horrific screams of animals at a German slaughter factory. Are those screams not a clear sign of their terror and trauma? And why should we care about the sufferings and traumas of other species when human beings experience so much suffering and trauma? If we consider the present and future realities of climate change, it is safe to say that human beings and other species will suffer from losses of viable habitats, reduced resources, and increased political violence within and between nations—violence that impacts other species. In my view, some of the suffering rightly falls under the heading of trauma. But the question remains: Why should we care about the traumas of other species? The Anthropocene Age reveals that that human survival and flourishing depends on a biodiverse Earth. Indeed, *our*

---

53. I recognize that literary writers such as Jack London can easily slip into projecting human attributes onto other animals, as he does with Buck. This is especially true when we encounter the silence of other species and fill this silence with our imaginations. Nevertheless, it is clear that some are motivated to empathically understand the experiences of other-than-human species. This empathy is an attempt to bridge the ontological rift, as well as eschew psychological defenses implicated in legitimating the instrumental use of other-than-human species.

54. London, *Call of the Wild*, 761–62.

55. London, *Call of the Wild*, 763.

56. London, *Call of the Wild*, 770.

collective assumptive worlds depend on a biodiverse earth. Put differently, a habitable Earth is the existential foundation of any and all semiotic or symbolically organized experience and, therefore, a foundation of any and all assumptive worlds. The loss of a habitable world, therefore, is unbearable and unclaimable, whether we are referring to human beings or other animals.[57] In short, the painful and traumatic unhousing of other species will eventually lead to the unhousing of human beings from our collective home—the Earth.[58]

White Fang and Trauma

The story of White Fang begins in the depth of winter in the Alaskan Territory, where it was so "cold that the spirit of it was not even that of sadness."[59] In the midst of this desolate landscape Bill and Henry were making their way on the Northland trail toward Fort McGurry when they noticed that wolves were following them. Bill realized when he went to feed the dogs he was one fish short and only later discovered that one of the wolves had sneaked into the camp, masquerading as one of the sled dogs.[60] Not long after, they noticed one of their dogs was missing, likely killed and eaten by the wolves.[61] Eventually, after losing two more dogs, Bill and Henry espy the leader, a large she-wolf, who obviously knew the ways of human beings because she was able to sneak into the camp at night and was aware enough to stay out of the range of the rifle.[62] Over a period of days, Bill went missing, as well as all the other dogs, leaving Henry to survive alone. When he had almost succumbed to exhaustion, Henry was rescued, and he told his rescuers about a large she-wolf leading a pack of wolves.[63]

57. Human beings can certainly imagine a world where human beings and other species are extinct, but we cannot possibly experience that world because an uninhabitable earth does not give rise to the capacities for symbolically organized experience.

58. Let me stress that this does not mean we should care for and about other species simply and solely because we need them to survive. This kind of thinking is instrumental, though it is a step in the right direction. As I have argued elsewhere in this book, the existential fact of the singularities of other species gives rise to the existential categorical command to respect and care for their singularities. Instrumental epistemologies are subordinate to personalizing epistemologies. See Macmurray, *Persons in Relation*.

59. London, *White Fang*, 385.
60. London, *White Fang*, 388.
61. London, *White Fang*, 390–91.
62. London, *White Fang*, 398–99.
63. London, *White Fang*, 407.

The story shifts to the relationship between the she-wolf[64] and One-Eye, a male wolf. This couple travels together, and eventually Kiche, the she-wolf, becomes pregnant. They find a lair for Kiche to give birth to a litter, and One-Eye becomes the caregiver—bringing food for Kiche and, later, the pups. One of the litter was a gray cub. Even before "his eyes had opened, he had learned by touch, taste, and smell to know his mother—a fount of warmth and liquid food and tenderness. She possessed a gentle, caressing tongue that soothed him."[65] This gray cub had brothers and sisters, and "in this time his brothers and sisters were one with him."[66] While becoming more conscious and exploratory, the gray cub "learned other attributes of his mother than the soft, soothing tongue . . . he discovered in her a nose that with a sharp nudge administered rebuke, and later, a paw, that crushed him down or rolled him over."[67]

Kiche, One-Eye, and the litter mates endure two famines. Eventually only the gray cub survives, despite desperate efforts by Kiche and One-Eye, who later dies trying to find meat. As his mother frantically searches for food, the gray cub ventures out of the cave into a strange world of new experiences. One of his explorations led him to encounter a weasel, and if his mother had not heard his cries and intervened, he would have been killed. The gray "cub experienced another access of affection on the part of his mother. Her joy at finding him seemed greater even than his joy at being found. She nuzzled him and caressed him and licked the cuts made in him by the weasel's teeth."[68]

London spends considerable time describing the early life of the gray cub. I think he did this for two reasons. First, he continually juxtaposes the wild/nature and civilization. Nature is indeed difficult. There is the constant search for food, the threat of famine, and the perils of other animals, including the most dangerous—human animals. There is, in the wilds, no cruelty. Yes, there is fighting and death, but killing other animals for food is simply based on the need to survive. There is, in other words, no gratuitous killing or fighting, which is not the case, as we have seen in the previous chapter, for human beings. Second, London wants the reader to obtain a picture of what life is like for a cub. Despite dangers and seemingly harsh corrections from his mother, the gray cub experiences the love and care of his mother.

64. In the wild, the leader of the pack is known as she-wolf. Once she returns to the Indian camp, we learn her name is Kiche, which means Sky Spirit.
65. London, *White Fang*, 422.
66. London, *White Fang*, 423.
67. London, *White Fang*, 423.
68. London, *White Fang*, 434.

He trusts his mother, for she has demonstrated time and time again her loyalty to his well-being. This is his assumptive world—a world that will radically change.

The cub, in one of his explorations, encounters human beings for the first time. He "had never seen man, yet the instinct concerning man was his. In dim ways he recognized in man the animal that had fought itself to primacy over the other animals in the Wild... The spell of the cub's heritage was upon him, the fear and the respect born of centuries of struggle and the accumulated experience of the generations. The heritage was too compelling for a wolf that was only a cub. Had he been full-grown, he would have run away."[69] One of the men stood over him as the "cub cowered closer to the ground."[70] The man laughed, "Look! The white fangs!"[71] His mother bounded into the camp and one of the men remembered her as Kiche—a wolf-dog who had previously lived among them. To his surprise, "The cub saw his mother, the she-wolf, the fearless one, crouching down till her belly touched the ground, whimpering, wagging her tail, making signs of peace."[72] Gray Beaver recalled that during the famine, Kiche had left the shelter of the camp in search of food. It was in the wild that she joined and later led the wolf pack and had a litter with One-Eye.

While in the presence of these men, White Fang felt utterly helpless. Without the protection of his mother, "He could do nothing to defend himself. If this man-animal intended harm, White Fang knew he could not escape it."[73] All that he could do was to let out a very low growl. Once they came to the main camp, White Fang was attacked by dogs. The men, wielding clubs and stones, intervened to save him from further harm. This is when White Fang thought, "This was power, power inconceivable and beyond the natural, power that was godlike."[74] White Fang was in awe of these gods as he submitted to their rule. The freedom he and his mother experienced in the wild was severely restricted. Both he and his mother were tethered to sticks.[75] Not many days after this, White Fang was allowed to move about the camp. He was curious and saw something strange. Gray Beaver encouraged him to move closer, and White Fang, having never seen

---

69. London, *White Fang*, 440.
70. London, *White Fang*, 441.
71. London, *White Fang*, 441.
72. London, *White Fang*, 442.
73. London, *White Fang*, 443.
74. London, *White Fang*, 444.
75. London, *White Fang*, 445.

fire, was burned: "It was the worst [physical] hurt he had ever known."[76] Gray Beaver and others laughed at him while his mother was snarling and raging, unable to come to the aid of her cub. In this moment, physical pain was separated from the exquisite pain of shame and powerlessness—this profound sense of shame would follow White Fang for life.[77] "He could not stand being laughed at. The laughter of men was a hateful thing."[78]

White Fang, while living in the wild, had never experienced shame, though he would find this a frequent experience among men who wished to dominate him (and other dogs). For instance, not long after his mother was freed to roam the camp, Gray Beaver, in paying a debt to Three Eagles, gave Kiche away.[79] White Fang was horrified when seeing his mother get in a canoe with Three Eagles. He leapt into the river, only to be lifted out and severely beaten—multiple times—by Gray Beaver. "The beatings that had gone before were as nothing compared with the beating he now received. Gray Beaver's wrath was terrible."[80] From these experiences, "White Fang learned the right to punish was something the gods reserved for themselves."[81] Later that night, grieving alone, White Fang was beaten again because he "sorrowed too loudly."[82]

Two traumas shattered his assumptive world. The first was the loss of his mother—the foundation of his sense of self and his experiences of affection, care, and protection. The second trauma was being beaten (numerous times) and humiliated. These relationships with Gray Beaver and others "was no soil for kindliness and affection."[83] The shattering of his assumptive world would result in another world, another code—to obey the strong."[84] White Fang's new "development was in the direction of power" and subjugation.[85] White Fang "crawled slowly, cringing and groveling in the abjectness of his abasement and submission. He crawled straight for Gray Beaver, every inch of his progress becoming slower and more painful. At last he lay at his master's feet, into whose possession he now surrendered himself,

---

76. London, *White Fang*, 447.
77. London, *White Fang*, 447.
78. London, *White Fang*, 473.
79. London, *White Fang*, 452.
80. London, *White Fang*, 453.
81. London, *White Fang*, 454.
82. London, *White Fang*, 454.
83. London, *White Fang*, 458.
84. London, *White Fang*, 458.
85. London, *White Fang*, 458.

voluntarily, body and soul."[86] White Fang, though, "had no affection for Gray Beaver. True, he was a god, but a most savage god . . . His primacy was savage, and savagely he ruled, administering justice with a club, punishing transgression with the pain of a blow, and rewarding merit, not by kindness, but by withholding a blow."[87] White Fang's assumptive world had shifted from the care, affection, and security of his mother to cruel subjugation.

White Fang adapted to the cruelty and the competition with other dogs. He became "morose and lonely, unloving and ferocious, the enemy of all his kind."[88] This was the result of enduring multiple traumas. Vulnerability would have been anathema, whether in relation to Gray Beaver or other dogs. In relation to Gray Beaver, since he was a god, White Fang would obey and submit. This is what one does in the face of a terrifying, traumatizing victimizer. In relation to other dogs, White Fang would seek to dominate them. It was a solitary world of survival—devoid of affection, care, mutuality, and protection.

This world White Fang adapted to was bad, but it was going to get worse. Gray Beaver traveled with White Fang and other dogs to Fort Yukon. A man named Beauty Smith plied Gray Beaver with whiskey, and whatever money Gray Beaver had earned in trade was dwindling. Eventually, Gray Beaver handed White Fang over to Beauty Smith, who was "a monstrosity."[89] Beauty Smith "was cruel in the way that cowards are cruel."[90] Even though Gray Beaver was cruel, the relation between him and White Fang entailed a kind of faithfulness, though White Fang felt betrayed by being handed over to Smith.[91] Smith teased, humiliated, and beat White Fang, all with the aim of getting him ready to fight other dogs and wolves for sport. White Fang never lost, making a lot of money for Smith, though in time no one would want to have their dogs or wolves fight him. White Fang "now became the enemy of all things, and more ferocious than ever . . . he hated blindly and without the faintest spark of reason."[92]

The last fight was with a bulldog, which White Fang had never encountered before. To shorten the story, the bulldog eventually sinks his teeth into White Fang's neck, slowly choking the life out of him. When Smith "saw White Fang's eyes beginning to glaze, he knew beyond a doubt

86. London, *White Fang*, 462.
87. London, *White Fang*, 466–67.
88. London, *White Fang*, 484.
89. London, *White Fang*, 487.
90. London, *White Fang*, 489.
91. London, *White Fang*, 490.
92. London, *White Fang*, 491.

that the fight was lost ... He sprang upon White Fang and began savagely to kick him."[93] A tall young man waded through the crowd, yelling, "You Cowards! You Beasts!"[94] Just as Smith was about to kick, the young man, Weedon Scott punched him in the face. Smith tried to intervene again, only to be punched again. Scott and his friend tried to release the stranglehold of the bulldog, while his owner sauntered up and told them not to break his dog's teeth.[95] Eventually, he was able to break the hold and release White Fang, who was nearly dead. Smith tried to reclaim White Fang, arguing that by law he owned White Fang. Scott was having none of this, telling Smith he had forfeited any rights because of his cruelty.[96] Nevertheless, Scott forced Smith to accept $150 for White Fang, which was far below the market value.

White Fang had undergone a series of traumas since he first encountered human beings, in particular Gray Beaver and, later, Smith. Beaten numerous times into submission, White Fang's assumptive world, which had developed in a relationship of care, affection, and mutual trust and fidelity, was shattered. These beatings evoked feelings of helplessness, shame, and rage, which he channeled into survival, aggression against other dogs, and solitariness. The world of men, especially these types of men who treated animals as property, became his new world—a world marred by loneliness, fear of vulnerability, carelessness, distrust, and infidelity. To survive trauma, let alone repeated traumas, is an achievement, manifesting considerable strength and resilience, but the price of survival is a kind of ontological loneliness—a loneliness that can only be bridged by love, but fear stands in the way of crossing. It is a fear associated with vulnerability. To experience love and care, one must be vulnerable, but for those who have worked to survive trauma, like White Fang, vulnerability is linked to horrific trauma. It is safer, but not satisfactory, to not cross that bridge.

Care, Love, and the Possibilities of Healing from Trauma

White Fang was clearly very vulnerable when he was freed from the clutches of the bulldog's mandibles. If Weedon Scott had not intervened, Beauty Smith would have almost assuredly killed him or simply let him die. As a result of Matt's [a friend of Weedon] and Weedon's care, White Fang healed quickly, but he presented a problem because he was ferocious toward the

---

93. London, *White Fang*, 500.
94. London, *White Fang*, 500.
95. London, *White Fang*, 502.
96. London, *White Fang*, 503.

other dogs in the camp.[97] Given his history of trauma, this was understandable, but for Weedon and Matt, this raised the question whether White Fang could be healed or brought back into the company of men and dogs. Weedon remarked, "What he needs is some show of human kindness."[98] Easier said than done.

After throwing White Fang a piece of meat, another dog went after it only to be quickly killed. Matt went to kick White Fang away only to be bitten himself. Matt said, "served me right ... What'd I want to kick 'm for? You said yourself he'd done right."[99] They went back and forth about whether it was better to kill White Fang, eventually deciding to opt for kindness and freedom. Weedon said, "We'll let him run loose and see what kindness can do for him."[100] Weedon, without a club or gun, walks gently over to White Fang. "White Fang was suspicious. Something was impending. He had killed this god's dog, bitten his companion god, and what else was to be expected than some terrible punishment."[101] Weedon was not quick enough to escape being nipped as he reached to pet White Fang on the head. Matt saw what had happened and went for his rifle, while Weedon pleaded for him to stop. They both noticed White Fang's ferocious growling when the gun appeared, which stopped when Matt put it down and returned when he picked it up again.[102] They agreed that White Fang was "too intelligent to kill."[103] I take this to mean that they believed and hoped that with some consistent, patient care White Fang would come to trust them.

After learning his lesson, Weedon sat down a few feet from White Fang. White Fang was puzzled, softly growling. London shifts to White Fang's internal observations:

> Then the god spoke, and at the first sound of his voice, the hair rose on White Fang's neck and the growl rushed up in his throat. But the god made no hostile movement, and went on talking. For a time White Fang growled in unison with him, a correspondence of rhythm being established between growl and voice. But the god talked on interminably. He talked to White Fang as White Fang had never been talked to before. He talked softly and soothingly, with gentleness that somehow,

97. London, *White Fang*, 504.
98. London, *White Fang*, 505.
99. London, *White Fang*, 506.
100. London, *White Fang*, 507.
101. London, *White Fang*, 507.
102. London, *White Fang*, 508.
103. London, *White Fang*, 508.

somewhere, touched White Fang. In spite of himself and all the pricking warnings of his instinct [worldview], White Fang began to have confidence in this god. He had a feeling of security that was belied by all his experiences with men.[104]

Weedon's patience, gentleness, and care offered White Fang experiences he had not felt before with men, though he had experienced them with his mother. A glimmer of the original affection, trust, fidelity, and security with his mother, which had long been suppressed as a result of traumas, began to make its way slowly, cautiously into his consciousness.

Anyone who has worked with human beings who have been traumatized knows it takes a long time to cross the bridge from traumatic defensiveness to intimacy. There are all kinds of fits and starts, progress and regress, which London portrays in Weedon's emerging relationship with White Fang. London provides numerous examples of White Fang's distrust and Weedon's patient, reliable kindness. After some days, Weedon reached down to pat White Fang's head, and White Fang "snarled and bristled and flattened his ears . . . He shrank down under it [yet] . . . he still managed to hold himself together. It was torment, this hand that touched him and violated his instinct."[105] White Fang did not snap at Weedon, though he hated being touched, which I would argue is because touch is linked to vulnerability and trauma. This is analogous to human beings who have been traumatized and who hate, yet long for, intimacy.

In time White Fang learned that the touch "was not physically painful. On the contrary, it was even pleasant, in a physical way."[106] Nevertheless, White Fang "continued to fear, and he stood guard, expectant of unguessed evil, alternately suffering and enjoying as one feeling or the other came uppermost and swayed him."[107] "It was," London wrote, "the beginning of the end for White Fang—the ending of the old life and reign of hate. A new and incomprehensible fairer life was dawning. It required much thinking and endless patience on the part of Weedon Scott . . . And on the part of White Fang it required nothing less than a revolution. He had to ignore the urges and promptings of instinct and reason, defy experience, give the lie to life itself."[108] Scott's consistent kindness and gentleness "had gone to the roots

---

104. London, *White Fang*, 509.

105. London, *White Fang*, 510. I think a better term than *instinct* is *assumptive world* because if it were instinct, White Fang would have been forced to behave out of it. It is the assumptive world of trauma that makes it difficult for him to accept and trust kindness.

106. London, *White Fang*, 511.

107. London, *White Fang*, 511.

108. London, *White Fang*, 512.

of White Fang's nature, and with kindness touched to life potencies that had languished and well-nigh perished. One such potency was love . . . But this love did not come in a day."[109] I would rephrase this and say that care and love create a relationship wherein one's potentialities can be actualized—potentialities that lie dormant as a result of traumas. For White Fang to actualize his potential for love and being loved, he had to begin to trust and be vulnerable. London masterfully portrays this struggle—a struggle that entails both actors. All of this is quite similar to the terrible traumas human beings face and the work of therapy. It often takes years of work, on the part of the therapist and the patient, for the patient to experience and to own experiences of being cared for. When this happens (and it is never a one-time situation but takes place again and again) it is indeed a revolution.

Weedon felt obliged to redeem White Fang "from the wrong [men] had done . . . It was a matter of principle and conscience. He felt that the ill done White Fang was a debt incurred by man and that it must be paid. So he went out of his way to be especially kind . . . Each day he made it a point to caress and pet White Fang, and to do it at length."[110] White Fang enjoyed this but continued to growl, though "with a new note in it,"[111] which only someone as attentive and caring as Weedon could detect. Previously, men like Gray Beaver and Smith had imposed their will on White Fang. They did not listen to or get to know him, which is all part of the reality of traumatic relations, whether we are talking about other human beings or other species. Weedon's care involved attending, listening, and learning about White Fang, not in any instrumental way but for the sake of White Fang—*volo ut sis* (I want you to be).

Even with this new relationship and experiences, White Fang "was too self-possessed, too strongly poised in his own isolation. Too long had he cultivated reticence, aloofness, and moroseness. He never barked in his life, and he could not now learn to bark a welcome when his god approached."[112] Yes, it was a revolution to let himself be loved, to be petted. But change does not happen in an instant; it is a long process, demanding patience and perseverance. To be sure, White Fang was deeply attached and dependent on Weedon, but he remained wary, distant and aloof, especially, and understandably, from other men and other dogs. This would eventuate in a crisis for Weedon and White Fang.

---

109. London, *White Fang*, 512.
110. London, *White Fang*, 513.
111. London, *White Fang*, 513.
112. London, *White Fang*, 514.

Weedon left Matt in charge while he made a trip to Circle City. White Fang had never been separated from Weedon and did not understand that he would return. He only noticed that before Weedon left he had packed a bag. White Fang became listless, refused to eat, and was sick. Matt was concerned and wrote a letter, telling Weedon, "That Damn wolf wont work. Wont eat. Aint got no spunk left. Mebbe he is going to die."[113] Weedon returned quickly and White Fang recovered within two days.

What happened worried Weedon. As an engineer, his time in Alaska was limited. He knew he was going to return home to California to be with his family. "What the devil can I do with a wolf in California?" Weedon asked Matt.[114] Weedon was torn yet leaned to leaving for California alone. Matt said, "From the way he cut up the other time you went away, I wouldn't wonder this time but he died."[115] Angry, Weedon replied, "Oh shut up!"[116] Weedon had decided to leave without White Fang, and he locked the front and back doors to the cabin. Before boarding the *Aurora*, Matt noticed White Fang sitting a few yards away. Puzzled, Weedon guessed that White Fang had jumped through the window in pursuit of his master. This was confirmed when Weedon felt the "fresh-made cuts on his muzzle."[117] Looking at White Fang, Weedon decided to take him home with him to California. There, White Fang would actualize more of his potentialities as he healed from past traumas.

Before shifting to White Fang's time with Weedon and his family, I want to say a bit more about White Fang's responses to Weedon's leaving. Recall that when White Fang was still a very young wolf, he had experienced a double trauma. First, his mother was given away by Gray Beaver. The only love, affection, and protection White Fang had ever known (his assumptive world) was being taken down the river. Second, when he tried to pursue his mother, White Fang was brutally beaten. When Weedon left to travel to Circle City, White Fang, in my view, experienced this as abandonment, not unlike his mother being taken. This time, however, White Fang had no interest in living in a world without love and affection. Yes, he could have transferred his affections to Matt, but, like those who suffer trauma, the first person to care is felt to be the only person who cares. It is an either/or situation for White Fang—live with Weedon, his savior, or die without him. White Fang had not yet made the change to believing that affection and love

---

113. London, *White Fang*, 516.
114. London, *White Fang*, 520.
115. London, *White Fang*, 521–22.
116. London, *White Fang*, 522.
117. London, *White Fang*, 523.

could come from other people. So, when Weedon left again, White Fang was desperate to find a way to stay with him. This desperation came from the belief that his life depended on the love and affection of Weedon Scott.

In the previous chapter, I mentioned how painfully disoriented Buck, who grew up in the bucolic setting of California, was when he arrived in the wilds of Alaska. Similarly, after docking in San Francisco, White Fang "was appalled . . . The streets were crowded with perils—wagons, carts, automobiles; great straining horses pulling huge trucks; monstrous cable and electric cars hooting and clanging though the midst, screeching their insistent menace after the manner of lynxes he had known in the northern woods."[118] Thankfully, the nightmare of the city would recede quickly as they made their way to the country, where Weedon's family awaited his arrival.

The family had a couple of dogs, "but White Fang was averse to friendship." All he asked of other dogs was to be left alone . . . His whole life he had kept aloof from his kind."[119] This said, during his months in Santa Clara, "Human kindness was like a sun shining on him."[120] One scene is worth quoting at length:

> White Fang had never been very demonstrative. Beyond his snuggling and the throwing of a crooning note into his love-growl, he had no way of expressing his love. Yet it was given to him to discover a third way. He had always been susceptible to the laughter of the gods. Laughter had affected him with madness, made him frantic with rage. But he did not have it in him to be angry with his love-master, and when that god elected to laugh at him in a good-natured bantering way, he was nonplussed. He could feel the pricking and stinging of the old anger as it strove to rise up in him, but it strove against love. He could not be angry; yet he had to do something. At first he was dignified, and the master laughed harder. Then he tried to be more dignified, and the master laughed harder than before. In the end, the master laughed him out of his dignity. His jaws slightly parted, his lips lifted a little, and a quizzical expression that was more love than humor came into his eyes. He had learned to laugh. Likewise he learned to romp with his master.[121]

White Fang, while in Alaska, had learned to be vulnerable enough to accept love from Scott. Nevertheless, he continued to be captive to the

---

118. London, *White Fang*, 524.
119. London, *White Fang*, 529.
120. London, *White Fang*, 537.
121. London, *White Fang*, 538–39.

painful humiliations of the past. As mentioned above, he was morose and was not playful with anyone. The love he continued to receive from Weedon and others in his family created a space for White Fang to let go of (not forget) past humiliations in favor of experiences of being loved. And this made it possible for him to actualize his capacities for laughter and play.

There was one more capacity to be birthed. White Fang growled but never barked, neither in love nor fear. Weedon would often go horseback riding, and White Fang would follow effortlessly behind. One morning, Weedon's horse bucked in fear and he fell, injuring himself. White Fang feared leaving him, but Weedon was insistent on White Fang going home to get help, which he did. Frantic, he tried growling to gain the attention of family members, to no avail. He became more desperate, and Beth, Weedon's wife, said, "He is trying to speak." In that instant, "Speech came to White Fang, rushing up in a great burst of barking."[122] The family realized that something had happened to Weedon, so they followed White Fang and found the injured Weedon.

White Fang would, on another occasion, save the family from a felon, though in the process he would be grievously wounded.[123] The family scrambled to get him the care he needed and White Fang recovered. The story ends with White Fang, now called Blessed Wolf, lying on the front porch while a litter of puppies plays with him—puppies that were the result of his going off with the family's collie in the woods one day while Weedon went horseback riding.

This story has what might be called a typical American happy ending. But I wish to stress that London took pains to describe the numerous traumas White Fang endured before being rescued by Weedon Scott. London also portrays the long process of change—change made possible by the patient, reliable, benevolent care of Weedon (and later his family) and the corresponding hard work on the part of White Fang to trust enough to be vulnerable in accepting this love, as well as to risk changing (e.g., playing, laughing, barking). Anyone who has been traumatized or worked with victims of trauma knows the road to healing (not cure) is long and difficult.

Conclusion

Throughout this book, while focusing on men and their relationships, I have returned repeatedly to the issue of the climate crisis. The apparatuses of racism (and other forms of oppression and marginalization), imperialism, and

122. London, *White Fang*, 541.
123. London, *White Fang*, 544.

capitalism negatively shape our relationships with each other, as well as our relationships with other species and the Earth. Our failures to recognize and mourn the destruction of other human beings and other species only serves to fuel more destruction. We continue to cling, like Ahab, to apparatuses that fuel racism and other forms of marginalization. In terms of other creatures, we slaughter billions of other species every year, deafened to their screams by capitalistic marketing. We experiment on various species without even a twinge of remorse for the sufferings they endure, rationalizing it is necessary to meet human needs and pleasures. We are destroying and have destroyed habitats as a result of extractive and exploitative imperialistic capitalism. Our contributions to climate change have and will continue to cause the extinctions of other species, silencing forever the voices of these singular beings. This is all quite grim, but we are obliged to face all of this and, unlike Frankenstein and Ahab, lament and mourn. Confronting ourselves and mourning, however, enable us to change the ways we relate to each other and other species, as Scrooge did. We can, like John Thornton and Weedon Scott, make inoperative the apparatuses that alienate us from othered human beings and othered species and, in rendering these apparatuses inoperative, we can develop our empathic and compassionate capacities to care for and about other species. Fictional characters aside, there are many, but not nearly enough, people—scientists, activists, lay persons, etc.—who demonstrate the courage, persistence, patience, and labor to understand and care for othered human beings and other species—animals, insects, and plants.

Recognizing these efforts can raise a sense of hope in the midst of a bleak future—hope for ourselves as human beings—existent and nonexistent—and hope for other species and the Earth. This said, our care for each other, for other species, and the Earth is not necessarily contingent on hope. John Thornton and Weedon Scott intervened to care for Buck and White Fang after observing how cruelly they were being treated. They did not stop Hal's or Beauty Smith's actions out of some future vision or hope. Rather, they were guided by the categorical, ethical command to care, regardless of whether that care resulted in Buck or White Fang surviving or thriving. It was their care for animals they did not know that made possible hope for Buck's and White Fang's well-being. *Care precedes and founds hope.* Hope is contingent on care, but the reverse is not true. In other words, care can exist in the midst of hopelessness, which is a crucial insight as we face a dire future. As boys and men (and, of course, girls and women), we are invited to dwell in the world, wherein we nurture the virtues of courage, patience, humility, and benevolence, which are necessary for our listening to and being moved by the voices of other human beings and other species. In being moved, we labor to care for the Earth and its inhabitants.

Bibliography

Agamben, Giorgio. *Homo Sacer: Sovereign Power and Bare Life*. Translated by Daniel Heller-Roazen. Stanford: Stanford University Press, 1998.
———. *The Open: Man, and Animal*. Translated by Kevin Attell. Stanford: Stanford University Press, 2004.
———. *Potentialities: Collected Essays in Philosophy*. Translated by Daniel Heller-Roazen. Stanford: Stanford University Press, 1999.
———. *State of Exception*. Stanford: Stanford University Press, 2005.
———.*What Is an Apparatus? And Other Essays*. Translated by David Kishik and Stefan Pedatella. Stanford: Stanford University Press, 2009.
Alexander, Michelle. *The New Jim Crow: Mass Incarceration in the Age of Colorblindness*. New York: New Press, 2010.
Alford, C. Fred. *Trauma and Forgiveness: Consequences and Communities*. Cambridge: Cambridge University Press, 2013.
Altman, Niel. "Black and White Thinking: A Psychoanalyst Reconsiders Race." *Psychoanalytic Dialogues* 10 (2000) 589–605.
———. "Whiteness Uncovered: Commentary on Papers by Melanie Suchet and Gillian Straker." *Psychoanalytic Dialogues* 14 (2004) 439–46.
Améry, John. "Torture." In *Art from the Ashes: A Holocaust Anthology*, edited by Lawrence L. Langer, 121–36. Oxford: Oxford University Press, 1995.
Anderson, Carol. *White Rage: The Unspoken Truth of Our Racial Divide*. New York: Bloomsbury, 2016.
Andrianova, Anastassiya. "Narrating Animal Trauma in Bulgakov and Tolstoy." *Humanities* 5.4 (2016) e84. https://doi.org/10.3390/h5040084.
Aralepo, Olatokunbo. "The White Male Therapist/Helper as (M)other to the Black Male Patient/Client." *Free Associations* 10 (2003) 382–98.
Arendt, Hannah. *Eichmann in Jerusalem: A Report on the Banality of Evil*. New York: Penguin, 1965.
———. *The Human Condition*. Chicago: University of Chicago Press, 1958.
———. *On Lying and Politics*. New York: Library of America, 2022.
———.*The Origins of Totalitarianism*. New York: Harvest, 1968.
———. *The Promise of Politics*. New York: Schocken, 2005.

Armstrong, Karen. *A History of God: The 4,000-Year Quest of Judaism, Christianity and Islam.* New York: Ballantine, 1993.

Bakan, David. *The Duality of Existence: Isolation and Communion in Western Man.* New York: Beacon, 1966.

Baldwin, James. *The Fire Next Time.* New York: Dial, 1990.

———. *Notes of a Native Son.* Boston: Beacon, 1984.

Barker, Ernest. *The Politics of Aristotle.* Oxford: Oxford University Press, 1971.

Baurecht, William. "To Reign Is Worth Ambition: The Masculine Mystique in *Moby-Dick*." *Journal of American Culture* 9.4 (1996) 53–62.

Beebe, Beatrice, and Frank Lachmann. "The Contribution of Mother-Infant Mutual Influence on the Origins of Self- and Object Representations." In *Relational Perspectives in Psychoanalysis,* edited by Neil J. Skolnick and Susan C. Warshaw, 83–118. London: Analytic, 1992.

Benjamin, Jessica. "Sameness and Difference: Toward an 'Over-Inclusive' Model of Gender Development." *Psychoanalytic Inquiry* 15 (1995) 125–42.

Black, Daniel. *The Coming.* New York: St. Martin's, 2015.

Bodin, Jean. *On Sovereignty: Six Books on the Commonwealth.* Seven Treasures, 2009.

Bollas, Christopher. *The Shadow of the Object: Psychoanalysis of the Unthought Known.* New York: Columbia University Press, 1987.

Bookchin, Murray. *Post-Scarcity Anarchism.* Edinburgh: AK, 2004.

Breitman, George, ed. *Malcolm X Speaks.* New York: Grove, 2024.

Brody, Sylvia. "Transitional Objects: Idealization of a Phenomenon." *Psychoanalytic Quarterly* 49 (1980) 561–605.

Bromberg, Phillip M. "Treating Patients with Symptoms—And Symptoms with Patience: Reflections on Shame, Dissociation, and Eating Disorders." *Psychoanalytic Dialogues* 11(6) (2001) 891–912.

Brown, Wendy. *Undoing the Demos: Neoliberalism's Stealth Revolution.* New York: Zone, 2015.

Bubeck, Diemut Elisabet. *Care, Gender, and Justice.* Oxford: Clarendon, 1995.

Buber, Martin. *I and Thou.* New York: Scribner, 1958.

Bunge, Marcia J. *The Child in Christian Thought.* Grand Rapids: Eerdmans, 2001.

Butler, Judith. *Precarious Life: The Powers of Mourning and Violence.* New York: Verso, 2004.

Butler, Smedley D. *War Is a Racket.* Port Townsend, WA: Feral House, 1935.

Camus, Albert. *The Plague.* New York: Vintage, 1991.

Capps, Donald. *Men and Their Religions: Honor, Hope, and Humor.* New York: Bloomsbury, 2002.

———. *Men, Religion, and Melancholia: James, Otto, Jung, and Erikson.* New Haven: Yale University Press, 1997.

Caputo, John. *What to Believe? Twelve Brief Lessons in Radical Theology.* New York: Columbia University Press, 2023.

Caruth, Cathy. *Listening to Trauma: Conversations with Leaders in the Theory and Treatment of Catastrophic Experience.* Baltimore: Johns Hopkins University Press, 2014.

———. *Unclaimed Experience: Trauma, Narrative, and History.* Baltimore: Johns Hopkins University Press, 1996.

Cholbi, Michael. *Grief: A Philosophical Guide.* Princeton: Princeton University Press, 2021.

Clebsch, William A., and Charles R. Jaekle. *Pastoral Care in Historical Perspective.* Northvale, NJ: Aronson, 1994.

Clinebell, Howard. *Basic Types of Pastoral Care and Counseling: Resources for the Ministry of Healing and Growth.* Nashville: Abingdon, 1984.

Coates, Ta-Nehisi. *Between the World and Me.* New York: Spiegel & Grau, 2015.

Colebrook, Claire, and Jason Maxwell. *Agamben.* New York: Polity, 2016.

Colman, Athena V. "Corporeal Schemas and Body Images: Fanon, Merleau-Ponty, and the Lived Experience of Race." In *Fanon, Phenomenology, and Psychology*, edited by Leswin Laubscher et al., 127–38. New York: Routledge, 2022.

Cone, James H. *The Cross and the Lynching Tree.* Maryknoll, NY: Orbis, 2011.

Connolly, William E. *Facing the Planetary: Entangled Humanism and the Politics of Swarming.* Durham: Duke University Press, 2017.

Corradi Fiumara, Gemma. *The Other Side of Language: A Philosophy of Listening.* London: Routledge, 1990.

Cox, Harvey. *The Market as God.* Cambridge: Harvard University Press, 2016.

Crutzen, Paul J, and Edward F. Stoermer. "The 'Anthropocene.'" *IGB Global Change Newsletter* 41 (2000) 17–18.

Cunsolo, Ashlee, and Karen Landman, K., eds. *Mourning Nature: Hope at the Heart of Ecological Loss & Grief.* Toronto: McGill-Queen's University Press, 2017.

Cupitt, Don. *Above Us Only Sky: The Religion of Ordinary Life.* Santa Rosa, CA: Polebridge, 2011.

———. *Radical Theology: Selected Essays.* Santa Rosa, CA: Polebridge, 2006.

Dalal, Farhad. *Race, Colour and the Process of Racialization: New Perspectives from Group Analysis, Psychoanalysis and Sociology.* New York: Routledge, 2002.

———. Racism: Processes of Detachment, Dehumanization, and Hatred. *The Psychoanalytic Quarterly* 75.1 131–61. https://doi.org/10.1002/j.2167-4086.2006.tb00035.x

Dardot, Pierre, and Christian Laval. *The New Way of the World: On Neoliberal Society.* New York: Verso, 2013.

De La Torre, Miguel A. *Embracing Hopelessness.* Minneapolis: Fortress, 2017.

Derrida, Jacques. *The Animal That Therefore I Am.* New York: Fordham University Press, 2008.

Des Pres, Terrence. *The Survivor: An Anatomy of Life in the Death Camps.* Oxford: Oxford University Press, 1976.

Dewey, John. *Art as Experience.* New York: Perigee, 1934.

Dickens, Charles. *A Christmas Carol.* E-Book: Animedia, 2013.

Dickinson, Colby. "The 'Absence' of Gender." In *Agamben's Coming Philosophy: Finding a New Use for Theology*, edited by Colby Dickinson and Adam Kotsko, 167–82. New York: Rowman & Littlefield, 2015.

Dinkel, Danae, and Kailey Snyder. "Exploring Gender Differences in Infant Motor Development Related to Parent's Promotion of Play." *Infant Behavior and Development* 59 (2020) e101440. https://doi.org/10.1016/j.infbeh.2020.101440.

Doehring, Carrie. *The Practice of Pastoral Care: A Postmodern Approach.* Louisville: Westminster John Knox, 2015.

Doucet, Marilyn, and Martin Rovers. "Generational Trauma, Attachment, and Spiritual/Religious Interventions." *Journal of Loss and Trauma* 15.2 (2010) 93–105. https://doi.org/10.1080/15325020903373078.

Douglass, Frederick. *Narrative of the Life of Frederick Douglass: An American Slave.* New York: Library of America, 1994.

Du Bois, W. E. B. *The Souls of Black Folk: Essays and Sketches.* 1903. Reprint, New York: Dover, 2016.

Dufour, Dany-Robert. *The Art of Shrinking Heads: On the New Servitude of the Liberated in the Age of Total Capitalism.* Cambridge: Polity, 2008.

Dykstra, Robert C. *Images of Pastoral Care: Classic Readings.* St. Louis: Chalice, 2005.

Easterly, William. *The Tyranny of Experts: Economics, Dictators, and the Forgotten Rights of the Poor.* New York: Basic Books, 2013.

Ellison, Ralph. *Shadow and Act.* New York: Vintage, 1995.

Engster, Daniel. *The Heart of Justice: Care Ethics and Political Theory.* Oxford: Oxford University Press, 2007.

Epstein, Helen. *Children of the Holocaust: Conversations with Sons and Daughters of Survivors.* New York: Penguin, 1988.

Erikson, Erik H. *Childhood and Society.* New York: Norton, 1952.

Faber, Roland. *The Mind of Whitehead: Adventure in Ideas.* Eugene, OR: Pickwick Publications 2023.

Fanon, Frantz. *Alienation and Freedom.* Edited by Jean Khalfa and Robert Young. London: Bloomsbury Academic, 2018.

———. *Black Skin, White Masks.* New York: Grove, 2008.

Fassin, Didier, and Richard Rechtman. *The Empire of Trauma: An Inquiry into the Condition of Victimhood.* Princeton: Princeton University Press, 2009.

Ferdowsian, Hope, and Debra Merskin. "Parallels in Sources of Trauma, Pain, Distress, and Suffering in Humans and Nonhuman Animals." *Journal of Trauma and Dissociation* 12 (2012) 448–68. https://doi.org/10.1080/15299732.2011.652346.

Flesberg, Evon O. *The Switching Hour: Kids of Divorce Say Good-Bye Again.* Nashville: Abingdon, 2008.

Fonagy, Peter. *Attachment Theory and Psychoanalysis.* New York: Other Press, 2001.

Fonagy, Peter, and Mary Target. "Attachment and Reflective Function: Their Role in Self-Organization." *Development and Psychopathology* 9 (1997) 679–700.

Forti, Simona. *Totalitarianism: A Borderline Idea in Political Philosophy.* Stanford: Stanford University Press, 2024.

Foster, John Bellamy. *The Return of Nature: Socialism and Ecology.* New York: Monthly Review, 2020.

Foucault, Michel. *Discipline and Punish: The Birth of the Prison.* New York: Vintage, 1979.

Frady, Marshall. *Martin Luther King, Jr.: A Life.* New York: Penguin, 2002.

Frank, Thomas. *One Market under God: Extreme Capitalism, Market Populism, and the End of Economic Democracy.* New York: Anchor, 2000.

Fraser, Nancy, and Axel Honneth. *Redistribution or Recognition? A Political-Philosophical Exchange.* New York: Verso, 2003.

Freis, Hans. "Faith and Knowledge." In *The Encyclopedia of Theology: The Concise Sacramentum Mundi*, edited by Karl Rahner, 418. New York: Crossroad, 1984.

Freire, Paulo. "Conscientisation." In *Conversion: Perspectives on Personal and Social Transformation*, edited by Walter E. Conn, 297–306. New York: Alba House, 1978.

Freud, Sigmund. "The Aetiology of Hysteria." In *The Standard Edition of the Complete Psychological Works of Sigmund Freud*, edited by James Strachey, 3:191–226. London: Hogarth, 1887.

———. "Mourning and Melancholia." In *The Standard Edition of the Complete Psychological Works of Sigmund Freud*, edited by James Strachey, 14:237–59. London: Hogarth, 1917.
Freyd, Jennifer J. *Betrayal Trauma*. Cambridge: Harvard University Press, 1996.
Gay, Peter. *Freud: A Life for Our Time*. New York: Anchor, 1988.
Gay, Ross. *Inciting Joy*. New York: Algonquin, 2022.
Gay, Volney P. *American Slavery: Privileges and Pleasures*. IPbooks, 2021.
———. *Freud on Sublimation: Reconsiderations*. SUNY Series on Religious Studies. New York: SUNY Press, 1992.
Gergley, György, and Zsolt Unoka. "Attachment and Mentalization in Infants: The Development of the Affective Self." In *Mind to Mind: Infant Research, Neuroscience, and Psychoanalysis*, edited by Elliot L. Jurist et al., 50–87. New York: Other Press, 2008.
Gerkin, Charles V. *An Introduction to Pastoral Care*. Nashville: Abingdon, 1997.
Gibson, Danjuma G. *Frederick Douglass, a Psychobiography: Rethinking Subjectivity in the Western Experiment of Democracy*. New York: Palgrave, 2018.
Gilligan, Carol. *In a Different Voice: Psychological Theory and Women's Development*. Cambridge: Harvard University Press, 1982.
Gilman, Sander L. *Difference and Pathology: Stereotypes of Sexuality, Race, and Madness*. Ithaca: Cornell University Press, 1985.
———. *Inscribing the Other*. Lincoln: University of Nebraska Press, 1991.
Giroux, Henry A. *Disposable Youth: Racialized Memories and the Culture of Cruelty*. London: Routledge, 2012.
Go, Julian. *Postcolonial Thought and Social Theory*. Oxford: Oxford University Press, 2016.
Goldberg, David Theo. *The Threat of Race: Reflections on Racial Neoliberalism*. Malden, MA: Wiley-Blackwell, 2009.
Graham, Larry Kent. *Moral Injury: Restoring Wounded Souls*. Nashville: Abingdon, 2017.
Grand, Sue. *The Reproduction of Evil: A Clinical and Cultural Perspective*. Northvale, NJ: Analytic, 2000.
Gray, J. Glenn. *The Warriors: Reflections on Men in Battle*. Omaha: University of Nebraska Press, 1970.
Grayling, A. C. *The History of Philosophy*. New York: Penguin, 2019.
Halevi, Yehuda. "Tis a Fearful Thing." www.sewgn.com/uploads/4/3/7/9/43793727/tis_a_fearful_thing.jpg.
Haley, Alex. *The Autobiography of Malcolm X*. New York: Grove, 1965.
Hall, Stuart. *Cultural Studies 1983: A Theoretical History*. Durham, NC: Duke University Press, 2016.
———. *Representation: Cultural Representations and Signifying Practices*. New York: Sage, 1997.
Hamington, Maurice. *Embodied Care: Jane Addams, Maurice Merleau-Ponty, and Feminist Ethics*. Urbana: University of Illinois Press, 2004.
Hardin, Harry T. "On the Vicissitudes of Freud's Early Mothering. I: Early Environment and Loss." *Psychoanalytic Quarterly* 56 (1987) 628–44.
———. "On the Vicissitudes of Freud's Early Mothering: II: Alienation from His Biological Mother. *The Psychoanalytic Quarterly* 57 (1988) 72–86. https://doi.org/10.1080/21674086.1988.11927204

Hardin, Harry T., and Daniel H. Hardin. "On the Vicissitudes of Early Primary Surrogate Mothering." *Journal of the American Psychoanalytic Association* 33 (1985) 609–29.

Hardt, Michael, and Antonio Negri. *Commonwealth*. Cambridge, MA: Belknap, 2009.

Hayek, F. A. *The Road to Serfdom: Text and Documents*. Vol. 2 of *The Collected Works of F. A. Hayek*. Chicago: University of Chicago Press, 2007.

Held, Virginia. *The Ethics of Care: Personal, Political, and Global*. Oxford: Oxford University Press, 2006.

Helsel, Philip Browning. *Pastoral Power beyond Psychology's Marginalization: Resisting the Discourses of the Psy-Complex*. New York: Palgrave, 2015.

Herman, Judith L. *Trauma and Recovery: The Aftermath of Violence—From Domestic Abuse to Political Terror*. New York: Basic, 1992.

Hillman, John. *A Terrible Love of War*. New York: Penguin, 2003.

Hiltner, Seward. *Preface to Pastoral Theology: The Ministry and Theory of Shepherding*. Nashville: Abingdon, 1958.

Hinds, Jay-Paul. *A Gift Grows in the Ghetto: Reimagining the Spiritual Lives of Black Men*. Louisville: Westminster John Knox, 2022.

Hochschild, Arlie Russell. *The Managed Heart: Commercialization of Human Feeling*. Berkeley: University of California Press, 2012.

Holifield, E. Brooks. *A History of Pastoral Care in America: From Salvation to Self-Realization*. 1983. Reprint, Eugene, OR: Wipf & Stock, 2005.

Holmes, Jeremy. *Attachment, Intimacy, Autonomy*. Northvale, NJ: Aronson, 1996.

Honneth, Axel. *Freedom's Right: The Social Foundations of Democratic Life*. New York: Columbia University Press, 2011.

———. *The Struggle for Recognition: The Moral Grammar of Social Conflicts*. Cambridge: MIT Press, 1995.

Human Rights Watch. *Racial Discrimination in the United States*, August 8, 2022. https://www.hrw.org/report/2022/08/08/racial-discrimination-united-states/human-rights-watch/aclu-joint-submission.

Hume, David. *On Suicide*. London: Oxford University Press, 1783.

Ibsen, Malte Frøslee. *A Critical Theory of Global Justice*. Oxford: Oxford University Press, 2023.

Illouz, Eva. *Cold Intimacies: The Making of Emotional Capitalism*. Cambridge: Polity, 2007.

Ingold, Tim. *The Perception of the Environment: Essays on Livelihood, Dwelling and Skill*. London: Routledge, 2022.

James, William. *The Principles of Psychology*. Vol. 1. New York: Holt, 1956.

JanMohamed, Abdul R. *The Death-Bound Subject: Richard Wright's Archaeology of Death*. Durham: Duke University Press, 2004.

Janoff-Bulman, Ronnie. *Shattered Assumptions: Towards a New Psychology of Trauma*. New York: Free Press, 1992.

Johnson, Cedric C. *Race, Religion, and Resilience in the Neoliberal Age*. New York: Palgrave Macmillan, 2016.

Johnson, Chalmers. *The Sorrows of Empire: Militarism, Secrecy, and the End of the Republic*. New York: Owl, 2004.

Johnson, Mark. *The Body in the Mind: The Bodily Basis of Meaning, Imagination, and Reason*. Chicago: University of Chicago Press, 1987.

Jones, David Stedman. *Masters of the Universe: Hayek, Friedman, and the Birth of Neoliberal Politics*. Princeton: Princeton University Press, 2012.

Josefson, Jim. *Hannah Arendt's Aesthetic Politics: Freedom and the Beautiful.* New York: Palgrave, 2019.
Joseph, Peniel E. *The Sword and the Shield: The Revolutionary Lives of Malcolm X and Martin Luther King Jr.* New York: Basic, 2020.
Keen, David. *Shame: The Politics and Power of an Emotion.* Princeton: Princeton University Press, 2023.
Keller, Catherine. *Political Theology of the Earth: Our Planetary Emergency and the Struggle for a New Public.* New York: Columbia University Press, 2018.
Kelley, Melissa M. *Grief: Contemporary Theory and the Practice of Ministry.* Minneapolis: Fortress, 2010.
Kendi, Ibram X., and Jason Reynolds. *Stamped from the Beginning: The Definitive History of Racist Ideas in America.* New York: Bold Type Books, 2020.
Kestenberg, Judith S., and Joan Weinstein. "Transitional Objects and Body Image Formation." In *Between Reality and Fantasy*, edited by Simon A. Grolnick and Leonard Barkin, 75–96. Northvale, NJ: Aronson, 1978.
King, Martin Luther, Jr. *The Autobiography of Martin Luther King, Jr.* Edited by Clayborne Carson. New York: Grand Central, 1998.
Kishik, David. *The Power of Life: Agamben and the Coming Politics.* Stanford: Stanford University Press, 2012.
Klein, Christopher. "Last Hired, First Fired: How the Great Depression Affected African Americans." *History.* August 2018, https://www.history.com/news/last-hired-first-fired-how-the-great-depression-affected-african-americans.
Klein, Naomi. *The Shock Doctrine: The Rise of Disaster Capitalism.* New York: Holt, 2007.
———. *This Changes Everything: Capitalism vs. the Climate.* New York: Simon & Schuster, 2014.
Kniess, Johannes. "Bentham on Animal Welfare." *British Journal for the History of Philosophy* 27 (2019) 556–72. https://doi.org/10.1080/09608788.2018.1524746.
Kocka, Jürgen. *Capitalism: A Brief History.* Princeton: Princeton University Press, 2016.
Kohn, Eduardo. *How Forests Think: Toward an Anthropology beyond the Human.* Sacramento: University of California Press, 2013.
Kolbert, Elizabeth. *The Sixth Extinction: An Unnatural History.* New York: Holt, 2014.
Kotsko, Adam, and Carlo Salzani. *Agamben's Philosophical Lineage.* Edinburgh: Edinburgh University Press, 2017.
Kovel, Joel. *The Radical Spirit: Essays on Psychoanalysis and Society.* New York: Free Associations Books, 1988.
———. *White Racism: A Psychohistory.* New York: Columbia University Press, 1970.
Krippner, Stanley, and Deirdre Barrett, "Transgenerational Trauma: The Role of Epigenetics." *Journal of Mind and Behavior* 40 (2019) 53–62.
Kris, Ernst. *Psychoanalytic Explorations in Art.* New York: International Universities, 1952.
Lakoff, George, and Mark Johnson. *Philosophy in the Flesh: The Embodied Mind and Its Challenge to Western Thought.* New York: Basic Books, 1999.
LaMothe, Ryan. "The Absence of Cure: The Core of Malignant Trauma and Symbolization." *Journal of Interpersonal Violence* 14 (1999) 1193–210.
———. "Autobiography in the Face of Social Death: Martin Luther King Jr., Sustaining Object/Process, and Radical Hope/Redemption." *Pastoral Psychology* 72 (2022) 289–303. 10.1007/s11089-22-01038-38.

———. *Care of Souls, Care of Polis: Toward a Political Pastoral Theology*. Eugene, OR: Cascade Books, 2017.

———. *The Coming Jesus and the Anthropocene*. Eugene, OR: Cascade Books, 2024.

———. "Literature and Social Pathologies: Ahab's Masculinity as a Distortion of Care and Faith." *Pastoral Psychology* 72 (2023) 49–63. https://doi.org/10.1007/s11089-22-01042-y.

———. "Male Pathological Grief in Mary Shelley's *Frankenstein* and Charles Dickens's *A Christmas Carol*: A Pastoral Psychological Perspective." *Pastoral Psychology* 72 (2023) 845–61.

———. "Men, the Ontological Rift, and the Possibility of Repair in Jack London's *Call of the Wild*: A Pastoral-Psychoanalytic Perspective." *Pastoral Psychology* (2023) 1–15.

———. *Pastoral Care in the Anthropocene Age: Facing a Dire Future*. Lanham, MD: Lexington, 2023.

———. *Pastoral Reflections on Global Citizenship: Framing the Political in Terms of Care, Faith, and Community*. Lanham, MD: Lexington, 2018.

———. "Pastoral Theology and the Problem of Political Violence." *Journal of Pastoral Theology* 33 (2021) 122–41.

———. *A Political Psychoanalysis for the Anthropocene Age: The Fierce Urgency of Now*. London: Routledge, 2024.

———. *A Radical Political Theology for the Anthropocene Era*. Eugene: Cascade, 2021.

Lane, Melissa. *The Birth of Politics: Eight Greek and Roman Political Ideas and Why They Matter*. Princeton: Princeton University Press, 2014.

Lartey, Emmanuel Y., and Hellena Moon. *Postcolonial Images of Spiritual Care: Challenges of Care in a Neoliberal Age*. Eugene, OR: Pickwick Publications, 2020.

Latour, Bruno. *We Have Never Been Modern*. Cambridge: Harvard University Press, 1993.

Layton, Lynne. *Toward a Social Psychoanalysis: Culture, Character, and Normative Unconscious Processes*. London: Routledge, 2020.

Lear, Jonathan. *Radical Hope: Ethics in the Face of Cultural Devastation*. Cambridge: Harvard University Press, 2006.

Lee, Ronald R., and J. Colby Martin. *Psychotherapy after Kohut: A Textbook of Self Psychology*. Hillsdale: Analytic, 1991.

Lester, Andrew D. *Pastoral Care with Children in Crisis*. Louisville: Westminster John Knox Press, 1985.

Lesutis, Gediminas. *The Politics of Precarity: Spaces of Extractivism, Violence, and Suffering*. London: Routledge, 2021.

Lev-Wiesel, Rachel. "Intergenerational Transmission of Trauma across Three Generations: A Preliminary Study." *Qualitative Social Work* 6 (2007) 75–94. https://doi.org/10.1177/1473325007074167.

Levi, Primo. *Survival in Auschwitz*. New York: Collier, 1960.

Levinas, Emmanuel. *Totality and Infinity: An Essay on Exteriority*. Pittsburgh: Duquesne University Press, 1969.

Linzey, Andrew. *Why Animal Suffering Matters: Philosophy, Theology, and Practical Ethics*. Oxford: Oxford University Press, 2009.

Litt, Carole J. "Theories of Transitional Object Attachment: An Overview." *International Journal of Behavioral Health* 9 (1986) 383–99.

London, Jack. *Call of the Wild*. In *The Unabridged Jack London*, edited by Lawrence Teacher and Richard E. Nichols, 759–831. Philadelphia: Running, 1981.

———. "The League of the Old Men." In *The Unabridged Jack London*, edited by Lawrence Teacher and Richard E. Nichols, 368–82. Philadelphia: Running, 1981.

———. *White Fang*. In *The Unabridged Jack London*. Edited by Lawrence Teacher and Richard E. Nichols, 383–548. Philadelphia: Running, 1981.

Lukács, Georg. *History and Class Consciousness: Studies in Marxist Dialectics*. Cambridge: MIT Press, 1968.

Lundestad, Geir. *The Rise and Decline of the American "Empire": Power and Its Limits in Comparative Perspective*. Oxford: Oxford University Press, 1990.

MacDonald, G. Jeffrey. *Thieves in the Temple: The Christian Church and the Selling of the American Soul*. New York: Basic Books, 2010.

MacIntyre, Alistair. *After Virtue: A Study in Moral Theory*. Notre Dame: University of Notre Dame Press, 1983.

Macmurray, John. *Conditions of Freedom: Being the Second Lectures on the Chancellor Dunning Trust, Delivered at Queen's University, Kingston, Ontario, 1949*. 1949. Reprint, London: Humanities, 1993.

———. *Persons in Relation: Being the Gifford Lectures Delivered in the University of Glasgow in 1954*.
. London: Humanities, 1991.

Malcolm, Hannah, ed. *Words for a Dying World: Stories of Grief and Courage from the Global Church*. London: SCM, 2020.

Mandela, Nelson. *Long Walk to Freedom: The Autobiography of Nelson Mandela*. New York: Little, Brown, 1995.

Mandeville, Bernard. *The Fable of the Bees: Or Private Vices, Publick Benefits*. New York: Penguin Classics, 1989.

Mantena, Karuna. "Showdown for Nonviolence: The Theory and Practice of Nonviolent Politics." In *To Shape a New World: Essays on the Political Philosophy of Martin Luther King, Jr.*, edited by Tommie Shelby and Brandon M. Terry, 78–104. Cambridge, MA: Belknap, 2018.

Marable, Manning. *Malcolm X: A Life of Reinvention*. New York: Viking, 2011.

Marcel, Gabriel. *The Existential Background of Human Dignity*. Cambridge: Harvard University Press, 2014.

Margalit, Avishai. *The Decent Society*. Cambridge: Harvard University Press, 1996.

Marshall, Joretta L. *Counseling Lesbian Partners*. Louisville: Westminster John Knox, 1997.

Mbembe, Achille. *Necropolitics*. Durham: Duke University Press, 2019.

McCarroll, Pamela R. "Listening for the Cries of the Earth: Practical Theology in the Anthropocene." *International Journal of Practical Theology* 24 (2020) 29–46.

McGarrah Sharp, Mindy. *Misunderstanding Stories: Toward a Postcolonial Pastoral Theology*. Eugene, OR: Pickwick Publications, 2013.

McGuire, Danielle L. *At the Dark End of the Street: Black Women, Rape, and Resistance—A New History of the Civil Rights Movement from Rosa Parks to the Rise of Black Power*. New York: Random House, 2011.

Melville, Herman. *Moby-Dick; or The Whale*. 1851. Reprint, E-book.

Michaelson, Eric O. *Martin Luther King, Jr.: A Comprehensive Biography of Martin Luther King, Jr.* Self-published, 2023.

Miller, Alice. *For Your Own Good: Hidden Cruelty in Child-Rearing and the Roots of Violence*. New York: Farrar, Straus & Giroux, 1990.

Miller, Walter James. Foreword to *Frankenstein*, by Mary Shelley, v–xviii. New York: Signet Classics, 2000.

Miller-McLemore, Bonnie J. "Climate Violence and Earth Justice." *International Journal of Practical Theology* 26 (2022) 329–66.

Mills, Charles W. *The Racial Contract*. Ithaca, NY: Cornell University Press, 1997.

Mitchell, Kenneth R., and Herbert Anderson. *All Our Losses, All Our Griefs: Resources for Pastoral Care*. Louisville: Westminster John Knox, 1983.

Moon, Zachary. *Coming Home: Ministry that Matters with Veterans and Military Families*. St. Louis: Chalice, 2015.

———. *Warriors between Worlds: Moral Injury and Identities in Crisis*. Lanham, MD: Lexington, 2019.

Moore, Jason W. "Name the System! Anthropocene & the Capitalocene Alternative." 2016 Bing Videos. https://jasonwmoore.wordpress.com/tag/capitalocene/.

Morris, Joshua. *Moral Injury among Returning Veterans: From Thank You for Your Service to a Liberative Solidarity*. Lanham, MD: Lexington, 2021.

Mounier, Emmanuel. *Personalism*. London: Routledge & Kagan Paul, 1952.

Neihardt, John G. *Black Elk Speaks: Being the Life Story of a Holy Man of the Oglala Sioux*. 1959. Reprint, Lincoln: University of Nebraska Press, 2014.

Neri, Erica, Simona Spinelli, Augusto Biasini, Marcello Stella, and Fiorella Monti. "Parenting Preterm Infants: Influence of Parental Gender and Dyadic Sensitivity on Infants' Cognitive and Interactive Development." In *Pre- and Postnatal Psychology and Medicine*, edited by Goetz Egloff and Dragana Djordjevic, 217–47. New York: Nova Medicine & Health, 2020.

Newmyer, Stephen T. *Animals, Rights and Reason in Plutarch and Modern Ethics*. New York: Routledge, 2005.

Niebuhr, H. Richard. *Faith on Earth: An Inquiry into the Structure of Human Faith*. New Haven: Yale University Press, 1989.

Novak, Michael. *The Spirit of Democratic Capitalism*. New York: Simon & Schuster, 1982.

———. *Toward a Theology of the Corporation*. Washington, DC: AEI, 1987.

Nussbaum, Martha C. *Justice for Animals: Our Collective Responsibility*. New York: Simon & Schuster, 2022.

———. *Political Emotions: Why Love Matters for Justice*. Cambridge, MA: Belknap, 2013.

Oates, Wayne E. *Grief, Transition, and Loss: A Pastor's Practical Guide*. Minneapolis: Fortress, 1997.

Oliner, Pearl M., and Samuel P. Oliner. *Toward a Caring Society: Ideas into Action*. Westport, CT: Praeger, 1995.

Oreskes, Naomi, and Erik M. Conway. *The Big Myth: How American Business Taught Us to Loathe Government and Love the Free Market*. London: Bloomsbury, 2023.

Park, Jeonghyun. *Pastoral Care for Survivors of a Traumatic Death*. Eugene, OR: Wipf & Stock, 2017.

Patterson, Orlando. *Rituals of Blood: The Consequences of Slavery in Two American Centuries*. New York: Basic, 1998.

———. *Slavery and Social Death: A Comparative Study*. Cambridge: Harvard University Press, 1982.

Patton, John. *Pastoral Care in Context: An Introduction to Pastoral Care*. Louisville: Westminster John Knox, 1993.

Payne, Les, and Tamara Payne. *The Dead Are Arising: The Life of Malcolm X*. London: Liverlight, 2020.

Peirce, Charles. *The Essential Peirce: Selected Philosophical Writings, 1893–1913*. Edited by the Peirce Edition Project. Bloomington: Indiana University Press, 1998.

———. *Peirce on Signs: Writings on Semiotic by Charles Sanders Peirce*. Edited by John Hoopes. Charlotte: North Carolina University Press, 1991.

Phillips, Kevin. *American Theocracy: The Peril and Politics of Radical Religion, Oil, and Borrowed Money in the 21st Century*. New York: Viking, 2006.

Pihkala, Panu. "Eco-Anxiety, Tragedy, and Hope: Psychological and Spiritual Dimensions of Climate Change." *Zygon* 53 (2018) 545–69.

Pistor, Katharina. *The Code of Capital: How the Law Creates Wealth and Inequality*. Princeton: Princeton University Press, 2019.

Poling James Newton. *Render unto God: Economic Vulnerability, Family Violence, and Pastoral Theology*. 2002. Reprint, Eugene, OR: Wipf & Stock, 2002.

Porter, Eduardo. *American Poison: How Radical Hostility Destroyed Our Promise*. New York: Knopf, 2020.

Porter, Roy. *The Faber Book of Madness*. London: Faber, 1991.

———. *A Social History of Madness: Stories of the Insane*. New York: Dutton 1991.

Prichard, Alex. *Anarchism: A Very Short Introduction*. Oxford: Oxford University Press, 2022.

Prozorov, Sergei. *Agamben and Politics: A Critical Introduction*. Edinburgh: Edinburgh University Press, 2014.

Pruyser, Paul W. *The Play of the Imagination: Toward a Psychoanalysis of Culture*. New York: International Universities, 1983.

Puryear, Stephen. "Schopenhauer on the Rights of Animals." *European Journal of Philosophy* 25 (2017) 250–69.

Rahner, Karl. "A Way to Faith." In *The Encyclopedia of Theology: The Concise Sacramentum Mundi*, edited by Karl Rahner, 496. New York: Crossroad, 1984.

Ramsay, Nancy J. "Compassionate Resistance: An Ethic for Pastoral Care and Counseling." *Journal of Pastoral Care* 52 (1999) 217–26.

Ramsay, Nancy J., and Carrie Doehring, eds. *Military Moral Injury and Spiritual Care: A Resource for Religious Leaders and Professional Caregivers*. St. Louis: Chalice, 2019.

Rank, Otto. *The Trauma of Birth*. 1929. Reprint London: Routledge, 2014.

Rieff, David. "Liberal Imperialism." In *The Imperial Tense: Prospects and Problems of American Empire*, edited by Andrew J. Bacevich, 10–28. Chicago: Ivan R. Dee.

Rizzuto, Ana-Marie. *The Birth of the Living God: A Psychoanalytic Study*. Chicago: University of Chicago Press, 1979.

Robinson, Cedric J. *Black Marxism: The Making of the Black Radical Tradition*. Raleigh: The University of North Carolina Press, 1983.

Robinson, Fiona. *The Ethics of Care: A Feminist Approach to Human Security*. Philadelphia: Temple University Press, 2011.

———. *Globalizing Care: Ethics, Feminist Theory, and International Relations*. Boulder, CO: Westview, 1999.

Rogers-Vaughn, Bruce. *Caring for Souls in a Neoliberal Age*. New York: Palgrave, 2016.

Rumscheidt, Barbara. *No Room for Grace: Pastoral Theology and Dehumanization in the Global Economy*. Eugene, OR: Wipf & Stock, 1998.

Saïd, Edward W. *Culture and Imperialism*. New York: Vintage, 1994.

———. *Orientalism*. New York: Vintage, 1979.

Sampson, Anthony. *Mandela: The Authorized Biography*. New York: Vintage, 2020.
Sandel, Michael J. *What Money Can't Buy: The Moral Limits of Markets*. New York: Farrar, Straus & Giroux, 2012.
Sanders, Cody J. *A Brief Guide to Ministry with LGBTAQIA Youth*. Louisville: Westminster John Knox, 2017.
Sawyer, Michael E. *Black Minded: The Political Philosophy of Malcolm X*. London: Pluto, 2020.
Schafer, Roy. *Aspects of Internalization*. Washington, DC: International Universities, 1990.
Scheib, Karen D. *Challenging Invisibility: Practices of Care with Older Women*. St. Louis: Chalice, 2004.
———. *Pastoral Care: Telling the Stories of Our Lives*. Nashville: Abingdon, 2016.
Schlanger, Zoë. *The Light Eaters: How the Unseen World of Plant Intelligence Offers a New Understanding of Life on Earth*. New York: Harper, 2024.
Schmitt, Carl. *Political Theology: Four Chapters on the Concept of Sovereignty*. Translated by George Schwab. Chicago: University of Chicago Press, 2005.
Segal, Hanna. "Notes on Symbol Formation." *International Journal of Psychoanalysis*, 38 (1957) 391–97
Sehgal, Parul. "The Case against the Trauma Plot." *The New Yorker*, January 3, 2022, 1–9.
Self, Will. "A Posthumous Shock: How Everything Became Trauma." *Harper's Magazine* (2022) 1–15. https://harpers.org/archive/2021/12/a-posthumous-shock-trauma-studies-modernity-how-everything-became-trauma/
Sevenhuijsen, Selma. *Citizenship and the Ethics of Care: Feminist Considerations on Justice, Morality and Politics*. London: Routledge, 1998.
Sheehan, Sean. *Anarchism*. Focus on Contemporary Issues. London: Reaktion, 2003.
Shelby, Tommie, and Brandon M. Terry, eds. *To Shape a New World: Essays on the Political Philosophy of Martin Luther King Jr*. Cambridge, MA: Belknap, 2018.
Shelley, Mary. *Frankenstein*. New York: Signet Classics, 2000.
Silva, Jennifer M. *Coming Up Short: Working-Class Adulthood in the Age of Uncertainty*. Oxford: Oxford University Press, 2013.
Singer, Peter. *Animal Liberation: A New Ethics for Our Treatment of Animals*. New York: Harper Collins, 1975.
———. *Ethics in the Real World: 90 Essays on Things That Matter*. Princeton: Princeton University Press, 2023.
Smiley, Tavis, and David Ritz. *Death of a King: The Real Story of Dr. Martin Luther King Jr.'s Final Year*. New York: Little, Brown, 2014.
Smith, Archie. *The Relational Self: Ethic and Therapy from a Black Church Perspective*. Nashville: Abingdon, 1982.
Soss, Joe, Richard C. Fording, and Sanford F. Schram. *Disciplining the Poor: Neoliberal Paternalism and the Persistent Power of Race*. Chicago: University of Chicago Press, 2011.
Spivak, Gayatri Chakravorty. "Can the Subaltern Speak?" In *Marxism and the Interpretation of Culture*, edited by Cary Nelson and Lawrence Grossberg, 271–313. Basingstoke, UK: Macmillan, 1988.
Stampfl, Barry. "Theorizing Canine PTSD." *Semiotics* (2012) 159–68. https://doi.org/10.5840/cpsem201216.
Stengel, Richard. *Mandela's Way: Lessons for an Uncertain Age*. New York: Broadway, 2018.

Stengers, Isabelle. *Making Sense in Common: A Reading of Whitehead in Times of Collapse*. Minneapolis: Minnesota University Press, 2023.
Stonebridge, Lyndsey. *We Are Free to Change the World: Hannah Arendt's Lessons in Love and Disobedience*. New York: Random House, 2024.
Strozier, Charles B., and Michael Flynn, eds. *Genocide, War, and Human Survival*. New York: Rowman & Littlefield, 1996.
Strozier, Charles B., and Michael Flynn, eds. *Trauma and Self*. New York: Rowman & Littlefield, 1996.
Taylor, Charles. *The Ethics of Authenticity*. Cambridge: Harvard University Press, 2018.
Taylor, Mark Lewis. *The Executed God: The Way of the Cross in Lockdown America*. Minneapolis: Fortress, 2015.
Tocqueville, Alexis de. *Democracy in America*. New York: Bantam, 2004.
Trepagnier, Barbara. *Silent Racism: How Well-Meaning White People Perpetuate the Racial Divide*. Boulder, CO: Paradigm, 2010.
Tronto, Joan C. *Caring Democracy: Markets, Equality, and Justice*. New York: New York University Press, 2013.
———. *Moral Boundaries: A Political Argument for an Ethic of Care*. New York: Routledge, 1993.
Tutu, Desmond. *No Future without Forgiveness*. New York: Doubleday, 1999.
Ugilt, Rasmus. *Giorgio Agamben: Political Philosophy*. Philosophy Insights. Humanities E-books, 2014.
van der Kolk, Bessel A., Lars Weisaeth, and Onno van der Hart. "History of Trauma in Psychiatry." In *Traumatic Stress: The Effects of Overwhelming Experience on Mind, Body, and Society*, edited by Bessel A. van der Kolk, Alexander C. McFarlane, and Lars Weisaeth, 57–76. New York: Guilford, 1996.
van der Kolk, Bessel A., Onno van der Hart, and Charles R. Marmar. "Dissociation and Information Processing in Posttraumatic Stress Disorder." In *Traumatic Stress: The Effects of Overwhelming Experience on Mind, Body, and Society*, edited by Bessel A. van der Kolk et al., 303–30. New York: Guilford, 1996.
van Deusen Hunsinger, Deborah. *Bearing the Unbearable*. Grand Rapids: Eerdmans, 2015.
Vinci, Tony M. *Ghost, Android, Animal: Trauma and Literature beyond the Human*. Perspectives on the Non-human in Literature and Culture. London: Routledge, 2019.
Viveiros de Castro, Eduardo. *Cannibal Metaphysics: For a Post-structural Anthropology*. Minneapolis: Minnesota University Press, 2017.
Wacquant, Loïc. *Punishing the Poor: The Neoliberal Government of Social Insecurity*. Politics, History, and Culture. Durham: Duke University Press, 2009.
Wade, Phillip. "Shelley and the Miltonic Element in Mary Shelley's *Frankenstein*." *Milton and the Romantics* 2.1 (1976) 23–25.
Waggoner, Matt. *Unhoused: Adorno and the Problem of Dwelling*. New York: Columbia University Press, 2018.
Wallace-Wells, David. *The Uninhabitable Earth: Life after Warming*. New York: Dugan, 2020.
Weber, Max. *The Protestant Ethic and the Spirit of Capitalism*. Translated by Talcott Parsons. 1930. Reprint, London: Routledge, 1992.
Welch, Sharon D. *After Empire: The Art and Ethos of Enduring Peace*. Minneapolis: Fortress, 2004.
West, Cornel. *Race Matters*. 1993. Reprint, New York: Beacon, 2017.

White, Edward A., ed. *Saying Goodbye: A Time for Growth for Congregations and Pastors*. New York: Alban Institute, 1990.
Whyte, Jessica. *Catastrophe and Redemption: The Political Thought of Giorgio Agamben*. SUNY Series in Contemporary Continental Philosophy. New York: SUNY Press, 2013.
Wilson, Edward O. *The Future of Life*. New York: Vintage, 2005.
Wilson, Sarah. "Melville and the Architecture of Antebellum Masculinity." *American Literature* 76 (2004) 59–87.
Wise, Tim. *Color-Blind: The Rise of Post-Racial Politics and the Retreat from Racial Equality*. San Francisco: City Lights, 2010.
Winnicott, D. W. *Playing and Reality*. London: Routledge, 1971.
Winspear, Jacqueline. *Leaving Everything Most Loved*. New York: Harper Perennial, 2014.
Wolin, Sheldon S. *Politics and Vision: Continuity and Innovation in Western Political Thought*. Expanded ed. Princeton: Princeton University Press, 2016.
Wollstonecraft, Mary. *A Vindication of the Rights of Women*. Mineola, NY: Dover, 1996.
Wood, David. *Reoccupy Earth: Notes toward an Other Beginning*. New York: Fordham University Press, 2019.
Wood, Ellen Meiksins. *The Origin of Capitalism: A Longer View*. New York: Verso, 2017.
Worden, J. William. *Grief Counseling and Grief Therapy: A Handbook for the Mental Health Practitioner*. 4th ed. New York: Springer, 2008.
Wright, Richard. *Black Boy*. Washington, DC: Library of America, 1991.
Wulf, Andrea. *The Invention of Nature: Alexander von Humboldt's New World*. New York: Vintage, 2016.
Zeddies, Timothy J. "Behind, Beneath, Above, and Beyond: The Historical Unconscious." *Journal of the American Academy of Psychoanalysis* 30 (2002) 211–22.

Index

Adorno, Theodor, 6, 32n5
affectional bonds, 5–9, 14, 19
African Americans, 122–35
    black sovereignty, 173, 175
    Civil Rights Movement, 119–21, 146n146
    and Eurocentrism, 94
    freedom and creativity, 189–90
    Jim and Jane Crow laws, 111–12, 119–20, 123, 132, 136–40, 141–46, 189, 241
    religious communities, 241
    representative democracy, 47
    resilience and resistance, 91n11
    soul murder, 152–53
    Southern apartheid, 111–12
    space of appearances, 131–32, 144–46; 157, 167, 186, 190
    white sovereignty, 169, 171
    See also being aggrieved; King, Martin Luther Jr.; Malcolm X; racism
Africans, 94, 101–2, 105n71, 116, 121, 169, 173, 194, 201–3, 205
Agamben, Giorgio
    and apparatuses, 4n12
    bare life, 89
    border between human and animal, 47, 214
    and depersonalization, 97
    exclusion of other species, 176
    and impotentiality, 85, 106–8, 135n87, 154–55, 198, 221–22
    and inoperativity, 84–85, 85n96, 110n86
    potentiality and actuality, 84–85, 99, 102, 105–8, 154, 154n14, 217, 222
    and sovereigns, 96
    state of exception, 134
agency
    civic agency, 39
    and freedom, 8, 99–101, 156, 170–72, 187, 199, 217, 221–23
    and other species, 91n12, 99n53
    political agency, 41–42, 99, 123, 126, 131–32, 145, 151, 155, 157–58, 159n30, 167, 170–71, 173, 179, 183, 188–89, 194, 200–201, 217
    and reason, 32, 123
    and sense of self, 136, 141–43
    social agency, 37, 167, 170
    and toxic masculinity, 90, 97, 114
Alford, Fred, 237
alienation, 224–26
Améry, Jean, 238–39, 241
anarchic self, 151–52, 168–76
Anderson, Carol, 123–24
Anthropocene Age, 63, 86, 86n99, 117, 208, 225, 243–44
anti-transformational objects, 61, 70–84

INDEX

apparatuses
    Agamben on, 4n12
    of imperialism and capitalism, 61–62, 85–86, 92–105, 113–14, 208–9, 225–26, 228
    and inoperativity, 84–85, 108
    of the ontological rift, 214–19, 222, 233
    patriarchal, 3–5, 28–30
    of the racial contract, 157, 167
    of racism, 111–12, 135, 144–45, 151–52, 178, 189–91, 255–56
    of slavery, 109–14, 110n86
    of society, 41, 107
    of sovereignty, 152, 171, 174–75, 209
    of toxic masculinity, 89–92
    of white supremacy, 168–76
Aralepo, Olatokunbo, 125
Arendt, Hannah, 131–32, 155n19, 168, 183–88, 196, 203
Aristotle, 3n10, 105–6, 106n73, 127, 154, 179–84
Armstrong, Karen, 62
art/arts, 181–83
assumptive worlds, 237–44, 246–49
autobiographies, 119–21
autocratic polities, 47–48

Bacon, Francis, 3n10
Baldwin, James, 105n71, 120, 125, 129, 152, 161–62, 241
barbarisms, 5, 61
bare life, 90, 96–97, 104, 105, 108, 115, 123n29, 125
Bartleby, The Scrivener (Melville), 85, 106–8, 222
beauty. *See* political aesthetics and beauty
behavior(s), 5, 9–11, 27, 57, 64–66, 92, 94–96, 101, 108, 122, 208
being "accepted," 164, 164n69
being aggrieved, 151–76
    apparatuses that undermine civic care and justice, 157
    experiences of, 164–67
    general perspective, 153–54
    parental care, 160–62
    white supremacy and sovereignty, 157–59

being valued, 155–56
belongingness, 126–27, 175, 180–82, 184, 186, 190–91, 194–97, 225–26
Benjamin, Jessica, 124–25
Bentham, Jeremy, 234
Black, Daniel. *See The Coming* (Black)
Black Legion, 160
Black Lives Matter, 133
Bodin, Jean, 133
Bollas, Christopher, 7n22, 21, 21n79, 61, 70–72, 71n52, 142, 181–82
Bourecht, William, 44–45
broken promises, 183–85
Buber, Martin, 182, 225
Bunge, Marcia, 33
Butler, Judith, 8, 103, 122–23, 128
Butler, Smedley, 42

Call of the Wild (London), 209–30
    alienation, 224–26
    civilization and the primitive (nature), 214, 223–24, 225, 227–28, 233
    inoperative love, 224–29
    love and repair in, 219–24
    ontological rift, 210, 214–19, 221–22, 225, 226–29
capitalism, 32–35, 40, 42–48, 52–53n89, 56, 57–58, 61–62, 73, 84–86, 84n93, 86n99, 90, 92–97, 94n22, 104, 121, 209, 215–16, 221–22, 225, 228, 256
Capps, Donald, 10–11n35
Caputo, John, 103
care, 5–6n17, 5–11, 49–56
    enviro-somatic caring, 72–73
    and faith, 6–7n20, 7, 11–14, 19–21, 31–42, 57
    foundations and practices of pastoral care, 35
    healing from trauma, 249–55
    and hope, 148, 256
    impersonal instrumental care, 90, 97, 102–3
    and love, 38n38
    pastoral theology and pastoral ministry, 30, 33–36, 102n61
    pathologies or distortions of, 34

INDEX

possibilities of healing from trauma, 232–33, 235, 249–55
presymbolic organizations of experience, 141–43
resilience and resistance, 108–16
singularities of other species, 225–29
and surrender, 21, 70–75
trauma and other species, 235–44
use value, 216
See also civic care and faith; faith
carelessness, 27, 29–30, 51, 53, 55–56, 97, 104, 112, 154, 228, 249
Caruth, Cathy, 236–37
catastrophic loneliness, 28, 57, 237
Charcot, Jean-Martin, 235
children
   apparatuses of racism, 189–90
   apparatuses of sovereignty, 169, 174–75
   art/arts, 181
   being aggrieved, 160–62
   freedom and creativity of parents in caring for, 187–88, 191
   potentialities actualized by care and love, 107, 154–55
   valuation, 156
Cholbi, Micheal, 67, 67n38, 80
Christianity, 61–62, 84, 84n93, 93n21, 140
A Christmas Carol (Dickens), 60–87
   anti-transformational objects, 70–84
   Christianity, 61–62, 84, 84n93
   love in, 64–75
   mammon complex, 61–62, 63, 70–86
   masculinity and the fear of vulnerability, 63–70
   process of change, 75–86
church, 145
civic care and faith, 38–42, 123–24, 155, 157, 167, 183
civilization and the primitive (nature), 214, 223–24, 225, 227–28, 233, 245
Civil Rights Movement, 119, 146n146
Clebsch, William, 140–41
climate change, 5, 5n15, 8, 86, 86n99, 178, 204–5, 208, 209, 210–11, 225–26, 228, 229–30, 233, 243–44, 255–56

Coates, Ta-Nahisi, 152, 161, 165
Colebrook, Claire, 85, 107, 222
collective precarity and vulnerability, 56n98, 61, 228
collective resistance, 112–14
collective traumas, 240–41
Colman, Athena, 238
colonial capitalism, 45, 62, 116, 225
colonization, 92–94, 168–69, 209
The Coming (Black), 92–117
   backdrop of, 92–95
   capacity for empathy, 116–17
   and depersonalization, 98–105
   resilience and resistance of ungovernable selves, 108–16
   and slavery, 92–105
   toxic masculinity, 95–117
compassion, 30, 61–63, 74–75, 117, 234
conceptualizations, 208–10
Cone, James, 125
Connolly, William, 99n53, 217n53
conscientization (Freire), 193
cooperation, 38–42, 49, 52, 54–55, 155
Corradi Fiumara, Gemma, 232
cosmos, 9, 103, 219, 226–27
courage, 186, 194–95, 198–99, 202
creativity, 181, 187–91, 196–97
Crow people, 147, 240–41
Crutzen, Paul, 86n99
cultural artifacts/objects, 33–35, 144
Cupitt, Don, 100

Dalal, Farhad, 124
Damon, Arwa, 241
deliberation, 179–80, 183–86, 189–91, 195, 205
democracy, 134
depersonalization, 90, 97–105, 111–15, 124–26, 157, 166–67
Derrida, Jacques, 47n64, 97, 214–15n40, 215
Des Pres, Terrence, 240
developmental theory (Erikson), 7n21, 40–41
Dickens, Charles. See *A Christmas Carol* (Dickens)
differentiation, 142–44
dignity, 200, 216
disidentification, 37, 124–25

divorce, 7
Du Bois, W. E. B., 94, 119

Easterly, William, 37n37
Ellison, Ralph, 35
empathy, 26–30, 74–75, 77–78, 81–83, 116–17, 234
Engster, Daniel, 36
enslaved persons, 90, 96–101, 104–5, 105n71, 123, 169n104, 186, 213, 216
environmental mother, 7n22
enviro-somatic caring, 21–22, 72–73
Epstein, Hellen, 240–41
Erikson, Erik, 7n21, 10–11n35, 40–41, 102n63
eudaimonia, 127
Eurocentrism, 92–95, 215
European Jews, 240–41
evil, 15–18, 20, 21, 22n84, 26, 28, 31–32, 53
excess, 90–91, 105, 105n71, 108–9, 111–16, 119, 127
existential insecurity, 100, 135, 218
existential insignificance and impermanence
  affectional bonds, 8–9
  afterlife, belief in an, 15n59
  Ahab's obsession, 55–56
  civic care and faith, 42
  defer aspects of precarity, 104
  embracing shared precarity, 226–28
  enslaved persons, 104–5
  enviro-somatic caring, 22
  evil, appellation of, 17
  experiences of beauty, 182–83, 190
  illusions of superiority, 218–19
  and inoperativity, 110
  invulnerability, 11, 28
  life and love, 28, 41
  of love, 74–75
  mammon complex, 61
  normative and historical unconscious, 129
  other species, 117, 229
  parental care, 14, 41
  patriarchal apparatuses, 28–30
  systems of objectification, 57–58
  toxic masculinity, 103
  and vulnerability, 70, 71
  white supremacy, 128
existential precarity, 22
  acceptance of, 16, 55–56
  aesthetics and beauty, 182
  affectional bonds, 8–9
  capitalist apparatuses, 57–58, 61, 228
  care and faith, 41–42
  climate change, 208, 226, 229–30
  and freedom, 155
  and inoperativity, 110
  of love, 74–75
  other species, 226–27
  patriarchal apparatuses, 28–30
  promise-making and promise-keeping, 183n25
experience of being, 21, 72–75, 142, 157
experiences, 180–83
exploitation, 89, 215, 225–26, 228

Faber, Roland, 180
faith
  anti-transformational objects, 70–71
  being aggrieved, 152–53
  and care, 6–7n20, 7, 11–14, 19–21, 31–42, 57
  civic care and faith, 38–42, 123–24, 155, 157, 167, 183
  contractual faith, 78
  developmental theory, 7n21
  grief and mourning, 6–9
  impersonal instrumental care and faith, 90, 97, 102–3
  and Niebuhr, 102n63
  pathologies or distortions of, 34
Fanon, Frantz, 35, 49, 89, 126n46, 238
Fassin, Didier, 236, 239
fear and anxiety, 8, 70, 73–74, 104–5, 161, 218
fidelity, 7, 71–75, 77
finitude, 7–9, 11, 60, 155
forgiveness, 183–86, 196, 203–4
Foucault, Michel, 4n12, 33
Frady, Marshall, 139
Francis of Assisi, 234

INDEX

Frankenstein (Shelley), 2–30
    care and faith, 11–14
    failure to grieve or mourn, 20–28, 30
    love in, 27–28, 29
    Victor's response to mother's death, 15–23
Fraser, Nancy, 133
freedom, 43, 217, 223, 246
    and agency, 8, 99–101, 156, 170–72, 187, 199, 217, 221–23
    and creativity, 187–91, 196–97
    experiences of, 154–57
    King's radical hope, 148
    Mandela's exercise of, 198–202
Freire, Paulo, 193
Freud, Sigmund, 8n25, 10–11, 91n12, 128, 235

Garvey, Marcus, 158–59, 171
Gay, Ross, 106n77
Gay, Volney, 181
generosity and hospitality, 61, 79, 81, 88, 179, 186, 190, 195–97, 203, 205–6
Gibson, Danjuma, 91n11
Gilman, Sandor, 33
God, 73–74, 142–43, 147
Godwin, William, 1
Goldberg, David, 121–22
good-enough parents, 41, 107, 152, 155–56, 170, 174, 187, 190–91
Grand, Sue, 237
grandiosity, 18–20, 20n74
grief and mourning, 2–11, 15–23
    affectional bonds, 5–9
    anti-transformational objects, 70–84
    as confirmation of personhood, 113
    failure to grieve or mourn, 20–28, 30, 88–89
    and faith, 6–9
    and isolation, 10, 17–19, 24–27, 27n105
    maladaptive grief, 4–5, 18, 21–24, 24n90
    pathological grief and mourning, 3–4, 11, 24n90, 67–68
    Scrooge's pathological grief, 67–68
    tasks/work of, 9–11, 15–19, 21–22, 28, 67, 73–75, 86
Grief Counseling and Grief Therapy (Worden), 5–6, 5n15

Halevi, Yehuda, 7–8
Hall, Edward, 95
Hall, Stuart, 33
Hardin, Harry, 8n25
Hardt, Michael, 38n38
Hegel, Georg Wilhelm Friedrich, 38–39
helplessness and powerlessness, 8, 16–19, 22, 28–29, 77, 105, 125, 237, 239, 247, 249. *See also* vulnerability
historical unconscious, 128–29, 208
Hobbes, Thomas, 39, 43, 168n96, 186
Holifield, Brooks, 48
Holocaust, 240–41
Honneth, Axel, 155
Hoover, J. Edgar, 139
hope, 7, 7n21, 53–54, 60, 76, 102, 102n63, 147–48, 148n156, 256
Horkheimer, Max, 32n5, 36n32
human animals, 5–6, 9, 97, 106, 154–55, 210, 214–15, 225, 228, 234, 245
human dominion, 47–48, 215, 234
humiliations, 122, 127, 135–40, 159, 160, 167, 195–96, 255
humming, 112–13
hysteria, 235

Ibsen, Malte, 32n5
identification, 37, 64–65, 116, 124–25, 130
identity, 90, 97, 100–101, 110, 126, 130, 135, 201–2
illusions of superiority and inferiority, 97, 100–101, 104, 109–10, 125–30, 135, 144, 159n30, 161, 167n95, 215–19, 221, 228, 235
illusions of white supremacy, 91, 121, 158, 171
imperialism, 32–35, 42–48, 56, 57, 221–22, 225, 228, 255–56
    Indigenous peoples, 45–47, 121, 209, 215
    toxic masculinity, 90, 95, 97, 104

impotentiality, 106–10
  Agamben's idea of, 85, 106–8, 135n87, 154–55, 198, 221–22
  being aggrieved, 157
  capacity for, 61, 106n76, 106n77
  human capacity for exercising, 111–12, 143–47, 154–57, 154n15, 170, 183, 187, 190, 196–97, 221–22
  and inoperativity, 108–10
  resilience and resistance, 116
Indigenous peoples
  aesthetics of togetherness, 197
  capitalist-imperialist mindset, 45–47, 121, 209, 215
  and Christianity, 62
  civilization and the primitive (nature), 214, 223–24, 225
  collective traumas, 240
  colonization, 168–69
  and Eurocentrism, 94–95
  personification of other species, 210
  singularity, denial of, 216
  sustaining objects, 147
individualism, 46
industrial slaughterhouse, 204, 232
infants, 7n21, 7n22, 8n25, 21, 21n79, 71–72, 71n52, 107, 141–44, 155–56, 181, 187–88, 191, 235, 238. See also parental care
inferiority. See illusions of superiority and inferiority
Ingold, Tim, 37n34, 91n12, 210
injustices, 216, 235
inoperative love, 108–13, 224–29
inoperativity, 61, 84–86, 108–15, 110n86, 144–49
instrumental epistemologies, 204, 209, 216, 221, 225, 229
integrity, 185, 198–99, 202
internalization, 129–30
interpersonal recognition, 41, 131, 145–46, 176, 183
interpersonal trust and fidelity, 71, 73–74
invulnerability, 11, 14, 15n59, 16, 20, 22, 28, 49, 55, 75
Israeli persecution of Palestinians, 241
I-Thou relationship, 146, 182, 225

Jaekle, Charles, 140–41
James, William, 10–11n35, 235
Jan-Bulman, Ronnie, 237
Janet, Pierre, 235
JanMohamed, Abdul, 105, 122
Jim and Jane Crow laws, 111–12, 119–20, 123, 132, 136–40, 141–46, 189, 241
Johnson, Mark, 238
Josefson, Jim, 183
Joseph, Peniel, 136–37
just distribution of resources, 133
justice, 24n90
justice and care, 62, 156–57

Keen, David, 128
Kelley, Melissa, 10
kindness, 250–52, 254
King, Alberta Williams, 136
King, Coretta Scott, 139
King, Martin Luther Jr., 135–49
  biographical details, 135–40
  love, theology of, 144–47
  radical hope, 147–48
  sustaining objects, 140–49
kingdom of God, 7n20, 156, 188, 219
Kniess, Johannes, 234
Kocka, Jürgen, 93
Kohn, Eduardo, 37n34, 46n62, 91n12, 210, 221n63, 234, 242
Kotsko, Adam, 99, 217
Ku Klux Klan, 138, 157n23, 158

Latour, Bruno, 47n64, 97, 214–15n40, 215
Layton, Lynne, 128
Lear, Jonathan, 147, 240
Levi, Primo, 239–40
liberalism, 32–35, 43, 46–47, 56, 57
Linzey, Andrew, 234
Little, Earl and Louise, 158–63, 167, 169, 171–72
London, Jack. See *Call of the Wild*; *White Fang*
loneliness, 18–19, 25–30, 57, 64, 249
loss(es), 1–5, 7–11, 15–17, 20–22, 29, 67–75, 247

love
    agency and freedom, 222–23
    in *Call of the Wild*, 219–29
    in *A Christmas Carol*, 64–75
    contractual faith relations, 78–79
    in *Frankenstein*, 27–28, 29
    inoperative, 108–13, 224–29
    King's theology of, 144–47
    and madness, 220–22
    and politics, 38n38
    resilience and resistance, 109–13
    in *White Fang*, 249–55

Macmurray, John, 38–39, 50–51, 131n70
madness, 220–22
maladaptive grief, 4–5, 18, 21–24, 24n90
Malcolm X, 151–76
    anarchic self, 151–52, 168–76
    biographical details, 151
    and internalization, 130
    and racism, 151–53, 157–62, 165–72
    See also being aggrieved
mammon complex, 61–62, 63, 70–86
Mandela, Nelson, 178–204
    childhood, 191–98
    freedom, exercise of, 198–202
    political aesthetics and beauty, 178–204
    transgression, 178–79, 191–204
Manifest Destiny, 42, 45
Marable, Manning, 157n23, 162, 166–67
Margalit, Avishai, 189
marginalization, 167, 255–56
Marx, Karl, 66, 95n32
Maxwell, Jason, 85, 107, 222
Mbembe, Achille, 122–23, 126, 131n72
melancholia, 10, 11n35, 20n74
Melville, Herman. See *Bartleby, The Scrivener*; *Moby-Dick*
memories, 8, 8n25, 17, 41, 69, 73–75, 79–81, 110–11, 136, 138, 171–72, 191–92, 236, 239
mental suffering, 235
mercantilism, 93
Merleau-Ponty, Maurice, 238
microaggression, 124
Miller, Alice, 33

Miller, Walter, 1–2, 3n11, 13n46
Mills, Charles, 94, 123, 130
misogyny, 4, 29–30, 173n113
Moby-Dick (Melville), 32–58
    care and faith, 35–42
    mutual personal recognition, 38–42
    pathological masculinity of Ahab, 32–35, 48–56, 57, 60
    semiotic systems, 42–48, 57
money, 61, 66, 69–70, 73–74
Monroe Doctrine, 42, 45
Moore, Jason, 86n99
Mqhayi, Krune, 194
Muhammad, Elijah, 173–74
multinaturalism, 46n62, 210
multiplicity, 180–81, 183–85, 190, 194, 228
murder, 114–16
mutual personal recognition, 38–42, 123n29, 131–32, 185, 185n35, 186, 188, 190, 192–97, 205

narratives and rituals, 142–44, 240
National Action Council, 200
nationalism, 86n99, 94
Nation of Islam, 172–75
Native peoples. *See* Indigenous peoples
nature
    as abstraction, 208–9, 208n5, 228
    and civilization, 214, 223–24, 225, 227–28, 233, 245
    dominion over, 4, 46–48, 57–58
    romanticizing, 229
    See also climate change; other species
Negri, Antonio, 38n38
Newmyer, Stephen, 234
Niebuhr, H. Richard, 6–7n20, 40, 102n63
non-reparability of relationships, 237
nonviolent resistance, 145–47, 151, 201
normative unconscious, 128
Nussbaum, Martha, 38n38, 234

objectification, 45–48, 57
object knowing, 38–41, 50–51
obsession, 31–32, 34, 44–57
ontological rift, 210, 214–19, 221–22, 225, 226–29, 233

ontological significance, 9, 98, 103
oppression and marginalization, 2, 34–35, 105, 121, 126, 132, 149, 151, 156, 175, 189, 191, 205, 234. *See also* othered persons and groups/Others; racism
"Orientals," 33, 95, 208
othered persons and groups/Others, 36–42, 58, 94–100, 104, 141, 157, 234
other species, 208–11, 214–19, 229–30, 232–35
    and agency, 91n12, 99n53
    apparatuses of racism and marginalization, 256
    communications of, 232
    empathy for, 116–17
    exclusion from the Human Family, 176
    injustices toward, 235
    love and madness, 221
    personification of, 210
    singularities of, 43n56, 204–5, 206, 208–9, 225–29, 232, 235, 244n58
    and trauma, 235–44

Paradise Lost (Milton), 12n37
paranoia, 128
parental care, 14, 41, 70, 71–73, 102n63, 142–44, 152, 154–56, 160–62, 169–70, 170–74, 187–91, 194
parental personal recognitions, 6–8, 107, 143, 155, 156
pastoral functions in Christian history, 140
pastoral theology and pastoral ministry, 30, 33–36, 102n61
pathological grief and mourning, 3–4, 11, 67–68
pathological masculinity of Ahab, 32–35, 48–56, 57, 60
patriarchy, 3–5, 3n10, 28–30, 172, 174–75
Patterson, Orlando, 89, 122
Payne, Les, 159
Peirce, Charles Sanders, 7n22, 242–43
personal knowing subordinate to object knowing, 39–41, 45, 50

personal recognition and knowing, 36–42, 37n37
personhood, 91, 91n12, 98–100, 110, 113–16
Pistor, Katharina, 93
play, 195–97
Plenty Coups, 147, 240
plurality, 98, 180, 183–85, 188, 194
Plutarch, 234
polis
    actualizing potentiality and impotentiality in the, 154–57
    aesthetics and beauty, 179–91, 197
    anarchic self, 152
    and care, 5n17, 36, 42, 102n61
    good-enough, 154–56
    space of appearances, 131, 145
    white sovereignty, 133–34
    zones of injustice or non-justice, 132–33
political aesthetics and beauty, 178–206
political agency, 41–42, 99, 123, 126, 131–32, 145, 151, 155, 157–58, 159n30, 167, 170–71, 173, 179, 183, 188–89, 194, 200–201, 217
political animals, 154
political belonging(ness), 126–27, 190–91, 201, 205
political power, Arendt's notion of, 132
political violence, 41, 151, 179, 186, 201, 243
political virtues, 185–86, 190–91, 194–96, 198, 202–4, 205–6
Politics (Aristotle), 179–80, 183
Porphyry, 234
Porter, Roy, 33
post-traumatic stress disorder, 236, 242n51
potentialities
    actualized by care and love, 107–8, 111, 154–56, 172, 174, 183, 185, 187–88, 252–53
    being aggrieved, 157
    mutual personal recognition creating spaces for, 196–97
    resilience and resistance, 116

potentiality and actuality, 84–85, 99–100, 102, 105–6, 154, 154n14, 217, 222
pre-representational organizations and experiences, 7, 7n22, 8n25, 21n79, 41, 71n52, 239
preservation, consolation, and consolidation, 140–41
presymbolic organizations of experience, 21, 72, 141–43, 156, 175, 181
prison life, 166–67, 202
privileges, 2, 3, 29, 101, 120–21, 124, 130, 138, 232
projection and denial, 125–30, 135, 218
promise-making and promise-keeping, 183–85, 190–91, 203
Prozorov, Sergei, 99, 217
Pruyser, Paul, 144
psychological suffering, 35, 48n67, 49, 109, 235–36
psychology of religion, 152–53
psychosocial development, 7n21, 11n35, 38, 102, 129, 143–44, 178
psychosocial dynamics of racism, 124–30
psychosocial responses to trauma, 241
Puryear, Stephen, 234

racial biases and privileges, 120–21
racial capitalism, 94
racial contract, 94, 103, 123–24, 127, 129–35, 138–40, 140–41, 146, 154, 157, 160–61, 165, 167, 171, 216–18
racism, 241, 255–56
    being aggrieved, 151–53, 154
    and capitalism, 94n22
    definition, attributes, and functions, 121–35
    inoperativity, 111–12, 144–49
    in King's childhood, 138–40, 143
    and Malcolm X, 151–53, 157–62, 165–72
    and Mandela, 197–201
    resiliency and resistance, 149
    toxic masculinity, 95

    ugliness of, 178–79, 180, 185, 188–90, 197–98, 204, 205
    of white sovereignty, 169–72
    See also Jim and Jane Crow laws
radical hope, 147–48
Rahner, Karl, 40
Rank, Otto, 235
Rechtman, Richard, 236, 239
reclamation, 79–81
redemption, 60–63, 210–11
relational trust, 7, 21, 72, 233, 237
relationships, 157, 224–25, 232–33
repair(s), 141, 184–88, 196, 209–10
representative democracy, 47
resiliency and resistance, 89–91, 91n11, 105–16, 135–36, 140–41, 149, 151–52, 175
respect, 195–97
rights of animals, 234
Robben Island, 202
Robinson, Cedric, 94

Saïd, Edward, 33, 94–95, 208–9, 229, 232n7
Sales, Ruby, 111–12, 141, 144, 169–71, 190, 229
Salzani, Carlo, 99, 217
Sampson, Anthony, 192–93, 198, 203–4
Sawyer, Michael, 172–73n113
Schafer, Roy, 129
Schlanger, Zoë, 232n6, 242n48
Schmitt, Carl, 133–34
Schopenhauer, Arthur, 234
science, 2–4, 3n10, 9, 12, 14, 15n59, 16–22, 28
secrets and maladaptive grief, 24
Segal, Hanna, 236
segregation, 138–39, 146
Sehgal, Parul, 236n21
Self, Will, 236n21
self-esteem, self-confidence, and self-respect, 143, 149, 155–59, 161, 165, 167, 169–75, 188
selfhood, 234
self-interests, 43–47, 57
self-knowledge, 67n38, 74–75, 80–83
self-limitation, 36–41, 49, 51–52
self-realization, 39–41, 43–44, 46

semiotic systems, 42–48, 57, 236–44
sense of self, 72–75, 239–40, 247
sensory perception, 179–80
separation, 142–43
shame, 26, 128, 247
Shelley, Clara, 2, 3n11
Shelley, Mary. See *Frankenstein* (Shelley)
Shelley, Percy, 2
Singer, Peter, 116–17, 232n5, 234
singularities, 37, 56, 167, 186, 215–18, 219, 221, 235
    of other species, 43n56, 204–5, 206, 208–9, 225–29, 232, 235, 244n58
sixth extinction event, 86, 86n99, 210
slavery, 89–91, 92–105, 95n32, 108–17, 215–16
slavocracy, 90, 100, 103, 113–16, 121, 185
social death, 89, 119, 122–23, 123n29, 134, 135, 140, 144
somebodiness, 141–43
soul murder, 152–53
soul(s), 97–98, 98n43, 104, 111, 166–67, 229
South Africa, 193–97, 200–204, 234
sovereignty, 96, 168–76, 209
space of appearances, 102n61, 131–32, 144–46, 155, 157, 167, 183, 186, 188, 190–91, 195, 204–5
Spivak, Gayatri Chakravorty, 232n7
Stampfl, Barry, 242n51
state of exception, 133–34
Stengel, Richard, 203
Stengers, Isabelle, 97, 215
Stoermer, Edward, 86n99
subjectivity, 21, 32, 32n5, 46, 49, 72, 85, 96, 130, 210, 222, 233, 234
subordination and subjugation, 3, 90, 97, 101–3, 123, 134, 157–58, 164n69, 216, 247–48
suffering(s), 33–35, 74, 76–78, 81–83, 84n93, 242, 256
superiority, 90, 125–30, 161, 215–19, 221, 235
Suppression of Communism Act, 200
surrender, 16, 21–22, 28–29, 32, 61, 70–75, 78, 80–81, 84, 86
sustaining objects, 135, 140–49
symbolization, 7, 142, 180–81, 236–44

Taylor, Charles, 43
Tocqueville, Alexis de, 131–34
togetherness, 180, 187, 190, 192, 194–97
torture, 238–39
totalitarianism, 168–71
toxic masculinity, 88–92, 95–105, 105–17
transformational objects, 7n22, 21–22, 23, 27–28, 70–74, 142
transitional objects, 142–45
trauma(s), 152–53, 232–33, 235–44, 247–49, 250–55
Trepagnier, Barbara, 124
trust, 7, 7n21, 40–42, 70–75, 77, 107–8, 216, 237–43, 250–52
Tutu, Desmond, 193, 203n118, 204

Ugilt, Rasmus, 105–6
ugliness, aesthetics of, 180, 184
ugliness of racism, 178–79, 180, 185, 188–90, 197–98, 204, 205
unclaimed experiences, 237–42
unconscious fear, 70, 97, 103–5
ungovernable selves, 90, 105–16, 127
utopias, 188

value/valuation, 103–4, 155–56, 216–19, 226–27, 234
Vinci, Tony, 233n9
A Vindication of the Rights of Women (Wollstonecraft), 1, 1n3
violence, 99–101, 104, 108, 111, 114, 126–27, 137–40, 161, 241
Viveiros de Castro, Eduardo, 37n34, 46n62, 91n12, 210, 221n63
vulnerability, 7–8, 11, 16–17, 17n65, 19, 21, 27–28, 29–30, 41, 61, 66, 67, 70, 71–75, 78–79, 237–42, 248, 249–55

Wade, Phillip, 12n37
War Is a Racket (Butler), 42
Weber, Max, 40, 51, 62
Western persons, 97, 97n38, 208, 215, 215n41
White Fang (London), 232–56
    assumptive worlds, 237–44, 246–49
    care, love, and possibilities of healing, 249–55

trauma and other species, 235–44
White Fang and trauma, 244–49
Whitehead, Alfred North, 180–87, 190
white racism, 124–29, 159–60, 159n30, 162, 167, 178
white sovereignty, 133–34, 157–59, 165, 168–76
white supremacy, 91, 92–94, 116, 123–24, 126–30, 157–59, 168–76, 185
Wilson, Sarah, 48
Winnicott, Donald, 7n22, 142–44, 155n17, 188
women, 2–4, 12–13, 13n46, 29, 47, 62, 122

Wood, Ellen Meiksins, 93–94
Worden, William, 5–11, 5n15, 15
Wright, Richard, 122, 129, 161

Zeddies, Timothy, 128
zone of justice (ethics), 99–100, 131–32, 146, 204–5, 217
zones of non-being, 89–90
zones of non-justice or injustice, 89, 96–97, 99, 104, 132–33, 134–35, 146, 216–17, 219, 229. *See also* bare life

www.ingramcontent.com/pod-product-compliance
Lightning Source LLC
Chambersburg PA
CBHW032058220426
43664CB00008B/1049